The Growth of European Mixed Economies
1945-1970

THE GROWTH OF EUROPEAN MIXED ECONOMIES
1945 - 1970

A Concise Study of the Economic Evolution of Six Countries

SIMA LIEBERMAN

Schenkman Publishing Company, Inc.

A Halsted Press Book

JOHN WILEY AND SONS

New York • London • Sydney • Toronto

Schenkman Publishing Company, Inc.
3 Mt. Auburn Place
Cambridge, Massachusetts 02138

330.94
L716g

Distributed solely by Halsted Press, a Division of
John Wiley & Sons, Inc., New York, New York

Library of Congress Cataloging in Publication Data
Lieberman, Sima, 1927-
    The growth of European mixed economics, 1945-1970.

    Bibliography: p.
    Includes index.
    1.   Europe — Economic conditions — 1945-   I. Title.
HC240.L52   197 b   330.9′4′055   77-4837
ISBN 0-470-99168-2 (Wiley)

78-6505

To helpful friends and distinguished colleagues,

T.C. Barker, The University of Kent, U.K.
C.A. Blyth, The University of Auckland, New Zealand
R.R. Edminster, The University of Utah, U.S.A.
H.J. Habakkuk, Oxford University, U.K.
H. Rosovsky, Harvard University, U.S.A.

CONTENTS

TABLES

CHAPTER   12.

INTRODUCTION

Comparative economic systems texts are still presenting to the reader in the 1970s a dualistic economic map of Europe. Market-oriented economies are distinguished from command-oriented economies. This simplistic categorization poorly hides political prejudices. Indeed, the basic idea this taxonomy purports to convey is that European economic systems differ fundamentally because of different political ideologies. The argument is that the neo-Capitalist "West" has retained the basic institutions of a non-planned market economy, while the Socialist or Communist "East" relies on planned systems which have little in common with those of the western democracies. Twentieth-century European Capitalism is thus associated with the preservation of a market economy while Socialism is supposed to rely exclusively on planned, command systems. The picture presented by this association of terms is not only misleading, but it also presents a very static view of economic life in Europe. It minimizes the perception of the dramatic and significant economic mutations which developed in Europe since the end of World War II and which still occur at the present.

The Yugoslav economic system, for instance, is usually regarded as a command-oriented economy and is thus grouped together with the systems of the U.S.S.R., Czechoslovakia and the German Democratic Republic. The French system, on the other hand, is explained in that part of the text devoted to the analysis of market-oriented economies such as those of the German Federal Republic, Italy, Sweden and the United Kingdom. And yet, a brief study of these systems will reveal that in the 1960s, the Yugoslav economic system resembled much more the French system than the economic systems then existing in the U.S.S.R. and in the other Comecon countries. Moreover, the Yugoslav economic system of 1965 was totally different from what it had been in 1948.

The comparative study of economic systems should not limit itself to an analysis of institutions existing during a given period of time, but should also recognize the importance of changes in these institutions over time.

Two important trends run through the eonomic history of postwar Europe. In the West, state intervention in economic life became stronger over time and national planning eventually became an inherent feature of post-1945 European Capitalism. In the Soviet bloc countries, important economic reforms followed gradually upon Stalin's death in 1953, the most spectacular ones being proposed by the Russian economist Yevsei Liberman in 1962. It is interesting to notice in this connection that the first "Eastern" country which adopted Liberman's ideas was the German Democratic Republic, the most faithful disciple of the U.S.S.R. The expulsion of Yugoslavia from Cominform in 1948 induced that country's government to transform its economic system into one which would more closely adhere to Marxist values as interpreted by Yugoslavs.

In Western Europe, as well as in the East, appalling shortages of food, fuel, raw materials and housing in the early postwar years presented problems which only the state could attempt to solve. The state alone was able to muster sufficient capital to undertake the task of reconstructing war-damaged economies. Although the extent of state intervention differed in the various economies of Western Europe, it grew over time. Public intervention in the economy was facilitated in certain instances by the existence of a large public sector of pre-war origin; this was particularly the case in Italy and West Germany. Extensive nationalizations enlarged the public sector in France and in the United Kingdom. Together with an expanding public sector, public investment, both in absolute terms and as a proportion of total investment, grew in all countries. A natural concomitant of large public investment was national economic planning. Planning characterized and molded the growth of many European market-oriented economies in the 1960s.

France initiated comprehensive national planning in Western Europe with its "indicative" Monnet Plan of 1946. Although the French plans were not mandatory, their support by both the public and the private sectors was obtained by the government by means of "legal bribes" such as tax exemptions and tax rebates, subsidies and advantageous loans.

Britain adopted a Five-Year Plan only in 1962, planning in that country having been made particularly difficult by recurring balance of payments crises. Although the West German social market economy purported to rely almost exclusively on market competition, it was not long before the Federation of German Industry, the *Verband der deutschen Industrie,* started engaging in effective planning. Industrial and banking oligopolies, as closely interconnected as in pre-war times, simply undertook covertly what the state refused to do openly. Although the government had no official plan to implement, it nevertheless actively assisted industrial expansion by means of subsidies, public loans, tax exemption and public investment.

In Italy, the first Five-Year Plan of 1966 was preceded by a great deal of partial planning by public and semi-public agencies. Comprehensive, large-scale planning for the development of the impoverished *Mezzogiorno* was approved as early as 1950 with the establishment of the *Cassa per il Mezzogiorno,* a public planning and investment agency.

The role of the state in the economy was boosted by the development of new industrial technology. Automation and electronics introduced major changes in methods of production and these changes required large amounts of capital. Firms sought to obtain the capital needed to replace costly outdated equipment by means of merger and amalgamation or asked for government assistance in the form of subsidies and privileged tax treatment. The establishment of EEC and EFTA and a rapidly growing world trade strengthened international competition and accelerated the trend toward industrial concentration. Western European economies became increasingly dominated by industrial and banking oligopolies which soon learned the American "monopoly game." The policy of limiting output and reducing the work force while raising prices, even in periods of weakening demand, brought "stagflation" to some of the western economies in the late 1960s. Government was forced to act more forcefully in order to maintain employment and purchasing power on the one hand, and relative price stability on the other.

The first part of this book, which covers the period 1945 to 1955, examines the problems of postwar economic reconstruction in six different countries. These countries, representing both Western and Eastern Europe, have been selected because of their economic, demographic, and political diversities. The second part of the book studies the pattern and speed of economic development in these countries since 1955. A necessarily brief sketch of the history of economic growth in the chosen countries in the period 1945 to 1970 will hopefully give sufficient evidence to support the thesis that political ideology had very little to do with the type of economic growth and the rate of economic growth experienced by the selected countries.

In all of these countries, war-inflicted destruction and damage were eliminated much faster than had been anticipated in 1945. Pre-war levels of output were attained and surpassed during the early 1950s. By 1955, East Germany and Yugoslavia had succeeded in building an entirely new industrial sector. The German Democratic Republic accomplished this feat in spite of a very poor endowment in industrial raw materials and fuels, in spite of recurrent waves of Soviet appropriations and in spite of a continuous loss of manpower to the other Germany. Yugoslavia industrialized in spite of the very heavy human and material losses it had suffered during the war and in spite of the great economic difficulties it faced in 1948 when a sudden Soviet world economic blockade deprived it of highly needed credits and imports.

Rapid industrialization also occurred at this time in both Italy and West Germany under Christian Democratic governments. France, under the guidance of its "indicative" plans, rapidly modernized its key industries; it was a citizen of a traditionally protection-minded country who, on May 9, 1950, introduced the proposal, later known as the Schuman Plan, which led to the establishment of the European Coal and Steel Community in 1951, the first step in the direction of a new European customs union. Although Britain was a laggard in the pace of growth in Europe, it succeeded, in spite of serious balance of payments difficulties, in maintaining a rate of growth which was much higher than the pre-war rate and in providing employment for its entire labor force.

A number of events in the early 1950s diminished European fears of a new world war and encouraged Europeans to actively develop their economies. The end of the Korean War, Stalin's death and the production of a hydrogen bomb by the Soviet Union reduced the probability of a direct American-Russian military confrontation in Europe. The new Soviet policy of peaceful co-existence with the non-Communist world, and the gradual passing of McCarthy-type political hysteria in the United States, produced an international *détente* which favored economic investment in many countries.

The gradual disappearance of European colonial empires following the end of World War II induced some of the Western European nations to give more importance to economic growth than to military power. By 1960, nearly all of the important colonial areas in Africa and

Asia had gained independence and European countries prepared to replace military dictate by economic influence in the former colonies.

The long agony of European colonialism in the 1950s did not bring to Western Europe the economic catastrophe predicted by right-wing imperialists. The economies of Western Europe continued to expand rapidly, experiencing at the worst brief and relatively mild recessions in the 1960s. Unemployment practically disappeared in these economies, even though population was growing. In some of the countries, shortages of labor led to a large influx of foreign workers, and it is interesting to notice that the West German trade unions never protested the presence of two million foreign workers in the country.

The "economic success" formula was not the same for the various countries under consideration. In the West, Italy and West Germany gave great importance to price stability; France, on the other hand, financed industrial expansion through inflation. In the East, the German Democratic Republic remained closed to American and West European capital, while Yugoslavia welcomed it. It is undeniable that the growth of intra- and extra-European trade after the mid-1950s allowed nations, both in Western and in Eastern Europe, to increase their import capacity, to produce more along lines of comparative advantage, and to benefit from rapidly rising productivity. In the West, international trade was boosted by the formation of the EEC and the EFTA. In the East, increased trade within the CMEA area followed the abandonment in the Communist world of Stalin's view that Socialist countries should be as self-sufficient as possible and should develop largely on the basis of their own resources.

If a common denominator must be identified to explain the success of these economies in the 1950s and 1960s, the most obvious feature is that they were neither true market-oriented, Capitalist economies, nor pure Socialist command systems. In fact, they were all mixed economies and it is the author's hope that the following chapters will allow the reader to gain a better insight of the complexity of growth causality in these "mixed European economies."

S. Lieberman

Salt Lake City

Part I
The First Postwar Decade

CHAPTER 1

ECONOMIC DUALISM
À LA FRANÇAISE

The leaders of the Resistance gave their country in 1944 a new dream. This was a dream about an economic and political future that would cause Frenchmen to forget the hardships and the shame of economic stagnation, military defeat and occupation by the German foe. The history of the French economy in the interwar period is largely one of stagnation and of government protection of the *status quo*. During the entire period 1913-1938, the French gross national product increased by only 6%.[1] This stagnation has been explained in terms of the inadequacy of population growth, the excessive reliance placed by French enterprise on governmental protection, the absence of technological and product innovation, and the lack of growth of the home market due to the conservative and traditional behavior of the French consumer. This lack of economic dynamism has been explained by Professor Landes as having been due in part to "too many tight-fisted peasants, too much expenditure on food, resistance to standardized products and aggressive selling."[2] The Depression of the 1930s plagued France until the start of the second world war. Throughout the decade, net investment in France remained close to zero. Industrial production, as late as 1938, was still about 25% below the level attained in 1929. France's inability to resist the German invader in 1940 must be attributed to a large extent to the fact that France never recovered from a decade-long period of industrial and demographic decline.[3]

The long years of occupation developed the "Spirit of Resistance." Leaders of the Resistance vowed to bring economic, social and political renewal to France. Their goals were determined not only by the memory of prewar stagnation, but were very much affected by the humiliation of German occupation. France's military defeat appeared to them to be obviously tied to the weak economy of the country, an economy which had suffered too long from inadequate investment, from inefficient production methods and from the conservatism of private enterprise. What the Resistance wanted was strong State action which would rescue the economy from the chaos caused by the war and transform it into a modern, industrial, competitive economy. In the immediate postwar period, the State was to solve the problems created by acute fuel and raw materials shortages, the collapse of the transportation system, and the lack of housing. Indeed, the war had caused a great loss of resources. The loss of capital equipment during the years of war was estimated to have been twice the value of the French gross national product in 1938. Wartime mass labor deportations to Germany had caused serious manpower shortages. A Frenchman described his country's economy after liberation in the following words:

> It was a ravaged France that left its prison. 115 major railroad stations had been destroyed or badly damaged. . . . We had had 12,000 locomotives; 2,800 of them remained. From Paris to Lyon, Marseilles, Toulouse, Nantes, Lille, Nancy, there were no more trains. Canals, riverways, and ports were unusable. Electric lines were cut. 3,000 ports had been blown up. Of every ten motor vehicles, nine could no longer run and the tenth was out of fuel. Airplanes? There weren't any.[4]

The reformist spirit of the Resistance naturally favored national planning for economic modernization. It was this spirit which led, shortly after liberation, to the creation of a Ministry of National Economy charged with the tasks of drafting and implementing national plans for economic reconstruction and modernization. The communist, socialist, and centrist M.R.P. leaders in the de Gaulle government agreed that rational and centralized planning was needed to facilitate rapid economic reconstruction. Given the existing economic chaos, planning appeared to be indispensable to mobilize and allocate resources efficiently. Planning, it was believed, would also prevent a return to the stagnant society of the Third Republic.

When de Gaulle, shortly after his 1945 election as Head of the Government, declared that he would bring about the "nationalization of credit and of electricity," he was simply explaining to the French people that nationalization would make the government's planning and modernization tasks more effective. Nationalization of large sectors of the economy had already been advocated as a political and economic necessity by the wartime National Council of Resistance, which in March 1944 had asked for "the return to the nation of the great monopolies in the means of production, the sources of energy, the mineral wealth, the insurance companies and the large banks." Although the nationalizations carried out in the period 1944 to 1946 were not as extensive as those demanded by the Resistance, the coal mines, the electric and gas industries, Air France, Renault, the Bank of France, the four largest deposit banks and thirty-two insurance companies were transformed into public enterprises. The government acquired direct control over 20% of the industrial sector.

In conformity with an old tradition going back to the days of the monarchist *ancien régime,* Frenchmen entrusted the State with the necessary power to improve the economy. But though in the early postwar years the Resistance and many Frenchmen had hoped that the State would be able to industrialize, modernize, and democratize the economy, the experience of the Fourth Republic showed that too many small industrialists, boutique owners, craftsmen, and *petit fermiers* expected that the State, following hallowed tradition, would be mainly concerned with the protection of the economic and social *status quo* and would not endanger the *situations acquises* of the small businessmen and peasants. Because of the strong conservatism of a large part of French society, the economic and social impact of France's moderniza-tion plans remained limited during the first postwar decade: these plans were unable to eliminate from the economy an old infrastructure based on inefficient, small family firms and family farms, surviving largely because of the weakness of competition prevailing in French markets.

It may justly be said that the Fourth Republic initiated a twentieth century industrial revolution in France. This revolution, the product of the efforts of State officials, of technocrats and of some large private enterprises, was however unable to by-pass the many problems of economic dualism. A large part of the French economy may have passed directly from the eighteenth to the twentieth century after 1945, but a large entrepreneurial class remained loyal to the typically nineteenth century, unprogressive, tradition-determined values and attitudes of the prewar *bourgeoisie.*

In spite of the continuing presence of small enterprises in the French economy, in spite of the gradual weakening of the spirit of the Resis-tance indicated by the withdrawal from government by the Com-munists in 1947 and by the Socialists two years later, nationalization and the type of economic planning initiated by Jean Monnet in 1946 succeeded in transforming France into a nation that would be able to compete in the 1960s with the industrial might of West Germany.

What is peculiar about the growth and the modernization of the French industrial sector in the postwar period is that they developed under conditions of recurring acute price inflation. Faced with the problems of severely limited resources, the early postwar governments decided to formulate reconstruction and modernization policies without the help of direct economic controls. Wartime controls rapidly disappeared after liberation. The government's resolve to reconstruct the economy without these controls forced M. Mendès-France, Minister of the National Economy and an advocate of economic controls, to leave the government in April, 1945. The views of his more conservative successor, René Pléven, were generally followed by the various governments of the Fourth Republic. France would rebuild its economy without the help of *dirigisme,* without rationing consumer goods and without recourse to heavy taxation to reduce excess demand. As a writer observed, "the French chose to do their rationing by means of rising prices."[5]

Inflation was the Fourth Republic's *enfant terrible.* Inflation brought *le Général* back to power in 1958. The Fourth Republic inherited from the Third excess liquidity in the hands of the public and a great impatience on the part of Frenchmen for higher standards of living at a time when the supplies of consumer and capital goods were still well below prewar levels. The resulting inflationary pressures were strengthened by a number of developments. Workers, shortly after the liberation of Paris, obtained a 40% wage increase, and a further increase followed in the spring of 1945. Although wartime price controls had not been cancelled, authorized price increases were so numerous that price inflation developed quite freely. Price controls were practically abandoned in 1948. Starting in 1945, consumer rationing was gradually eliminated. Poor weather conditions in 1946 and 1947 slowed down agricultural recovery and added strength to inflation, an inflation further fueled by freely expanding bank credit, resource hoarding and governmental deficits covering about a third of public expenditures.[6] The magnitude of the early postwar inflation is best shown by the fact that in the fall of 1948, prices were about eighteen to twenty times what they had been ten years earlier. During this period, the increase in wages and salaries tended to lag behind that of prices. Wages and salaries rose between eight and twelve times during the decade 1938 to 1948. The acute inflation of the period 1945 to 1948, a period during which many prices were rising by as much as 50% per year, came to a temporary end in 1949. The Korean war brought a new wave of inflation to France, and between 1950 and 1957 consumer prices increased at an average annual rate of 5.3% per year.[7] Table 1.1 shows the trend of French wholesale prices in the period 1945 to 1950.

TABLE 1.1

INDEX OF WHOLESALE PRICES
1938 = 100

December		December	
1945	469	1948	1,974
1946	846	1949	2,002
1947	1,217	1950	2,409

Source: Ministère des Finances: *Inventaire de la Situation Financière,* 1951, Paris, p. 144.

To the non-military causes of France's almost chronic inflation during the first postwar decade must be added, besides the impact of the Korean war, the more prolonged economic effects of France's military operations in Indo-China. Politically, the war in Indo-China led to the strengthening of France's centrist and right-wing parties. With the exodus of the Communists from the government, France's attitude toward Ho Chi Minh became more hostile in spite of the Vietnamese leader's repeated offers of a non-violent settlement of differences between the French *colons* and the Vietnamese nationalists. Under the Schuman government, formed in November 1947, the Ministry of Overseas France became ultra-colonialist. The war continued, and drained resources away from non-military sources. On December 28, 1950, for instance, the French National Assembly discussed a government proposal to increase military expenditures from 449 billion francs to 780 billion in 1951. It is interesting to note that the resulting deficit was to be covered in part by United States aid amounting to 255 billion francs, of which 140 billion francs were to be in the form of military aid.[8]

It is within this background of inflation that the first French economic plan, the Monnet plan, was launched in 1946 to cover the period 1947 to 1950.

The Monnet Plan: 1947-1952

In 1945, M. Jean Monnet submitted to General de Gaulle the draft of a plan detailing economic goals the country should achieve in 1950. The objectives of M. Monnet's plan were not limited to the attainment of certain levels of output. For M. Monnet, the modernization of the economy was as important as the fulfillment of quantitative production targets. He wrote to the General:

> The reconstruction of France not only requires the repairing of war damage, but also the modernization of equipment and methods of production. France, in order to live, needs to reconstruct what was destroyed during the war. But in order to take her rightful place in a world where technical improvements have changed rapidly, she must alter the conditions of production. Without this modernization she will be unable to raise the standard of living of the French people. . .[9]

Monnet believed that, given the extent of war damage and the severity of fuel and raw materials shortages, it would be difficult, if not impossible, for the government to invest in the short-run sufficiently to help in the rebuilding of the entire economy. During the period of the plan, public investment would rather focus on the reconstruction and expansion of key economic sectors whose increased production would in turn facilitate further industrial and agricultural development. Monnet's strategy was to obtain "considerably increased quantities of coal, electricity, steel and cement, a sufficiently mechanized agricultural system to ensure that the population is fed, and finally, a transportation network in keeping with the above."[10] The improvement of the highly deficient housing conditions and immediate increases in the production of consumer goods received low priorities.

The Monnet Plan, extended in 1948 to 1952 in order to terminate with the final year of Marshall Plan aid, gave investment priority to six key sectors in the economy. These chosen sectors covered coal, electricity, steel, cement, farm machinery and transportation. Fuel and fertilizers were later added to the list. The Plan initially contemplated a production increase in the selected sectors of 25% above 1929 levels by 1950. These targets were lowered in 1948 to a 10% output increase in 1950 above 1929 production levels. At the same time, as mentioned, the duration of the plan was extended by two years.

The most interesting feature of the Monnet Plan and of the plans that succeeded it was that the output targets specified in these plans were indicative rather than binding on public and private enterprises. To the extent that the plans met with success, it was largely because both government and private enterprise agreed with them and because representatives of the various interest groups in the nation had participated in their formulation. This planning procedure had been proposed by Monnet in 1945. It was Monnet's belief that:

> Since the execution of the plan will necessitate everyone's collaboration, it is essential that all important sections of the community participate in carrying it out. For this reason, the proposed procedure brings together in each sector the responsible administrators, the best qualified experts and the representatives of the professional trade unions.[11]

For each economic sector, the details of planning were left to the determination of modernization committees made up of officials of the Planning Commission, the heads of pertinent private firms, officials of public enterprises, union leaders and professional experts.[12] It should be noted that the decisions made by these committees were, to use the French expression, entirely "indicative" and the commitments of the participating committee members were entirely voluntary.

On the whole, the Planning Commission obtained the loyal cooperation of private enterprise. This may have been due to a number of factors. Since public enterprise supported the Commission's goals, private firms were encouraged to follow suit. Private and public entrepreneurs understood the imperative need to modernize and rebuild the economy. Their willingness to attempt the achievement of prescribed goals was also secured by the government through an extensive system of rewards and incentives taking the form of tax relief, tariff concessions, government contracts, and perhaps most important of all, advantageous government loans. During the first postwar decade, the private capital market remained, as a result of war and inflation, quite limited. Firms, private and public, had to depend heavily on the government as the main supplier of funds for investment. The Planning Commission, having control over the allocation of these investment funds and being able to facilitate or hinder private lending, obviously possessed enormous persuasive power over enterprises.

> The government encouraged private investments in "approved" sectors by guaranteeing the bond issues of certain firms. These guarantees were extended to some private firms whose projects came under the

modernization and equipment plans, but most of them applied to the bond issues of nationalized enterprises. More important, the government sometimes used its influence to obtain medium-term bank credit for private or nationalized forms. . . . In quantitative terms, the principal method for implementing the investment plan in the early years was the provision of public funds under favorable conditions from a number of budgetary or para-budgetary accounts. . . . The difficulties of obtaining private funds were intensified by the inflation which got under way shortly after liberation. Individual and business savings were wiped out; this was particularly damaging since the family enterprise (typical of large parts of French industry and trade) traditionally resorted to internal financing of its investments. [13]

Although not all of the targets of the Monnet Plan were attained in 1952, the plan was on the whole fulfilled with success. As shown in Table 1.2, coal output in 1952 attained 95.7% of the planned output target; electric power reached 94.9% of its goal. Cement and petroleum production exceeded their output targets. Steel output in 1952 was, however, only 87.2% of the planned output. Nitrogenous fertilizers reached an output of 285,000 tons in 1952, an output short of the Plan's target, but an output which was more than double the output of 1946. Although the output of tractors reached only 63% of the planned output in 1952, the increase in tractor production during the period covered by the Plan was quite substantial. France had produced only 2,000 tractors in 1946; the output climbed to 14,200 in 1950 and to 25,300 in 1952.

Not only were quantitative targets established in 1946 attained with reasonable success so that the economy was provided with sufficient key resources to allow economic expansion in later years, but planning also resulted in major qualitative changes in the economy. The prewar technologically backward steel industry had undergone complete transformation by 1952 so that at the termination of the Monnet Plan, France had acquired a modern and efficient steel industry. The coal mines were producing in the early 1950s more coal than during any prewar time on the basis of 30% fewer workers. [14] Petroleum refining capacity exceeded by over three times prewar figures, while electric power plants had doubled their generating capacity. [15]

The planning procedure underlying France's first economic plan was not based on sophisticated econometric analyses. Statistical information was limited and it was through informal discussion of vol-

TABLE 1.2
FRENCH INDUSTRIAL OUTPUT FOR SELECTED YEARS

Item	Actual Production					Planned Output Target
	1929	1938	1946	1950	1952	for 1952
Coal million tons	55.0	47.6	49.3	52.5	57.4	60.0
Crude Steel million tons	9.7	6.2	4.4	8.7	10.9	12.5
Cement million tons	6.2	3.6	3.4	7.2	8.6	8.5
Petroleum million tons	0.0	7.0	2.8	14.5	21.5	18.7
Electricity billion kwh.	15.6	20.8	23.0	33.1	40.8	43.0
Tractors 1,000 units	1.0	1.7	1.9	14.2	25.3	40.0
Nitrogenous Fertilizer 1,000 tons	73.0	177.0	127.0	236.0	285.0	300.0

Source: Commissariat Général du Plan de Modernisation et d'Equipement, *Rapport sur la réalisation du plan de modernisation et d'équipement de l'Union française,* Paris, 1953.

untarily exchanged information that the members of the modernization committees tried to decide on an optimum rate of growth for their
particular economic sector. The committees did not try to determine
rates of growth that would conform to the wishes of the head of the
government. Rather, the modernization committees estimated natural
rates of growth and then, through a consensus of opinion, the committees endeavored to detail the expansion of every pertinent firm within
the sector necessary to obtain the desired aggregate growth rate. This
highly informal planning system succeeded. Large investments in the
selected basic industries allowed the nation to solve the severe problems of resource shortages. The linkage effects of the six favored
industries allowed in turn further economic expansion on a more
balanced basis.

The Monnet Plan not only brought about a significant increase in
industrial production, but also resulted in a rapid increase in employment. In 1952, the number of employed persons was 20% higher than
it had been in 1938.[16] This increase represented an addition to the
prewar labor force of about 2 million workers and an increase of about

80 million work-hours per year. Employment increases were not general or identical for the various sectors of the economy. In the textile and foodstuff industries, employment in 1952 was about the same as it had been in 1938. The coal and railroad transportation industries actually had fewer workers in 1952 than in 1938. On the other hand, between 1946 and 1952, employment in the chemical industries increased by 20%, while it increased by at least 30% in the electrical, engineering, ceramic and construction industries.[17] In the case of the petroleum industries, the increase in employment attained 120%.

FIGURE 1
EMPLOYMENT IN FRANCE
1930=100

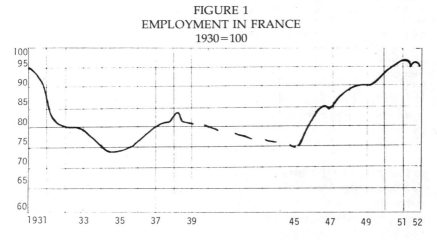

Source: Comité National de la Productivité, *Actions et Problèmes de Productivité*, Paris, 1953, p. 471.

The most significant contribution of the Monnet Plan was, however, the increase in productivity which resulted from the modernization of a large sector of the economy. The Monnet Plan concentrated on large investments for capital formation and there has usually been a close relationship between capital formation and technological progress. It has been estimated that for the period 1949 to 1959, France had the third largest average growth rate of labor productivity in Western Europe; West Germany obtained the highest and Italy the second highest growth rate.[18]

The Monnet Plan was successful in many ways. The participation of union leaders in the discussion of the modernization committees probably explains the decline of strike activity after 1948. The participation of organized labor in the planning process was, however, reduced in the 1950s when the largest French trade union, the *Confédération Générale du Travail,* feeling that its cooperation was sought by the government for purely political reasons, decided to withdraw from the planning agency. The informal committee discussions also encouraged the development of a phenomenon new to French enterprise. The heads of rival firms started abandoning their traditional secretiveness about production data and showed willingness to exchange technical and economic information. Planning also spurred the French entrepreneur to modernize and to become productivity-conscious. Finally, by making large investment and modernization in key industries possible, the Monnet Plan secured a strong foundation on which further industrialization could be built.

TABLE 1.3
GROWTH RATES OF REAL GROSS DOMESTIC PRODUCT,
EMPLOYED LABOR FORCE AND
LABOR PRODUCTIVITY IN SELECTED COUNTRIES
1949 - 1959

| | Annual Percentage Rates of Growth | | |
	Real GDP 1954 Prices	Employed Labor Force	Labor Productivity
France	4.5	0.1	4.3
West Germany	7.4	1.7	5.7
Italy	5.9	1.1	4.8
Netherlands	4.8	1.2	3.6
United Kingdom	2.4	0.6	1.8
United States	3.3	1.2	2.0

Source: United Nations, *Economic Survey of Europe in 1961,* Part 2, "Some Factors in Economic Growth in Europe During the 1950s," Geneva, 1964, Table 4, pp. 11-12.

The Trade Unions, Politics and Inflation

Liberation brought about the revival of two principal trade union federations in France. The largest was the Communist-dominated *Confédération Générale du Travail,* the CGT, whose membership in the spring of 1946 exceeded 5 million. The *Confédération Française des Travailleurs Chrétiens,* the CFTC, attracting mostly members of the political Catholic center, counted at that time about 750,000. A new organization, the *Confédération Générale des Cadres,* appealing mostly to supervisory employees and technicians, was formed in 1946. The diverse political ideologies of these organizations, the continuing inflation, and the wage-freeze which lasted until February 1950 kept political protest rather than the pursuit of economic goals the principal *raison d'être* of French organized labor in the days of the Fourth Republic.

Until the end of 1948, political disagreement among and within labor groups plagued the French economy with repeated strike activity and led to further divisions within the labor movement. Labor's turmoil was mainly due to political differences between Communists and non-Communists within the CGT. As early as 1946, railroad, postal and communications workers had abandoned this organization. The unsuccessful generalized strike of November 1947 further weakened the CGT when Socialists and other non-Communists in that organization decided to establish a new confederation, the *CGT-Force Ouvrière.*

Between January and November 1947, the retail price index had risen from 856 to 1336. Wages lagged far behind prices. During the last six months of the year, wages rose by 19% while prices increased by 51%. Although inflation had plagued the economy since liberation, the economic situation of the workers was worse than in earlier years. Major strikes developed in November in Paris, in Marseilles, and in the coal-mining area. The departure of the Communists from government and the tough anti-Communist position of M. Schuman induced the CGT to order a number of strikes, strikes which shut down the coal mines, most of the large metallurgical plants, the ports and some railroads. The strikes failed and in December the CGT-FO was formed. French trade unionism was now split into three main groups: The CGT had become the labor organization of the Communist Party; the CGT-FO was largely under the influence of the Socialists, while the CFTC was linked to the centrist M.R.P. party. A mixture of Gaullists, ex-Communists and Vichyite labor leaders organized in October the strongly pro-de Gaulle *Confédération du Travail Indépendante,* the CTI.

Inflation, though temporarily stopped in 1950, rendered the unions less interested in collective bargaining than in obtaining from government periodic increases in the legal minimum wage which would support subsequent union demands for higher wages. Unfortunately, the economic impact of frequent increases in the legal minimum wage was soon nullified by concurrent increases in prices. Although in Feburary of 1950 the Bidault government finally allowed the re-establishment of free collective bargaining in France, it was only in 1955 that the French worker finally succeeded in recovering his prewar real wage.

The price-wage merry-go-round continued during the 1950s. In August 1950, the Pléven government authorized a minimum legal wage for the Parisian area of seventy-eight francs per hour. This measure resulted in a general wage increase throughout the country and in January 1951, the hourly wage index stood 13% higher than it had been six months earlier. Price increases, largely due to the higher costs of imported raw materials and to the hoarding of commodities by firms and individuals, left the French worker with an unchanged purchasing power. Unions started pressuring for further wage increases and a series of strikes followed in February and March. On March 23rd, the Queuille government increased the legal minimum wage for Paris to eighty-seven francs per hour. Workers in certain public industries were granted a 10% wage increase. Unfortunately, prices continued to rise. The price of wheat increased by 33.5% in August. On September 8, 1951, the legal minimum wage was again increased by 15%, which lifted it to 100 francs per hour. As in previous instances, price increases left the worker's real income unchanged. A law of July 18, 1952, provided for a sliding scale for the determination of the minimum wage. In February 1954, the latter attained 115 francs per hour and reached 121.50 francs in October. [19]

Inflation, the political division of organized labor and opposition to improved labor-management relations by the strongly autocratic and conservative employers' association, the *Conseil National du Patronat Français,* the CNPF, weakened the contribution the unions could make to the improvement of the economic position of their members. During the first postwar decade, the fruits of economic expansion were largely appropriated by the profit earners. The purchasing power of the average hourly wage in July 1955 was 7% below that of 1937. If in 1955 the real income of the French wage-earner was higher than it had been before the war, this was due to the fact that the length of the work-week had increased since 1945 and also to the various financial benefits received by workers as a result of new social welfare legislation passed immediately after liberation. Until at least 1955, increases in real wages did no result from any increase in the purchasing power of hourly wages. This explains the pessimism of the French working-class during the early 1950s and the continuing strength of the CGT in spite of the events of 1947. A poll taken in 1950 showed that 71% of the French wage-earners felt that their living standard had diminished in comparison with that of 1939. This view had not substantially changed five years later. Salary and wage-earners, asked whether their standard of living had improved during the last five years, answered in 1955 as shown in Table 1.4.

TABLE 1.4

POLL OF EMPLOYEES

	Yes	No	Did not work or did not answer
Wage-earners	38%	52%	10%
Salaried employees	54%	37%	9%
Supervisory employees	61%	33%	6%

Source: L. H. Parias, *Histoire du Peuple Français*, Nouvelle Librairie de France, Paris, 1967, p. 563.

The economic expansion of the 1950s did not diminish the traditional disparities in the standard of living of the *Français populaire*, the *Français classe moyenne* and the *Français dirigeant*. These disparities played a major role in maintaining the political instability which characterized the Fourth Republic.

The Hirsch Plan: 1954-1957

The recurrent waves of inflation experienced by the Fourth Republic had many undesirable effects on the French economy. Inflation undoubtedly hurt French foreign trade and resulted in foreign exchange scarcities which slowed down the modernization of the economy. Inflation forced the government to continue an undesirable policy of subsidies which tended to perpetuate the psychological *immobilisme* of many French entrepreneurs. By undermining the confidence of the people in their government, inflation contributed to political instability and to a lack of confidence in the future by both producers and consumers. The continuous rise in prices was a heavy burden for retired people living from a private or public pension; those depending exclusively on public pensions were simply forced into poverty. Inflation also caused serious social unrest as wage and salary earners compared the development of their standard of living with those of the merchants or other profit takers.

And yet, economic expansion continued in the midst of inflation. Indeed, economic activity tended to decline in times of governmental efforts to stabilize prices as in 1949, 1952 and 1958. Many Frenchmen believed that inflation had become the *sine qua non* of economic progress. The 1930s had been barren of economic innovation. Economic stagnation had not stimulated economic thought. The inflationary days of the Fourth Republic were, on the other hand, filled with new ideas and with the willingness to experiment and to change. A manifestation of this new postwar desire to renew production and distribution methods was economic planning. The pragmatic approach of Jean Monnet brought to France a rapid reconstruction of key industries and gave assurance to the United States that American aid had prevented the entire socialization of the French economy as desired by the then strong political Left.

The goals of the Hirsch Plan were much broader. Planning extended over the entire economy and the plan covered agriculture and construction as well as manufacturing. The planners not only strove for a 25% increase of the national product above 1952 levels, but also gave importance to the development of more efficient methods of production in order to allow France to compete with other industrialized nations. During the period of the Second Plan, industrial production was to increase by 30%, while agricultural output was to expand by 20%. The plan also aimed for a 60% increase in construction. Some of the production targets and their fulfillment appear in Table 1.5.

With the exception of petroleum production, handicapped by the Suez affair, most targets of the Hirsch Plan were not only attained in 1957, but even surpassed. During the period of this plan, industrial output grew at a yearly rate of over 9%. Although agricultural output as a whole achieved an increase of only 18.5%, the production of wheat and meat surpassed the assigned targets. The construction of dwelling units also exceeded the figure in the forecast. The production of automobiles had a 76% increase instead of the planned increase of 20%.

Causes of Economic Growth

The rapid economic expansion of France during the first postwar decade was the result of the interaction of two main factors, i.e., demographic growth and productivity increases.

In 1901, France counted 40.6 million inhabitants. In 1946, French school children were still learning that there were 40 million people in

TABLE 1.5.
PRODUCTION TARGETS

	Actual Production		Second Plan Target	Fulfillment as % of Target
	1952	1957		
Coal million tons	57.4	59.1	61	97
Electricity million kwh.	40.8	57.5	55	105
Petroleum million tons	21.5	25	30	83
Steel million tons	10.9	14.1	14	100
Cement million tons	8.6	12.5	10.8	115
Meat 1,000 tons	2,065	2,500	2,500	100
Wheat million *quintals*	84.2	110	95	116
Housing Units completed	74,920	270,000	240,000	111

Source: Commissariat Général du Plan de Modernisation et d'Equipement, *Rapport d'éxecution du Plan de Modernisation,* Paris, 1958, p. 6.

their country, and to be more exact, 40.3 million. During the inter-war period, the French population had actually diminished and a continuation of this trend in the postwar period could well have meant biological suicide. The trend was, however, suddenly reversed after the war in spite of difficult economic conditions. Between 1946 and 1955, the population started expanding by an average of 340,000 persons per year. This expansion in population was not due to any net immigration, but resulted entirely from an excess of births over deaths. The yearly rates of population growth in this period varied between 0.7% and 1.2% and are therefore not spectacular in themselves. Of much greater interest than the quantum of these rates is the causality of the sudden reversal in the population trend. Population started increasing after the end of the war because of the interaction of a rapidly falling death rate and a rise in the birth rate. Improved economic conditions after liberation, the impact of new social welfare measures enacted by de Gaulle's Provisional Government and by the Fourth Republic, and better public health and public sanitation systems explain to a large extent the fall in mortality rates. The rise in the number of births may have been due to better economic conditions in the country, but may also have manifested a definite postwar rupture from prewar attitudes and values. It seemed that Frenchmen, in spite of the political instability of the Fourth Republic, acquired, nevertheless, new confidence in their future and in the future of their children.

Population growth was of vital necessity in the process of economic reconstruction and expansion of an under-populated country. Equally important was the gradual lowering of the average age of the population. The age structure of the population changed between 1946 and 1955. During this period there occurred an 0.6% increase of persons over sixty-five years of age and a 3.5% increase of persons under twenty. At the same time, a continuous flow of people from the rural areas to the cities boosted the percentage figure of urban population in total population from 52.4% in 1936 to 56% in 1954 and to 67.3% in 1962. The *rajeunissement* of the French population and the fact that more Frenchmen lived in urban centers were factors undoubtedly favorable to further industrial expansion and modernization.

If economic growth is interpreted as a continuous growth in *per capita* output of goods and services, economic growth then means a continuous increase in labor productivity. For the period covered by the Monnet and Hirsch Plans, the real gross national output of France increased by about 4.5% per year, while the yearly average rate of growth of the employed labor force was only 0.3%. The growth of the country's real gross national product is therefore mainly attributable to increases in labor productivity.

France regained the 1938 level of national income as early as 1948; in 1950, France's national income reached that of the peak year 1929. Many Frenchmen in 1950 felt that from then on, national income would expand with great difficulty. There was, indeed, an alarming slowdown of economic activity in 1952 and 1953. Then, with a great momentum, national income attained unprecedented peaks throughout the rest of the decade. In 1961, national income was 87% larger than it had been in 1938 and 57% larger than that of 1929.

Figure 2 shows the principal demographic trends in France in the period 1930 to 1960.

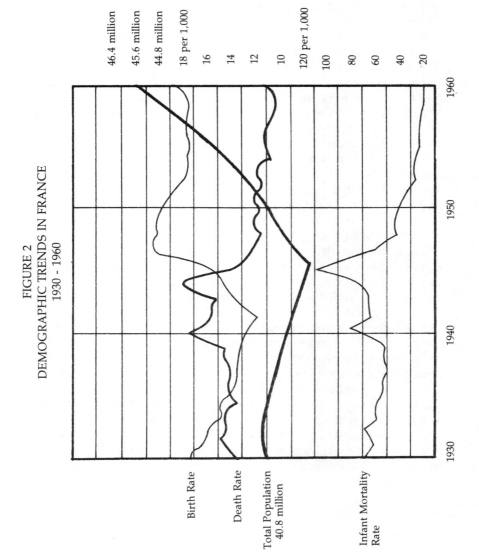

FIGURE 2
DEMOGRAPHIC TRENDS IN FRANCE
1930 - 1960

Figure 3 shows the remarkable postwar growth of French national income and industrial output. It should be noticed that for the period 1929 to 1955, the index of industrial output increased by only 18%. For the same period, the industrial output index increased by 61% in the United Kingdom, by 70% in Italy and by 86% in Western Germany. The low French figure reflects the difficult heritage postwar France received from the years of stagnation in the 1930s.

FIGURE 3
GROWTH OF INDUSTRIAL AND
NATIONAL OUTPUT: 1929-1960

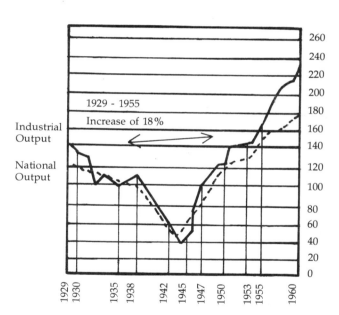

The beneficial increases in productivity experienced by the French economy were the direct result of the emphasis given by French planners to the modernization of the economy. Though a large part of the economy continued to be bound to traditional and inefficient methods of production and distribution, productivity advances in key industries gave France in the 1950s one of the highest labor productivity growth rates in Western Europe. These gains in productivity were achieved in spite of the adverse economic effects of the Korean war, of the war in Indo-China and of the later rebellion in Algeria, in spite of the 1956 Suez crisis and in spite of inflation.

Inflation was particularly damaging to the export industries and hindered both the growth of productivity in this sector of the economy and the growth of export capacity. While the 1938 volume of imports was regained as early as the spring of 1946, the volume of exports regained the 1938 level only in 1948. Inflation weakened the competitiveness of French products in world markets and induced French producers to give preference to the home market where prices were rising more rapidly than abroad. Inflation also strengthened the home demand for imports and contributed to the maintenance of a balance of payments deficit. France retained a large deficit in its balance of payments on current account until 1954, a deficit which varied between over $2 billion in 1946 and about $1 billion in 1951. The decline in the deficit after 1951 was not so much due to a decline in imports and growth of exports as to the large military expenditures of the United States in France.

During the early postwar years, trade and exchange controls, the governmental requisitioning of French private investments abroad and emergency American and English loans allowed France to import the foodstuffs and raw materials needed for economic recovery. Marshall Plan aid added to the import capacity of the country. Because the succeeding governments of the Fourth Republic, with the Pinay government as an exception, were unwilling or unable to secure price stability through effective fiscal and monetary policies, bilateral trade agreements and official devaluations of the franc became the chief instruments by means of which government attempted to correct the country's external difficulties.

The immediate effect of devaluation was to allow French exporters to receive a larger amount of home currency for every unit of foreign exchange earned. Devaluation thus allowed them to reduce the prices of their exports in terms of foreign currencies and placed them in a stronger competitive position in the international market. Devaluation also raised import prices expressed in home currency and therefore reduced the French demand for imports.

The exchange rate between the French franc and the American dollar had been fixed in December 1945 at 119.07 francs to the dollar. This rate of exchange was accepted by the I.M.F. in 1946 as the franc's official parity. Though during 1946 and 1947 France experienced a much more severe price inflation than its main trading partners, the dollar price of the franc was not altered. It was felt that since the country's imports were already down to an essential minimum and that since, at least in the short-run, export sales could not be increased because of production capacity constraints, devaluation would be unable to reduce the balance of payments deficit. However, in 1948, the single dollar rate of the franc was replaced by a complicated system of multiple rates. First of all, an official rate of 214.39 francs to the dollar applied to most dollar transactions. For tourist trade transactions, the applicable exchange rate was determined by a legal "free exchange market." In this market, the prices of the American and Canadian dollars, those of the Portuguese escudo and of the Swiss franc, were allowed to exceed the official rates of these currencies. In April 1949, the free market dollar rate reached 330 francs to the dollar. After the devaluation of the British pound in September 1949, a single exchange rate for all transactions was reintroduced and a new official dollar rate was fixed at 350 francs to the dollar. This new rate represented a devaluation of about 22% from the prior official rate. No further devaluation of the franc then took place until 1957.[20]

The devaluations of 1948 and 1949 furthered the expansion of French exports. From 1948 on, the rate of growth of French exports surpassed the rate of growth of imports. With 1938 as a base year, the index of the volume of imports grew from 29.7 in 1945 to 105 in 1950 and 132 in 1954. The corresponding indices for export volumes were 9.6 in 1945, 173 in 1950 and 206 in 1954.[21]

An Evaluation of French Industrial and Agricultural Growth

France, when compared to other major Western European industrial nations, was neither among the leaders nor among the laggards in industrial growth. During the 1950s, West Germany, Austria, Italy and the Netherlands experienced a faster expansion of industrial output than did France. During the period 1948 to 1954, the industrial output of West Germany almost trebled; that of Austria more than doubled; it nearly doubled in Italy. Industrial production grew by 51% in the Netherlands but by only 22% in France. France's industrial growth was, however, superior to that of Belgium, the United Kingdom and Sweden. The industrial output and employment indices of these countries appear in Table 1.6.

TABLE 1.6
INDUSTRIAL OUTPUT AND EMPLOYMENT INDICES, 1948-1954
1950=100

	West Germany		Austria		Italy	
	Output	Empl.	Output	Empl.	Output	Empl.
1948	55		63		79	
1949	79		84		87	
1950	100	100	100	100	100	100
1951	119	108	114	105	113	101
1952	128	112	115	103	116	101
1953	139	116	117	101	127	101
1954*	154	125	140	108	137	106

	Netherlands		France		United Kingdom	
	Output	Empl.	Output	Empl.	Output	Empl.
1948	81		90		87	
1949	91		94		93	
1950	100	100	100	100	100	100
1951	104	103	109	102	105	102
1952	106	100	108	101	101	102
1953	117	103	109	99	106	103
1954*	123	106**	110	100	105	106

	Belgium			Sweden	
	Output	Empl.		Output	Empl.
1948	98			92	
1949	98			95	
1950	100	100		100	100
1951	115	104		104	102
1952	112	102		103	99
1953	112	101		105	96
1954*	117	100		95	98

Sources: United Nations, Department of Economic Affairs, *Economic Survey of Europe in 1953*, Geneva, 1954, p. 219 and *Economic Survey of Europe in 1954*, Geneva, 1955, p. 199, 204. *1954 output figures are those for the third quarter of 1954. **June 1954 (all other employment data for 1954 taken as of September)

The data in Table 1.6 show that the average annual rate of growth of industrial output was 14.1% for West Germany, 11% for Austria, 8.2% for Italy, 6% for the Netherlands, 2.8% for France, 2.5% for the United Kingdom, 2.5% for Belgium and 0.4% for Sweden. With the exception of Italy and of the United Kingdom, it appears that during the first half of the 1950s, the rate of growth of industrial output was closely correlated to the rate of growth of industrial employment. West Germany and Austria showed the largest gains in employment during these years and also had the largest growth of industrial production. Industrial employment remained practically unchanged in France and Belgium and declined in Sweden.

The relatively poor performance of French industry should not be ascribed entirely to inflation and to the under-industrialization of the country at the end of the war. Demographic factors have also been important explanatory variables affecting the French postwar experience. In 1954, France recorded a century of population stagnation. As early as the second half of the nineteenth century, the French rate of natural increase of population had neared zero, while it was at least 1% per year for most other European countries. Not only did the population fail to expand, but its age structure tended to deteriorate. Since 1910, the share of population in the age group 15 to 59 years had steadily diminished. The data show that this share was 63.6% during the second decade of the century and 60.6% during the period 1930 to 1950.[22]

Technological progress and industrial expansion usually require high rates of population and labor force increase, since necessary changes in the occupational distribution of labor tend to be facilitated by a large yearly influx into the labor force of young, adaptable and trainable or trained young persons. In France, young men entering the labor force represented a smaller share of the total labor force than in other countries. A rapid increase in the labor force is also necessary if some industries are to expand without forcing a concurrent contraction in other economic activities. Population stagnation in France resulted in undesirable rigidities in the French productive structure. The lack of adequate growth of the labor force explains to a large extent why the French engineering industry did not expand during the period 1930 to 1955, while it doubled in West Germany and in the United Kingdom.

Demographic stagnation has also tended to discourage private investment. In a demographically stagnating economy, the growth of some sectors may necessitate the contraction of other areas in the economy. Private investors in sueh an economy are faced by larger investment uncertainties than investors in a generally expanding economy. When we add the unfavorable effects demographic stagnation has had on investment to the unfavorable effects inflation had on private saving, the data in Table 1.7 become quite understandable.

TABLE 1.7
PER CAPITA GROSS NATIONAL PRODUCT BY MAJOR COMPONENTS
IN FRANCE, THE UNITED KINGDOM AND WESTERN GERMANY
1952

GPN = 100

	France	United Kingdom	Western Germany
Gross National Product	100	100	100
Private Consumption	73	71	66
Investment	12	13	24
of which: Gross fixed capital formation	13	14	19
Civil Public Expenditure	5	4	5
National Defense	10	12	5

Source: United Nations, Department of Economic Affairs, *Economic Survey of Europe in 1954*, Geneva, 1955, p. 176.

The economic situation of France in the early 1950s was well described in a speech delivered by M. Mendès-France on December 30, 1951. The French statesman pointed out that although aggregate production in other European countries had surpassed 1929 levels, French production in 1951 was still smaller than that of 1929. Wages had been adjusted to prices ten times since liberation, but price inflation continued. The French consumer was unduly burdened by an inefficient system of indirect taxation then yielding 69% of France's revenue, when indirect taxes before the war amounted to only 55% of the public revenue. Finally, M. Mendès-France accused the government of subsidizing industry too generously and too indiscriminately and of relying too much on American aid, *espoir suprême et suprême pensée.* [23] Mendès-France did not exaggerate. The First and Second Modernization Plans were unable to transform and modernize the French economy. Old methods of production and of distribution continued to prevail in many economic sectors. Traditional ways and traditional attitudes remained particulary strong in agriculture.

It was not the *Code Civil* of 1803 alone which subjected over one-half of the arable land in France to an excessive number of minuscule and economically inefficient holdings. The extreme fragmentation of farming lands in many areas of France marks the survival of medieval practices and traditions originating in the ancient manorial system of agriculture. The tenth-century custom of allowing each peasant family in the manorial village to possess and cultivate various narrow strips of land dispersed throughout the fields of the *pars massaricia* survived the Revolution and five Republics.

Extreme fragmentation of land holdings developed in the course of time in the Loire Valley, the Northeast, Burgundy, the Béarn, the Rhône Valley and Limagne. In this latter area, the average size of the *parcelle* amounted to 0.08 hectares.[24] In the early 1950s the average French farmer owned about 42 scattered *parcelles* whose complete land area represented 14.5 hectares, i.e., 34.8 acres. This excessive fragmentation of the land retarded the modernization of agricultural practices since fragmentation of holdings often rendered mechanization and rational land use impossible. The uneconomic use of farms resulted in an exodus of the younger elements of the farm population; the consequent rural labor shortage added to the difficulties of the agricultural sector. One writer described land fragmentation as follows:

> A great many of the small parcels which make up a farm are too narrow and irregular in shape to permit them to be worked efficiently. Some are located a long way from the farm buildings. . . . Many parcels are completely surrounded by other parcels and so can be reached only by crossing another man's field. The haphazard location of these parcels takes no account of the slope of the land and so makes rational soil erosion control impossible. The amount of time spent going to and from these lots represents a considerable amount of unproductive labor and reduces the production per man hour. According to one study on this point it was estimated that for 10 hours of work the time actually spent working the soil was 9½ hours on consolidated holdings and only 8 hours on a parcelized farm.[25]

A land consolidation law, passed by the Vichy government in March 1941, was re-enacted by the de Gaulle government in 1945 but did not lead to any noticeable reallocation of holdings for the purpose of land consolidation until 1953. By October 1950, consolidation under the provisions of the law had not been initiated in 25 departments and had barely started in 39. The strong *amour de la terre* of the French peasant made him reluctant to give up ownership of small plots of land inherited from his ancestors. This phenomenon explains why agricultural recovery after 1945 was much slower than the recovery of industrial production. In 1952, total agricultural output was only 3% higher than it had been in 1938. Throughout the 1950s, agriculture remained one of the weakest sectors in the economy. While it employed one-third of the working population, it generated less than one-fifth of national income.

The indices in Table 1.8 show that in many respects French agricultural practices remained very inferior to those of Western Germany, Denmark and the United Kingdom.

TABLE 1.8

AGRICULTURE IN FRANCE: INTERNATIONAL COMPARISONS
1954

France = 100

	Production per active male	Production per hectare of agricultural area	Yields per milking cow per year	Use of Fertilizer per hectare of agricultural area
France	100	100	100	100
Denmark	203	200	169	292
Western Germany	120	170	135	341
United Kingdom	207	117	136	177
Italy	47	110	85	76

Source: United Nations, Department of Economic and Social Affairs, *Economic Survey of Europe in 1954*, Geneva, 1955, p. 184.

Fragmentation of land and slowly changing methods of production did not, however, characterize the entirety of French agriculture in the 1950s. In the industrial north, large-scale farming utilizing advanced techniques resulted in crop and livestock yields that compared favorably with those of Western Germany. Agriculture was not as technologically advanced in Alsace, Lorraine and in the intensive-production belt along the Mediterranean coast; still, output per man and per hectare in these regions reached the levels obtained in Western Germany. Throughout the rest of France, agriculture tended to remain under-developed and tied to traditional practices. The agricultural sector, just like the industrial one, was unable to escape economic dualism.

The Fourth Republic saw the successive withdrawal from government of members of the strong Communist and Socialist parties. With them went the Resistance dream of modernizing the entire French economy. After 1947, more conservative governments chose to maintain a bourgeois democracy in France and an economic system which should not differ too much from that of the Third Republic. These governments were equally frightened by Communists and Gaullists. The para-military pomp of the Gaullist R.P.F. ceremonials definitely had a Fascist flavor and the centrist M.R.P. leaders were quite concerned by the enthusiasm shown for de Gaulle by the many shopkeepers, artisans and former Vichyites that formed France's *petite bourgeoisie*. In 1947, thousands of Frenchmen started acclaiming de Gaulle as France's Man of Destiny, as France's indispensable *Fuehrer*. These were the people who disliked and opposed any social or economic change; these were the men and women who would never accept the Resistance-inspired economic revolution. Planning and American aid brought change to parts of the economy. In many sectors, however, economic life remained tied to old practices, attitudes and values.

NOTES

1. OEEC, *Progress and Problems of the European Economy* (Paris, January 1954), p. 94.
2. D.S. Landes, "Observations on France, Economy, Society and Polity," *World Politics*, vol. 9 (1957), p. 335
3. W.C. Baum, *The French Economy and the State* (Princeton: Princeton University Press, 1958) p. 15.
4. J. Lecerf, *La Percée de L'Economie Française* (Paris: B. Arthaud, 1963), pp. 11-12.
5. R.V. Rosa, "The Problem of French Recovery," *Economic Journal* (June 1949), pp. 154-170.
6. Baum, *The French Economy and the State*, pp. 43-46.
7. Report for the Joint Economic Committee, 85th Congress, 2nd Session *Economic Policy in Western Europe*, (reprinted by Greenwood Press, New York, 1968), p. 13.
8. A. Werth, *France, 1940-1955* (London: R. Hale, Ltd., 1956), p. 499.
9. C. De Gaulle, *War Memoirs: Salvation 1944-46* (New York: Simon & Schuster, 1960), p. 369.
10. Commissariat Général du Plan de Modernisation et d'Equipement, *Rapport Général sur le Premier Plan de Modernisation et d'Equipement* (Paris, 1947), p. 24.
11. De.Gaulle, *War Memoirs: Salvation 1944-1946*, p. 372.

12. For further details about French planning procedure see J. Hackett and A. M. Hackett, *Economic Planning in France* (Cambridge: Harvard University Press, 1965); J. S. Harlow, *French Economic Planning* (Iowa City: University of Iowa Press, 1966); V. Lutz, *French Planning* (Washington: American Enterprise Institute, 1965); P. Bauchet, *Economic Planning, The French Experience* (New York: Praeger, 1964).

13. Baum, *The French Economy and the State,* pp. 26-27.

14. Comité National de la Productivité, *Actions et Problémes de Productivité* (Paris, 1953), p. 472.

15. W.C. Peterson, "Planning and Economic Progress in France," *World Politics,* vol. 9 (1957), pp. 351-382.

16. Comité National de la Productivité, *Actions et Problèmes de Productivité,* p. 471.

17. *Ibid.,* p. 472.

18. A. S. Vasconcellos, and B.F. Kiker, "The Performance of the French Economy Under Planning: 1949-1964, *Economics of Planning,* vol. 8 (1968), pp. 157-104.

19. Institut National de la Statistique et des Etudes Economiques, *Mouvement Economique en France, 1944-1957* (Paris, 1958).

20. L.B. Yeager, *International Monetary Relations* (New York: Harper & Row, 1966), pp. 395-403.

21. Baum, *The French Economy and the State,* p.88.

22. United Nations, Department of Economic Affairs, *Economic Survey of Europe in 1954* (Geneva, 1955), p. 175.

23. Werth, *France, 1940-1955, pp. 551-552.*

24. *H. Brousse, Le Niveau de Vie en France* (Paris: Presses Universitaires de France, 1949), p. 84.

25. F.O. Sargent, "Fragmentation of French Land: Its Nature, Extent and Causes," *Land Economics,* vol. 28 (August 1952), p. 218.

CHAPTER 2

THE TEUTONIC PHOENIX RISES FROM ITS ASHES
WESTERN GERMAN ECONOMIC RECONSTRUCTION AND EXPANSION
1945 - 1955

The Yalta and Potsdam Agreements

On June 5, 1945, the commanders-in-chief of the Allied Powers — Eisenhower, Zhukov, Montgomery and de Lattre de Tassigny — proclaimed in Berlin the details of the unconditional surrender of the whole German nation. Germany, with a population of over 60 million, was to be occupied by the armies of four countries and was to be governed by four governments entertaining very different views about its political and economic future.

The idea of an unconditional surrender not only by the German armed forces buy by all of the German people had been urged by Roosevelt during his meeting with Churchill at Casablanca in January, 1943. Roosevelt's proposal was accepted two years later by Churchill and Stalin when all three met at Yalta in the Soviet Union in the early days of February, 1945. The Yalta protocol stated that "we have agreed on common policies and plans for enforcing the unconditional surrender terms which we shall impose together on Nazi Germany after German armed resistance has been finally crushed." At Yalta, the Big Three found no difficulty in agreeing on a number of resolutions affecting postwar Germany. National Socialism and all its agencies would be eliminated and German militarism would be destroyed. Germany was to be burdened with reparation payments in the form of confiscations of capital equipment, levies on current output and the use of the labor of German war prisoners. The Yalta protocol declared: "The United Kingdom, the United States of America, and the U.S.S.R. shall possess supreme authority with respect to Germany. In the exercise of such authority they will take such steps, including the complete disarmament, demilitarization, and the dismemberment of Germany as they deem requisite for future peace and security. . . ."

There were, however, major issues on which the Big Three could not agree. The problem of a western Polish frontier revealed discord in the views of the three heads of state. The Soviet Union, declaring that it would keep the Polish territories it had annexed in 1939, proposed to compensate Poland by allowing it to annex German lands situated east of the Oder and Western Neisse rivers and Stettin. The U.S.S.R., by an agreement of Arpil 21, 1945, proceeded to allow Poland to govern these territories, although the negotiators had concluded in Yalta that the fixation of a permanent western Polish border should be determined at a Peace Conference in which Germany would participate. Another border problem involved the establishment of military zones of occupation in Germany. A tripartite European Advisory Commission formed by the Big Three had spent most of 1944 working on a protocol establishing three postwar zones of occupation in Germany. The protocol of November 14, 1944, was ratified at Yalta a few months later, and at Yalta, Stalin was persuaded to agree to a French zone of occupation. Under these agreements, Berlin received special treatment since it was to be governed jointly by the Allies. In Berlin, a Control Commission formed by the commanders-in-chief of the Big Three was to issue orders affecting the whole of Germany, while each commander-in-chief became the supreme authority in his respective occupation zone. At Yalta, it was finally agreed that France would participate in the Control Commission.

Another major problem which was not finally settled at Yalta was the matter of German reparation payments. There was general agreement among the discussants that Germany should help rebuild economies victimized by German military occupation, particularly the Soviet economy. German destruction of human life and economic wealth in the Soviet Union had been particularly severe. The western half of European Russia and virtually all of Belorussia and the Ukraine had been systematically devastated. Between twenty and twenty-five million Russians had perished during the war. The war had brought about the destruction of 60% of the Soviet mining and metallurgical industries; only 45% of the 1940 steel producing capacity was still usable after the war. At Yalta, the Soviet delegation made it clear that the U.S.S.R. would make maximum use of the German economy to reconstruct the badly damaged Soviet economy and demanded that "the German national economy should, first, be deprived for two years of the use of all its factories, heavy machinery, machine tools, rolling stock and foreign investments and, secondly, should make annual reparation payments for ten years in manufactures or raw materials." [1]

The Anglo-Americans at Yalta did not accept the Soviet point of view. The Anglo-American delegation did not agree to the Soviet demand of $20 billion total German reparation payments. Roosevelt, having at that time rejected most of the Morgenthau Plan proposals, took the view that sufficient industrial capacity had to be left to Germany so that it would be able to finance, by means of exports, the imports of foodstuffs and raw materials it badly needed. The final Conference communiqué stated in a very vague fashion that Germany would "make compensation in kind to the greatest extent possible."

Following Germany's surrender, the Big Three met again in July 1945, at Potsdam in Germany. The Conference started on July 16 with Truman taking the position of Roosevelt who had died on April 12. During the course of negotiations, Attlee replaced Churchill. France was not invited to participate in these meetings. Although France was now granted a fourth zone of occupation in Germany, including the coal rich Saar valley, the cold-shouldering of France left General de Gaulle with lasting ill-feelings toward his Anglo-American allies.

With no German government in existence at this time, the negotiators could not draft a peace treaty with Germany. Instead, a final "protocol of proceedings" proclaimed the joint resolutions of the chief negotiators. Germany was to be completely disarmed and de-militarized, and to prevent a revival of aggressive militarism, as had happened after World War I, German industrial capacity was to be curtailed. The highly oligopolistic industrial and banking structures of Nazi Germany were to be decentralized and decartellized, but, contrary to the much discussed Morgenthau Plan, Germany would still be treated as an economic unit by the new military governments. Germany was not to be dismembered as had been planned at Yalta, and the military zones of occupation were to be only a temporary arrangement pending a final peace treaty with Germany which would restore political unity to the country. The onset of the Cold War prevented, of course, the realization of these 1945 goals.

The Potsdam negotiators left the details of German reparation obligations as vague as they had been enounced at Yalta. The Potsdam protocol did not explicitly allow the occupying powers to satisfy their indemnification claims against Germany through the use of forced German labor.

German industrial capacity not deemed essential to a peacetime economy by the military commanders would be dismantled and appropriated by the military authorities to satisfy the claims of their nations against Germany. Each military government was to appropriate surplus capital equipment in its zone. In this way, the Soviet Union was allowed to satisfy the claim it had presented at Yalta from German areas under its control. When the Soviets protested that the western powers had acquired control of over 60% of German industry, the negotiators resolved that 10% of the industrial facilities dismantled in the western zones would be automatically delivered to the Soviet Union and that a further 15% would be exchanged against Soviet deliveries of foodstuffs and raw materials. Removals of capital equipment were to end within two years. This agreement avoided the necessity for the negotiators to fix the quantum of German war reparations in terms of money. Although reparations obligations were to be satisfied on a zonal basis, the negotiators fully expected that their commanders-in-chief, acting jointly, would coordinate their economic policies in order to allow the entire German economy to rebuild and develop in order to "assure the production and maintenance of goods and services required to meet the needs of the occupying forces and displaced persons in Germany and essential to maintain in Germany average living standards not exceeding the average of the standards of living of European countries." The rapidly forming fissure between the Soviet Union and its wartime allies defeated the Potsdam scheme, and the growing tensions between the occupying powers brought first an economic partition of Germany and eventually, a political one.

In March 1946, the four Allied Powers reached an agreement concerning the industrial capacity Germany would be allowed to retain under the Potsdam resolutions. On the whole, German heavy industry was to be reduced to between 50% and 55% of its 1938 capacity. The production of commodities necessary for a war economy was either forbidden or subjected to drastic limitations. German industry was not permitted to produce certain machine tools, radio-transmitting equipment, aircraft, seagoing vessels, ball-bearings, arms and ammunition, synthetic rubber, or various other products of the chemical industry. The output of steel could not exceed 7.5 million tons, about 30% of the prewar output. Chemicals which were allowed could not surpass 40% of the 1938 output.[2] The agreement provided that over 1,500 factories in the U.S. and U.K. zones would be dismantled for appropriation by the victorious powers. An Inter-Allied Reparations Agency was established in Brussels to distribute these appropriations among several claimants. It was not long until these policies were severely criticized in western Europe. The *Economist* in England viewed them as "an "unparalleled essay in international machine wrecking . . . as anachronistic and dangerous as the primitive and spontaneous machine-smashing of the Luddite age."[3]

The March resolutions were ignored in the Soviet and French zones where the military governments proceeded to appropriate a maximum of industrial facilities. The Russians promptly confiscated half of the industrial plants in their zone and levied heavily on the output of whatever remained. During the second half of 1945 neither the Soviet Union nor France appeared very much interested in implementing the Potsdam provisions regarding German economic unity. No foodstuffs or raw materials were shipped from the Soviet zone to the other zones and in May 1946, American military authorities temporarily suspended deliveries of German capital equipment to the Soviet Union. Less than one year after the Potsdam meetings, Churchill was warning at Fulton about the menace of the "Iron Curtain" and urging the "free world" to be strong enough to resist Communist threats.

The German Economy: 1945-1948

Many German cities had been extensively damaged by British-American bombings. The largest part of Frankfurt am Main, Dresden, and Leipzig had been completely destroyed. Allied bombs had crippled transportation facilities. In the British zone of occupation, only 10% of the railroad installation had escaped war damage. Industrial output in the various zones was only a small percentage of prewar levels; at the end of 1945, the American zone produced only 10% of the 1936 industrial ouput.[4] And yet, Germany had not been as seriously damaged by the war as initial observations tended to suggest. Under the debris of bombed factories, most of the machinery remained intact or subject to easy repair. Selective bombing had spared many German installations. The Allies left the I.G. Farben headquarters in Frankfurt am Main untouched, even though three-fourths of the city lay in ruins. It has been estimated that war-time destruction of industrial capacity amounted to only 10% for metallurgy, 10% to 15% for the chemical industry and about 20% for textiles.[5] Wartime industrial losses were more than offset by the Nazi additions to productive capacity during the years of war. The economy suffered more from the break-down of the transportation system, the lack of housing, the chaotic financial situation and the inflow into Germany of millions of "ethnic Germans" expelled from Poland, Czechoslovakia and other central European areas, than from the destruction of productive capacity. Indeed, it was the existence of excess productive capacity that allowed West Germany to develop rapidly after 1948.

In spite of the bombings and ground fighting, most of the German labor force was still well-nourished in May 1945. A surprisingly large stock of foodstuffs and raw materials, extracted from the countries Germany once controlled, still existed in Germany at the time of surrender. But the standard of living worsened rapidly from then on, partly because of the production restrictions imposed on Germany. A serious food shortage developed in 1946. In the Anglo-American zones, many Germans had to survive on the basis of food rations representing less than 1000 calories per day. West Germans were not yet able to utilize export earnings to import needed foodstuffs. To avoid mass starvation in their zones, the U.S. and Britain were forced to finance foodstuff imports amounting to about $700 million per year. Matters worsened when coal shortages developed during the winter of 1946, forcing many factories to stop operations.

On September 6, 1946, James F. Byrnes, American Secretary of State, in a speech delivered at Stuttgart, declared that it was the policy of the United States to help in the improvement of the German standard of living and thus implicitly rejected the Soviet position that German reparation payments should command top priority in Allied policies regarding Germany. Byrnes urged that "Germany must be given a chance to export goods in order to import enough to make her economy self-sustaining." In December of 1946, a British-American resolution provided for a fusion of the British and American zones of occupation and Bizonia was established on January 1, 1947. In fact, Byrnes had offered to merge the economies of the United States' zone with those of any or all the other zones for the sake of German economic unity; but only the British accepted the American proposal. The merging of the French zone with the other two was delayed until April, 1948. The Anglo-American arrangement provided for a Joint Export-Import Agency (JEIA) for Bizonia which was funded with $121 million. This agency was to develop German exports and to utilize their proceeds to finance necessary imports.

The inconsistencies in the occupation policies of the four Allied Powers became quite obvious during a Foreign Ministers Conference held in Moscow in March 1947. The French strongly opposed any liberalization of the level-of-industry agreements for Germany. France's Bidault refused to support the furtherance of German economic unity. Although Molotov supported the idea of restoring economic unity to Germany, he claimed that the creation of Bizonia had violated the terms of the Potsdam Agreement and in order to allow the Soviet Union to obtain its $10 billion war indemnification from Germany, Molotov asked that the Allied Powers should levy on current German output for a period of about twenty years. Molotov also demanded that the Soviet Union should be allowed to participate in a quadripartite agency in charge of administering the Ruhr. The American Secretary of State, George C. Marshall, felt that the Soviet demands would render Germany "an economic poorhouse in the center of Europe."[6] Marshall and Bevin argued that the acceptance of Molotov's proposals would force the Anglo-Americans to carry the burden of reparation payments to the U.S.S.R.

The sharp disagreements between the Big Four at Moscow announced the beginning of the Cold War. The Moscow Conference also rendered the economic and political division of Germany inevitable. Following this conference, Great Britain and the United State simply decided to administer Bizonia independently of the other two Allied Powers and started changing occupation policies still influenced by the Morgenthau Plan. In spite of strong French protests, level-of-industry restrictions were liberalized so that the industrial output in the Anglo-American zones could increase to its 1936 level. On May 25, 1947, an Economic Council was established in Germany for Bizonia. Although the dismantling of capital equipment continued in the western zones, the number of German plants subject to confiscation in Bizonia was sharply reduced.

These measures did not, however, help the stagnating economies of the western zones very much. Fuel and raw materials shortages and a continuous inflow of millions of refugees from the East turned feeding and housing problems into a nightmare. The uselessness of money as a means of exchange, largely because of a general expectation of a currency reform which did not arrive until mid-1948, and the resulting hoarding of assets by individuals and firms, seemed to make economic recovery hopeless. A journalist travelling at this time in Germany observed:

> In Hanover, I took the tram outside the station and for upwards of an hour, as I travelled past mile upon mile of houses gutted by bombs and fire, all I could see of what had once been a city was a vast mound of dust and rubble. At Bremen it was the same: little piles of bricks and stones, and as far as the eye could reach not a single house that was still intact. In Cologne, in Hamburg, in Frankfurt, in Berlin, in Munich, in Dresden, the same experience was repeated. The rations we lived on were absurd. At Essen, I stayed with a family where the young daughter went out to work in the morning with nothing but a slice of bread and a tomato to last the whole day.[7]

These sad economic conditions were, of course, not peculiar to Germany alone. The situation was no better in Italy, Greece, Yugoslavia, Poland and the U.S.S.R. Millions of Europeans would not have survived the hardships of 1946 in the absence of American economic aid. American aid in excess of $2 billion, distributed by the United Nations Relief and Rehabilitation Administration, benefited countries liberated from German occupation. Even the enemy countries, mainly Germany and Japan, received American gifts of civilian supplies worth about 3.5 billion.

Further American aid to Europe was proposed by Secretary of State Marshall in his Harvard University speech of June 5, 1947. Marshall suggested that if the European countries would be willing to work out a joint economic recovery program, the United State would finance the European effort. The Soviet Union and other countries of Eastern Europe decided not to accept Marshall Plan aid, while sixteen European countries, including West Germany, represented by the Allied commanders-in-chief, proceeded to draft a recovery program for presentation to the United States government. On July 12, the delegates of these countries formally declared that "the German economy should be integrated into the economy of Europe in such a way as to contribute to a raising of the general standard of life.''[8] In the spring of 1948, West Germany was admitted as a member of the Organization for European Economic Cooperation (OEEC), established on April 16, 1948. While East Germany was one of the countries that had been forced to follow the Soviet resolution of reconstructing without Marshall Plan funds, West Germany was to receive about $1.4 billion in Marshall Plan aid.

The Monetary Reform and the Beginning of the Social Market Economy: 1948 - 1951

Only a comprehensive system of rationing and wage and price controls had allowed the Nazi government to suppress a major German wartime inflation. During the war, large-scale government spending had resulted in a sharp increase in German monetary wealth while real wealth steadily declined. Between 1936 and 1945, the Reich debt grew from RM 30 billion to 800 billlion. During this period, the currency in circulation expanded from RM 5 billion to 50 billion and bank deposits increased from RM 30 billion to 150 billion.[9]

Pending a quadripartite solution to the threat of serious inflation, the Allied Powers decided to retain temporarily most of the Nazi economic controls. It was only logical for Germans to expect that sooner or later the ruling military governments would order a general currency reform in order to re-establish a sound monetary system. in Germany. This expectation gave cause to a general belief that in an undefined future, the value of the Reichsmark would be drastically reduced. Any currency reform would reduce the money supply and a rumor circulated in the country that this reform would probably destroy up to 90% of the existing money supply. The direct result of these expectations was a flight from the Reichsmark, and individuals and firms started hoarding assets.[10] Firms were reluctant to sell goods for money which could become practically worthless within a few weeks. It has been estimated that during 1947 and early 1948, about half of the current output in Bizonia was hoarded by firms, while the other half was sold to special customers. The average consumer found almost no goods in the market.[11]

1946 and 1947 passed and the four occupying powers were still unable to agree on a German currency reform program. In the Soviet Zone, an immediate reorganization of the banking system had taken place at the end of the war; five new state banks replaced the private commercial banking system and a blocking of bank deposits effectively reduced the money supply in the eastern zone of occupation. In the western zones, the reorganization of the prewar banking system was only completed in 1948 after differences in American and British policies were finally reconciled.

The Americans, remembering that Hitler's acts of aggression had been supported by the enormous concentration of banking and industrial power that had developed in Germany since Bismarck's days, interpreted the Potsdam Agreement as obligating the occupying powers to decentralize the German banking system in order to limit the degree of control German banks had acquired over industry. The United States Military Government felt that European peace would be served best by establishing in Germany a new banking system largely patterned after the American Federal Reserve System. The *Reichsbank* and the oligopolistic *Grossbanken* were to be eliminated. Instead of a new national central bank, state central banks were to be created, one for each German state or *Land*. This *Landeszentralbank* was to serve the particular *Land* as a banker's bank. An American banking reform proposal was presented in November 1945 to the Allied Control Council in Berlin. This plan defined the functions of the projected state central banks. They were to be initially financed by each *Land* government, although eventually, private banks in each *Land* would provide the capital of the state central bank. These banks were to perform many of the services of a central bank. They were to regulate the reserve requirements of private banks, hold their reserves as deposits, regulate interest and discount rates and engage in open-market operations. They were to act as the fiscal agent of the *Land* government and were to supervise clearing and settlement transactions of banks within the *Land*. They were not to have the power to issue notes, nor could they determine their own monetary policy. Instead, an Allied Banking Board and a *Land* Central Bank Commission, the latter representing the various state central banks, were to formulate general currency and banking policies for all of the *Laender*. These two agencies were to have exclusive control over the issuance of currency. Under the American plan, private banks were not allowed to maintain branches outside of the *Land* in which the head office was located.

Although the French and Russian members of the Control Council supported the American proposal of decentralizing the German banking structure, the British delegate took a different position and argued for the creation of a new central banking mechanism. The American plan failed to obtain unanimous support during the final discussions of October 1946.

The Americans then proceeded to implement their plan unilaterally in their zone of occupation. In each *Land* of the U.S. zone, a *Land* central bank was created. The board of directors of these banks included representatives of industry, agriculture, labor, trade and government.

In May 1947, branches of the *Deutsche Bank, Dresdner Bank,* and *Commerzbank* in the American zone of occupation were transformed into a large number of small, independent banks, operating under different names.

The French, following the American example, also established *Land* central banks in their zone, but left it to the determination of each *Land* to decide whether the ownership of such banks would be private or public. Branches of the *Grossbanken* in the zone were also changed into new, independent banks.

The existing banking system in the British zone was left practically intact until 1948. British policy continued to emphasize the need for centralized control over any new system of German banking, and in the British zone of occupation, the military government took it upon itself to act as the central bank. Head offices for the *Reichsbank,* the *Deutsche Bank,* the *Dresdner Bank* and the *Commerzbank* were set up in Hamburg to replace former Berlin headquarters. In October 1947, following the creation of Bizonia, a banking agreement was finally reached by the British and the Americans. The British consented to replace the *Reichsbank* in their zone by *Land* central banks and to decentralize the *Grossbanken;* the Americans agreed to the creation of a new central banking agency that would coordinate monetary and banking policies in the eight *Laender* of Bizonia. The French joined this agreement and on March 1, 1948, the *Bank Deutscher Laender* was established in Frankfurt. This was to be a banker's bank for the Land central banks. It was to hold the legal reserves of these banks, rediscount paper for them and lend them money. It was also given the exclusive power to determine monetary and banking policies for the western zones and to issue currency. It was to deal primarily with the *Land* central banks, the central banks of other countries, and after the establishment of the German Federal Republic, with its government and agencies. [12] Its capital was subscribed by the various *Land* central banks and its board of directors was formed by presidents and officials of these banks. It was not allowed to establish branches or subsidiaries or to engage in commercial transactions.

Following the establishment of this new banking system in the western zones of occupation, different from the banking system in the Soviet zone, economic separation between these two areas was further accentuated by the establishment of a new monetary system for the western zones in June 1948.

The American authorities in Germany had presented as early as 1946 a detailed currency reform proposal to the Control Council in Berlin but, largely because of Soviet objections, no general agreement was ever reached. Meanwhile, the large volume of currency in circulation and the expectation of a drastic curtailment in the supply of money had made money a useless means of exchange in the western zones of occupation. Cigarettes rather than Reichsmarks became the accepted means of exchange. Goods were traded either by barter or at very high prices in the black market. No one wanted to hold money. Professor Lutz describes the situation as follows:

> Individuals and business firms acquired most of the commodities they wanted by exchange against commodities they had to offer, and a whole series of exchanges were sometimes necessary to obtain the desired commodity. Every firm had several specialists, called "compensators," on its staff. If, for example, cardboard for packing was needed, the compensator might be obliged to barter the plant's own products for typewriters, the typewriters for shoes, and the shoes for cardboard. All this was not only illegal but involved tremendous costs. . . Workers and employees also insisted on being paid partly in kind, and bartered the commodities they received against others which they needed. Most people had no inducement to earn more money than was required to buy the rations at prices which were, on the whole, still fixed at the pre-war level. It was profitable for a man to be absent one or two days a week from his job if he could use the time to cultivate his own garden, to forage in the countryside for food, or to operate in the black market. . . . By the middle of 1948, the economy had reached a state of paralysis resulting in near-starvation for a large part of the population. [13]

In June 1948, the military commanders of the three western zones finally ordered for their zones the long delayed currency reform. This reform was effectuated between June 20 and June 26. The general goal of the reform laws was to reduce currency in circulation and bank deposits amounting to about 130 billion *Reichsmark* (RM) to about 12 or 13 billion of a new currency named the *Deutsche Mark* (DM). The currency reform was decreed independently of any German approval, and as a German historian put it: "Thus, in the case of the Federal Republic, we have the completely paradoxical position that, instead of money being created by the State, the State was created by money." [14]

The reform program did not establish a single rate of exchange between the old *Reichsmark* and the *Deutsche Mark*. During the week of currency reform, each individual was allowed to exchange 40 RM notes for 40 new DM notes. Furthermore, individuals and firms were ordered to deposit RM note holdings into special accounts. The aggregate of these RM note deposits and existing RM bank deposits was then transformed into a DM bank balance at the exchange rate of 10 RM to 1 DM. The owner of this balance was allowed free disposal over 50% of this new DM bank balance and the remainder was blocked.

On October 1st, it was ordered that 70% of the blocked bank accounts would be cancelled, 20% would be released and 10% would continue being blocked. This measure transformed the rate of exchange to 10 RM for 0.6 DM. However, all private debts were to be paid at the 10 to 1 rate; in this way, creditors obtained an advantageous exchange rate.

During the reform week of June, firms were allowed to receive 60 DM per employee at the 10 to 1 rate. If firms lacked sufficient RM holdings to obtain the new currency, they still could receive 60 DM per employee at the 1 to 1 rate. After that week, firms were forced to sell if they needed more DM funds. This caused goods that had been hoarded to appear suddenly on the market.

RM balances held by state and local governments and by other public agencies were cancelled. To enable these agencies to continue their operations, they were granted a gift of DM equivalent to their semi-annual receipts in the period October 1, 1947, to March 31, 1948. The military governments of the three western zones were also granted an endowment of 770 million DM.

The currency reform rendered worthless a large part of the assets of commercial banks. Claims against the Reich and deposits held in other banks were cancelled. Commercial loans were transformed at the 10 to 1 ratio. On the liability side, customers' demand and time deposits were transformed into DM initially at the 10 to 1 ratio, and as of October 1, 1948, at the 16 to 1 ratio. Still, the reform placed private commercial banks in a position where liabilities greatly exceeded assets. In order to strengthen these banks, the reform program provided that these banks would receive claims against the *Laender* amounting to the difference between their assets and their liabilities plus capital.

The currency reform was severely criticized, both on economic and social grounds. The amount of DM in circulation, excluding bank loans, reached about 12.3 billion by the end of 1948. Private bank loans extended during the second half of 1948 amounted to about 5 billion DM. It has been contended that the reform resulted in the creation of too much money. More particularly, it has been pointed out that the reform created potentially inflationary commercial bank reserves. As of June 20, 1948, these banks had been ordered to hold 10% reserves against demand deposits and 5% against time deposits. The reform laws also vested these banks with DM credits which gave the banks large excess reserves.[15] Given the fact that the "free accounts" of firms were released only gradually, in this period firms started borrowing heavily from the banks. In spite of the large liquidity of the commercial banking system in June, private banks started borrowing from the central banking system in order to maintain reserves supporting short-term commercial loans of DM 4.4 million outstanding in December. The rapid expansion in the money supply, combined with the eagerness of West Germans to convert rising personal money incomes into real assets, brought about price increases. Prices rose by about 10% during the second half of 1948. Early in November, the *Bank Deutscher Laender* finally decided to curb inflation. Minimum reserve requirements for demand deposits were raised from 10% to 15% for certain commercial banks, and commercial banks were requested not to expand their loans beyond the level of October 31, 1948. The discount rate was left unchanged at 5% and the rate of interest charged by private banks remained at between 6% and 9%. Prices started stabilizing in December.

It was also argued that the currency reform laws resulted in a more unequal distribution of wealth. Holders of claims against the Reich were impoverished while hoarders of real assets were not affected by the reform program. Holders of private claims were favored in comparison to owners of bank deposits. In spite of the unequal treatment given to those who kept their savings in money and those who kept them in the form of land, buildings or commodities, the average German had reason to feel that the currency reform brought about an immediate improvement in living conditions. Professor Lutz describes the rapid economic change following the reform as follows:

> On June 19th, a Saturday, not a single article could be seen or had in the retail shops. On June 21st the shops were full of goods: housewares, textiles, cameras, etc. These stocks had been withheld, because with the knowledge that the reform was imminent, no trader wanted to sell against RM and be left with RM balances. The supply of goods in retail shops, which had never been large since the end of the war, had completely dried up in the months preceding the reform . . . The development which took place during the following six months can, however, not be ascribed solely to the currency reform. The return to the free market economy for almost all industrial products (the most important exceptions being coal, iron and steel), and the Marshall aid which began to arrive in larger amounts toward the end of the year, share with the currency reform the merit of having brought about a remarkable revival of the German economy.[16]

The deterioration of relationships between the Soviet Union and its former wartime allies had become quite apparent at the Moscow and London Conferences of March and December 1947. The accusations traded between the delegates of the Western Powers and those of the Soviet Union announced the end of quadripartite government of Germany. This end was dramatized on March 19, 1948, when, during a meeting of the Control Council in Berlin, Marshal Sokolovsky of the U.S.S.R. read to the other delegates a list of Soviet charges against their policies in Germany, then rose and left the meeting. During the following weeks, Soviet policy in Germany took on a more threatening character. The Soviet controlled radio and press started asserting that all of Berlin was part of the Soviet zone of occupation. Soviet military authorities started subjecting road and rail traffic moving between Berlin and the western zones to irregular but increasingly frequent difficulties. Finally, on June 16, the Russians left the Berlin Kommandatura in protest against alleged American discourtesy.

On June 18, the western military commanders informed Marshal Sokolovsky that on June 20, a new currency would be introduced into the western zones of occupation, but that Berlin would remain for the time being outside the area of currency reform. On the following day, Sokolovsky announced that the new western marks would not be allowed to circulate in the area of Greater Berlin, a city which "comes within the Soviet zone of occupation and is economically part of the Soviet zone." On June 22, a currency reform was proclaimed for the Soviet zone and all of Berlin. On June 24, the western military authorities resolved that both new western and eastern marks would be allowed to circulate in the western sectors of Berlin. The Russians, declaring this resolution to be illegal, proceeded to block all traffic between Berlin and the western zones. The Berlin blockade became one more step in the direction of a politically divided Germany. Suddenly Berlin was not the symbol of Prussian militarism and Nazidom; in the matter of a few days, it had become a bastion of beleaguered European democracy. General Clay's airlift scheme to save Berlin quickly transformed the German enemy of 1945 into a 1948 ally of the Western Powers. Although the Berlin blockade ended on May 5, 1949, its political and economic repercussions were to last for years to come. The blockade turned American attention away from the goal of elimination of Nazism; this objective was replaced by a new mission, the containment or weakening of Soviet influence in Germany. Most Germans were only too eager to acclaim and support this mission. One writer observed:

> The increasing virulence of the West's denunciations of the Soviet Union now began to overshadow any criticisms of the Nazis. Immediately, the latter began to feel that they had been justified. Was it not they who had been the first to perceive the fundamental wickedness of Moscow and had sacrificed everything in their struggle against it? Had not the Nazi leaders tried to warn the West against its mistake, and to win it over to a common struggle against Bolshevism? . . . Whether they approved or disapproved all Germans saw the matter in this light.[17]

This political climate induced the Western Powers to hasten the transformation of that part of Germany they controlled into a new state which would not hesitate to become a loyal ally of the West. On June 4, 1948, representatives of Great Britain, the United States, France and the Benelux countries met in London to study a proposed international authority for the Ruhr. It was agreed during that meeting that the three commanders-in-chief in Germany would be instructed to organize with the help of the heads of the eleven *Laender* in West Germany, a

German Constituent Assembly responsible for the drafting of "a democratic constitution which will establish for the participating states a governmental structure of federal type which is best adapted to the eventual re-establishment of German unity at present disrupted. . . ." At the request of the military commanders, the Ministers-President of the various *Laender* in the three western zones met at Koblenz during July 8 to 10. These German statesmen decided to oppose the calling of a constituent assembly because the formulation of a constitution for only part of Germany would facilitate the final partition of the country. Instead, it was decided that delegates of the various state parliaments would gather in a Parliamentary Council which would draft a *Basic Law*. This *Basic Law* was to be a provisional constitution that would be effective only until improved political conditions would allow the drafting of a constitution for the whole of Germany. The Parliamentary Council met at Bonn on September 1, 1948, and an initial draft of the *Basic Law* was presented to the military authorities on February 13, 1949. The document became law on May 23 after certain objections to the initial draft by the military commanders were finally settled.

The *Basic Law* was not the constitution of a sovereign state. The occupying authorities reserved to themselves extensive powers in the governance of West Germany. On December 28, 1948, an International Authority for the Ruhr had been set up and on January 17, 1949, an Allied Military Security Board was established at Koblenz "to ensure the maintenance of disarmament and demilitarization" in Germany. Furthermore, an *Occupation Statute* proclaimed by the military governors was to enter into effect simultaneously with the *Basic Law*. Under the Occupation Statute, the Allied Powers retained extensive control in certain areas of governance. This control was to be exercised by a non-military Allied High Commission which took over the functions of the military governments in June 1949. Following West German elections for a federal parliament on August 14, 1949, the two houses of a new West German federal parliament were constituted, the *Bundestag* and the *Bundesrat*. Professor Theodor Heuss was elected Federal President; the leader of the Christian Democratic Union, Dr. Konrad Adenauer became Federal Chancellor. On September 21, 1949, the three western powers recognized the establishment of the German Federal Republic. The Soviet Union was not long in retaliating, and on October 7, 1949, its zone of occupation became the German Democratic Republic.

Over a year earlier, in April 1948, Professor Ludwig Erhard, Director of the Economic Council of Bizonia, had announced to the German people the establishment in West Germany of a new economic policy, the policy of *Soziale Marktwirtschaft*. Literally translated, this term means "social market economy," a free enterprise system subjected to the pursuit of certain social objectives. The social market economy and the currency reform of mid-1948 became the main pillars on which the rapid economic recovery of West Germany was built. Adenauer, inclined like most Germans to stress the proverbial German *Tuechtigkeit* as a principal determinant of the West German economic miracle, wrote in 1957:

> We were compelled to start reconstruction in a state of complete devastation and with a productive capacity largely destroyed through the effects of war. We found ourselves isolated from the world economy and had a largely useless currency. Gratefully, we remember the aid we received in those difficult times from those countries which only shortly before had been our enemies. Among them, The United States took the leading postition . . . then came the Marshall Plan. It gave us the chance to close many gaps which the war had left in our productive plant and to get the productive process under way again. But primary credit must be given to the initiative of German management and the unflagging assiduity of German labor . . . Another important factor in our economic recovery was the currency reform of 1948. And the social market economy — the policy which has determined economic decisions of the federal government since its founding in 1949 — played a major role in our economic recovery. [18]

Erhard proposed to establish in West Germany a truly competitive market economy, free from domination by government or private monopolies. Economic forces were to be allowed to operate freely, subject only to such limitations that would ensure the social as well as the economic development of the country. Erhard tended to emphasize more the need for free enterprise than the social obligations of the state. Thus, Erhard asserted that:

> It is indispensable that every class in our society, in fact, every single citizen should be conscious of the fact that he should not inveigh against the "capitalists" and should not make the state alone responsible for his social existence, but that it is his duty to cooperate in the shaping of his own and our common future. [19]

After the hardships and the economic chaos Germans endured during fifteen years of command economy, under both the Nazi and the Allied governments, they were quite willing to accept Erhard's proposals. Although many German economists feared that the sudden removal of rationing and price and wage controls in times of high scarcity would lead to hyperinflation and economic collapse, Erhard's policies succeeded, partly because of the impact on the economy of exogenous developments such as the Korean War. Throughout the 1950s, West German industrial production expanded in a prodigious fashion.

The removal of controls and the currency reform had an immediate impact on the volume of industrial output. The index of industrial production in Bizonia increased by 53% between June and December, 1948.[20] West German industrial production more than doubled in the period 1948 to 1951, and in 1951, the Federal Republic produced the pre-war agricultural output. By mid-1951, the volume of German exports was six times larger than it had been in 1948; this is shown in Table 2.1.

TABLE 2.1

INDEX OF INDUSTRIAL PRODUCTION IN THE FEDERAL REPUBLIC
1948 - 1951

	1948	1949	1950	1951
		1936	= 100	
Total Industrial Output	63.0	89.8	113.7	136.0
Capital Goods	51.3	82.7	114.5	152.5
Consumer Goods	53.6	85.9	113.1	131.9
Building	——	88.3	110.1	129.3

Source: *Statistisches Jahrbuch,* Statistisches Bundesamt, Wiesbaden, 1952, p. 209.

Before the end of Adenauer's administration, the German Federal Republic had become the third largest steel-producing country in the world and was second only to the United States in the export of engineering products. It ranked third among the world's shipbuilding countries.

The increase in industrial production allowed German exports to expand rapidly. By 1951, the volume of West German exports had surpassed the prewar level. But although the value of exports in the period 1948 to 1951 increased by an average of about $3 billion per year, the value of imports continued to exceed that of exports and West Germany's balance of trade remained negative. It worsened during the winter 1949-1950 when West Germany liberalized its imports from the O.E.E.C. countries in conformity with the policy of that organization. The outbreak of the Korean War in the summer of 1950 brought apprehensions of a wider war; industrial firms, fearing future short-ages of raw materials, started buying heavily in world markets. Boom-ing imports from the O.E.E.C. countries soon exhausted West Germany's overdraft facilities with the European Payments Union and the country was forced to seek a special credit from the Union amount-ing to $120 million. Import liberalization had to be suspended in February 1951.

The initial impact of the Korean War brought about an increase in West German imports; the war, on the other hand, soon turned out to be a blessing for the export industries of the Federal Republic. West German industry, being barred by the Potsdam Agreement from the production of any kind of military equipment, possessed excess capac-ity that could be utilized for an expanded production of capital goods. After 1948, relative price stability in the country and the modernization of plant facilities, largely financed through foreign aid, made West German industrial products very competitive in world markets. The war generated a large demand for industrial products West Germany could sell promptly and on very competitive terms. The existence of excess capacity in the capital industries allowed German producers to meet the booming demand for West German products. Production and exports were in turn encouraged by means of the fiscal policy of the federal government and the tight money policy of the *Bank Deutscher Laender.* Not only did the German industrialist receive privileged tax treatment, but his exports also benefited from West German's price stability made possible by the policies of the central bank and by the passivity of organized labor.

The rapid rise of exports allowed West Germany to repay as early as May 1951 the whole of the $120 million credit it had obtained from the European Payments Union. From then on, the country was able to develop a growing surplus on current account.

The West German economic miracle of the 1950s cannot be ex-plained alone in terms of wise West German economic policies or in terms of German *Tuechtigkeit.* Major credit must also be given to a happy coincidence of events exogenous to the West German economy, events which succeeded in drastically transforming that economy during the fourteen years of Adenauer's rule.

First of all, West Germany benefited paradoxically from the fact that it had lost the war. While France and the United Kingdom were draining resources into the maintenance of a costly military establishment, the Federal Republic did not have to support its own military forces until the mid-1950s. West Germany, unlike other European nations, was thus able to devote almost the entirety of its resources in the early postwar period to internal economic reconstruction and development. Occupation costs were not unduly burdensome and were largely offset by the large spending in the country by the occupying forces. And though the Allied Powers continued to dismantle West German factories until 1950, these confiscations did not constitute a crushing blow to West German industry and in the long run, they helped in the modernization of this industry.

Foreign aid made the process of reconstruction much easier. West Germany started receiving Marshall Plan aid shortly after its currency reform, and under this program, the country received about $1.4 billion from the United States. Total American aid to West Germany until the beginning of the Korean War amounted to about $3.5 billion. The amount of foreign aid received by the Federal Republic contributed in a major way to its success in foreign trade.

Millions of ethnic Germans living in a number of Central and Eastern European countries started fleeing westward to Germany as the Red Army approached from the east during the last months of World War II. They were soon joined by the *Sudeten* Germans from Czechoslovakia and by Germans expelled from the territories annexed by Poland. These refugees tried at first to settle in East Germany but the poverty of this area forced most of them to move westward once more. By September 1950, almost eight million destitute refugees from East Germany had entered the territory fo the Federal Republic. Though most of them arrived in West Germany in the immediate postwar period, at a time when the economy was still very weak, the refugees did not remain an undesired burden on the West German economy for very long. Most of them were of working age; many of them were engineers, physicians, school teachers and skilled workers. Lensmakers from the Zeiss works in the Soviet zone or glassworkers from Czechoslovakia brought valuable skills to Bizonia. The refugees were willing to work hard and for low wages. Those who had lost all their wealth in the former homeland were anxious to rebuild their original economic and social status and accepted whatever work conditions were offered. As employees, their discipline was excellent and they willingly accepted Adenauer's dictate to "work hard and obey." They tended to resent strikes and thus discouraged labor unions from making large wage demands. The constant increase in the number of these refugees promoted wage stability and facilitated the expansion of West German industry. Throughout the 1950s, the rate of growth of wages remained lower than that of output and the resulting higher profit rate made it easier for German firms to expand operations on the basis of self-finance.

Two endogenous developments further contributed to the rapid recovery and growth of the West German economy. A high investment-national income ratio allowed continuous increases in output and employment. This high rate of investment was stimulated by appropriate monetary and fiscal policies.

Throughout the 1950s, the rate of investment in West Germany stood much higher than that of other European countries. During this period, total domestic fixed investment in the Federal Republic represented about 22% of its GNP, while in the United Kingdom, the corresponding figure was only 16.6%.[21] The West German high rate of investment was in part made possible by relatively low private consumption-national income ratios. On the average, for the decade 1950-1960, private consumption in West Germany represented only 59% of the GNP, compared with 65% for the United Kingdom.[22]

West Germans were very successful in selling an expanded output in world markets because their country was not experiencing the rate of inflation developing in competing economies. Relative price stability gave a definite advantage to West German exports and their expansion induced in turn further output and employment increases.

Price stability in West Germany became from the start the main objective of the *Bank Deutscher Laender.* As stated by the London *Economist,* "no sterner guardian of a country's currency can be found than the Bank Deutscher Laender."[23] In support of this view, the Bank's President, Dr. Vocke, affirmed that "the government itself is interested that such an agency be guided. . . . simply and objectively by the goal of keeping the currency stable."[24] During its seven years of existence, the Bank's pursuit of price stability reflected the priority given by its management to the improvement of West Germany's external position. The overriding concern was to expand West German exports in order to render the country less dependent on foreign aid. To encourage exports, inflation had to be curbed. The monetary policy of West Germany in the years 1948 to 1955 can readily be understood when viewed as an efficient tool utilized for the recapture of lost foreign markets and the building up of international reserves. The improvement of the balance of payments, rather than the furtherance of domestic economic growth, became the chief concern of the central bank.[25]

West Germany's hard-money policy was quite successful. Though prices rose immediately after the removal of controls in 1948, they remained relatively constant between 1951 and 1957. With 1949 as the base year, the wholesale price index of industrial goods rose from 91 in June 1948 to 104 in December of that year. By June 1950, it had fallen to 96. The Korean War increased the index to 124 in December 1951, but it did not rise above that level until 1958. The cost-of-living index followed a parallel trend.

In regard to fiscal policy, the view that Adenauer's government entirely rejected Keynesian prescriptions for economic growth misinterprets rather than explains West Germany's social market economy. Fiscal policy was extensively used to quicken capital formation and to facilitate the expansion of selected economic sectors. In the 1950s, taxation absorbed as much as 35% of the GNP. Large tax revenues allowed government to build up budgetary surpluses providing investment funds to both the public and the private sectors of the economy. It has been estimated that between DM 35 and 40 billion were lent by West German public authorities to the private sector in the period 1949 to 1957. Public funds financed the development of agriculture, coal mining, housing and shipbuilding. Government loans for the construction of houses carried a rate of interest as low as 1%. Furthermore, as noticed by Professor Roskamp:

> An extensive and complicated system of tax exemptions influenced the direction of flow of investible funds, and probably to some degree also the volume of that flow. Many features of this system of tax incentives persist up to the present time. The tax exemptions granted between 1949 and 1957 for the purpose of capital formation have been estimated at 28 billion DM. There can be no doubt that this was effective in changing and directing the preferences of private investors.[26]

The West German tax system attempted above all to encourage the growth of private saving and investment and to direct investment funds into desirable channels. Large tax exemptions were allowed for investment in business, housing and shipbuilding. The tax laws favored the aggressive entrepreneur and induced him to re-invest a large part of his profits; they discriminated against the weaker salaried groups in society. Considerable income inequality was permitted in order to stimulate the growth of aggregate supply while holding down the level of domestic demand.

Commenting on the West German income tax laws of 1949 and 1950, Professor Wallich remarks:

> Top bracket rates were, in effect, reduced for all those able to save. Independent businessmen were given special advantages, as compared with earners of high salaries, through the deductibility of what in many cases were living expenses and the possibility of building up capital in the business. These advantages were so pronounced that they must have exerted strong pressure upon anyone at all able to do so to go into business by himself . . . the granting of most of these tax concessions in a form benefiting saving and investment had extraordinarily favorable implications for private capital formation.[27]

Wallich further remarks:

> The incentive elements in the German picture — free markets, tight financial policies, and pro-business taxation — created an economy with certain well-defined characteristics. The German system gave freedom to the strong . . . For the weak only a minimum of consideration was shown. A floor was put under them through the comprehensive social security system. But the payments, though accounting in the aggregate for almost 40% of the budget, were desperately small for many individuals. Beyond this bare minimum the strong were not weighed down by the burden of carrying the weak. The times were too hard to permit fairness to everybody. It was a question of giving the strong a chance of saving themselves in the hope that if they succeeded they would later pull the others along.[28]

Decartellization and Codetermination

West German economic growth in the 1950s was indeed impressive. The Federal Republic had the highest rate of growth of real GNP in Western Europe and in spite of a continuing inflow of millions of refugees, the country also maintained the highest average annual rate of growth of GNP per capita.

As was noted, the happy coincidence of a number of events over which the Germans had little or no control were major contributive forces bringing about the amazing expansion of the West German economy in the 1950's. American aid in the early postwar years more than offset the losses due to Allied dismantling of West German plants. The Cold War brought an early end to the punitive policies of the Western Powers and the Korean War became a boon to West German export industries. The economy of the Federal Republic further benefited from the fact that the country did not have to support a military establishment of its own and this allowed West Germany to devote almost all of its resources and manpower to internal economic development. Until 1958, West German contributions to finance occupation costs and other defense expenditures never exceeded 5.6% of the GNP. Even the currency reform of 1948 was imposed on West Germany by the occupying authorities.

It has also been argued that the speed of the West German recovery was further facilitated by the breaking up of the traditional German oligopolistic industrial and financial structures. In spite of German opposition, industrial deconcentration was ordered by the Allied authorities in 1947, more for political than for economic reasons. Large industrial concerns such as *Krupp, Klockner, Flick, Gutehoffnungshuette, Hoesch, Reichswerke,* and *Otto Wolff* were transformed into a larger number of small independent firms. The gigantic *Vereinigte Stahlwerke,* which in prewar times produced 40% of Germany's steel, was broken up into thirteen metallurgical companies and nine mining companies. The large commercial banks were dealt the same fate. The three prewar banking giants, the *Deutsche Bank,* the *Dresdener Bank* and the *Commerzbank* were replaced, at least for a few years, by thirty independent, regional banks.[29]

The transformation of an economy characterized by government controls and a high degree of banking and industrial concentration into a more competitive free market economy has been credited with bringing to West Germany a more efficient allocation of resources which made possible the superior West German economic performance. According to this view, Erhard's qualified *laissez-faire* policies are at the base of the *Wirtschaftswunder.* Professor Sohmen states:

> With all due respect to all other factors, biological, sociological and metaphysical, the conclusion is nevertheless inescapable that only more efficient resource allocation can explain the difference between West

> Germany's rate of growth and that of other countries in a comparable
> state of development . . . the postwar German experience seems to
> suggest that it is feasible to intensify competition sufficiently to make an
> economy perform markedly better than under alternative forms of social
> organization.[30]

This argument has encountered a great deal of criticism. It is undeniable that governmental interference with the German social market
economy kept it from becoming the classical *laissez-faire* economy.
Through public investment, loans to the private sector, subsidies and
tax exemptions, the West German government implicitly utilized
economic planning and economic policies designed to achieve certain
economic goals such as price stability and a high ratio of capital formation to gross national product. The existence of a relatively large public
industrial sector also facilitated centralized control of economic activity.

Another development, exogenous to the West German economy,
played as vital a role in the rapid growth of the West German economy
as Erhard's resource allocation reforms. This was the spectacular increase in West Germany's population after 1945. The increase was
principally due to the influx of about 10 million refugees from the East,
which boosted the West German population from 39.3 million in 1939
to 49.6 million in 1954. Looking at the impact of this immigration on the
West German economy, Professor Wallich states:

> A population increase of this kind was almost bound to bring an
> increase in national income, by one route or another. The new people
> had to be housed, clad and fed, and along with their demand for goods
> they brought their manpower, if nothing else, to augment the supply
> . . . The refugees intensified competition wherever they went . . . The
> refugees increased the mobility of the population as a whole . . . They
> had no local ties where they first landed and were willing to move in
> response to market factors. The great outpouring of production from the
> Ruhr and other industrial centers would never have been possible with-
> out a substantial flow of population to the expanding industries. . . .
> Finally, the refugees have played an undeniable role in maintaining a
> high and expanding level of demand.[31]

Throughout the 1950s, the inflow of refugees fed a large pool of
unemployed from which industry could draw skilled workers, willing
to work long hours for whatever wage was offered. Most of these men,

anxious to rebuild wealth or status lost in their homeland, were reluctant to participate in strikes or any other work-stopping activity. Their acceptance of the work conditions offered by employers contributed to wage stability. This stability was also furthered by the rapid rise in unemployment following the currency reform of June 1948. With the disappearance of the barter and black market economies, firms started dismissing employees whose services became redundant. The continuously expanding number of refugees entering the Federal Republic and the unwise policy of settling them at first in relatively unpopulated rural areas boosted the numbers of unemployed. In June 1953, refugees represented 34.8% of the population of Schleswig-Holstein, a predominantly agricultural area with no excess demand for labor. Refugees constituted 23.4% of the population of Bavaria but only 16.8% of that of industrial, labor-hungry Nordrhein-Westfalen.[32]

TABLE 2.2

GERMAN FEDERAL REPUBLIC: LABOR FORCE

	Ratio of Working Population to Total Population	Ratio of Numbers Employed to Total Population
1949	31.4	28.8
1950	32.3	28.9
1951	33.1	30.1
1952	34.3	31.4
1953	34.9	32.3
1954	35.9	33.4
1955	36.7	34.9

Source: Deutsche Bundesbank, Monthly Report, Vol. 12, No. 1, January, 1960.

Between June 1948 and June 1949, unemployment rose from 450,000 to over 1.2 million. By March 1950, unemployment had increased to 1.8 million and except for seasonal variations, remained at that level in 1953. The winter 1953-1954 registered as many as 2 million unemployed. Though unemployment increased, so did employment. There were about 13.5 million employed in June 1948, 14.7 million in 1951, 15.2 million in 1952 and 16.5 million in 1954. Between 1948 and 1954 the employed labor force was expanding at an average annual rate of 3%. Unemployment during this period could not be reduced since the yearly rate of growth of the total labor force was about 5%. . The West German economy was not yet able to absorb the large accretions to its labor force generated by events over which it had little control.

In spite of the large numbers of unemployed, the economy benefited from a steadily increasing ratio of numbers of people employed per one hundred inhabitants. The increase in the numbers employed, coupled with relative wage stability, facilitated the rapid growth of domestic investment, production and exports.

Wages and salaries represented 65.6% of the national income during the first half of 1950, profits and other income claiming the balance of 35.4%. Two years later, these figures were respectively 61.9% and 38.1%.[33] Though in later years labor's share was slightly increased, it is undeniable that, in Wallich's words:

> For the economy as a whole labor's muted and unaggressive policy has been an inestimable advantage. It has, in the first place, made a major contribution to the stability of the new currency . . . in the second place, labor's restraint has helped to make and keep exports competitive . . . the final and probably most decisive contribution, however, has been to the financing of the investment boom. By allowing wages to lag behind profits, labor made it possible for business to engage in large-scale self-financing. The inequality of the income distribution, favoring the higher incomes where proportionately more savings accrue, was the essential condition of the high rate of investment.[34]

The investment boom allowed in turn an increase in the number of employed which between 1950 and 1962 rose from 13.8 million to over 21 million and reduced the number of unemployment to 142,000 by 1962.

Another major determinant of West Germany's production boom was the persistence in the 1950s of harmonious management-labor relations. The absence of strikes on the West German labor scene cannot be entirely explained in terms of the continuous inflow of work-seeking refugees. Codetermination, a West German institution which placed trade union men on the board of directors of key industrial concerns and allowed a union representative to occupy the position of a top manager, brought about peaceful management-labor relations, an experience which was not shared by other major industrial nations in Western Europe.

The concept of codetermination was formulated in Germany as early as 1925 in a little book titled *Sociology of the Trade Union Movement,* by Karl Zwing.[35] Zwing's proposed economic reforms gave the disagreeing factions of the Weimar Republic Socialists a new alternative for social and economic organization which neither followed Marxist doctrine nor the principles of "bourgeois democracy." Zwing could not agree with the radical Socialists who wanted to rebuild Germany in the image of the Soviet Union and who demanded that all political and economic power should belong to workers' and soldiers' committees. Neither did he align himself with the Socialist majority which was inclined to accept the "bourgeois democracy" established by the Weimar Constitution and the process of collective bargaining between employers and trade unions as the proper means to obtain better working conditions for wage earners. He did not propose the abolition of the institution of private property. Instead, he suggested that workers should participate as equals to management in the control of industry. If Zwing rejected the Marxist demand of workers' ownership and domination, he asked that workers and managers should be given the same number of votes in the determination of any social and economic policy affecting any industrial or commercial enterprise. For Zwing, it was not sufficient for unions and management to determine jointly how the firm's earnings would be shared by workers and owners. Workers should have the right to co-determine the entirety of the firm's policies. The workers' right to an equal voice in the determination of any policy that could affect them is justified by Zwing's *Gemeinschaftsprinzip*, Zwing felt that enterprises should serve the the *Gemeinschaft* or community, which in turn allows these firms to exist. Owners, managers and workers are simply servants of the *Gemeinschaft* and discharge their duties to the community as equals. "Everything comes from the community; everything goes back in the service of the community."[36] As servants of the community, neither managers nor workers should attempt to dominate or dictate in the formulation of the firms' economic and social policies. Both Marxism and bourgeois democracy offended Zwing's *Gemeinschaftsprinzip* since the ideologies of these systems furthered an unequal participation of managers and workers in the economic decision-making process.

Zwing's proposals were incorporated in 1928 in the program of the German Socialist trade union federation. The details of the program appeared in a book titled *Economic Democracy*, which emphasized the goal of joint decision-making

The Nazi labor code established the owner or the top manager of a firm as the supreme decision-maker, provided, of course, he was

"Aryan." There was to be only one leader for any given firm and leadership could not be delegated. The Nazi labor code with its *Fuehrerprinzip* was abolished in 1945. It was not long before union leaders and Socialists started arguing again for the implementaton of *Mitbestimmung*, codetermination. In 1947, a number of bills containing codetermination provisions were drafted by legislators in various *Laender* and some of these bills were voted into law. American and British vetoes suspended the effectiveness of these laws.

The Basic Law of May 1949 gave the West German federal government authority to legislate in labor matters; in the field of labor legislation, federal law superseded state laws. In April 1951, the Bundestag made codetermination in the mining, steel and coal industries part of the federal corporate law. Codetermination practices that had been implemented with success in the industries of the Ruhr since 1947 were now given the durability of law.

In the fall of 1946, the British military authorities established a Steel Trustee Association whose principal task was to deconcentrate the iron and steel industry of the Ruhr and to reorganize the various plants into independent and competing firms. A German, Heinrich Dinkelbach, was given the responsibility of carrying out this program. Union leaders were demanding at this time the nationalization of the Ruhr industries. Dinkelbach, in an attempt to persuade the unions to stop pressing for the nationalization of heavy industry, offered the latter equal seating on the board of directors of the new companies to be formed. Dinkelbach further proposed that each company would have a Labor Director, appointed by the union, who would discharge the functions of an industrial relations manager for the company. Though union leaders accepted the Dinkelbach scheme with enthusiasm, they overlooked the fact that the arrangement fell quite short of the Zwing proposals. Even though a major company official was to be a union man, the largest part of the decision-making process remained firmly in the hands of management. The Dinkelbach plan was, however, quite successful and brought about an era of harmonious labor-management relations which allowed the steel industry to rebuild a full year before the receipt of Marshall Plan aid.

The law of 1951 made the Dinkelbach plan mandatory for the iron-mining, steel-producing and coal industries. The law gave labor unions, rather than labor in general, the right to nominate five of the eleven members of the *Aufsichtsrat* of a firm, the board of directors responsible for the formulation of general policies for the firm. The actual management of the concern was placed in the hands of a management board, the *Vorstand,* consisting of a Technical Director, a Business Director and a Labor Director. The latter was to be a union man.

A law of 1952 extended a modified version of codetermination to all industrial enterprises not covered by the law of 1951. Under the 1952 law, only one-third of the seats on the board of directors of firms covered by this statute were to be controlled by unions and the law did not require these firms to have a union appointed Labor Director.[37]

Agriculture

Military destruction, the collapse of the transportation system, manpower losses, fuel, fertilizers and seed shortages, and the loss of agricultural imports from East German territories under Polish and Russian rule resulted in serious foodstuff shortages in the years 1945 to 1948. In the western zones of occupation, the average daily caloric intake during the winter 1945-46 amounted to between 700 and 800 calories. In West Germany, the decline in agricultural output from its prewar level was due both to a reduced acreage under cultivation and to a deterioration of agricultural yields.[38]

Immediately after the war, shortages of fertilizers and manpower and the worthlessness of the Reichsmark limited the speed of recovery of agricultural output. In those days of monetary uncertainty, farmers were more interested in hoarding and in building up stocks of farm animals than in selling their products for currency no one wanted to hold. Agricultural growth was further retarded by two principal factors, one economic in nature and the other social. For centuries, land tenure in West Germany had been characterized by relatively free peasant tenancy of small and medium-size farms. In prewar times, unlike the situation prevailing east of the Elbe river where the largest part of agricultural production took place on the large *Junker* estates, the representative farm of the west did not exceed ten hectares. A farm of this size did not allow an efficient use of modern methods of production and did not supply the farmer and his family with an adequate income. Hence, the West German farmer was forced to work on a part-time basis in the non-agricultural sector of the economy. The economic efficiency of these farms was further weakened by excessive farm fragmentation. A holding of eight or ten hectares was often fragmented into a large number of non-contiguous parcels and traveling to and from them took as much as a fourth of the farmer's working time.[39]

The attachment of most Western German farmers to tradition was a further impediment to rapid increases in agricultural productivity. As one writer put it:

> Even under more favorable conditions, the traditionalism of most German farmers would have made changes slow and difficult. To them, agriculture was a way of life rather than merely an economic enterprise . . . Furthermore, the predominant type of agriculture, a highly variegated mixed farming, was not one to which specialization or mechanization could be easily applied. The typical German farmer in 1945 preferred horses to tractors and the labor of his wife and children to that of a machine.[40]

If agricultural output reached its prewar volume in 1950, it was largely due to rapid increases in yields made possible by the availability of fertilizers and seeds after 1948. The acreage devoted to the production of human-consumption crops was still smaller in 1949 than the corresponding area before the war, as shown in Table 2.3

TABLE 2.3
WEST GERMANY: ESTIMATED ACREAGE AS A PERCENT
OF CORRESPONDING 1938 ACREAGE

	1948	1949
Bread Grains	85	84
Feed Grains	77	80
Potatoes	99	97
Fodder Roots	113	112
Sugar Beets	121	128
Permanent Meadows	100	102
Permanent Pasture	102	99

Source: G.F.R., Ministry of Food, Agriculture and Forestry, *Agrarstatistische Unterlagen*, Bonn, April, 1951.

Though occupation authorities attempted to implement plans designed to increase the acreage devoted to human-consumption crops and tried to persuade the farmers to cut back on their acreage planted with fodder crops, German farmers, at least until 1948, tended to ignore these directives and continued to emphasize the rearing of animals which were used to replenish herds destroyed by the war or which were disposed of profitably in the black market.

Yields and acreage statistics for the years 1945 and 1948 are not very reliable. During these years, the Allied Powers continued to burden farmers with old Nazi production directives. The farmers were forced to deliver part of their output to the authorities at low official prices. In a situation where the local currency had lost practically all value, the farmer was induced to underestimate his crop. The output of grain he reported did not include the grain he secretly fed to his animals. The statistics became more accurate following the currency reform of 1948 and the abandonment of the controlled economy.

TABLE 2.4

WEST GERMANY: CROP YIELDS
100 Kilograms per Hectare

	Bread Grains	Fodder Grains	Total Grain	Potatoes	Sugar Beet
1938	21.9	23.0	22.3	185	327
1948	19.8	17.6	18.8	205	300
1950	23.7	22.5	23.1	244	362
1959	30.4	27.2	29.0	215	285
1962	31.3	30.9	31.1	261	328

Source: G.F.R., *Deutschland Heute*, Presse-und Informationsamt, Wiesbaden, 1965, p. 352.

After 1948, improving conditions in the non-agricultural sectors of the economy induced many farmers to sell their farms in order to work full-time in industry. Between 1950 and 1961, the total number of full-time agricultural workers fell by 40% from 3.9 million to 2.3 million. Many farms that were sold in this period were bought by farmers eager to consolidate and increase the size of their holdings. During these years, the number of farms up to ten hectares in size diminished by 26%, while the number of farms varying in size between 10 and 50 hectares increased by 13%.[41] Still, at the start of the 1960s 72.8% of West German agricultural holdings were made up by farms of less than 10 hectares in size. In 1961, 21.5% of all West German farms possessed between 0.01 and 0.5 hectares of land.[42]

Though agricultural output increased, it did not increase as rapidly as the output of the other sectors of the economy. In the 1950s, the relative share of agriculture in the national income thus tended to decline and individual incomes in the agricultural sector tended to remain lower than in industry.

NOTES

1. A. Grosser, *Germany in Our Time* (New York: Praeger, 1971), p. 28.
2. A. Grosser, *The Colossus Again* (New York: Praeger, 1955), p. 87.
3. "The German Crisis": *Economist* (London: April 6, 1946).
4. H. Zink, *The United States in Germany, 1944-1955* (New York: D. Van Nostrand Co., 1957), p. 254.
5. Grosser, *The Colossus Again*, p. 86.
6. *New York Times*, April 1, 1947.
7. H. Abosch, *The Menace of the Miracle* (New York Monthly Review Press, 1963), p. 3.
8. Grosser, *Germany in Our Time*, p. 67.
9. H. Moeller, *Zur Vorgeschichte der DM* (Basel: Kyklos-Verlag, 1961), p. 216.
10. H. Sauermann, "The Consequences of the Currency Reform in Western Germany," *The Review of Politics*, Vol. 12 (1950), pp. 178-179.
11. F.A. Burchardt, and K. Martin, "Western Germany and Reconstruction," *Bulletin of the Oxford University Institute of Statistics*, vol. 9 (1947), p. 405.
12. E.E. Emmer, "West German Monetary Policy, 1948-1954," *Journal of Political Economy*, LXIII (February, 1955), pp. 52-69.
13. F.A. Lutz, "The German Currency Reform and the Revival of the German Economy," *Economica*, vol. 16 (May 1949), p. 122.
14. F. Pritzkoleit, *Die Neuen Herren* (Desch, 1955).
15. R. E. Emmer, "West German Monetary Policy, 1948-1955," *Journal of Political Economy*, LXIII (February 1955), p. 55.
16. F. A. Lutz, "The German Currency Reform and the Revival of the German Economy," *Economica* (May 1949), pp. 131-132.
17. Abosch, *The Menace of the Miracle*, p. 22.
18. K. Adenauer, "Perspective of Germany," *Atlantic Monthly*, 200:110-13 (March 1957).
19. L. Erhard, *Deutsche Wirtschaftspolitik* (Düsseldorf: Econ Verlag, 1962), p. 551.
20. Statistisches Amt des Vereinigten Wirtschaftgebietes, *Statistische Monatszahlen* (Bonn: December 1948).
21. R. G. Opie, "Western Germany's Economic Miracle," *Three Banks Review* (March 1962), p. 6.
22. *Ibid.*, p. 8.
23. "Germany's Boom," *Economist* (August 13, 1955), p. 523.
24. W. Vocke, "Aktuelle Fragen der Notenbankpolitik," *Gesundes Geld* (Frankfurt: F. Knapp, 1956), p. 127.
25. J. Hein, "The Mainsprings of German Monetary Policy," *Economia Internazionale*, vol. 17 (May 1964), p. 320.
26. K. W. Roskamp, "Competition and Growth—The Lesson of West Germany: Comment," *American Economic Review*, vol. 50 (December 1960), pp. 1015-18.
27. H. C. Wallich, *The Mainsprings of the German Revival* (New Haven: Yale University Press, 1955), p. 129.
28. *Ibid.*, p. 130.
29. S. Lieberman and J. Short, "The Indestructible German Grossbanken," *Rivista Internazionale di Scienze Economiche e Commerciali*, No. 10 (October 1970), pps. 998-1016.
30. E. Sohmen, "Competition and Growth—The Lesson of West Germany," *American Economic Review*, vol. 49 (December 1959), pp. 986-1003.
31. Wallich, *Mainsprings of the German Revival*, pp. 282-284.
32. *Statistisches Jahrbuch fuer die Bundesrepublik Deutschland* (Wiesbaden, 1954), p. 48.

33. Bank deutscher Laender, *Monthly Report* Frankfurt, May. 1954).

34. Wallich, *Mainsprings of the German Revival,* pp. 299-300.

35. K. Zwing, *Soziologie der Gewerkschaftsbewegung* (Jena: *Gewerkschafts-Archiv, 1925).*

36. *Ibid.,* p. 53.

37. W. H. McPherson, "Codetermination in Practice," *Industrial and Labor Relations Review:* 8(499-519, July 1955; P. Fisher, "Labor Codetermination in Germany," *Social Research,* 18:499-85 (December 1951).

38. G. F. R., *Deutschland Heute,* Presse-und Informationsamt (Wiesbaden, 1965), p. 339.

39. U. S.-British Bipartite Food and Agriculture Panel, *Food and Agriculture U.S.-U.K. Zones in Germany* (Berlin, February, 1947), pp. 5-6.

40. H. G. Schmidt, "Postwar Developments in West German Agriculture, 1945-1953," *Agricultural History,* 29:147-59 (October 1955).

41. *Deutschland Heute,* p. 346.

42. P. Mueller, "Recent Developments in Land Tenure and Land Policies in Germany," *Land Economics,* 40:267-75 (August 1964).

CHAPTER 3

ECONOMIC SOCIALIZATION IN THE UNITED KINGDOM
FROM DALTON TO BUTLER

The policies of Mssrs. Dalton, Stafford Cripps and Gaitskell, the Labour Chancellors of the Exchequer in the period 1945 to 1951, as well as those of Mr. Butler, the Conservative Chancellor from the end of 1951 to the end of 1955, were governed by two principal goals. The first was the maintenance of a high and stable level of employment in conformity with the provisions of the 1944 White Paper on *Employment Policy.* [1] The second objective, as important as the first for a country highly dependent on a large volume of foreign trade, and often conflicting with full employment policies, aimed at a continuous improvement of the British balance of payments.

Both the Labour and the Conservative governments were determined to prevent a return to the unemployment conditions which had plagued British society during most of the interwar period. The memory of the interwar economic stagnation which kept about 10.5% of the labor force unemployed had not vanished and induced many politicians to embrace Keynesian full-employment policies and to accept economic ideas which would have been considered quite revolutionary a few decades earlier.

The Keynesian idea of raising the level of aggregate demand through public intervention in order to assure a satisfactory level of employment cannot be inflexibly followed in an open economy, an economy highly dependent on exports for the obtainment of necessary foodstuffs and industrial raw materials. After the latter part of the eighteenth century, the United Kingdom had to import even larger volumes of fuel, food and raw materials to survive. Exports of commodities, exports of invisible services such as banking, insurance and shipping services, dividends and interests earned on British overseas investments, and borrowing abroad financed the country's vital imports.

The United Kingdom started experiencing balance of payments difficulties as early as the 1920s. The country was unable at that time to offset the decline in its coal and cotton exports through an expansion in the export of new products. American and German competition started reducing British overseas markets. The decision of the British government to return to a Gold Standard system at the prewar parity in 1925 overvalued sterling and lowered the competitiveness of British export industries. A current account surplus could only be maintained because of persistent conditions of unemployment in the country. With higher levels of employment and home demand, large deficits would have accumulated, given the poor performance of British exports. In the thirties, the United Kingdom's position deteriorated and current account deficits prevailed during most of the decade in spite of low level of national income and in spite of tariff increases.

The war further worsened the country's balance of payments. War production required a reduction in exports to about one-third of their prewar value. During the years of war, American lend-lease supplies compensated for Britain's loss of import capacity, but lend-lease assistance came to a sudden end in August, 1945. At this time, British export industries were seriously handicapped through war destruction of factories, roads and port facilities; the existing productive capacity was paralyzed by serious shortages of fuel, food and raw materials. Traditional sources of invisible exports had also been weakened during the years of war. To finance the war effort, 25% of British overseas investments, amounting to over 1 billion pounds, had to be sold off and the dividend and interest earnings from these investments were lost. Furthermore, the country's international debt had increased during the war from 476 million pounds to 3,335 million pounds. Freight earnings were considerably reduced through the destruction of 18 million deadweight tons of British merchant ships by German bombs and German U-boats. All of these wartime calamities made the United Kingdom the world's largest debtor in 1945.

The Labour government of 1945 had promised to engage in planning and to keep "a firm constructive hand on our whole productive machinery" in order to do away with the economic difficulties and the social miseries developed by the capitalist system of the interwar period.[2] Although the government desired a high degree of economic interventionism, it did not advocate the establishment of a totally controlled economy. The belief was that government could bring about and maintain a satisfactory level of employment by managing aggregate demand, and particularly aggregate investment, without need for the elimination of all capitalist institutions in the system. Public control over basic sectors of the economy, achieved by means of nationalization, was to facilitate the development of efficient economic planning and of efficient investment. Postwar socialist theories supported the establishment of a mixed economy in which the nationalization of key industries would assure that a maximum of industrial activity would be carried out in the public interest and not for the sake of private profit alone.

What Labour economists minimized or failed to see clearly was that full employment policies and policies aiming at the stabilization of the country's balance of payments could conflict. To a large extent, it was felt that continuing American financial aid would take care of Britain's external problems and that therefore there was no reason to fear the price and income effects of expanding demand and output on the balance on current account. In time, the government found out that the inconsistent pursuit of both full employment and external balance was forcing it to repeatedly revise and downgrade investment plans whenever economic growth threatened to diminish insufficient international reserves. This "stop-go" pattern of policy was detrimental to both long-run and short-run planning and some economists believe that "Britain would probably have enjoyed more rapid and more productive capital formation had the difficult position of her international reserves not forced stop-go policy." [3]

The most dramatic expression of the Labour government's program was the series of nationalizations of basic industries which started shortly after 1945. National boards or commissions were established to administer the nationalized industries. The public take-over of industries started with the Coal Industry Nationalization Act of 1946 which placed the entire national production and distribution of coal under the administration of a National Coal Board; the latter was endowed with 150 million pounds to modernize and reorganize an old industry which had been deprived of modern capital equipment for too long and which had to face the wage demands of a militant labor force.

In the same year, a Steel Board was created for the purpose of directing the reconstruction and the development of a still privately owned industry, an industry which was, however, subject to many wartime governmental controls. In 1946, the railways and canal transportation were also nationalized and a Transport Commission was charged with the task of improving rail and road transport in the country. In 1947, an Electricity Bill nationalized the production and distribution of electricity and a British Electricity Authority was set up on April 1, 1948. The Steel Bill of 1948 provided for the nationalization of 107 major steel concerns in the country and although these companies retained their identity, they were in effect administered by the new Iron and Steel Corporation of Great Britain, a public agency.

By mid-1951, the Labour government had nationalized the Bank of England, rail and road transport, the commercial airlines and the production and distribution of coal, electricity, natural gas and iron and steel.

Nationalization affected about 20% of British industry. It undoubtedly facilitated government's management of the economy. Total demand could be more effectively controlled through changes in public expenditure in the large nationalized sector. The government's philosophy was that adjustments in public investment, coupled with the continuation of wartime direct controls, would provide the authorities with the necessary and sufficient tools required for the maintenance of a high, but not excessive, level of demand. Nationalization was not intended to weaken the profit-making system in the private sector. Labour leaders argued that nationalization would facilitate efficient economic planning and would help to maintain full employment conditions throughout the economy; nationalization would thus strengthen rather than weaken the private sector of the economy.[4]

The Labour Party had inherited from the war an extensive system of direct controls. Among the major controls still in existence in 1945 were the rationing of consumer goods, controls over private investment and over the allocation of industrial fuels and of raw materials to manufacturing concerns, and import and price controls. The Party was eager to retain these various controls as instruments of planning, instruments which could also be used to control postwar inflationary pressures. Some of these controls were to remain in existence until the 1950s.

Extensive rationing of consumer goods had been imposed during the years of war and wartime rationing was not only retained after 1945, it was extended during the early postwar years to foodstuffs that had never been rationed before. Bread, which had never been rationed during the war years, was rationed in July, 1946. Potatoes followed suit in November of the following year. Milk remained a rationed commodity until May 1950. It was only in September 1953, that sugar was derationed. Meat and bacon continued to be rationed until July 1954. Food rationing finally came to an end in 1954, but coal continued to be rationed until July 1958.[5]

Until the early 1950s, the government attempted to regulate the flow of private investment, quantitatively and qualitatively, through a number of control devices. There were financial controls over foreign exchange transactions and over capital issues by private firms; the government acted as a quasi-monopolist in the import of industrial fuels, raw materials and machinery, and allocation quotas limited the flow of these materials to manufacturing concerns and thereby limited their growth. Building licenses regulated investment in new plants and equipment.

Unitl 1950, most basic foods, industrial raw materials and manufactured products were imported through government purchase. Two thirds of all British imports were bought by the government in 1946. The newly established Raw Cotton Commission acquired in that year the exclusive right to import raw cotton. Although during the late 1940s the share of private traders in the country's foreign trade tended to grow, private imports remained subject to severe licensing regulations until 1953. A great backlog of unsatisfied demand for imports and inadequate public holdings of international reserves, particularly of American dollars, resulted in complete import control during the first postwar years. Marshall Plan aid, the import liberalization policy of the O.E.E.C. in 1949 and the establishment in 1950 of the European Payments Union allowed the government to relax import restrictions for commodities bought in non-dollar countries, while dollar imports were further restricted. Rapidly rising import prices due to the impact of the Korean War resulted in a serious balance of payments crisis in 1951. New import restrictions were quickly imposed on both dollar and non-dollar imports and it was only in 1953 that the government decided to start a policy of gradual decontrol. Discrimination against dollar imports ended only in 1959.[6]

Price controls were a natural complement of import controls and like the latter, they remained quite extensive until 1953. Although gradually relaxed in 1949 and 1950, they were increased in 1951 to check the

Korean inflation. Controls over food prices ended in 1953. Price controls over coal, rents, bus and railway fares continued to exist.

The "Cheap Money" Policy of Dr. Dalton

The first postwar Chancellor came to power at a time when the country's exports had been reduced to a fraction of their prewar level and when the loss of overseas income, the necessity of repaying the sterling debt that had accumulated during the war, and the deterioration in the terms of trade required exports to rise by at least 75% of their prewar volume to allow the country to import sufficiently to survive.[7] The condition of the British economy in 1945 has been described as follows:

> When the war ended, a quarter of the country's manpower was in the armed forces. The government was spending over half the national product. Civilian output was heavily curtailed. Gross investment was negligible. Consumer's expenditure, though higher than at the worst period during the war, was still only 90 percent of its pre-war level, being restricted by high taxation, and even more severely by rationing and shortages. Since 1942, the balance of payments deficit had been met by lend-lease. To further the war effort, exports had been reduced in the middle years of the war to a third of their pre-war volume . . . in 1945 the volume of exports was still less than half pre-war. Invisible earnings too had been greatly reduced by the disposal of British assets overseas to pay for the war. Notwithstanding the low level of imports, the foreign deficit in 1945 amounted therefore to about ten percent of the national product.[8]

Inflationary pressures had grown during the war years. Rationing and shortages had boosted consumers' savings from a prewar 5% of disposalbe income to 25% at the height of the war. In spite of high levels of taxation, people had saved unprecedented large fractions of their earnings. Firms also accumulated large liquid funds during the war, being unable to invest in plant, equipment and raw materials. These abnormal wartime savings supported a high level of excess demand which threatened the economy with serious inflation. No currency reform program was carried out after 1945 to reduce excess liquidity in the economy; instead, the government decided to rely on the battery of physical controls it retained in order to fight inflation. The Chancellor seemed to be more preoccupied with the possibility of a recurrence of a 1919-1921 type of postwar deflation than with the dangers of imminent inflation. He apprehended the possibility of a condition of serious unemployment in 1948 when, upon taking office, he stated that, "the risk of inflation now is less than the risk of deflation later."[9]

Dalton believed that in order to achieve a speedy economic recovery on the basis of full employment, private and public borrowing should not be burdened with high interest rates. He thought that a reduction in short- and long-term rates of interest would benefit the economy in different ways. A fall in rates would reduce the interest-cost of the public debt and would encourage an expansion of public finance for reconstruction purposes. Since most of the sterling balances held in London by other countries were held in the form of Treasury bills, a reduction of the Treasury bill rate would benefit the balance of payments. Finally, the cheap money argument affirmed that low rates of interest would boost private investment and maintain a high level of employment.

The rate of interest on Treasury bills was halved in October, 1945. Conversions of long-term public issues brought the long-term rate down to 2.5%. Rates on government loans were also reduced and local authorities were able to borrow from the Local Loans Fund at rates as low as .75%.[10] Critics pointed out that Dalton's monetary policy was not anti-inflationary. It was not meant to be; inflation was to be checked through devices such as price and import controls, rationing and regulated allocations of raw materials. Meanwhile, Dalton's policy allowed the Labour government to halve interest payments on the public debt. The government's confidence in its ability to control inflation was such that income taxes were reduced in 1946 and the wartime excess profits tax was abolished in the same year.

A sufficiently large American loan was counted upon to solve Britain's balance of payments problems. The famous Dollar Loan Agreement was signed by President Truman in July, 1946. It had been estimated that it would take from three to five years for British exports to reach the planned target of 175% of their prewar volume. Meanwhile, with due consideration being given to the effects of worsening terms of trade, it was believed that during the same period Great Britain would accumulate a balance of payments deficit of 1.2 billion pounds. The government's objective was to cover this deficit through the American loan.

Under the terms of the 1946 Loan Agreement, the British indebtedness to the United States for the value of lend-lease supplies granted by the Americans to the United Kingdom during the years of war was written off, with the exception of $650 million worth of supplies received by Britain after lend-lease had been ended in August, 1945. The totality of the American loan amounted to $4.4 billion; out of this figure, $650 million was to be applied to the settlement of Britain's lend-lease indebtedness. This left a net credit of $3.75 billion. The Agreement provided that Britain would start paying a 2% rate of interest on the loan in 1951, but that interest payments would be waived if the country's earnings of foreign exchange should drop in any year below their 1936-38 average. The principal was to be repaid over a period of fifty years. These terms were quite generous but other terms in the Agreement brought Britain a serious foreign exchange crisis in the following year.

The Agreement forced Britain to accept immediately all of the resolutions of the free trade 1944 Bretton Woods Agreement. For a country whose export capacity was still weak in relation to its import requirements, the acceptance of this Agreement condition was, as *The Economist* put it, "a bitter pill to swallow." [11] What caused the greatest apprehension in the country was the government's promise to restore full convertibility of the pound within one year after the signing of the Agreement. It was claimed that full convertibility of sterling and the acceptance by Britain of non-discriminatory trade policies had been imposed by the United States more for the sake of American economic advantage than for the purpose of strengthening the British economy.

The American loan was supplemented by a Canadian loan of $1.25 billion, extended to Great Britain under identical conditions. These lines of credit became available to Britain in July 1946 and the country promptly took advantage of them to boost its imports. Between July 1946 and June 1947, the United Kingdom's imports from the dollar area rose to $1.54 billion; during the same period, British exports to the dollar area totalled only $340 million. It was soon recognized that the credits were being drawn upon at a dangerously high rate and it was feared that they would be exhausted long before 1951.

Other developments further burdened the British balance of payments. In February 1947, a fuel crisis resulted from insufficiencies in coal production. A harsh winter had reduced the output of coal to such an extent that electric power to industrial users had to be cut off. Production and transportation were crippled for several weeks and the country suffered an export loss of 200 million pounds.[12] The terms of trade continued to deteriorate while the general world scarcity of dollars stregthened the dollar appetite of foreign holders of sterling balances. When full convertibility of sterling was announced on July 15, 1947, countries with current sterling earnings tried to convert their pounds into dollars as quickly as possible. To prevent a total exhaustion of British dollar holdings, convertibility had to be ended on August 20. The terms of the Dollar Loan Agreement had to be suspended and severe restrictions on dollar imports followed in September.

Inflation and rising unemployment compounded the problems of the economy in 1947. Taking 1963 as the base year, the retail price index had risen from 49 in 1945 to 54 in 1947. The wholesale price index rose by 7% from 51 to 58. Unemployment increased from 179,000 in 1945 to 537,000 in 1947. The level of unemployment in 1947 reached a postwar peak.[13] The government's reaction to these developments was not spectacular. In April, excise taxes and death duties were raised and distributed dividends were taxed in October. Investment cuts of 200 million pounds were announced in the Fall.

Dr. Dalton resigned in November; a critic evaluated his policies as follows:

> Here was a country with over 1 million men in the Forces, over 2 million in Government service, no coal to export, a flowing tide of monetary inflation, foreign exchange reserves being used up at a rate which would completely exhaust them in fifteen months, and apparently no new ideas about what to do.[14]

This is a harsh evaluation. Industrial output had surpassed the 1938 level in 1946.[15] In addition to achieving rapid economic reconstruction, the government, determined to minimize poverty in the country, brought the passage in 1946 of of the National Insurance Act and of the National Health Service Act. By the time Dr. Dalton resigned, the country's wartime economic wounds were healed and the government could plan for new growth.

Sir Stafford Cripps' "Dirigisme"

The fuel crisis of February 1947 gave cause to loud criticism of the government's ability to manage the economy. The government reacted by revising and centralizing its planning apparatus. In March, Sir Stafford Cripps, then President of the Board of Trade, announced the establishment of an inter-departmental planning staff, headed by a Chief Planning Officer. This planning agency was charged with the tasks of co-ordinating government planning, of reviewing existing plans and of formulating future plans. An Economic Planning Board was set up to supervise the implementation of the economic plans and to act in an advisory capacity. Representatives of industrial management and of the trade unions were to be seated on this Board.

The procedural innovations did not bring economic peace. The convertibility crisis of August 1947 followed the fuel crisis by only six months. The new crisis induced the Prime Minister to elevate Sir Stafford Cripps to the position of Minister for Economic Affairs, a position Sir Stafford retained when he followed Dr. Dalton as Chancellor of the Exchequer on November 13. As one writer put it, "no minister before or since, even during the war years, had as great power to direct the economy as Sir Stafford Cripps.[16]

The new Chancellor, although an enthusiast of democratic planning based on an extensive use by government of physical and financial controls, felt that an efficient management of the economy required close cooperation and clear mutual understanding between government and society as a whole. As President of the Board of Trade, Sir Stafford had been very successful in obtaining voluntary export targets from industry. As Chancellor, Sir Stafford showed great skill in having industry, commerce and the trade unions support policies of voluntary price and wage restraint. He was particularly successful in the achievement of wage stagility within the period ending with the Korean War.

During the quarter of a century between 1924 and 1949, the strongest wage increases in Britain occurred during the periods 1939 to 1942 and 1945 to 1948. During both these periods, wages increased at the average rate of about 10% per year.[17]

The United Kingdom, unlike the United States, had not imposed a wage freeze during the war period. Price ceilings had been established in July 1941, and the government had hoped that with price stability, organized labor would not press for higher monetary wages. Indirect controls contributed to the stabilization of wage pressures on both sides of the labor market. Compulsory assignment of labor to industries facing manpower shortages curbed inflationary wage trends in those industries,[18] Compulsory arbitration of management-labor disputes was adopted in the summer of 1940 and the binding decisions of the National Arbitration Tribunal also played a major role in the stabilization of wages. Labor's awareness of the war's dangers probably also induced labor leaders and workers to forego aggressive wage demands.

Once the war had ended, however, voluntary wage restraint seemed less patriotic and less necessary to workers. Labor unions started pressing for higher wages. In spite of the continuation of compulsory arbitration, rising import prices, rising costs and the rising prices of controlled commodities made wage increases unavoidable; during the first three postwar years, trade unions succeeded in obtaining the wage increases they demanded.

It was to Sir Stafford Cripps' credit that the unions decided to support the government's wage stabilization policy in the period 1948 to 1950. The government, in a White Paper titled a "Statement on Personal Incomes, Costs and Prices," issued in February 1948, demanded wage and salary stability in order to facilitate a badly needed expansion of exports. Wage increases were to be disallowed except as compensation for increased productivity or when granted as a means to attract labor to undermanned essential industries.[19]

The British *Trades Union Congress* decided to support the government's wage policy. The acceptance of government policy by the T.U.C. was given, however, subject to certain conditions. Labor demanded that collective bargaining should remain free of governmental regulation; wage increases were to be allowed where existing incomes were below a reasonable standard of subsistence; wage increases were also to be allowed when justified by increases in output. The acceptance by unions of voluntary wage restraint and their willingness to have the government act as arbitrator in wage disputes were the major factors supporting the income stability that prevailed in the country until the outbreak of the Korean War in the summer of 1950. Average weekly earnings had risen by 10% between April 1947 and April 1948; they rose by only 5% between April 1948, and April 1949. For two and a half years, labor gave its support to the government program, even though prices were rising faster than wages and in spite of the devaluation of the pound in September 1949. Although devaluation threatened an increase in the cost of living, the General Council of the T.U.C. still recommended in November 1949 that trade unions refrain from pressing for higher wages until the end of 1950. In January 1950, a majority of unions voted to accept the General Council's re-commendations. The T.U.C. decided, however, to change its policy by mid-year. On June 28, just before the outbreak of war in Korea, the General Council announced that a "greater flexibility in wage movements" was needed.[20]

Price and wage stability greatly contributed to the export and production boom of 1948. Of equal importance for the growth of output was the receipt of President Truman's Interim Aid at the end of 1947, followed in 1948 by Marshall Plan assistance. Although economic aid received by Great Britain under the European Recovery Program of 1948 effectively ended with the Korean War, it allowed the British economy to survive the disastrous convertibility crisis of 1947.

Sir Stafford Cripps counteracted the crisis by re-establishing and tightening controls over foreign exchange transactions and imports. Import restriction allowed him to reduce the British deficit with the dollar area; the Chancellor achieved the development of a British surplus with the sterling area and the latter in turn had a surplus with the dollar area. By December 1948, Great Britain attained for the first time in the postwar period an overall balance on current account.[21]

There were, however, serious weaknesses in the economy. The country was still unable to earn sufficient dollars to pay for imports from the United States and Canada and was unable to replace these imports by imports from the sterling area. As one writer put it, the British balance of payments statistics did not reveal a true equilibrium "since this would imply that a sterling asset was just as good as a dollar debt and it was the fact that this was not so which constituted the dollar problem."[22]

With improved supply conditions in 1948, import restrictions were relaxed together with a general reduction in governmental controls. This happened at a time when the export boom and the accumulation of unsatisfied wartime consumer demand threatened inflation. The government had abandoned Dalton's cheap money policies and was following not very anti-inflationary neutral monetary and fiscal policies. Sir Stafford's 1948 budget did not raise the level of taxation. Although a once-for-all special levy on wealth was imposed and although some indirect taxes were raised, tax revenue was left practically unchanged because of a compensatory reduction in income taxes which benefited mostly the low income groups.

At the end of 1948, the beginning of a recession in the United States caused a sharp fall in British exports. The resulting drop in British foreign reserves was aggravated by a flight from sterling caused by a public statement of the United States Administration recommending the devaluation of the pound.[23] In the fall of 1949, the British government decided to devalue the pound in such a way that British exports would substantially benefit. In violation of the regulations of the International Monetary Fund, the pound was devalued by 30.5% on September 18, 1949, its value falling from $4.03 to $2.80

The United Kingdom could only gain by such a devaluation if the volume of foreign purchases of British goods increased by more than the percentage drop in the dollar price of sterling and if the new rate of exchange prevented an increase in the value of British imports. Devaluation had as its principal goal the expansion of exports. The gain from devaluation could only be realized if the sterling prices of exports did not rise and if British exporters were prepared to sell abroad a sufficiently larger volume of British commodities. With unchanged sterling prices, and with the dollar prices of British exports now 30.5% less than before devaluation, British exporters had to expand their sales abroad by more than 30.5% of pre-devaluation sales if they were to earn more dollars than they earned before September 18.

The devaluation was criticized as being excessive. Many of the countries in the sterling area and the Scandinavian countries devalued in turn by as much as Britain, but Canada, France, Germany, Italy and Belgium devalued their currencies by a smaller percentage. It was believed that the severe devaluation of the pound would force the United Kingdom to devote a much larger part of its resources to exports in order to allow the country to purchase the pre-devaluation volume of imports; this, it was held, would add to inflationary pressures in the country.[24]

However the devaluation was successful. The sterling area deficit with the dollar area was turned into a $40 million surplus during the first quarter of 1950. The British balance with the sterling area improved.[25] British gold and dollar reserves increased from $1,425 million at the end of September 1949, to $2,422 million at the end of

June, 1950.[26] During the entire period 1948 to 1957, the balance of payments on current account showed a deficit in only three years. Surpluses in these years exceeded deficits by over 0.5 billion pounds. These surpluses were not used, however, to expand the country's international reserves; instead, they were used to pay off some of the country's international debts and as investments overseas. In the words of Professor Youngson;

> The pressure to invest this surplus abroad was very great. The result was that insufficient was available to strengthen the reserves. They were always inadequate. And time and time again a comparatively small change in British prices, in foreign confidence in sterling, in the level of activity at home, in the willingness of markets overseas to buy British goods, or in the terms of trade caused hasty internal adjustments because the reserves were not large enough to permit the authorities to watch heavy inroads being made upon them without anxiety.[27]

Devaluation, by making imports more expensive for British buyers and by diverting resources from home to export use, threatened inflation. To avoid this possibility, the government, following its traditional stop-go policy, announced in October that cuts in investment and public expenditure of about 280 million pounds would be made in 1950.[28]

Sir Stafford Cripps remained Chancellor of the Exchequer after the election of February 1950. Illness forced him to resign in October. During his period in office, the economy had finally achieved a substantial surplus in its balance of payments in spite of the ending of Marshall Plan aid in 1950; full employment had been maintained. Looking at the period 1947 to 1950, G.D.N. Worswick summarized the economic achievements of the labour government by noticing that:

> The volume of industrial production in 1950 was 30 percent higher than in 1947; the volume of exports was 60 per cent higher, and had reached the target of "75 percent above pre-war." In 1950 the balance of payments was in surplus to the extent of 229 million pounds as compared with a deficit of 545 million pounds in 1947. At the end of 1950, the United Kingdom was fully solvent and able for the first time since the war to dispense with outside aid. At home personal consumption had been raised by 5 percent since 1947, the number of new houses provided since the war had passed the million mark, and there had been a general extension of the social services, including health and education. Finally, there had been continuous full employment.[29]

The successful performance of the economy was not entirely due, however, to the wisdom of government policy. The recovery of the American economy in the spring of 1950 contributed probably more than devaluation to the British export boom. The continuing use of extensive import controls remained of crucial importance in the government's attempt to improve the balance of payments. As late as 1950, most British imports were still subject to government control. Careful government control over investment and high levels of taxation were needed to prevent inflation. In spite of the much advertised November 1948, "bonfire" of controls by the Board of Trade, economic activity during Sir Stafford Cripps' period of tenure remained subject to tight governmental regulation and control. One cannot but wonder what would have happened to this economy had Sir Stafford decided to follow the example given by Dr. Ludwig Erhard in West Germany.

The Korean War and "Butskellism"

Industrial recovery in the United States after the 1949 recession and the rapid recovery of West Germany and Japan boosted world-wide industrial production and resulted in large imports and stockpiling of raw materials in those countries months before the outbreak of war in Korea.[30] The war simply intensified the international scramble for raw materials whose prices shot up. The index of British import prices rose by 25% during 1950 and increased by a further 25% during the first half of 1951. British imports in 1951 cost 1.1 billion pounds more than a year before. The resulting loss of international reserves was worsened in March by the Iranian seizure of the British oil refineries at Abadan. The seizure forced the United Kingdom to spend 100 million pounds more each year to buy oil from other sources.

During 1950 and the early months of 1951, booming world demand for materials such as wool, rubber and tin had substantially increased the dollar earnings of many countries contributing to the sterling area dollar pool. But although the dollar earnings of the sterling area were rising, so were sterling area dollar imports. By mid-1951, world raw materials prices started to fall and the dollar earnings of the sterling area began to diminish. The countries earning these dollars continued, however, to import from the United States and Canada at twice the rate of 1950, so that instead of expanding, the sterling area dollar pool started to shrink.

Though British export prices increased during this period, their rate of increase was only half the rate of price increase of imports. The end result was that the British balance of payments surplus of 307 million pound in 1950 became a 365 million pound deficit in 1951.

To make matters worse, the government announced in September 1950 that defense expenditures would be raised from about 750 million pounds a year to 3.6 billion pounds for the three years 1951 to 1953. In January, the amount of these expenditures was revised and increased to 4.7 billion pounds.

It was under these unfavorable circumstances that Mr. H. Gaitskell became Chancellor of the Exchequer in October 1950, a position he retained for only one year. He was succeeded by Mr. R. A. Butler after the Conservative Party's victory in the 1951 election.

Rearmament required a larger public use of a number of industrial raw materials subject to serious shortages. The government felt that increases in taxes alone would not be able to generate adequate supplies of aluminum, nickel, zinc, copper and steel. Although purchase taxes on consumer goods embodying relatively large amounts of metal were doubled, Gaitskell's 1951 budget did not provide for large income tax increases. To obtain more tax revenue, the government raised the profits tax from 30% to 50%.[31] Price controls followed in July, and Mr. Butler, upon taking office, ordered new import cuts.

Mr. Butler's policies continued those of his predecessors. "Butskellist" policies continued to rely on import controls and fiscal policy to bring the country out of the 1951 balance of payments crisis.[32]

Immediately upon taking office, Mr. Butler ordered major import cuts, and additional import reductions were imposed in January and March 1952. This was a major departure from the 1949 O.E.E.C. policy which had advocated import liberalization between member countries. Following this policy, the United Kingdom had liberalized over 90% of its private imports from O.E.E.C. countries in 1950. Mr. Butler reduced this percentage to 61% at the end of 1951 and to 44% at the end of 1952. Similar restrictions on imports were adopted by the sterling area countries.[33]

The Labour government's rearmament program had added strength to the inflationary pressures in the economy. In order to avoid the undesirable effect of inflation on exports, Mr. Gaitskell had urged the banks to limit their lending. An increase in the corporate profits tax and the elimination of certain depreciation allowances were to reduce private investment expenditure. While public expenditure, mainly on defense, increased between 1950 and 1951, consumers' expenditures were reduced, fixed investment in 1951 did not rise above the 1950 level, and the volume of exports actually fell. A large increase in imports brought about a balance of payments crisis, and the government resolved to bring about a drastic reduction in imports through new controls.

These policies were followed by Mr. Butler. Import restrictions were immediately imposed. Restrictions on investment were not abandoned. To fight the slump burdening the textile and clothing industries, the 1952 budget reduced income taxes, but a concurrent reduction of food subsidies by over 150 million pounds a year left the consumers' purchasing power unchanged. Restrictions on the purchase of consumer durable goods on the basis of installment payments appeared for the first time. Mr. Butler's only economic policy innovation at the time was to increase the Bank of England discount rate from 2% to 2.5% in November 1951, and to 4% in March 1952. These deflationary policies did not help exports; they fell, together with industrial output. The fall of exports was, however, more than offset by a concurrent fall of imports, partly due to the effect of the new import restrictions, partly to the 1952 decline in home demand. The 1952 decline of imports brought a surplus in the balance of payments by the end of the year. Improving terms of trade helped the country to retain this surplus during the two following years.

Continuing traditional stop-go policies, Mr. Butler attempted to revive home demand and to stimulate investment and production in his 1953 budget. Reductions in income and purchase taxes resulted in the largest increases in consumption expenditure since the end of the war. Investment expenditure and manufacturing output also expanded rapidly. Although imports were rising in 1953 and 1954, exports rose sufficiently to maintain the balance of payments surplus.

The rapidly increasing investment in industrial plant and equipment started subjecting the economy to strong inflationary pressures in the Fall of 1954. Inflationary forces were clearly of the "demand-pull" rather than of the "cost-push" type. Until the end of 1954, wages did not rise faster than productivity.[34]

Home demand and investment continued to expand in 1955. Exports continued to rise, but they failed to keep up with the increase in imports and a balance of payments crisis occurred once again. As in prior instances of balance of payments difficulties, the government took action to eliminate the external deficit and to reduce inflation. The Bank rate was increased to 4.5%, public investment plans were cut back, credit restrictions were strengthened and, in October, purchase taxes were raised. Although a balance of surplus was obtained in the following year, Butler's 1955 deflationary policies reduced the country's rate of economic growth and stopped for three years the expansion of manufacturing output. The Conservative Chancellor, just like the earlier Labour Chancellors, sacrificed economic growth for the sake of external balance. Table 3.1 shows that during both 1951 and 1955 — years of accumulating balance of payments deficits — home demand, as shown by total domestic expenditure contracted; Gross Domestic Product exhibited either a decline or a smaller rate of increase.

TABLE 3.1

UNITED KINGDOM: YEARLY CHANGES
IN DEMAND AND SUPPLY
(£Million, 1958 Prices)

	1947	1948	1949	1950	1951	1952	1953	1954	1955
Demand									
Consumers' expenditure	−71	238	351	−179	−64	578	546	564	129
Public expenditure	−21	183	0	247	355	105	−15	−115	−26
Fixed capital formation	188	198	126	10	10	269	234	168	146
Stock accumulation	−259	−160	−365	890	−550	70	−81	259	−69
Total domestic expend.	−163	459	112	968	−249	1022	684	876	180
Exports	650	341	493	−40	−82	160	225	260	195
Total Final expend.	487	800	605	928	−331	1182	909	1136	375
Supply									
G.D.P.	527	539	574	675	−42	899	767	732	362
Imports	40	262	31	253	−289	283	142	404	13
Total Supplies	487	800	605	928	−331	1182	909	1136	375

Industrial Growth During the First Postwar Decade

It has often been stated that the growth and competitiveness of British industry were handicapped in the 1950s and 1960s by the continued use of obsolete plants and equipment and by the lack of interest on the part of British management in the adoption of new methods of production and distribution. At a time when the West Germans were rebuilding their factories on the basis of the most modern and efficient techniques, too many British firms continued to operate with outdated prewar equipment. Technological progress in Britain compared poorly with that of other countries in Western Europe.[35] Excepting the automobile, aircraft and oil technology industries, most British manufacturing firms were relatively small and 'tended on the whole to respond slowly to the challenge of technological advance. Many of these firms, "employing few more workers than Mr. William Lever's Bolton grocery business in the 1880s," lacked the necessary resources to finance research and were not large enough to induce their management to invest in more efficient production techniques.[36] Poorly talented managers may have failed to perceive the potential of new techniques, even when their adoption was justified. Although generalizations are often faulty, the background and the value system of a large part of British management are well described by John and Anne-Marie Hackett in the following way:

> The "cult of the amateur" is not the monopoly of high officials. "It is well known," writes Mr. Shanks, "that if one wants to reach the top in British industry it is usually fatal to admit any specialist expertise. Otherwise one is apt to find oneself put in charge of a specialist advisory department . . . and there one is liable to stay." The fact that a degree in engineering is still often considered, even in industry, as inferior to a training in classics or letters must severely deflect many brilliant scientists away from careers in industry.
>
> The same lack of systematic training on the job which is held against the Civil Service in Britain is to be found in the private sector. Although scientific management is taught at all levels in modern branches of industry like electronics, chemistry and oil technology, this is by no means true in many of the traditional branches such as shipbuilding, machine tools and building construction . . . It was not until 1963 that a business school was planned for higher ranks of industry.
>
> The problems in the nationalized industries are similar to those in the private sector.[37]

Competent and innovative management tended to be associated with the large industrial firms of the aircraft, automobile and oil processing industries. A series of amalgamations among firms in these industries, along with, in some cases, American control, brought to these firms important economies of scale and falling per-unit costs. Elsewhere, however, managerial inflexbility, combined with the production planning difficulties resulting from the governmental stop-go policies, caused a rate of growth of industrial output which remained far below the corresponding rates in other countries. Full employment further restricted the expansion of industrial output in Britain by limiting the annual rate of growth of the labor force.

From Table 3.2 it appears that production in manufacturing industry rose on the average in the period 1946 to 1955 by 3.4% per year. However, the yearly rate of growth for the entire industrial output was only 1.8%.[38] Employment in manufacturing during this period increased by about 0.17% per annum, labor productivity in manufacturing increasing therefore by 3.23% per year. For industry as a whole, including mining, construction, and the production of electricity, gas and water, the average yearly rate of growth of labor productivity was about 2%. This rate placed Britain in the early 1950s at the bottom of a list of nine Western European countries.

TABLE 3.2
INDUSTRIAL PRODUCTION AND EMPLOYMENT IN
MANUFACTURING: 1956 - 1955

	Manufacturing Production Index: 1963 = 100	Total Industrial Output Index 1963 = 100	Employment in Manufacturing In millions
1946	52.2	67	7.11
1947	55.2	66	7.57
1948	60.3	70	7.70
1949	64.1	73	7.85
1950	68.5	76	8.05
1951	71.4	76	8.27
1952	68.8	75	8.02
1953	73.1	79	8.26
1954	78.0	84	8.68
1955	83.0	84	8.68

Source: The Times, *The British Economy Key Statistics*, 1900-1970, Tables C and E.

Technological backwardness and managerial mediocrity explain to a large extent Britain's relatively poor productivity record. They burdened both private and nationalized industries. In one of the largest nationalized industries, British Railways, large losses in the period 1948 to 1955 were mostly due to the fact that management was unable to determine which railroad lines had been the sources of these losses over the years. It has been reported that:

> As late as 1959, it was still a mystery just where the massive losses were being incurred. In that year the railways were subjected to the scrutiny of the Select Committee of Nationalized Industries, the Report of which echoed the plaintive admission of the Permanent Secretary to the Ministry of Transport that: "We find one of the most difficult things in the Ministry is to discover where money is actually lost . . ."[40]

Employers' associations as well as trade unions exhibited a great lack of interest in the improvement of both industrial relations and methods of production. Until 1964, four organizations represented the employers. These were the British Employers' Confederation, the National Association of British Manufacturers, the Federation of British Industries and The National Association of Chambers of Commerce. Representing different groups of employers and different parts of their activities, these organizations were both weak and over-conservative. Their conservatism was shared by the trade unions. The memory of the massive unemployment conditions of the 1930s permeated the minds of trade union leaders with the fear that technical progress endangered job security. This state of mind also affected the attitudes of officials of the Trades Union Congress who in the 1950s remained suspicious of plans to modernize means of production and distribution.[41]

Agriculture

World War II forced the British government to undertake a major effort to raise the country's agricultural output. As German submarines started threatening Britain's imports of foodstuffs and agricultural raw materials, and as the volume of these imports had to be reduced because of a lack of sufficient shipping facilities, a generous policy of grants and subsidies to farmers was initiated in order to raise efficiency and production in the agricultural sector. It was felt that national survival required a rapid expansion of domestic agricultural output and that this expansion should be achieved regardless of cost. This view continued to prevail in the early postwar years. Military strategists argued in the late 1940s that the world's political instability dictated a higher degree of independence from foreign sources of foodstuff supplies. The 1947 convertibility crisis and the accompanying dollar shortage caused many British economists to argue that, given the country's incapacity to earn sufficient dollars to pay for its dollar imports, the latter should be reduced through an import-replacement program which encouraged the growth of home agricultural output.[42] Professor Robinson warned that in time, primary export countries would attempt to industrialize and that these industrialization efforts would force them to consume more of their own primary products. Hence, these countries would export smaller volumes of agricultural products while their demand for British manufactured products would also decline. The United Kingdom should therefore protect itself from the effect of deteriorating terms of trade for manufactured goods by gradually increasing its own agricultural output.[43] The 1946 decline of cereal imports and the resulting rationing of bread seemed to support the predictions of these economists. Government decided to continue to encourage the growth of domestic agricultural output, not through a system of tariffs or import quotas as was done on the Continent, but through a scheme of production grants and subsidies.

The Exchequer started assisting the British farmer through a number of direct production grants. Financial assistance was given for the ploughing of old grassland, for the purchase of fertilizers, for investment in new drainage systems and for the acquisition of machinery.[44]

The main form of public aid to agriculture was a program of price subsidization provided by the Agriculture Act of 1947. The principal aim of this Act was "the promotion of a stable and efficient agriculture capable of producing such part of the nation's food and other agricultural produce as in the national interest it is desireable to produce in the United Kingdom. . . ."[45]

Under the terms of the Act, the government attempted to obtain desired levels of agricultural output by guaranteeing the prices of roughly 90% of Britain's agricultural output.[46] Guaranteed prices were to be reviewed each year by a joint committee formed by representatives of the Ministry of Agriculture and the National Farmers' Unions. The actual market prices of these products were to be determined by the interaction of free market demand and supply forces and could be reduced by low-cost imports. If in any given year the actual market prices of a protected commodity should fall below its guaranteed price, the government would compensate the farmer for the difference. This system of deficiency payments encouraged the British farmer to expand production under conditions where agricultural imports entered the country free of tariff restrictions and of large customs duties at prices which were from 25% to 30% lower than British agricultural prices. The provisions of the Act induced the farmer to continue production even in times when the market price of his product fell below production costs.

The cost of these subsidies was not small. It amounted to 140 million pounds in the period 1954-1955. If this policy allowed British consumers to purchase foodstuffs at prices which were generally lower than those prevailing on the Continent and raised the income of British farmers, it burdened British taxpayers between 1947 and 1952 with a cost of 820 million pounds.[47]

With the passage of the Agriculture Act of 1947, the government announced a five-year plan for the expansion of agricultural output which called for a net increase in output of 20% over current levels. Targets were not fulfilled in time for all the commodities covered by the plan. While the output of livestock products increased according to plans, Table 3.3 shows that there was a drop in the output of potatoes and oats, while the output of barley remained constant. The relatively poor performance of crops was probably due to the fact that the area of arable land in the country declined from 19 million acres in 1946 to 17.5 million acres in 1955.[48] The effects of a diminishing area under crops were partially offset by an increased utilization of industrial inputs in agriculture, the value of these inputs in terms of 1954 prices having risen from a prewar figure of 231 million pounds to 456 million pounds in 1955.[49]

Although Britain almost doubled the use of industrial inputs in agriculture, the country's growth rate of gross agricultural output was not among the largest of such rates for Western European countries. In the 1950s, Italy, France, Denmark, Western Germany and Finland had larger growth rates. Agriculture, of course, does not usually exhibit the same close correlation between output and inputs of labor and capital as does industry; in most countries, the rate of growth of agricultural output is still affected by such non-marketable inputs as weather conditions. The data, however, show that in those countries with growth rates larger than that of Great Britain, the agricultural sector received a larger share of total investment than in Britain.[50]

TABLE 3.3

AGRICULTURAL PRODUCTION IN THE UNITED KINGDOM
INDICES FOR SELECTED YEARS
1939 = 100

	1946-1947	1954-1955
Wheat	119.1	168.6
Rye	390.0	390.0
Barley	256.6	293.3
Oats	149.6	125.8
Potatoes	208.6	150.3
Sugar Beet	165.0	164.9
Milk	106.2	137.6
Eggs	83.6	142.9
Beef and Veal	92.9	137.9
Mutton and Lamb	72.3	93.3
Pigmeat	48.5	174.0
Wool	79.4	100.0

Source: Agricultural Economics Research Institute, *The Agricultural Register New Series, Changes in Economic Pattern*, Oxford 1957, pp. 9-10.

TABLE 3.4

AGRICULTURAL PERFORMANCE IN SELECTED
WESTERN EUROPEAN COUNTRIES: 1949-1959

	Growth Rate of Gross Output %	Percentage Share of Agr. Sector in Gross Investment %	Growth Rate cf Labor Productivity %
Italy	3.5	13	4.7
France	3.1	11	4.9
Denmark	3.0	8.5	4.9
Western Germany	2.7	8.5	5.5
Finland	2.4	13	4.2
United Kingdom	2.0	4.5	3.8
Netherlands	1.8	6	3.8
Austria	1.1	14	1.8
Belgium	0.9	4	4.6
Norway	0.6	8.5	3.1

Source: United Nations, Economic Commission for Europe, *Some Factors In Economic Growth in Europe During the 1950s*, Geneva, 1964, Ch. III, p. 28.

In Retrospect

During the first postwar decade, as well as throughout the 1950s, the United Kingdom appeared at the bottom of a list of European countries showing rates of growth of gross national product, employed labor force and labor productivity. For the decade of the 1950s, the data are shown in Table 3.5.

Economists generally believe that international differences in rates of economic growth are in large part due to international differences in rates of fixed capital formation. Fixed capital formation contributes to overall economic growth in two principal ways: it enlarges the volume of capital equipment available to an economy, facilitating an increase in production; and it also helps the growth of technological progress. The quantum of fixed capital formation during a given period of time depends, of course, on the ratio of total investment, public and private, to gross national product during this period of time. The data show a positive correlation between rates of growth of investment in the European countries considered and the expansion of gross national product. Among the industrialized countries of Western Europe, the United Kingdom had both the lowest yearly rate of overall economic growth and the lowest investment ratio.

The low British investment ratio was due to a number of factors. Private saving was much weaker in the United Kingdom than elsewhere in western Europe. The low British private saving rate can be explained in part by the fact that taxation attained higher levels in Britain than in other countries and that high rates of taxation may have discouraged private saving. Taxes were high in the United Kingdom because of the government's inability to borrow sufficient funds to finance public investment. In the early postwar period, Britain's cheap money policy hampered public long-term borrowing and induced the government to finance a large part of government investment out of tax revenues. Furthermore, as Professor Kaldor pointed out, the British private saving ratio could also have been depressed by the country's low rate of growth of per capita income. When an economy grows rapidly, the share of profits in total national income tends to rise; since profit earners tend to save a larger proportion of their earnings than wage earners, a rapid rate of overall growth will tend to raise the saving ratio. The opposite tends to occur when the rate of economic growth is low.[51]

TABLE 3.5

GROSS INVESTMENT RATIOS, GROWTH OF DOMESTIC PRODUCT,
EMPLOYED LABOR FORCE AND LABOR PRODUCTIVITY IN
SELECTED COUNTRIES: 1949-1959

Compound Annual Percentages Rates of Growth

	Gross Investment Ratio: Constant Prices	G.D.P.	Employed Labor Force	Labor Productivity
Western Germany	24.2	7.4	1.6	5.7
Austria	23.3	6.0	1.1	4.8
Greece	17.8	5.9	1.5	4.3
Italy	21.9	5.9	1.5	4.8
Turkey	——	5.9	2.4	3.4
Yugoslavia	23.2	5.5	1.1	4.4
Iceland	30.9	5.4	1.5	3.8
Spain	——	5.2	0.8	4.3
Switzerland	——	5.2	1.5	3.7
Netherlands	25.0	4.8	1.2	3.6
France	20.6	4.5	0.1	4.3
Finland	30.0	4.2	0.7	3.4
Portugal	16.2	4.1	0.6	3.5
Luxembourg	23.7	3.8	0.8	3.0
Norway	32.6	3.4	0.3	3.1
Sweden	21.4	3.4	0.5	2.9
Denmark	17.5	3.2	1.0	2.2
Belgium	16.9	3.0	0.3	2.7
United Kingdom	16.1	2.4	0.6	1.8
Ireland	17.9	1.3	-1.1	2.4

Sources: United Nations, Economic Commission for Europe, *Some Factors In Economic Growth in Europe During the 1950's* Geneva, 1964, Ch. II, Tables 4 and 6.

Growth in the United Kingdom was also often accompanied by relatively long periods of excess demand which indicated the existence of supply limitations; supply shortages tended in turn to reduce the rate of capital formation. Similar manifestations of excess demand did not exist in Italy and occurred only briefly in Western Germany. In the United Kingdom, the government was very much concerned that conditions of excess demand could lead to balance of payments difficulties; this induced it to follow temporary policies of demand restraint which often caused an under-utilization of resources, another cause for a low rate of capital formation. In the United Kingdom, authorities were particularly afraid that excess demand could lead to cost and wage inflation. Britain had good reason to be afraid of wage inflation since it did not possess the large manpower reserve of Western Germany and Italy. Wage inflation would have added to Britain's export difficulties and would have threatened the country's external balance. Although France also witnessed periods of excess demand, the government in France did not show the concern of its British counterpart to maintain balance of payments stability.[52] Frequent short-term investment restraints imposed by the British government tended to limit investment demand as well as investment supply.

The British rate of economic growth was also adversely affected by labor factors. Full employment conditions and a low rate of growth of the labor force created a rigid employment structure and induced management to hoard labor. During periods of falling demand, British firms, instead of releasing their excess labor to other firms or industries, tended to retain their entire labor force out of fear that if they lost part of it, they would be unable to recuperate the laid-off labor force during periods of rising demand. Assuming that the government's commitment to a policy of full employment would continue, British firms preferred, during periods of slackening demand, to reduce the weekly work load of their employees rather than to utilize a smaller labor force more efficiently. This policy did not encourage the development of a more efficient utilization of labor and did nothing to boost labor productivity. Labor unions, in turn, probably still influenced by memories of the 1930s, continued to insist on the maintenance of restrictive practices which hampered the growth of labor productivity. With its labor force fully employed, the United Kingdom, unlike Italy or Western Germany, was unable to move workers easily from low productivity industries to sectors where labor could be more productive. The endemic housing shortage further added to labor's immobility.

Given the obstacles to an efficient utilization of capital and labor inputs in the United Kingdom, the slow growth of the British economy during the first postwar decade becomes understandable.

NOTES

1. Cmd. 6527
2. Labour party election manifesto, *Let us Face the Future*, 1945, p. 4
3. R.E. Caves, *et al.*, *Britain's Economic Prospects* (London: George Allen & Unwin Ltd., 1968), p. 16.
4. H.A. Clegg and T.E. Chester, *The Future of Nationalization* (Oxford: Oxford University Press, 1955), Ch. 1.

5. J.C.R. Dow, *The Management of the British Economy, 1945-1960* (London: N.I.E.S.R., 1964), pp. 146-149.

6. G. Ray, "British Imports of Manufactures," *National Institute Economic Review* (May 1961):36-41.

7. P.E.P., Political and Economic Planning, *Britain and World Trade* (London: 1947), p. 61.

8. Dow, *The Management of the British Economy*, p. 14.

9. Lord H. Dalton, *High Tide and After: Memoirs, 1945-1960* (London: Muller, 1962), p. 165.

10. C.M. Kennedy, "Monetary Policy," *The British Economy, 1945-1950, ed.*, G.D.N. Worswick and P. H. Ady (Oxford: Oxford University Press, 1952), pp. 188-206.

11. *The Economist* (London, December 8, 1945), p. 821.

12. A.J. Youngson, *Britain's Economic Growth, 1920-1966* (London: George Allen & Unwin Ltd., 1967), p. 164.

13. *The Times, The British Economic Key Statistics, 1900-1970* (London, 1972), Table E, p. 8.

14. Youngson, *Britain's Economic Growth*, p. 168.

15. Industrial output in 1946 surpassed the 1938 level although the industrial labor force in 1946 was smaller than that of 1938. D. Seers, "National Income, Production and Consumption," *The British Economy, 1945-1950*, p. 38.

16. Dow, *Management of the British Economy*, p. 33.

17. The period 1924 to 1939 was characterized by chronic unemployment and by relatively stable wage rates; the decade 1939 to 1949 was one of sustained full employment with the wage index increasing from 101 in 1939 to 193 in 1949. See A. Flanders, "Wages Policy and Full Employment in Britain," *Oxford Institute of Statistics*, vol. 12 (July-August 1950), pp. 225-242.

18. The Restriction of Engagement Order of June, 1940, made workers in the engineering, coal-mining and building industries, as well as in agriculture, unable to leave their jobs unless specifically allowed to do so by the Ministry of Labor. The Essential Work Order of 1941 limited the right of employers to discharge employees and restricted the rights of the latter to leave their job. See P.E. Sultan, "Full Employment on Trial: A Case Study of the British Experience," *The Canadian Journal of Economics and Political Science*, vol. XIX (May 1953), pp. 210-221.

19. Cmd. 7321, February 1948.

20. T.U.C. Proceedings (1950), pp. 266-67.

21. The data show a deficit in the current balance of 300 million pounds in 1946, a deficit of 450 million pounds in 1947, equilibrium in 1948 and a surplus of 50 million pounds in 1949. United Kingdom, *"Blue Book," National Income and Expenditure* (1957).

22. M. Hall, "The United Kingdom After Devaluation," *American Economic Review*, vol. 40, (December 1950):864-875.

23. T. Balogh, "The International Aspect," *The British Economy, 1945-1950*, p. 499.

24. R. Triffin, *Europe and the Money Muddle* (New Haven: Yale University Press, 1957), p. 75.

25. J.R. Sargent, "Britain and the Sterling Area," *The British Economy, 1945-1950*, pp. 531-549.

26. H.M.O.S., *United Kingdom Balance of Payments, 1946-1954* (1954), Cmd. 9291.

27. Youngson, *Britain's Economic Growth, 1920-1966*, p. 171.

28. *House of Commons Deb.* (October 24, 1949), pp. 1018-19.

29. G.D.N. Worswick, and P.H. Ady, *The British Economy in the Nineteen-Fifties* (Oxford: Clarendon Press, 1962), pp. 1-2.

30. United Nations, *Economic Survey of Europe in 1950* (Geneva, 1951). pp. 5-6.

31. Dow, *Management of the British Economy*, p. 59.

32. "Butskellism" — a funny term made up of the names Butler and Gaitskell — was the traditional Labour government policy which supported both government management of the level of aggregate demand and the existence of a relatively free economy. See, S. Brittan, *Steering the Economy* (London: Penguin Books, 1969), pp. 187-190.
33. Worswick and Ady *British Economy in the Nineteen-Fifties*, p. 88.
34. During 1954, the wage-rate index rose by 4.3%; productivity per person employed in manufacturing rose by 6.7%. R.F. Harrod, "The British Boom, 1954-1955," *The Economic Journal* (March 1956), pp. 1-16.
35. S. Pollard, *The Development of the British Economy, 1914-1967* (London: E Arnold, 1969), p. 419.
36. P. Donaldson, *Guide to the British Economy* (Harmondsworth: Penguin Books, 1965), p. 80.
37. J. Hackett and A.M. Hackett, *The British Economy* (London: George Allen & Unwin Ltd., 1967), p. 34.
38. In Key Statistics, the aggregate industrial production index covers production in manufacturing, mining, construction, electricity, gas and water. On the basis of industrial output data covering manufacturing and construction, but excluding textile production, R.J. Nicholson calculates an average yearly rate of growth of industrial output for the period 1948 to 1955 of 4.5% and a rate of growth of industrial labor of 1.8%, resulting in a per annum rate of growth of industrial labor productivity of 2.7%. R.J. Nicholson, *Economic Statistics and Economic Problems* (London: McGraw-Hill, 1969), pp. 217-221.
39. The rates of growth of industrial labor productivity in the period 1950-1955 were 6.2% for the German Federal Republic, 4.4% for Italy, 4.2% for France, 4.4% for Switzerland, 4.2% for the Netherlands, 3.2% for Norway, 2.8% for Sweden, 2.5% for Belgium, 2.0% for the United Kingdom. See J. Knapp and K. Lomax, "Britain's Growth Performance; The Enigma of the 1950s," *Lloyd's Bank Review* (1964), pp. 1-24.
40. Donaldson, *Guide to the British Economy*, p. 101.
41. Hackett, *The British Economy*, p. 37.
42. C.H. Blagburn "Import-Replacement by British Agriculture," *Economic Journal* (March 1950), pp. 19-45; Notes by E.A.G. Robinson and R.L. Marris, *Economic Journal* (March 1950), pp. 177-181 and (March 1951), pp. 176-179; Note by G.D.A. MacDougall, *Economic Journal* (September 1950), pp. 629-631.
43. E.A.G. Robinson "The Future of British Imports," *Three Banks Review* (March 1953).
44. P. Gregg *The Welfare State* (London: G.G. Harrap & Co., 1967), pp. 180-181.
45. H.M.S.O., cmd. 6996 (1947).
46. J.A. Mollett, "Britain's Postwar Agricultural Expansion: Some Economic Problems and Relationships Involved," *Journal of Farm Economics*, vol. 41 (February 1959), pp. 3-15; W.H. Heath, "Agricultural Price Policy in the United Kingdom," *Journal of Farm Economics*, vol. 33 (August 1951), pp. 311-319.
47. J.R. Raeburn, "The Food Economy of the United Kingdom in Relation to International Balance of Payments Problems," *Journal of Proceedings of the Agricultural Economics Society*, vol. VIII, No. 1 (June 1948), p. 35.
48. *Key Statistics*, Table D.
49. Mollett, "Britain's Postwar Agricultural Expansion," p. 7.
50. United Nations, Economic Commission for Europe, *Economic Survey of Europe in 1961*, Part 2 (Geneva, 1964), pp. 27-30.
51. N. Kaldor, "Economic Growth and the Problem of Inflation," *Economica* (August 1959), pp. 212-226.
52. United Nations, Economic Commission for Europe, *Economic Survey of Europe in 1958*, Ch. III, *Economic Expansion and External Balance of Western European Countries* (Geneva, 1959), pp. 1-35.

CHAPTER 4

ALCIDE DE GASPERI AND THE NEW RISORGIMENTO

Eighteen months after September 8, 1944, the day when General Eisenhower and Marshal Badoglio agreed to the unconditional surrender of Italy to the Allied Powers, the German-created "Republic of Salo" finally collapsed. During that year and a half, Italy was ruled by very different governments. In the North, Mussolini ruled his Italian Social Republic under German supervision. In the South, the Royal Government had declared war on Germany on October 13, 1944. In the southern areas under Allied control, towns were openly governed by anti-Fascist Committees of National Liberation, CNL's. In the North, these Committees had to operate secretly and were actively engaged in armed resistance against the German occupying forces. The Committees were formed by members of the six political parties that had been active in the Resistance. The Communists, the Socialists and the Action Party constituted the Left of the movement. Besides a small group of southern Labor Democrats, the Christian Democrats represented a centrist position. The Liberal Party, though anti-clerical, was the most conservative group. The Action Party and the Labor Democrats did not long outlive the end of the war, but the political and economic history of Italy in the period 1945 to 1955 was largely written by the surviving four parties.

To most Italians, the summary execution of the *Duce* by partisans on April 28, 1945 meant the end of an unpopular war, and also announced the reunification of the northern and southern parts of the country after months of fighting and destruction. Fascist Italy had finally disappeared and although the various anti-Fascist parties did not always support the same policies for the solution of social and economic problems, they nevertheless shared a desire for political and economic renewal. Communists and Socialists, as well as Christian Democrats and Liberals, demanded agrarian and educational reforms, the elimination of monopolies and the participation of workers in the industrial decision-making process, a more equitable taxation system, economic development of the impoverished South, and administrative decentralization throughout the country. It seemed that their wishes for a drastic socio-economic change were to be fulfilled when in June 1945 Prince Umberto nominated Ferruccio Parri for the premiership. Parri, a leader of the Action Party and of the northern Resistance, had distinguished himself under the alias of "General Maurizio" in the fight against the Germans. The Parri Government included members of all six Resistance parties. The Socialist Pietro Nenni and the Liberal Manlio Brosio became Vice-Premiers, The Communist Palmiro Togliatti headed the Ministry of Justice and the Christian Democrat, Alcide De Gasperi, became Minister of Foreign Affairs. In November internal disputes brought an early end to this Government. Signor De Gasperi was asked to form a new government. Though leftists viewed him as a clerical, De Gasperi was able to retain Italy's premiership for the following seven years. During this period, Christian Democrats largely determined economic and political policy in both West Germany and Italy; in many respects, policies in the two countries followed a parallel course.

Italy, unlike West Germany, was able to sign a Peace Treaty with the Allied Powers. The treaty of February 10, 1947, compelled Italy to pay $100 million as war reparations to the Soviet Union and an additional $260 million to Yugoslavia, Greece, Ethiopia and Albania. Italy had to surrender a large part of its fleet to the Allied Powers. Territorially, the country agreed to renounce all claims to its possessions in Africa, granted its Adriatic islands and most of Venezia Giulia to Yugoslavia, and granted the Dodecanese Islands to Greece. The treaty did not settle the Italo-Yugoslav dispute over the Trieste area; in 1954 when the matter was finally decided, Italy received the city of Trieste and Yugoslavia most of the city's hinterland.

Another major difference between West Germany and Italy is that Italy is a much poorer country than the German Federal Republic. Italy's postwar economic development was greatly handicapped by three major factors: resource poverty, excessive dependence on agriculture and over-population. Neither the West-German nor the French postwar economic experiences were affected by all of these factors.

Italy is extremely poor in coal, iron and oil resources. The country's industry is therefore almost entirely dependent on fuel and raw materials imports. A large part of Italy's imports consist of coal, iron ores, oil, phosphates, copper and other non-ferrous metals, cotton, wool, wood-pulp and cellulose. The country's mineral wealth consists of mercury, sulphur and marble and the extraction of these is difficult and costly. Poverty in coal has been partially offset by adequate sources of hydro-electric power in the North, sources which were rapidly developed after 1948. The postwar discovery of large natural gas deposits in the Po Valley was a major boon to the country's postwar industrialization efforts. Italy's poverty in industrial resources explains why, in comparison to other major Western European countries, the general level of industrialization in Italy was low, both before and after the war. In 1949, the ratio of agricultural to industrial income was near unity in Italy; the ratio was 1 : 1.3 for West Germany, 1 : 3.2 for the Netherlands, 1 : 1.6 for France.[1]

Agricultural resources are equally poor. Almost 80% of Italy's area is formed by hills and mountains. The soil is generally poor and rainfall is inadequate, varying from 35 to 20 inches per year from north to south. Over 92% of the total area of the country has been used for agriculture and forestry so that there are practically no unexploited land resources in Italy. 37.6% of the cultivated area consists of mountain land and an additional 41.1% is composed of hills.[2]

As Table 4.1 shows, over 41% of all Italian farms in existence before the Agrarian Reform of 1950 measured less than 10 hectares. As one writer put it:

> Although there are more than 9 million farm properties in Italy, the vast majority of them are very small. according to post-war (but pre-land reform) statistics, among privately-owned farms those of under half a hectare accounted for 35.6 percent of the total number but for only 4 percent of the total area thus owned, while all farms of up to 5 hectares accounted for 93% of the total number and 31% of the privately-owned area.[3]

Not only were there too many inefficiently run small farms, but the latter were often subject to land fragmentation. A representative holding of four or five hectares was often made up of some vineyards and potato fields in the hills, wheat fields on the plain and orchards near the village where the farmer lived. Excessive land fragmentation has been mostly due to the effects of the inheritance laws passed in 1866, laws based on the Napoleonic Code which provided that every heir was entitled to a proportionate share of the parental farm.

TABLE 4.1

DISTRIBUTION OF PRIVATELY-OWNED REAL PROPERTY BY
SIZE GROUPS: 1946 (Before the Land Reform)

Size Group Hectares	Properties		Area	
	Number	Percent	Total Hectares	Percent
Up to 0.5	5,138,851	54.0	874,989	4.1
0.5 - 2	2,795,122	29.4	2,882,992	13.3
2 - 5	950,070	10.0	2,943,375	13.6
5 - 10	330,733	3.5	2,289,669	10.6
10 - 25	192,815	2.0	2,945,482	13.6
25 - 50	60,874	0.6	2,104,427	9.7
50 - 100	28,381	0.3	1,956,450	9.1
100 - 200	12,918	0.1	1,782,112	8.3
200 - 500	6,556	0.1	1,946,595	9.0
500 - 1,000	1,440	——	971,159	4.5
1,000 and over	502	——	875,701	4.2

Source: G. Medici, *Politica Agraria, 1945-1952*, Bologna, Zanichelli, 1952, p. 24.

Agriculture has been and is Italy's main source of employment. In 1936, the census showed that 48% of the working population earned a livelihood in the agricultural sector. This agricultural population represented about 45% of the entire Italian population. In 1954, 42.4% of the working population was still engaged in agriculture, while 31.6% of the working population had industrial occupations. In 1954, agriculture contributed 26% to the national income, while industry's contribution, amounted to 40%.

This great dependence on agriculture caused serious employment problems in Italy. In a country where practically every inch of arable land had been exploited for decades, yearly additions to the labor force had to be absorbed by industry or had to be removed from the economy through emigration if unemployment was not to rise.

During the decade 1945 to 1955, the Italian population increased by an average of about 400,000 persons per year. These increases were largely due to steadily falling mortality rates. The most rapid demographic increase during this period took place in the South and in the Islands, the poorest regions in the country.[4]

The continuation of massive unemployment in Italy during the first postwar decade has been diversely explained. Writers have explained this unemployment in terms of the disappearance of prewar Fascist public works and the loss of colonies; in terms of statutory impediments to the mobility of labor in existence until 1961; and in terms of the more capital-intensive methods of production adopted by north-ern industrialists in response to the high wage demand of trade unions.[5] Professor Hildebrand believes that although there was no deficiency in the aggregate demand for labor, unemployment re-mained high during the 1950s largely because of imperfections in the labor market. During this period, the continuing exodus of workers from the agricultural sector did not result in a efficient redistribution of these workers in non-agricultural sectors because of the effect of old statutory impediments to internal migration. These statutes, passed in the period of Fascism, prevented many unemployed from obtaining employment in the secondary and tertiary sectors. In these sectors, labor-saving equipment was adopted by employers to keep costs from rising in view of the aggressive wage demands of trade unions.[5]

The secondary and tertiary sectors remained unable throughout the 1950s to absorb a significant portion of the country's yearly working population increases. Emigration proved unable to syphon off Italy's entire surplus population, and massive unemployment resulted. Throughout the decade of the 1950s, the numbers of registered unem-ployed remained close to 10% of the total labor force. To the registered unemployed should be added the non-registered unemployed, though no figures exist for the latter. Underemployment, or disguised unemployment, particularly serious in the agricultural South, was another consequence of over-population.

TABLE 4.2

REGISTERED UNEMPLOYMENT: 1946-1955

Year	Number	Index: 1948 = 100
1946	1,655	77.3
1947	2,025	94.5
1948	2,142	100.0
1949	1,941	90.6
1950	1,860	86.8
1951	1,938	90.5
1952	2,073	96.8
1953	2,151	100.4
1954	2,197	102.6
1955	2,161	100.9

Since the latter decades of the nineteenth century and until the establishment of the Fascist State, emigration was Italy's demographic safety-valve. Mussolini and World War II temporarily stopped emigration, thereby reinforcing population pressures in the country; but after the war, and with the encouragement of Italy's government, emigration resumed, reaching 193,513 in 1947, 188,840 in 1949 and 170,271 in 1949. Emigration still represented only about one-third of the yearly increase in population.[7]

Open Inflation and Economic Chaos: 1945 - 1947

Italy's industrial and agricultural production has always been highly dependent on imports of necessary raw materials. Mussolini's alliance with Hitler during World War II brought a serious curtailment of imports to Italy. Germany was a poor supplier of the coal, crude oil and other basic raw materials needed by Italy to maintain its output. In 1942, Italy imported only 17% of the crude oil it had imported in 1938. Industrial production declined rapidly during the years of war. There was, however, one exception. During these years, the government directed available resources to the engineering industries producing war equipment; the productive capacity and output of these industries actually increased during the war. The resulting distortion in the pattern of investment burdened the economy with serious problems at the end of the war.

Industrial and agricultural production were further crippled by war-inflicted damage. Industry suffered most in southern and central Italy where the fighting had lasted longest. In Campagna and Tuscany 90% of the iron and steel industry was destroyed through military action. In 1945, central Italy was able to produce only 67.5% of the prewar electric power output, the South only 41.7%. The North was less severely affected by the war; largely due to partisan protection, electric power installations in the North were left practically untouched by the fighting and the northern iron and steel industries suffered only a 15% loss. The war inflicted the greatest damage on the poorer, less industrialized regions of Italy and contributed to the accentuation of the traditional economic differences between North and South. Italy's transportation system and the country's housing suffered severely from bombing and ground fighting. Taking 1938 as the base year, the index of industrial production was 23 in 1945.[8]

M. Grindrod has described in the following terms the economic conditions of Italy in 1945:

> Conditions when the war ended were, to say the least of it, extremely unfavourable. For the past twenty months the country had been divided in two, with dual administrations in every department of affairs. Damage to national territory and property was reckoned to have reduced it to about two-thirds of its pre-war value. Air raids and destruction during the fighting had been responsible for vast scale damage to buildings, roads, railways, ports, and electrical installation. The disruption of internal communications for many months after the war aggravated local shortages of food and other supplies. Damage to shipping had reduced the active merchant fleet to about a tenth of its pre-war tonnage. . . . In terms of available foreign currency to cover essential imports of food and fuel Italy was bankrupt. Prospects for agriculture were particularly gloomy: shortage of fertilizers throughout the latter part of the war had exhausted the soil, livestock was seriously depleted through war demands, German looting and lack of fodder, thousands of acres of olive groves, vineyards and orchards had been destroyed, while much of the land normally under cultivation was requisitioned or in a dangerous state because of uncleared minefields.[9]

Not only did Italians suffer from extensive destruction to housing and to means of transportation during the years of war, but these years also plagued them with severe price inflation. Large governmental deficit spending, largely financed by the *Banca d'Italia*, inflated the note issue of this institution while real output was continuously declining. The inflation of the money supply was particularly severe in the liberated South where the change to Allied military government had swept away the Fascist wage and price control system and where the re-establishment of independent trade unions allowed the latter to contribute to the strengthening of the price-wage spiral. After liberation, the still lower prices in the North started adjusting to the higher southern price level, but on the whole, between the end of 1945 and mid-1946, price increases remained modest. People held on to their lire balances, hoping that American liberation would soon bring an end to war-time scarcities; the inability of firms to increase production because of fuel and raw materials shortages also limited their demand for credit.

The soaring war-time issue of bank notes placed the public and the commercial banks in a highly liquid position. Between 1938 and 1945, the amount of bank notes in circulation expanded 18 times. In 1945, bank notes represented 71.6% of the total money supply, i.e., currency and bank deposits. On the other hand, real gross national product in 1945 was about half of what it had been in 1938.[10] In table 4.3, it appears that the ratio of the money supply to current gross national product increased from 27.7% in 1938 to 55.4% in 1944 and 46.8% in 1945.

TABLE 4.3

MONEY SUPPLY IN RELATION TO GNP
(Billions of Lire)

Years	Currency	Money Supply (Currency + Bank Deposits)	Current GNP	% of Money Supply to Current GNP
1938	22.1	42.2	152.8	27.7
1944	274.0	380.0	686.0	55.4
1945	419.0	587.0	1,254.0	46.8
1947	716.0	1,234.0	5,992.0	20.6
1957	1,897.0	4,808.0	14,805.0	32.5

Source: P. Baffi, Monetary Developments in Italy, *Banca Nazionale del Lavoro Quarterly Review*, December 1958, p. 417.

Without any mandatory reserve requirements for commercial banks, the continuous rise in the liquidity of the commercial banks expanded their lending potential. During the 1945-1946 pause in inflation, the public started exchanging bank notes for bank deposits and this further increased the lending potential of the banks.

The external value of the lira started falling during May 1946, forcing the government to change the official dollar rate of the Lira from the 1945 rate of 100 to the dollar to 225 to the dollar at the end of 1946 and to 350 in August 1947. From June 1946 on, wholesale prices started climbing at an average of 9.4% per month until September 1947. The new inflation was fed by a number of factors. The expectation of a currency reform induced Italians to transform their wealth into real assets and the flight from the lira increased money velocity. Between March 1946 and September 1947 industrial production doubled, financed by a rapid expansion in commercial bank credit. The resumption of demand for bank credit, coupled with a low elasticity in the domestic supply of foodstuffs, industrial raw materials and fuel, resulted in a rapid increase in raw materials prices. Consumer goods prices soon joined the upward price movement. The ratio of bank loans to commercial bank deposits rose from 42% in June 1946 to 75% in September 1947. Private demand for credit rather than deficit financing by government was now mostly responsible for the inflation. Wage increases of over 20% granted between October and December 1946 added fuel to the inflationary process. In the fall of 1947, the monetary authorities decided to stop inflation by blocking the excess liquidity of the banks through the introduction of a system of obligatory bank reserves. The government succeeded in stopping the inflation without resorting to currency reform. For the next thirteen years, Italy was to enjoy price stability.

Monetary Stability and Reconstruction: 1947 — 1950

Italy, unlike West Germany, decided against a currency reform as a means of stabilizing the value of the lira. Professor Luigi Einaudi, Vice President of the Council of Ministers and Minister of the Budget in the De Gasperi government of May 1947, must be credited with the distinction of having been the main architect of the new monetary policy initiated in the fall of 1947. This policy had a twofold aim and its goals were to be achieved by very conventional methods, methods that proved to be quite successful. In order to stop the inflation, the lending power of the commercial banks had to be reduced; also, a limit had to be imposed on the ability of the Treasury to finance government deficits by borrowing from the Central Bank. An Inter-Ministerial Committee on Credit and Saving was charged with the task of formulating over-all monetary policy and the Central Bank was given the responsibility of enforcing this policy.

On August 22, the Committee announced a new system of obligatory bank reserves, reserves whose purpose was to freeze whatever excess liquidity remained in the banking system following the 1946-1947 inflationary burst. As of September 30, 1947, all commercial banks were required to keep reserves against all their deposits. Reserves were fixed at about 25% of all deposits in existence on September 30.

Decrees of December 1947 and May 1948 prohibited Treasury borrowing from the Central Bank unless it was allowed to do so by special statutory provisions indicating specific sums of money. A number of subsidiary provisions further increased the power of the government in the management of the money supply. Commercial bank loans exceeding one-fifth of the capital of the lending bank could only be made with the authorization of the Central Bank. In order to facilitate an expansion in exports, the lira-dollar exchange rate was raised from 350 to 575 lire to the dollar.

Einaudi's simple system not only brought monetary stability to Italy for over a decade, but also facilitated the maintenance of a high rate of economic growth in the 1950s. Professor Hildebrand cites the following figures:

> The year 1948 ushered in the longest period of sustained economic expansion in modern Italian history, with comparatively stable prices prevailing throughout. Through 1961, increases were recorded in every single year for both real gross national product and industrial production . . . What these figures show above all else is that between 1948 and 1961 real gross domestic product jumped 119.6 percent in total, and 102.5 percent per resident, while the output of industry soared by 214.5 percent - a record that would be difficult to equal, let alone exceed, anywhere else in the world. In the same period, real gross investment climbed 222.4 percent, while from 1950 the real value of exports of goods and services advanced 291.6 percent . . . So calculated, total real product grew 5.86 percent a year, and per resident, 5.23 percent; while industrial output expanded at an impressive 8.81 percent.[11]

The rapid reconstruction of the economy after 1948 is particularly remarkable in light of the fact that the Italian economy inherited from the years of war a serious imbalance between capital and manpower. During the war, investments were concentrated on the engineering industries producing war supplies, while investment in other industries was practically nil. While war requirements brought about an over-expansion of engineering and textile industries, the neglect of other industries meant that in later years, these industries were unable to absorb part of the unemployed labor force. Italy's post-war unemployment problem was worsened by the return to the homeland of thousands of Italians who had lived outside of Italy during the war. These included people who had migrated to the former Italian colonies, workers who, freely or under duress, had migrated to Germany, and thousands of prisoners of war freed by the Allied military authorities. These returnees increased the numbers of an economically active population whose size had probably increased by as much as 900,000 since 1936. The Italian labor force of 1945 was confronted by an industrial production which in 1945 was only 23% of what it had been in 1938, by an impoverished agricultural sector, by a largely destroyed transportation system and by booming prices. The electric power available in 1945 was only about two-thirds of that available in 1938 and coal imports had declined from 12 million tons to 5.9 million.

Industrial reconstruction was facilitated by three key factors: UNRRA and later Marshall Plan aid, price stability throughout the 1950s and increases in industrial labor productivity. Between 1948 and 1952, Italy received about $1.5 billion in Marshall Plan aid. Total American aid to Italy during this period was markedly larger, amounting to $2.3 billion.[12] This aid allowed the country to obtain needed foodstuffs and raw materials at a time when its foreign reserve holdings had been exhausted.

Price and wage stability after 1948 facilitated production and the growth of exports. The existence of a large army of unemployed had a restraining influence on wage increases, and after 1948 both nominal and real wages remained quite stable.

TABLE 4.4
WHOLESALE PRICES, REAL WAGES AND SALARIES INDICES

For Prices 1953 = 100
For Wages and Salaries 1938 = 100

	Prices General	Raw Materials	Finished Goods	Farm Products	Real Wages	Real Salaries
1947	98	88	103	89	88.0	62.4
1948	104	92	108	93	108.4	78.7
1949	98	93	101	93	108.6	80.0
1950	93	93	92	95	113.2	80.4

Sources: Prices: United Nations, *Statistical Yearbook 1956*, New York 1957, p. 458. Wages and Salaries: A. Capanna, Economic Problems and Reconstruction in Italy, II, p. 35

In spite of wage and salary stability, labor costs of production nevertheless increased as social security payments became larger. Non-wage payments rose from about 27% of the earned wage in 1947 to 34.5% in 1950. This added cost of production was offset by industrial labor productivity increases of about 7-8% per year during the same period. Increase in industrial productivity was facilitated by the fact that the government had inherited from the interwar period a large public industrial sector. In 1945, the State owned about 80% of the shipbuilding industry, 40% of the railroad rolling-stock production and 60% of the pig iron furnaces.[13] This gave the government the ability to lead in the modernization of industrial facilities. Military defeat allowed a drastic reduction in public expenditures for the armed forces and the colonial administration, and permitted the government to divert real resources from military use to economic development after 1945.

The reconversion of Italian industry to peacetime uses was largely effectuated by a government agency created as early as 1933, *L'Instituto per la Ricostruzione Industriale,* IRI. Initially, IRI had been set up to protect the interests of depositors in a number of banks facing financial difficulties. It soon became a holding company, controlling activities in various sectors of the economy and financing these activities either through long-term loans or by buying new shares of stock issued by companies in the IRI empire. Toward the end of the 1940s, IRI's interests focused mainly on communications, electricity, shipping and shipbuilding, steel and engineering. At the end of the 1950s, IRI's steel companies produced more than 50% of the nation's crude steel output. IRI controlled the country's television and radio stations as well as the commercial airlines.

One of IRI's main objectives during this period was to protect the engineering industries which had been over-expanded during the war; an equally important aim was to support the labor force of these industries which had become much larger than that which could be efficiently employed. IRI's policies in this regard were in harmony with the provisions of agreements entered into by employers' associations and trade unions shortly after liberation, agreements which prohibited the dismissal of industrial workers in Northern Italy. After this arrangement was abolished by a law of September 1946, trade union contracts continued to provide that dismissals of workers would require, at least until 1950, the approval of "workers' committees." For ten years after the war, IRI's policies continued to prevent the dismissal of workers in its plants, even though purely economic considerations made dismissals desirable. IRI's determination to keep on payrolls thousands of workers active in plants which could not be profitably reconverted to peacetime uses was dictated by social and political considerations. Though this policy undoubtedly retarded the growth of industrial productivity, it prevented the worsening of an already serious unemployment situation.

Another major public holding company was the *Ente Nazionale Idrocarburi,* ENI. ENI was set up in 1953 to control various public and semi-public concerns, among them, the *Azienda Generale Italiana Petroli*, AGIP. In 1948 and 1949, AGIP began the development of natural gas resources in the Po Valley, a development which expanded Italy's natural gas output from 510 cubic meters in 1950 to 5.1 billion in 1958.

By the end of the 1950s, ENI's control extended to more than 200 concerns which included oil refineries, fertilizer and artificial rubber plants, as well as gasoline service-stations and motels.

The State's control over a large part of the industrial sector explains why gross investment, taken as a percentage of national income, steadily expanded in the period 1947 to 1950, rising from 17.7% in 1947 to 20.0% in 1950. Government not only encouraged private investment through a program of subsidies to private enterprise, but also contributed directly to aggregate investment. In 1947, an Engineering Industry Fund was established to finance the reorganization and modernization of engineering industries. The State initially contributed 8 billion lire to the fund; by the end of 1949, its contribution exceeded 50 billion lire. The State also granted over 120 billion lire to the IRI Endownment Fund to facilitate the reorganization and reconversion to peacetime use of a number of industrial concerns. Industrial investment was further encouraged by the government by allowing private entrepreneurs to utilize Marshall Plan and Export-Import Bank funds to finance on favorable terms the import of American machinery.

Spurred by public investment, industrial production rapidly increased. Industry was able to catch up with a backlog of technical advances whose utilization had been hindered by the war and by early postwar difficulties. The existence of excess capacity in a number of industries facilitated the expansion of output as the availability of raw materials improved. According to OEEC data, total industrial production in 1948 already exceeded the 1938 output; industrial output in 1950 was 126% that of 1938.[14] Agriculture recovered more slowly. Taking 1938 as the base year, agricultural output indices show 77.8 in 1947, 90 in 1949.

The economic expansion which followed the monetary stabilization of 1947, the Czechoslovak *coup d'état* of February 1948, and the coming of Marshall Plan aid assured De Gasperi's Christian Democrats a great victory in the first postwar elections for the national Chamber of Deputies and the Senate. This victory allowed De Gasperi to form a Cabinet on May 23, 1948, in which Christian Democrats dominated and which had no Socialist or Communist representation. On May 11,

1948, Professor Luigi Einaudi, the principal architect of Italy's monetary stabilization policy of 1947, was elected President of the Republic for a term of seven years.

The ability of the De Gasperi government to formulate and implement economic reform policies improved as the political and economic strength of its principal foe, the Communist Party, weakened after 1948. The slow deterioration of Communist strength is shown by the history of Italian organized labor in the late 1940s. In 1944, a single trade-union federation had been established by the various anti-Fascist parties. The *Confederazione Italiana del Lavoro*, CGIL, was soon dominated by Communists. The Communist Party did not hesitate to utilize the CGIL for the furtherance of its political aims. Once Communists no longer sat in the De Gasperi Cabinet, the Communist Party abandoned all pretense of cooperating with the government and embraced a policy of political and economic sabotage. A student's attempt to assassinate Togliatti induced the CGIL to call a general strike to take place in July 1948. The strike was not successful but during the remainder of the year, the CGIL continued to order a number of economic strikes. Non-Communist elements within the CGIL started opposing these tactics. In August, Catholic and non-Communist leaders in the CGIL decided to abandon this organization in order to form a new trade-union federation, the *Confederazione Italiana dei Sindicati Lavoratori*, CISL. This new organization was led by a Christian Democrat, Giulio Pastore, In June 1949, a second dissident group abandoned the CGIL to form the *Federazione Italiana del Lavoro*, FIL, an organization which in April 1950 became the *Unione Italiana del Lavoro*, UIL. The UIL was largely formed by Social Democrats and Republicans.

Although the CGIL remained Italy's largest trade-union federation, the Communist monopoly power over organized labor had come to an end. This development strengthened traditional employer and state authoritarianism in the field of labor relations. While union leaders remained mostly interested in broad social and political reforms, the employers' absolute rule over matters such as work conditions, pace of work and job assignment remained unimpaired.[15] Labor's docility, partly explained by the continuous presence of a large pool of unemployed, and the direct control of the government over a large sector of the economy were the principal explanatory factors of the economic *Miracolo* of the early 1950s. The Italian economic boom of the period

1948 to 1955 was particularly surprising since it was characterized by rapid economic growth concurrent with serious unemployment and by governmental control and intervention without planning and without nationalization.

The Beginning of the Italian Economic Miracle: 1950 — 1955

Until 1948, most of the 1.8 billion dollars Italy obtained as aid from the United States through UNRRA, Interim-Aid and the Export-Import Bank had been utilized to finance imports of foodstuffs and to a lesser extent, imports of fuel and of basic materials. Additional inflows of foreign capital were needed to re-equip and modernize Italy's industrial plants. The renewal of the country's industrial facilities was made possible by the 1.3 billion dollars allocated to Italy under the European Recovery Program. 20% of the Marshall Plan aid Italy received between April 1948 and December 1951 financed imports of industrial equipment from the dollar area. Imported new machinery went mostly to the power industry, the steel industry and the engineering industries. Marshall Plan aid not only allowed Italian industries to acquire new equipment, but it also supplied them with normal stocks of coal, crude oil and cotton. It allowed the country to return to an unrationed distribution of power early in 1950 and helped in the speed-up of the process of factory reconversion. Table 4.5 shows the rapid growth most industries were able to enjoy during the years 1948 to 1955.

With 1938 as the base year, industrial output expanded from 150 in 1952 to 164 in 1953, 181 in 1954 and 197 in 1955. By mid-1956, aggregate industrial output had doubled its 1938 level. During the period 1948 to mid-1956, the output of electricity increased by 68%. The output of natural gas became 37 times larger. While the output of the metallurgical industry was still below pre-war level in 1948, it surpassed that level by 124% by mid-1956. Pig iron output expanded four times in this period and the output of steel almost trebled.[16]

The rapid expansion in industrial production brought about a marked rise in national income. The pre-war income level was surpassed as early as 1949 and by 1955, national income, evaluated in terms of constant prices, was 54% higher than in 1938. Per capita income in 1955 was one-third higher than it had been before the war.

The expansion in national income allowed the De Gasperi government to put into effect the economic reforms it had prepared in earlier

TABLE 4.5

INDEX NUMBERS OF INDUSTRIAL PRODUCTION

1938 = 100

Industry	1948	1949	1950	1951	1952	1953	1954	1955
Mining	83	92	103	124	150	179	210	241
Power	146	134	159	188	198	210	229	246
Metallurgy	86	85	105	135	150	149	173	213
Engineering	105	118	129	142	155	171	179	204
Chemical	101	117	140	184	185	227	284	314
Rubber	103	115	132	152	142	160	194	202
Textile	100	102	109	116	108	116	117	104
Leather	75	78	85	79	90	90	92	85
Food Processing	96	113	136	140	147	150	157	268
Building Materials	91	96	120	129	138	162	175	207
Timber	95	103	123	139	161	167	173	176
Paper	72	90	105	113	112	127	132	143
Total Index	102	110	126	144	150	164	181	197

Source: Banco di Roma, *Ten Years of Italian Economy, 1947-1956*, Rome, 1957, p. 69.

TABLE 4.6

NET NATIONAL INCOME: ITALY

Years	Thousands of millions Lire of 1955 purchasing power	Lire per capita of 1955 purchasing power	Per capita income indices, 1955 purchasing power 1938 = 100
1938	7,666	177,643	100
1945	4,148	92,022	52
1948	7,157	154,991	87
1949	7,815	168,293	95
1950	8,926	190,857	107
1951	9,188	195,356	110
1952	9,665	204,205	115
1953	10,540	221,671	125
1954	11,014	230,505	130
1955	11,789	245,994	138

Source: G. Tagliacarne, *Income, Investments and Consumption*, in *Ten Years of Italian Economy, 1947-1956*, *op. cit.* p. 98.

years. In August 1950, a ten-year plan for the economic development
of the South was announced.

It must be clearly understood that if the economic reforms of 1950
were made possible by the rapid expansion of Italian industry, industrial gains were not typical of all regions in Italy. Italy, probably to a
larger extent than any other country in Western Europe, was and is
characterized by sharp spatial differences in the development of indus-

try. Industrial activity in Italy has remained concentrated in the northern part of the country. In 1951, 67.5% of all industrial workers lived in the North, while only 15.4% lived in Central Italy and 17.1% in the South and in the islands. While over 25% of the economically active population of Milan was engaged in industrial activity in the early 1950s, only 7% were so engaged in Naples. Not only was industry lacking in the *Mezzogiorno,* but its agriculture was markedly inferior to that of the North. In most of Central and Southern Italy, industrial backwardness was not offset by any non-industrial efficiently organized economic activity. The primitive cereal-growing and pastoral economy of the southern and central regions suffered from inadequate means of transportation, from an underdeveloped trade and credit system and from a rate of population growth that was higher than that of the wealthier North. For most southern workers, the only alternative to poorly paid and often seasonal agricultural occupations was emigration, and emigration had been drastically curtailed during the years of Fascist rule and of war. Not only was the man-land ratio more adverse in the agricultural *Mezzogiorno* than in the industrial North, but war destruction was more extensive in the South than in the North, worsening thereby the southern tragedy of human misery. In 1947, agricultural unemployment in the northern province of Venetia was calculated at 9%; Tuscany, 4%; Piemonte, 2%; and Liguria, 1%. In the southern provinces, Puglia had an unemployment rate of 50%; Lucania, 37%; Calabria, 33%; and Sardinia, 42%.

During the early postwar years, governmental reconstruction efforts had focused on the rebuilding of means of transportation and on the development of electric power generation in the North. While in 1947 the government spent 2.6 billion lire in the northern and central areas of the economy, the South and the islands received only 1.5 billion lire. In the same year, agricultural credit extended by the State amounted to 1.5 billion lire in the northern and central provinces, but was only .3 billion lire for the *Mezzogiorno.* [17] During the following years, however, the De Gasperi government started realizing that in order to rescue the southern economy from its traditonal condition of poverty and backwardness something more than the public financing of land reclamation projects and of irrigation systems had to be undertaken. It also became evident that the governmental policy of encouraging private investment in the South through tax incentives and other preferred treatment had not borne satisfactory fruit. If the standard of living in the *Mezzogiorno* was to come closer to that of the industrial North, a radical transformation of economic and social conditions in the South was unavoidable and this task could only be performed by a comprehensive and adequate public attempt to change and modernize the entire economic structure of the South.

On August 10, 1950, the Italian parliament entrusted the execution of this project to a Fund for Extraordinary Works of Public Interest in Southern Italy, the *Cassa per il Mezzogiorno*. The fund was financed by an initial allocation of one trillion lire, and was to operate for a period of ten years. Its existence was extended by two years in 1952, and the fund was given an additional allocation of 280 billion lire. A similar program for Northern and Central Italy was also set up in 1950 with an initial grant of 200 billion lire. The financing of the *Cassa* was made possible by two loans of $10 million each granted by the International Bank for Reconstruction and Development in 1951 and 1953. Another loan of $70 million was extended by the International Bank in 1955.

The main goal of the *Cassa* was to develop the South and Sicily both agriculturally and industrially. In the early 1950s, the largest part of the *Cassa*'s expenditures went into agricultural investment, i.e., land reclamation, irrigation systems, soil conservation and land reform. The remainder was spent for the building of social overhead capital such as roads, railways, ferries, aqueducts, dams and electric power stations. While at the start of the program 77% of the fund's investments were devoted to the improvement of agriculture, about 75% of these investments went into the development of a modern economic infrastructure at the end of the decade. During the 1950s, the fund invested about 125 billion lire per year in the South; another yearly 125 billion lire were invested by various governmental and private sources. Though the sum of these figures appears to be impressive, the total amounted to less than 10% of average annual gross domestic investment during the 1950s. This portion of yearly aggregate domestic investment went to an area containing about 37% of the total population. Though critics of the program contended that the government's investment efforts in the *Mezzogiorno* were not sufficient, the establishment of the *Cassa* was clearly an important and major attempt to expose the tradition-ruled southern economy to an inflow of external investment whose magnitude could perhaps shock the heretofore immutable, neo-feudal agricultural economy of the South into self-sustaining change and growth.

For decades, a whole matrix of geographical, social and economic factors had made the industrialization of the *Mezzogiorno* difficult. A brief indication of some of these factors will reveal the difficult problems the economists and sociologists of the *Cassa* had to solve. Culturally-determined attitudes, habits and values are not easily changed within a period of years, even through the application of compulsion. The twentieth century did not succeed in obliterating the cultural heritage impressed upon the South by the old Bourbon kingdom of the Two Sicilies. From the past, the regions of Abruzzi and Molise, Campania, Apulia, Lucania, Calabria, Sicily and Sardinia inherited a neo-feudal, tradition-determined way of life which formed a very different society from the dynamic, progress-oriented population of the northern provinces. Even in the 1970s, many southerners still feel that the central government has tried to force upon them a civilization imported from the North, an alien way of thinking and an alien way of life.

The strength of southern tradition is shown by educational and career preferences in the *Mezzogiorno*. In the 1950s, the southern middle-class youth remained largely uninterested in technical and business careers; their choice was safe governmental positions. This occupational preference demanded a training based largely on the humanities. In 1952, of every ten young people above the age of 14 attending school, eight attended schools providing a humanistic education in the South against five in the North. While the South accounted for about 37% of the total population, it provided 52% of all graduates from law faculties in 1952, but only 27% of the graduates from engineering schools. Furthermore, many engineers trained in the South migrated to the North in search of better careers, and this brought the South a continuous loss of a large part of its educated youth whose talents could have been used in commerce and industry.

Another equally important difficulty was the persistence of a high rate of illiteracy in the South. In the early 1950s, illiteracy rates were only 2% in Lombardy and 7% in Tuscany, but they were 32% in Calabria and 25% in Sicily. Low income levels in the South are mostly to blame for the fact that about 24% of the southern population was illiterate.[18]

Geographical factors have also hindered industrialization in the South. One such factor is the inadequate supply of electric power and of fuel in the *Mezzogiorno*. Southern Italy and the islands lack rivers carrying a continuous large flow of water throughout the year. The result was that per capita consumption of electricity in 1950 was 138 kwh in the South, compared to 603 kwh·in the North. The hope that the Abruzzi region would supply new sources of oil had to be abandoned in the mid-1950s. With a poor endownment in human and non-human resources, the achievement of industrialization in the South seemed to be an over-ambitious goal.

The De Gasperi government tried to enlist the participation of northern private enterprise in the realization of this goal. Private firms investing in the South were given preferential tax treatment and other attractive advantages. Up to 50% of the profits of any Italian firm could be exempted from income taxation if these profits were reinvested within a period of five years in the construction, expansion or renewal of an industrial plant in the *Mezzogiorno*. Building materials, machinery and other capital goods imported into the South for industrial use were free of customs duties until mid 1965. Preferential freight rates on State railways were granted for the transport of industrial supplies to the South. For distances of over 1,000 kilometers, the reduction in freight rates amounted to as much as 50%. A law of October 6, 1950, ordered public agencies to obtain at least one-fifth of their purchases from southern firms. A variety of other measures further encouraged private concerns to establish themselves in the South.[19] In many instances, the State became a shareholder in private enterprises and made direct financial contributions to them.

With more than half of the active population engaged in agriculture in the South, major attention had to be given to the improvment of agricultural conditions in an area containing about 19 million inhabitants, an area with a larger population than those of some of the smaller countries of Western Europe. Persistent rural poverty and increasing peasant unrest in Calabria induced the Italian parliament to enact the first land reform law in May 1950.

Agrarian Reform

Agriculture remained Italy's most important industry in the 1950s. Although agricultural output in 1945 was only 60% of what it had been in 1938, and even though the postwar lack of fertilizers, machinery and appropriate human skills reduced the already wretched pre-war living standard in the overpopulated rural sector by 63%, over 40% of the total Italian population aged ten years and above still worked in the agricultural sector ten years after the end of the war.

The process of agricultural reconstruction ended in 1950 when the level of agricultural output approximated what it had been in 1938. The expansion of agricultural output in the period 1945 to 1950 was, however, based on the utilization of traditional methods of production and no productivity gains were registered during this period.

The Agrarian Reform laws of 1950 introduced for the first time a period of agricultural modernization and rationalization. The 1950s saw a rapid development of efficient and mechanized methods of production, and a large increase in the use of fertilizers and of selected seeds. During this period, the government made major efforts to improve the skills of the rural population. A law of October 16, 1954, allowed the government to spend one billion lire per year during a five year period in order to advance funds to farmers which would cover 50% of the purchase price of select vegetables, cereal and fodder seeds. By 1955, the utilization of nitrogenous fertilizers was 210% higher than in 1938; the consumption of fertilizers based on potassium was 287% higher.[20] Agricultural productivity started rising by an average of 4.1% per year and in 1955, agricultural output exceeded that of 1938 by 24%.

The Agrarian Reform laws pursued two principal objectives for the sake of raising land productivity. One of the goals was the consolidation of excessively fragmented ownership units. In an already overpopulated rural sector where land hunger was large, a decrease in the total number of ownership units could have led to violent peasant reaction. The goal of consolidation was soon abandoned because of its political undesirability. The second objective of the laws, the subdivision of large estates, could, on the other hand, be attained with peasant support; the laws therefore concentrated on the breaking-up of inefficiently operated *latifundia*.

The first statutory provision introducing land reform was the Sila Act of May 1950. It allowed the expropriation of ownership units exceeding 300 hectares on the Sila Plateau of Calabria. Property owners were indemnified through compensation in the form of government bonds carrying a rate of interest of 5% and redeemable in 25 years. The value of the expropriated land was evaluated for indemnification purposes on the basis of the official taxation value of the land in

1947. About 534,000 hectares were expropriated under the Sila Act for subdivision into small holdings of 5 to 6 hectares that were sold by the government to landless rural workers or to peasants whose land was not sufficient to support their family. Before the new small farms were assigned to new owners, an Agency for the Development of the Sila was given the task of improving the land and of building "usable" farms with appropriate farm buildings and dwellings. The new assignees were to pay for the land received in 30 yearly installments, title to the land being retained by the Agency until payment in full was made. During the 30 year period, the assignee had to agree not to sell, rent, lease or subdivide the land, and to join for a period of 20 years any co-operative formed by the Agency.

The Sila Act was followed by the Stralcio Act of October 1950. This statute provided that all landowners earning from their land a taxable income of 30,000 lire and over in pre-war values would be subjected to some degree of expropriation. Only part of their holdings would be confiscated, the extent of the land subject to expropriation depending on the owner's income derived from the entire holding and on the average per-hectare income from cultivated land. Only holdings above a certain size were subject to expropriation, the maximum exempted size varying from region to region. Large estates operated in an efficient manner could escape expropriation. Indemnification conditions and the terms of sale to new owners were similar to those stipulated by the Sila Act.

Expropriation was carried out in areas characterized by the existence of *latifundia*, extensive cultivation, rural overpopulation and rural poverty. The Stralcio Law was applied mainly to areas in Apulia, Lucania, Campania, Lazio, Abruzzi and Molise, Romagna and Sardinia. At the end of 1950, Sicily enacted its own regional land reform program.[21]

The achievement in 1956 of the *Enti di Riforma*, the agencies responsible for the implementation of the land reform laws, are shown by these data: 800,000 hectares of land had been expropriated, 40,000 pieces of agricultural machinery had been introduced, 4,500 miles of road were built and 587,000 hectares of land were granted to new owners who also received 50,000 head of cattle. Although in 1955 the total acreage under wheat in Italy was 5.6% smaller than that of 1938, the yield per hectare during this period rose from 14.8 quintals in 1938 to 19.6 quintals in 1955.[22]

Professor P. Germani has evaluated the land reform program in these words:

> The reform has not only effected a redistribution of property, but has also performed a far-reaching work of land and agricultural improvement, radically altering the social and economic structure of the zones concerned. In compliance with modern technique, intensive cultivation replaces the former extensive systems of cultivation cr the *latifundia;* the equipment for the processing of agricultural produce completes the cycle of farm work; farm houses and buildings are erected and whole villages come into being.[23]

Repeated criticism of the agrarian reform program has, however, emphasized the fact that the latter has tended to replace inefficient *latifundia* by inefficient *minifundia.* The idea is that Italy's agricultural export possibilities "cannot be developed unless Italian agriculture is made more efficient and increased efficiency can be attained in many areas only through specilization and mechanization on reasonably large units."[24]

The Agrarian Reform undoubtedly achieved desirable social changes for thousands of impoverished southern peasants. It was, however, unable to do away with the massive rural unemployment of the *Mezzogiorno.* Though the program achieved invaluable improvements in human and non-human capital, it also created an excessive number of farms too small to be worked efficiently. The promotion of a subsistence type of farming hindered the development of specialized, commercial agriculture in the *Mezzogiorno* and because of this, the Agrarian Reform laws tended eventually to intensify the economic disparity between North and South.

Conclusion

The first postwar decade saw in Italy, as well as in France, a gradual weakening of the enthusiasm for economic and social reform that had been developed by the Resistance during the years of fighting. Marshall Plan aid strengthened the voice of conservatism in both countries, and in both countries, the Communist Party started losing political and economic ground after 1947. Members of the centrist parties were leading the governments of Italy, France and West Germany. De Gasperi and Adenauer, both Christian Democrats, remained in office long enough to allow their social and economic ideas to take root in their countries. The French political leadership, although frequently subject to change, was largely drawn from the centrist MRP and this allowed French economic and social policies to remain consistent. Industrial reconstruction and expansion was rapid in all three countries. Agricultural development was slower in all of them; the Italian record differed in the continuation of large unemployment in rural Italy. Although the program of the *Cassa per il Mezzogiorno* failed to equalize economic conditions throughout the country, it was a bold attack on Italy's traditional agrarian backwardness. De Gasperi's government must be given credit for having introduced a major program of agricultural development which was not duplicated either in France or in West Germany.

NOTES

1. A. Capanna, "Economic Problems and Reconstruction in Italy, Part I," *International Labour Review*, vol. LXIII (June 1951), p. 610.

2. G.G. D'Aragona, "A Critical Evaluation of Land Reform in Italy," *Land Economics* (February 1954), p. 12.

3. M. Grindrod, *The Rebuilding of Italy* (London: Royal Institute of International Affairs, 1955), p. 167.

4. M. Carlyle, *Modern Italy* (London: Hutchinson University Library, 1957), Ch. 2.

5. See V. C. Lutz, "The Growth Process in a Dual Economic System," *Banca Nazionale del Lavoro Quarterly Review*, vol. 11 (September 1958), pp. 279-324; A. Molinari, "Unemployment Statistics in Italy," *Banca Nazionale del Lavoro Quarterly Review*, vol. 5 (April-June 1952), pp. 76-88; M.D. Clark: "Governmental Restrictions on Labor Mobility in Italy," *Industrial Labor Relations Review*, vol 8. (October 1954), pp.3-18; G.H. Hildebrand, *Growth and Structure in the Economy of Modern Italy* (Cambridge: Harvard University Press, 1965), Ch. VII.

6. Hildebrand, *Growth and Structure in the Economy of Modern Italy*, pp. 187-188.

7. A. Capanna, "Economic Problems and Reconstruction in Italy, Part I," p. 615.

9. Grindrod, *The Rebuilding of Italy*, p. 38.

10. Hildebrand, *Growth and Structure in the Economy of Modern Italy*, pp. 15-17.

11. *Ibid.*, p. 47

12. US., Department of Commerce, *Survey of Current Business* (October 1952), p. 10.

13. United Nations, E.C.E., *Economic Survey of Europe Since the War* (Geneva, 1953), pp. 75-78.

14. OEEC, Statistical Bulletins, Industrial Statistics (Paris, 1960), p. 9.

15. O. Ornati, "The Italian Economic Miracle and Organized Labor," *Social Research* vol. 30 (1963), pp. 519-526.

16. Banco di Roma, *Ten Years of Italian Economy, 1947-1956* (Rome, 1957), pp. 72-77.

17. G. Savemini, *Scritti Sulla Questione Meridionale*, G. Enaudi ed. Turin, (1955).

18. S.H. Franklin, "Social Structure and Land Reform in Southern Italy," *The Sociological Review*, (November 1961), p. 324; V.C. Lutz, "Development Problems in Southern Italy: The Second Conference of the *Cassa per il Mezzogiorno*," *Banca Nazionale del Lavoro*

Quarterly Review (January — June 1954); G. Ruffalo: "The Italian Parliamentary Inquiry into Poverty," *Banca Nazionale del Lavoro Quarterly Review* (January-June 1954).

19. F. Vochting, "Industrialization or 'Pre-Industrialization' of Southern Italy?", *Banca Nazionale del Lavoro Quarterly Review* (April-June 1952).

20. P. Germani, "Italy's Postwar Agriculture," *Ten Years of Italian Economy*, 1947-1956, pp. 33-62.

21. L.M. Belotti, "An Analysis of the Italian Agrarian Reform," *Land Economics* (May 1960), pp. 118-128; G.G. D'Aragona, "A Critical Evaluation of Land Reform in Italy," *Land Economics* (February 1954), pp. 12-20; C. Vanzetti and F. Meissner, "The Agrarian Reform in Italy," *Land Economics (May 1953), pp. 142-154.*

22. E. Attilo, "Le Funzioni degli Enti di Riforma," *Politica ed Economia*, (December 1957), pp. 5-7.

23. P. Germani, "Italy's Postwar Agriculture," p. 39.

24. D'Aragona, "A Critical Evaluation of Land Reform in Italy," p. 19.

CHAPTER 5

THE "OTHER" GERMANY

The Potsdam resolutions of 1945 explicitly allowed the dismantling of German industrial installations by the occupying powers as a form of war reparation payment by the Germans. Unlike the earlier Yalta Agreement, the Potsdam protocol entirely omitted provisions permitting German indemnification to take the form of levies on current German output or the use of forced German labor.

The occupation policies pursued by the Soviets in East Germany promptly revealed that the U.S.S.R. understood the Potsdam Agreement to be simply a supplement to the Yalta determinations, an addendum which in no way superseded any of the Yalta resolutions.

The Potsdam Agreement allowed each occupying power to extract its share of German compensation from the zone it occupied in Germany, and during the eight years which followed the end of the war, the Soviet Union proceeded to exploit the East German economy in order to obtain from the latter the war indemnification the U.S.S.R. had asked for at Yalta.[1] Soviet dismantling of East German industrial, commercial and transport facilities proceeded in successive waves until 1954, even though Marshal Sokolovsky had announced as early as May 21, 1946, that Soviet dismantling and appropriations in the Soviet zone of Germany had ended.[2] Between 1945 and 1954, over 1,300 factories and about 4,500 miles of railroad track were removed from the Soviet zone for shipment to the Soviet Union.[3]

The western tourist who has visited the German Democratic Republic in recent years is quite aware of the fact that the people he observed in East Berlin, Desden or Leipzig, although apparently well-fed, do not dress with the elegance of Germans in Hamburg, Munich or Wiesbaden. In the cities of the Democratic Republic, the automobile traffic, the quality and variety of wares displayed in shops and the menus in the restaurants compare poorly with their counterparts in West Germany. If this tourist had by chance visited the German Democratic Republic in the early 1950s and then again in the late 1960s, he would have had to acknowledge that economic progress in the country was quite visible,

120

though the standard of living had not yet attained that of the German Federal Republic. And yet, back in his homeland, our tourist would report with the conviction of the "expert" that "the government in East Berlin could learn something in Bonn." Our hypothetical traveler was in all likelihood not aware that in the late 1960s the German Democratic Republic, a country the size of New York State, was the tenth largest industrial nation in the world and the second largest industrial power in the Soviet bloc.[4] Although the East German economy is much smaller than the West German one, it produced in 1965 more steel per capita than Italy, and also on a per capita basis, more electric power than West Germany and more cement, television sets and refrigerators than Britain.[5]

But even the knowledge of these facts would not have altered, in all probability, our visitor's evaluation of East German economic performance because he could not adequately perceive the signficance of this economic achievement in the light of the tremendous handicaps faced by the East German economy during the first postwar decade. To properly assess the performance of this economy, it is not sufficient to merely compare East and West German production data, as so many economists have done. East Germany had a territory quite poor in industrial raw materials, had suffered much more extensive war damage than West Germany, was burdened by excessive reparation obligations to the Soviet Union at a time when West Germany was receiving billions of dollars of American aid, was weakened over more than a decade by serious losses of manpower. Nevertheless, the economy of the German Democratic Republic witnessed an "economic miracle" in the 1960s, which in many ways, compares quite advantageously with the much advertised *Wirtschaftswunder* of the German Federal Republic.

The East German Economy in 1945

The German Democratic Republic covers an area of 46,600 square miles, an area representing about one fourth that of the German Reich in 1938. Its territory comprises the old German provinces of Mecklenburg, Brandenburg, Sachsen-Anhalt, Saxony and Thuringia, as well as part of Pomerania. Before the war, this area produced less than 3% of the total hard coal output of the Reich, less than 1% of its coke and less than 5% of its iron ore. The East German economy also lacked important fuels such as oil and natural gas and was poorly endowed with sources of hydro-electric power. Except for large deposits of lignite, East Germany was poor in supplies of industrial fuel. Over 90% of its coke requirements had to be imported, largely from the Ruhr area. Obviously, the importance of metallurgy in East Germany was quite minimal. In 1937 the area that eventually became the Federal Republic produced 97% of the pig iron output of the Reich and 91% of its unfinished steel.[6] This does not mean, however, that prewar East Germany was industrially underdeveloped. It is often erroneously believed that in prewar times East Germany was an agricultural area, exporting foodstuffs to Western Germany in exchange for manufactured products. In 1939, the area that ten years later became the German Democratic Republic contained 22% of the entire German population, produced 26% of the aggregate German agricultural output and 24% of total German industrial production.[7] This area had a well-balanced economy, but one that would encounter serious difficulties, once cut off from its traditional sources of industrial raw materials and trade in West Germany and the territories east of the Oder-Neisse line. Before 1939, while West German industry concentrated on the products of heavy industry, e.g., iron, steel and chemicals, the East German economy specialized in labor-intensive, light industry production. Skilled East German workers produced two-thirds of the country's textile machinery, one-third of the national output of precision tools and optical equipment, over 80% of the country's office equipment and almost half of the country's clothing.[8] East Germany was also well endowed with potassium deposits and in 1937 it produced about 57% of the total German potash output. This wealth in potash was the base of the synthetic fertilizer-oriented chemical industry which before the war exported large quantities of nitrogenous and potash-based fertilizers, soda and potash to the other regions of Germany.

Before the war, the area of the German Democratic Republic produced, in relation to the Reich's total, 39% of the bread-grain, 41% of potatoes and 60% of the sugar-beet output.[9] A surplus of cereals and sugar-beet was produced on the large *Junker* estates in Mecklenburg and Brandenburg. Further south, small and middle-sized holdings engaged in a varied type of agriculture. The hills of Thuringia, the Harz and the Ore Mountains were covered by firs which provided the raw material base of a developing timber products industry. Prewar East Germany exported to the other regions of the Reich cereals, potatoes, sugar-beet, pork meat and paper pulp, and imported from these regions vegetables, dairy products, beef meats and cattle fodder. It appears that prewar East Germany was a net importer of foodstuffs.

Even before the war had ended, the large-scale destruction of major East German cities and the immigration of thousands of German-speaking persons moving westward from Rumania, Czechoslovakia, Poland and other Eastern European countries resulted in a massive relocation of people from urban centers to the countryside. Land hunger induced East German peasants and rufugees to start taking possession of lands belonging to Junkers who had been killed during the war or who had otherwise disappeared. In September 1945, the governments of the five *Laender* established in the Soviet zone of occupation initiated a land reform program. Farms exceeding 100 hectares in size were confiscated for subdivision and redistribution to the peasantry. In this way, over 800,000 new small farms, averaging 7.3 hectares in size, could be distributed to land-hungry new farmers, the majority of whom were refugees from central and eastern European areas.[10] Furthermore, according to Order No. 124 of October 30, 1945, issued by the Soviet military commander, other types of land holdings were to be expropriated for redistribution to the people. Properties belonging to the Reich or to the German military establishment, properties owned by governments or citizens of countries that had supported Germany during the war, properties belonging to active and influential members of the Nazi party and properties of persons specially designated by the Soviet authorities were to be confiscated and redistributed in part to the people.[11] About three million hectares of land were expropriated in 1945, representing about one-third of the cultivated land area in the Soviet zone[12] Two-thirds of the appropriated land were immediately granted to individual farmers; land thus obtained could not be resold, subdivided, leased or mortgaged without the consent of the authorities; the remainder was shared by the *Laender*, local governments and the Red Army. Building and livestock were allocated to the new grantees, but agricultural machinery was generally transferred to Soviet-type machine-lending stations or M.A.S. — the *Maschinen-Ausleihstationen*. The redistribution of all expropriated land was completed in January 1949. The land reform resulted in a large increase in the number of farms whose size varied between .5 and 50 hectares, although the average size of the new holdings was only 4 hectares.[13]

TABLE 5.1

SIZE OF LAND HOLDINGS IN EAST GERMANY

	As % of all holdings	
	1939	1946
Under 5 hectares	9.2%	10.7%
5 - 20 hectares	31.8	56.6
20 - 50 hectares	22.4	21.5
50 - 100 hectares	8.4	4.6
over 100 hectares	28.2	3.6
	100.0	100.0

Source: German Democratic Republic, Planning Ministry, *Der Freie Bauer*, June 23, 1950.

The large, efficiently-run *Junker* estates were thus replaced by a large number of small farms operated by "new farmers", who too often lacked adequate skills and experience and who frequently did not possess the necessary tools, animals and seed to produce on the basis of efficient techniques.

Not only was the East German economy relatively poor in basic resources, particularly so in comparison with the economy of West Germany, but the eastern economy was further impoverished by the war which had been more destructive in the East than in the West. Allied bombing and massive destruction inflicted by the advancing Red Army, followed by pillaging and looting during the first months after the end of hostilities, reduced the industrial capacity of East Germany to 42.9% of its prewar level, while industrial capacity in West Germany in 1945 was 80% of what it had been in 1936.[14] In the Soviet zone, the surviving industry faced a great shortage of raw materials, so that available capacity could not always be used. What remained of usable industrial facilities was also subject to Soviet dismantling and appropriations. Railroad tracks, machinery of all kinds, stocks of raw materials, bureau installations and university laboratories were taken by the Russians at a time when 60% of the transportation facilities in the Soviet zone and 2.9 million dwellings in this area had been completely destroyed.[15]

Even though we should only accept the most conservative estimates of war damage to industry, we must still recognize that the large-scale destruction of transportation facilities, the massive bombing of cities such as Dresden, Leipzig and Plauen, the lack of fuel and industrial raw materials and the inflow of large numbers of refugees brought enormous economic hardships to the Soviet zone of occupation in Germany, hardships made worse by the absence of foreign aid and by continuous Soviet appropriations.

As the Soviet Union Goes, so Goes Walter Ulbricht

East Germany's postwar history was molded by both the political and economic policies of the U.S.S.R. and by those of East Germany's principal political party, the Socialist Unity Party. The joining, on April 21, 1946, of East Germany's Socialists and Communists into a single political party, the *Sozialistische Einheitspartei Deutschlands,* the SED, was achieved by giving both groups an equal voice in the new organization. Two men were elected to be joint chairmen of the SED; Wilhelm Pieck, a verteran Communist, and Otto Grotewohl, the leader of the Soviet Zone Social Democrats. Two vice-chairmen were also elected in 1946. One was the Socialist Max Fechner; the other was the Communist Walter Ulbricht. The party's executive committee, the *Vorstand,* was composed by an equal number of Socialists and Communists. The parity principle was extended to the party's fourteen-member *Zentralsekretariat.* At the time of its founding, the SED claimed to pursue its own philosophy, a philosophy that was not guided by Leninism. This was not to last very long.

At the party's Second Congress in September 1947, Ulbricht announced that the SED was to become a "Party of a new Type." At that time, not all party members understood the meaning Ulbricht attached to those words; however, their significance became clear to all one year later. A number of reasons have been advanced to explain the *Vorstand's* decision in 1948 to transform the SED into a Leninist party. The expulsion of Yugoslavia from the Soviet bloc in 1948 and the intensification of the Cold War following the Berlin blockade probably induced SED leaders to seek a closer alliance with the Soviet Union. Another equally strong reason was Ulbricht's dominant position in the party. As Stalin's trusted and loyal ally, Ulbricht enjoyed Russian support and this support gave him *de facto* leadership in the SED. The party thus embraced Leninism in 1948 and accepted guidance from the Communist Party of the Soviet Union.[16] The party's organization was "sovietized." A *Politbüro* replaced the *Zentralsekretariat* and Walter Ulbricht became its General Secretary, a position which was similar to that occupied by Stalin in the U.S.S.R. The SED abandoned the parity principle and during the following years the number of Social Democrat leaders in the party was gradually reduced; only 59% of the Social Democrats which had joined the SED in 1946 still held membership in the party in 1953.

Unlike Tito, Ulbricht never questioned nor hesitated to follow the Soviet dictate. His loyalty to the Soviet Union gave him a power tenure which outlasted that of Adenauer in the Federal Republic. In spite of political and economic difficulties, Ulbricht's determination to duplicate Russian political and economic actions in East Germany and to defend these actions in the face of Soviet exploitation, assured his political longevity. In the days of Stalin, East German policy faithfully imitated the Russians by giving emphasis to nationalization, the development of heavy industry and economic self-sufficiency. Following the Russian example, production was stimulated by "carrot and stick" policies. Decorations and some privileges were given to "labor heroes" who had exeeded the work norms set by efficiency engineers; those who could not meet them were given reprimands, fines and even imprisonment. The Russian "Stakhanov system" was faithfully copied in East Germany where it was known as the "Hennecke system."

The Soviet-like attempt to repeatedly raise quantitative targets of production subjected East Germany's industrial workers to higher production norms against which they apparently reacted on June 16 and 17, 1953. It is indeed curious that the strikes of June 17 followed by only one week the SED's announcement of a "New Course" program, new policies which paralleled those launched in the U.S.S.R. under the same name after Stalin's death. The SED *Politbüro* declared on June 9 that more importance would be attached henceforth to the production of consumer goods, that work norms would be relaxed, that interzonal travel would be liberalized and that private initiative would receive more encouragement. Eight days later, workers went on strike in various parts of the Democratic Republic. Western writers promptly reported these events as showing a "rising of workers in East Berlin and of people throughout the Soviet Zone of Germany." [17] Actually, it appears that at most 5.5% of East Germany's industrial workers went on strike on June 17. [18] The Eastern press blamed Western agitators for the disturbances and a number of Western newspapers supported their contention. In England, the *Manchester Guardian* of June 18, 1953, pointed out that "in the case of East Berlin, it may be true that the riots have been partly spurred on from the Western sectors."

Ulbricht's political strength was not weakened by these events. On the contrary, the June riots resulted in a purge of SED leaders who in the past advocated the adoption of major politico-economic reforms. Ulbricht did not tolerate the presence of men in the party who espoused revisionist policies, i.e., policies different from his own. The SED consequently expelled from its ranks reformers such as Wilhelm Zaisser, Minister for State Security, Max Fechner, Minister of Justice, and Rudolf Herrnstadt, editor-in-chief of the SED publication *Neues Deutschland.*

Ulbricht's adhesion to Soviet views manifested itself again in 1956. Khrushchev's attacks on Stalin at the Twentieth Congress of the Soviet Communist Party must have shocked Stalinist Ulbricht. And yet, within one week after the end of this Congress, Ulbricht published in *Neues Deutschland* an article which in essence repeated Khrushchev's contentions. In its issue of July 31, 1956, *Neues Deutschland* attacked the Stalinist "cult of personality" and asserted that excessive reliance on top leadership had in the past resulted "in a crippling of initiative and the hindering of independent study of new social problems." These statements were published to show the apparent compliance of the East German government with the new Soviet policy. In fact, Ulbricht's pronouncements did not bring about a change in his policies. Neither Herrnstadt nor Zaisser were cleared of charges and brought back into the party. On the contrary, Ulbricht continued expelling from the SED and punishing men who dared to propose politico-economic reforms he had not authored. Dramatic party excommunications took place during the second half of the 1950s. Dr. Wolfgang Harich, an SED academic, and his group of reformers were brought to trial and jailed in 1957. Reformist *Politbüro* members such as Karl Schirdewan, Fred Oelssner and Ernst Wollweber were dismissed from their positions because of "factionalism against their party." Although Ulbricht was not applauding Khruschev's attacks on the "cult of Stalin," he went on consolidating the"Ulbricht cult."

The death of Wilhelm Pieck, then President of the German Democratic Republic, in September 1960 further increased Ulbricht's power. Following Pieck's death, the one-man presidency was replaced by a collective presidency organized as a Council of State and Ulbricht became its Chairman. Ulbricht was now the supreme source of power and authority in the country.

East Germany's economic development in the postwar period was determined by the policies of this man. It was Ulbricht's determination to fully integrate the East German economy into the economic system of the Soviet bloc that ultimately explains the structure of East Germany's economy in 1970.

Reconstruction and Development During the Years of Soviet Exploitation

During the first eight years after the end of the war, the East German economy remained subject to recurring and unpredictable waves of Soviet appropriations of East German wealth. The Soviet military command in Germany was not responsible for the continuous dismantling of East German capital. The Russian military government seemed to favor an early end to this dismantling in order to maintain the productive capacity of the Soviet zone of occupation for the lasting benefit of the Soviet world. However, Russian political officers in Germany, reporting directly to Moscow and acting independently of Soviet military directives, followed the theory that a maximum of appropriations was necessary to facilitate the rapid economic reconstruction of the Soviet Union and that it was in the interest of the U.S.S.R. to weaken Germany as much as possible. No exact data have ever been published to show how much the Soviet Union took as reparation payments from the East German economy. It has been estimated that Soviet dismantling may have taken half of the 1936 industrial capacity of East Germany and that for certain heavy industries, confiscation probably amounted to two-thirds of the prewar capacity.[19]

During the first months of occupation, Russian military teams proceeded to dismantle industrial and commercial facilities according to their own evaluation of what could be of use in the U.S.S.R. No central plan seemed to guide their activity. About two hundred East German factories were dismantled during the spring and summer of 1946 for shipment to the Soviet Union. Most of this dismantling affected chemical, textile and paper-producing plants. In 1947, the occupying forces started transferring to the Soviet Union a large number of electric power plants and mining machinery. In the same year, 32% of the existing railroad track in the Soviet zone was appropriated and shipped to Russia.[20] In 1948, the synthetic rubber works at Schkopau were appropriated by the Soviets.

Soviet dismantling during the years 1945 to 1948 was carried out for the exclusive benefit of the Soviet Union; little attention was given to the effects of dismantling on the East German economy. The removal of important machinery often left industrial plants in an unusable state because the confiscated machinery could not be replaced. The Russians seemed to be most interested in appropriating plants and machinery in the lignite mining, artificial rubber, fertilizer and precision and optical instruments industries. Dismantling reduced by two-fifths the productive capacity of lignite mining and created serious shortages of East Germany's main industrial fuel.

On June 5, 1946, the Soviet Military Administration issued an order which transformed about two hundred major East German industrial firms into branches of Soviet enterprises. The management of these *Sowjetische Aktien-Gesellschaften,* usually known as S.A.G., was placed in Russian hands. Most of their output, representing between one-third and one-quarter of the total East German industrial production, was shipped to the Soviet Union. These deliveries were, of course, valued at very low prices.[21] Most of these firms were returned to German ownership in 1952 and 1953, but were emptied of inventories and equipment prior to their transfer to the Democratic Republic. By 1954, all the SAG enterprises had reverted to the German Democratic Republic, except for one. *S.A.G. Wismut,* in charge of uranium mining in East Germany, which became a joint Soviet-German enterprise, responsible for the exploitation of uranium mines in the Ore Mountains and Thuringia.

Until January 1954, the German Democratic Republic continued to satisfy war obligations to the U.S.S.R. by means of deliveries of current output. Levies on current industrial output in 1946 and 1947 for shipment to Russia may have represented between 65% and 70% of the Soviet zone's current industrial production.[22] The value of these levies was calculated in terms of 1936 prices, even though producing firms had to finance production costs by paying current prices. To the burden of these deliveries was added that of the occupation costs which East Germany had to finance. These costs were much higher than in West Germany and lasted until January 1959. Occupation costs took the form of deliveries of East German commodities to the Soviet military and were not treated as part of East German reparation payments.[23]

East German reconstruction was also retarded by the Soviet removals of practically all of the usable railroad rolling stock. Since the railroad was the principal means of transportation in the area, the Russian confiscation of miles of railroad track, locomotives and other equipment seriously crippled intra-zonal transportation and trade. This made the problem of raw materials and foodstuff shortages more difficult to solve. The disintegration of East Germany's traditional trade with West Germany and with the territories located east of the Oder-Neisse line further weakened the East German economy. In 1939, the area that became the Soviet zone of occupation exported 49% of its total product to the rest of Germany and imported from the latter 55% of its consumer goods.[24] The bulk of East Germany's industrial fuel and raw materials came from the western part of the country; West German coal, iron and steel supplied the light industries of East Germany. The partition of Germany brought an end to this important inflow of West German raw materials. The autarkic policies of the Soviet world and the lack of hard currency holdings in East Germany made it impossible for the Democratic Republic to import these raw materials from other sources. Partition was also more burdensome for the German Democratic Republic than for the Federal Republic for another reason. While West Germany was eventually able to trade with the economically advanced countries of the world, partition forced East Germany to trade almost exclusively with the relatively poor economies of the members of the Soviet bloc.

To the economic losses suffered by East Germany through Russian confiscations of capital equipment and of current output, to the losses due to the collapse of normal East German trade, must be added the serious economic difficulties brought about by the large losses of skilled manpower which for sixteen years weakened the East German economy. The erection of the Berlin Wall in August 1961 finally brought to an end a mass exodus of about three million people, which was largely induced by the economic disparities between East and West Germany. This outflow of manpower caused East Germany to lose between one and one and a half million persons of working age and resulted in difficult labor shortage problems in the German Democratic Republic.[25]

A reasonable appraisal of East German economic performance must recognize the great handicaps that plagued the East German economy at least until G. Malenkov's "New Course" policies of 1953, if not until the late 1950s. Over a span of eight years, East Germany paid to the U.S.S.R. the war indemnification which should have been paid by the entire Germany that had been at war with the Soviet Union. East Germany continued to make these payments practically until 1960. While Soviet dismantling was crippling the East German economy, West Germany was receiving over 4 billion dollars in aid from the United States.

Soviet exploitation did not bring with it an inefficient economic administration in East Germany. The Soviet military command ruled through German administrative bodies set up shortly after the end of the war. Later on, administrative powers were given to five *Laender* governments. Soviet policy, as implemented by the German administrative agencies, aimed at a full mobilization of all economic resources, human and non-human, within the zone. In July 1945, factory and store owners, as well as managers of private and public enterprises were given the order to resume their immediately activities. In September, a population survey was conducted to ascertain the identity of every person of working age. To obtain a consumer's ration card, individuals had to show that they were employed or that they were at least listed with an official employment agency. These measures brought about much faster economic recovery in the Soviet zone than in the western zones. Taking 1936 as the base year, the index of industrial production in the Soviet zone during the first quarter of 1948 was 63, while it was about 49 for the other zones.[26] Lack of raw materials, the non-availability of the excess industrial capacity which existed in Western Germany and the end of East Germany's ability to import from the West during the second half of 1948 handicapped East German economic growth with burdens which did not exist in the West German economy. Still, at least until 1948, economic recovery seems to have proceeded faster in the East in spite of Soviet dismantling, a crippled transportation system and serious fuel shortages.

In the Soviet zone, limited economic planning had a start toward the end of 1945, when a first, short-term plan was formulated to take care of the most pressing needs of the population; this plan covered the first quarter of 1946. This type of short-term planning was continued until 1948 when a Six-Months Plan for the second half of 1948 became a first step toward longer-term, more comprehensive planning. In 1948, a Two-Year Plan for 1949 and 1950 was adopted. The Plan called for an increase in total East German output of 81% above the 1936 volume. Average labor productivity was to rise by 30% between 1947 and 1950. Investments were to benefit the raw materials, energy, machinery and transport industries. The Plan aimed principally at a start in the construction of heavy industries which could help East Germany's light industries to overcome the effects of the end of raw materials imports from West Germany. According to East German data, these goals were reached within one and one-half years after the formulation of the plan.[27] The general willingness of East Germans to work hard for the rapid reconstruction of their country explains to a large extent the apparent success of the East German planners. Nevertheless, the efficiency of their planning was handicapped by the unpredictable and recurring Soviet appropriations and by the adherence of SED leaders to the Stalinist "ton ideology," i.e., the importance attached to the attainment of production targets expressed in terms of units, weight or volume, without much consideration being given to the quality and efficiency of production and the sufficiency of demand for whatever was produced.

A first Five-Year Plan was enacted in 1950. It prescribed an increase in industrial output of 190% which was to double East German industrial output between 1936 and 1955. The plan gave priority to the development of fuel, energy, metallurgy and machinery industries.[28]

Until the mid-1950s, East German planning aimed at the building of a variety of heavy industries which would compensate East Germany for the loss of its access to West German industrial markets. The East German literature appearing in those days repeatedly stressed the urgent need to eliminate the "economic disproportions" brought about by the partition of Germany. At a time when the Soviet bloc governments interpreted the Stalinist dogma to mean that socialist countries should be as self-sufficient as possible, and at a time when the activities of the Council for Mutual Economic Assistance (the CMEA, also known as COMECON, a Communist duplicate of the O.E.E.C.) were so limited that they tended to discourage economic specialization, the East German pursuit of economic autarky was not only understandable from a political point of view, but was also extremely well-considered given the economic conditions in East Germany. Indeed, Germany's partition had deprived East Germany of its usual sources of coal, iron and steel. This meant that during the 1950s, the supplies of industrial fuels in the Democratic Republic were unable to keep up with the demand for these materials, even though East German scientists had succeeded in producing a metallurgical coke derived from lignite. Because of fuel and raw material shortages, the aggregate metallurgical output in 1950 had not as yet reached its 1936 level.

It is indeed amazing that the Two-Year Plan and the first Five-Year Plan were carried out with some success. Not only was the East German economy continuously weakened by Russian levies on current output, but the Democratic Republic had also to endure the adverse effects of a declining population during the first half of the 1950s. In 1939, the area of the Federal Republic, including West Berlin, counted 42.1 million people. This population increased to 49.6 million in 1950 and to 52.1 million in 1955. This represented an increase of about 25%. In 1939, the area of the Democratic Republic, including East Berlin, had a population of 16.7 million. In 1950, this population had increased to 18.4 million, but then declined to 17.8 million in 1955.[29] This loss of population was mainly due to emigration from the Democratic Republic. Between 1948 and 1955, East Germany lost about 10% of its population to West Germany. This meant that economic plans were carried out in the face of continuous labor shortages.

The ability of state employment agencies to assign workers to any activity subject to labor shortages, the traditional diligence and skills of the population and the end of reparation payments in 1954 helped the East German economy to overcome demographic and other handicaps. Between 1950 and 1953, new steel works were built at Calbe an der Saale, with blast furnaces entirely fuelled by lignite. New plants at Fuerstenberg an de Oder, able to produce about 60% of the iron needs of the country, were completed during the first Five-Year Plan period. At Riesa, Henningsdorf and other locations, prewar iron and steel plants were increased in size and provided with new machinery. Improving trade relations with the Soviet Bloc countries allowed the Democratic Republic to import Soviet iron ore and Polish coke. As shown in Table 5.2, the output of pig iron increased threefold between 1950 and 1953, while crude steel production more than doubled.

TABLE 5.2

PRODUCTION INDICES FOR PIG IRON AND STEEL

	1936	1950	1951	1952	1953
Pig Iron	59	100	101	196	320
Steel	111	100	155	189	217

Source: German Democratic Republic, *Zehn Jahre Volkswirtschaft der D.D.R.*, Berlin-E, 1959, p. 98.

The Western literature in the late 1950s emphasized the fact that during the period 1950 to 1955, the gross national product of the German Federal Republic experienced larger growth than that of the Democratic Republic. Professor Kolmey has argued that although East Germany gave priority to the growth of industrial raw materials production, in terms of raw materials output per capita, the Democratic Republic in the 1950s lagged behind the Federal Republic. He indicates that per capita output of coal was 148.6 kilograms in East Germany, 2,504.7 kilograms in West Germany; the respective figures were 92.7 and 300.5 kilograms for iron ore and 84.5 and 315.8 kilograms for pig iron.[30] Professor Stolper, comparing West and East German production data in the 1950s, writes: "In the one case in which a Communist and a free economy are historically, culturally and economically comparable, there is no evidence whatsoever that the Communist economy has grown faster, even on a per capita basis."[31] Comparisons of East and West German production data are, however, of no great significance because the two German economies were not economically comparable. The much larger West German economy had experienced minimal and short-lived dismantling by the western occupation authorities; it was rich in industrial raw materials and benefited from large inflows of American dollars and of skilled manpower from the East. The smaller and poorer East German economy, deprived of any type of foreign aid, was weakened by Soviet appropriations until 1954, by high "occupation costs" until 1959 and by a continuous loss of manpower until 1961. Although Stolper recognizes that increases in per capita product were in many cases similar in both Germanies, he seems to fail to perceive the significance of this achievement in the case of East Germany.

As shown in Table 5.3, East German industrial output did expand during the period of the first Five-Year Plan. East German data reported an increase of 189.6% in gross industrial output between 1950 and 1955. Professor Kolmey has calculated this increase as only 90%. According to East German data, data which have been accepted as statistically reliable in both West Germany and the United States, the output of electricity in the Democratic Republic increased from 19,466 million kwh in 1950 to 28,696 million kwh in 1955. This expansion in the output of electric power was mostly due to the building of new power plants at Stalinstadt, Trattendorf, Elbe and Calbe. During the same period, the output of cement doubled and the number of diesel locomotives built in East Germany almost tripled.[32]

TABLE 5.3

INDICES OF INDUSTRIAL OUTPUT IN THE
GERMAN DEMOCRATIC REPUBLIC
1950 = 100

	Total Industry	Metallurgy	Light Industry
1950	100	100	100
1951	122.6	124.5	120
1952	142.3	151.3	131.7
1953	159.6	177.6	141.8
1954	176.0	198.5	157.8
1955	189.6	214.8	166.3

Source: *Statistisches Jahrbuch der D.D.R., 1955,* Berlin-E, 1956, p. 125.

It is true that these achievements in industrial production were obtained at the expense of the consumer and of the farmer. In 1955, the gross national product attributable to agriculture was still below the prewar level and the output of consumer goods was only three-fourths of what it had been in 1936. Still, the lack of industrial resources, Russian appropriations and the absence of foreign aid render the increase in East German industrial output a remarkable feat. East German industrial output increases were mostly due to increases in labor productivity; according to the calculations of Professor Kolmey, labor productivity in those years rose faster in the Democratic Republic than in the Federal Republic.[33]

Agriculture

Although in 1946 the official policy still purported to protect the East German farmer owning between 50 and 100 hectares of land, Ulbricht's loyalty to Stalinist practices led the East German authorities, as of 1948, to eliminate the East German *"kulak"* and to do away with privately owned farms whose size varied between 20 and 100 hectares.

In order to "build Socialism" in the rural sector, the burden of obligatory, low priced deliveries to the state and the rate of taxation imposed on large farmers were raised to force these farmers into bankruptcy. Privately owned farms of 50 to 100 hectares covered 470,000 hectares of land in 1946; by 1950, these farms extended over only 274,000 hectares.

The Two-Year Plan for 1949 and 1950 and the first Five-Year Plan imposed detailed production, harvesting and marketing directives on farmers. Every farmer was instructed what to plant and how much to plant. At the end of each week, every farmer had to report to the mayor of his village what he had done during that week and he received from that official work directives for the following week.[34] Obligatory delivery quotas were fixed before the results of the harvest were known. Surpluses had to be sold to a public agency at fixed prices. Fearing that the showing of a surplus would bring about an increase in the delivery quota, farmers were not motivated to increase their productivity. On the small farms, labor productivity was kept low by the lack of skills of the new farmers, the scarcity of equipment and the effects of excessive government regulations. The Soviet dismantling of factories producing fertilizers and their appropriations of large quantities of potatoes, farms animals and other farm produce, further impeded any rise in agricultural productivity.

In order to bring about the socialization of agriculture and an increase in agricultural productivity, agricultural production cooperatives, *Landwirtschaftliche Produktionsgenossenschaften* or LPGs, were created in 1952. At the same time, Ulbricht's government declared that private farms exceeding twenty hectares were to be regarded as undesirable "capitalist enterprises."[35] By the end of 1952, about two thousand agricultural cooperatives were in existence; three years later, there were three times as many. In 1953, these cooperatives and a small number of state-owned farms cultivated 26% of the tilled land area of the Democratic Republic. This percentage increased to 33% in 1957; still, by 1959, more than half of the cultivated area in the country remained in private ownership.

From the start, the East German government favored the LPGs in many ways. Government-owned machine-tractor stations had to satisfy the needs of the cooperatives before their equipment could be used by independent farmers. LPG members benefited from reduced taxes and lower delivery quotas. Private farmers, on the other hand, were subjected to higher taxes and more burdensome deliveries to the goverⁿment. A result of this policy was that thousands of East German farmers abandoned their land and fled to the West, allowing the East German government to confiscate their abandoned farms.

The East German cooperative was not a duplicate of the Soviet *kolkhoze* and it was not a state-owned enterprise. Members of an LPG retained the title to the land they had placed in the cooperative and could sell it or bequeath it to their heirs.[36] The LPG's leadership was freely chosen by the members of the cooperative and did not necessarily belong to party officials.

There were three different types of LPGs. Under the Type I arrangement, farmers simply pooled their arable land for joint cultivation, while they retained individual control over their pastures, animals and machinery. Under Type II, equipment and buildings were also pooled and pasture land could also be used jointly. Under Type III, all possessions were pooled, including livestock and pastures. Under each LPG type, the farmer was allowed to retain half an acre of land for personal use, and under Type II, he was also allowed to retain two cows, two breeding sows, five sheep and an unlimited number of small animals.

A number of state-owned farms, *Volkseigenes Gut* or VEG, had been established in 1949 to operate on public land, largely for research purposes. The VEGs had to deliver quality seed and animals to the LPGs and act as experimental stations. About 500 of these farms cultivated an area representing only about 4% of the total cultivated area.

TABLE 5.4 AGRICULTURAL OUTPUT: SELECTED ITEMS

In 1,000

	Head of Cattle	Wheat (tons)	Sugar Beet (tons)	Potatoes (tons)
1938	3,653.3	1,547	5,412	13,567
1950	3,614.7	1,163	5,460	13,711
1955	3,759.5	1,211	5,712	11,194

Source: *S.J.D.D.R., Suppl. 1967*, pp. 12-13.

As shown in Table 5.4, by 1955, agricultural productivity on both private and socialized farms was still far below that of 1936. The first Five-Year Plan had aimed at a 57% increase in agricultural output. The realized increase attained only 44%. Most of the Plan's agricultural targets were not reached. Agricultural yields in East Germany in 1955 remained well below corresponding yields in the Federal Republic.

The poor performance of the LPGs during their early years of operation has been explained by the East Germans in terms of the lack of skills of the participating farmers and the poverty of the farms which they pooled.

The First Postwar Decade in Retrospect

1955 marked the end of a decade of Soviet exploitation in East Germany. It was also the end date of East Germany's first Five-Year Plan. The targets set by the Plan were attained in the industrial sector; they were not reached in the agricultural one. While industrial output apparently doubled between 1950 and 1955, agriculture stagnated and agricultural productivity remained low in both the private and socialized agricultural sectors. The emphasis given to the development of heavy industry and the inadequacy of agricultural production created a low standard of living; according to western writers in the 1950s, this standard would soon force the East Germans to rebel against their government.[37] Their prediction that the East German economy would soon collapse proved to be false. Erroneous evaluations of the vitality of the East German economy were mostly due to a poor understanding of the East German economic system. This system was viewed in the West as one dominated by state ownership and by over-centralized, dogmatic and inflexible planning. This was not so. Although the government, as was earlier observed, continued many Stalinist policies even after Stalin's death, it must be remembered that only a part of the economy operated under public ownership. In 1950, the public sector contributed only half of the country's total produce. While state enterprises contributed 71% of the total industrial output in that year and 84% of the country's transportation, private ownership produced 87% of the agricultural output and 68% of all construction; this is illustrated in Table 5.5. State enterprises could not be blamed for inefficient production. Economic growth during those years was largely generated by the public sector. The poor performance of East German agriculture was due to the fact that most of this output was produced by small, inefficient, privately held farms.

The role of private enterprise in the economy was not insignificant. The government recognized the desirability of allowing private entrepreneurs to maintain and freely manage their businessess. This tended to indicate that the Ulbricht government was not as dogmatic and inflexible as many critics believed it to be. In many instances, the

TABLE 5.5

PERCENTAGE OF GROSS SOCIAL PRODUCT CONTRIBUTED
BY NATIONALIZED ENTERPRISES

	Industry	Construction	Agriculture	Transport Communica- tions	Trade
1950	70.7	31.6	12.6	83.5	62.1
1955	78.9	56.0	25.0	87.7	83.8
1960	84.5	78.0	80.1	92.6	86.6

Source: *S.J.D.D.R., 1967*, p. 37.

state acquired part-ownership in privately held firms, contributed capital, and allowed the initial owners to continue managing the firm, free of government interference.[38]

Following the death of Stalin, the U.S.S.R. gradually abandoned the dogma of national self-sufficiency. Increased trade between the C.M.E.A. countries allowed the latter to give more importance to the effects of comparative advantage in production. This allowed East Germany to secure the raw materials necessary for economic expansion and to depart from the Stalinist pattern of industrial development. A new emphasis on light industry production revitalized the East German economy and transformed it in the 1960s into a major supplier of manufactured products within the C.M.E.A. area.

TABLE 5.6

EAST GERMAN GROSS SOCIAL PRODUCT
1950 - 1960

	(Constant Prices)	
	GSP Index 1950 = 100	Annual Rate of GSP Increase: %
1950	100	24
1951	124	13.5
1952	141	7.1
1953	151	10
1954	166	9
1955	181	4.4
1956	189	4.8
1957	198	11.6
1958	221	10.9
1959	245	6.1
1960	260	3.8

Source: *S.J.D.D.R., 1967*, p. 21.

But even before Stalin's death, the East German economy, in spite of the serious obstacles to expansion then in existence, recorded remarkable growth rates. Although the East German concept of the Gross Social Product is somewhat different from the western definition of the Gross National Product, the internal consistency of the data still allow us to obtain a measure of East German economic growth during the early 1950s. The data in Table 5.6 show a high rate of over-all growth during the period of the first Five-Year Plan.

NOTES

1. It has been estimated that between 1945 and 1954, the U.S.S.R. appropriated 25% of the East German industrial output to satisfy Soviet war indemnification claims. W. Stolper, "The National Product of East Germany," *International Review for Social Sciences*, vol. 12 (1959), p. 153. A study of East German reparation payments to the Soviet Union indicates that during the period 1945 to 1960, East German reparation deliveries to the Soviet Union amounted to $19.3 billion in terms of 1938 prices. Compensation exceeding $17 billion had already been made as early as 1953. It appears that the Soviet Union extracted from East Germany nearly double the compensation it had asked at Yalta. H. Kohler, *Economic Integration in the Soviet Bloc* (New York: Praeger, 1965), p. 29.

2. J.E. Smith, *Germany Beyond the Wall* (Boston: Little, Brown & Co., 1967), p. 85; Kohler, *Economic Integration in the Soviet Bloc*, Ch. 1.

3. A Grosser, *Germany in Our Time* (New York: Praeger, 1971), p. 64.

4. E. Richert, *Das Zweite Deutschland, Ein Staat Der Nicht Sein Darf* (Guetersloh: Sigbert Mohn Verlag, 1964), p. 121.

5. D. Childs, *East Germany* (New York: Praeger, 1969), p. 136.

6. G. Roustang, *Developpement Economique de l'Allemange Orientale* (Paris: SEDES, 1963), p. 11.

7. B. Gleitze, *Wirtschaftsprobleme der Besatzungszonen* (Berlin-W, 1947), p. 17.

8. German Federal Republic, *Sowjetische Besatzugszone von A bis Z* (Bonn: Bundesministerium fuer gesamtdeutsche Fragen (henceforth BFGF) 1966), p. 206.

9. F. Wunderlich, "Agriculture and Farm Labor in the Soviet Zone of Germany," *Social Research* (June 1952), pp. 198-219.

10. M. Kramer, *Die Landwirtschaft in der SBZ* (Bonn, 1957); W. Ulbricht, "Die Demokratische Bodenreform," *Neues Deutschland* (Berlin-E; 2 September 1955).

11. German Democratic Republic, *Zehn Jahre Volkswirtschaft der Deutschen Demokratischen Republik* (Berlin-E, Verlag Die Wirtschaft, 1959), Ch. 2. In 1945 and 1946, East German authorities still assured the "large" farmer, i.e., the farmer owning between 50 and 100 hectares of land, that his property would not be confiscated and that he would be protected by the government. Kramer, p. 22. See also W. Ulbricht, *Zur Geschichte der neuesten Zeit*, vol. I (Berlin- E; Dietz Verlag, 1955), p. 377.

12. Kramer, *Die Landwirtschaft in der SBZ*, p. 10.

13. German Democratic Republic, Die Landwirtschaft in der DDR, *Heute und Morgen* (Dresden, 1965), p. 21.

14. German Democratic Republic, *Zehn Jahre Volkswirtschaft der Deutschen Demokratischen Republik*, Ch. 2. H. Kohler, however, feels that East German estimates have grossly overvalued the extent of war damage in East Germany in order to minimize the effects of Soviet dismantling on the economy. Industrial growth in East Germany during the war

years could mean, according to Kohler, that industrial capacity in 1945 may have been equal to that of 1936, if not higher. See Kohler, *Economic integration in the Soviet Bloc*, p. 13.

15. German Democratic Republic, *Zwanzing Jahre ein Freies Land (Dresden: Voelkersfreundschaft-Verlag, 1965), p. 8. See also Richert, Das Zweite Deutschland*, p. 123.

16. *Geschichte der Deutschen Arbeiter Bewegung* (Berlin-E: Dietz Verlag, 1966), p. 269.

17. C.G. Anthon, "Stalinist Rule in East Germany," *Current History* (May 1963), p. 267.

18. D. Childs, *East Germany* (New York: Praeger, 1969), p. 32.

19. Kohler, *Economic Integration in the Soviet Bloc* (New York: Praeger, 1965), p. 29. the industrial capacity of East Germany in 1946 was only 30% of what it had been ten years earlier and that in that year, 90% of the East German current output was appropriated for shipment to the Soviet Union. W. Friedmann, *The Allied Military Government of Germany* (London: Stevens & Sons, 1947), pp. 192-193.

20. B.F.G.F., *Sowjetische Besatzungszone von 1945 bis 1954* (Bonn: 1956), p. 58.

21. B.F.G.F., *Die Stellung der SAG in der Wirtschaft der Sowjetzone im Jahre 1951* (Bonn, 1952), p. 15.

22. *Europa-Archiv 1949*, No. 7, p. 2032.

23. H. Apel, "East German Miracle?," *Challenge*, vol. 12, No. 2 (November 1963), p. 11.

24. Deutsches Institut fuer Wirtschaftsforschung, *Vierteljahreshefte zur Wirtschaftsforschung*, (Bonn, 1952), p. 60.

25. W. Stolper, "Labor Force and Industrial Development in Soviet Germany," *Quarterly Journal of Economics*, vol. 71 (November 1957), pp. 518-545.

26. U.N., Economic Commission for Europe, *Economic Bulletin for Europe*, III (Geneva, 1949), p. 43.

27. German Democratic Republic, *Zehn Jahre Volkswirtschaft der Deutschen Demokratischen Republik* Ch. 2.

28. *Documents of the SED* (Berlin-E: Dietz Verlag, 1952), Part III, p. 133.

29. German Democratic Republic, *Statistisches Jahrbuch fuer die Deutsche Demokratische Republik 1956* (Berlin-E, 1956), p. 20.

30. G. Kolmey, "Special Features of the Development of Industry and Foreign Economic Ties in the German Democratic Republic, " *Problems of Economics* (November 1958), pp. 4-45.

31. W.F. Stolper, "The National Product of East Germany," *Kyklos*, vol. XII (1959), pp. 131-166 at p. 136.

32. German Democratic Repubic, *Statistisches Jahrbuch 1964* – henceforth, S.J.D.D.R. (Berlin-E: Staatsverlag der D.D.R., 1964), pp. 148-161.

33. Kolmey, "Special Features of the Development of Industry."

34. *Die Wirtschaft* (Berlin-E, March 30, 1950).

35. German Democratic Republic, *Chronologische Materialen zur Geschichte der S.E.D.* (Berlin-E, 1956), p. 116.

36. Roustang, *Developpement Economique de l' Allemange Orientale,* p. 61.

37. E.L. Dulles, *One Germany or Two* (Stanford: Hoover Institution Press, 1970), p. 85.

38. Smith, *Germany Beyond the Wall*, pp. 101-106.

CHAPTER 6

YUGOSLAVIA IN AND OUT OF COMINFORM

On the eve of World War II, Yugoslavia still exhibited many features of pronounced economic backwardness. 77% of the population depended on agriculture for a livelihood and agriculture accounted for 53% of the national income[1] The great majority of the peasants cultivated scattered strips of land whose total area added to less than 10 hectares. One-third of the land holdings in the country were of less than 2 hectares, and another third did not exceed 5 hectares.[2] A subsistence peasant economy covered most of Serbia as well as the entirety of Bosnia-Herzegovina, Macedonia and Montenegro. Unlike the situation in Hungary and East Germay, no aristocratic land-owning group in Yugoslavia possessed and cultivated large estates. The prevailing egalitarian distribution of small farms and a highly illiterate peasant population kept the rural sector tied to primitive methods of agriculture.[3] During the interwar period, the government had done little to improve conditions in the overpopulated agricultural sector and the latter continued to be characterized by low crop yields, a primitive monoculture based on cereals, solidly entrenched socio-economic traditions and poverty.

Industry had developed in some of the northern and western parts of the country, particularly around Ljubljana in Slovenia and Zagreb in Croatia. This industry had developed largely under the ownership and direction of foreign capital or of the state. Probably half of the capital invested in Yugoslav industry in the late 1930s was foreign-owned. Foreign interests controlled almost the entirety of the metal mining industry, 97% of the cement industry, 67% of the chemical industry, 81% of the textile industry and 51% of the food processing industry.[4] The State owned and operated iron foundries and steel works, as well as coal mines and sugar refineries. Very little industrial activity was in the hands of private Yugoslav entrepreneurs in 1939. The nationalization of industry in 1946 did not bring about a major change in the industrial organization of the country. Although the prewar industrial sector was small, it was not insignificant. It contained important mining and smelting industries and large cement and timber processing industries whose products were exported. The steel industry, however, was small and the economy lacked non-ferrous metal processing industries.

Poor means of transportation and of communication kept the internal market small and the country economically backward. A plurality of languages, religions and traditions tended to compartmentalize the economy and to prevent industrial growth. Yugoslavia had had not only two alphabets, three religions and four major languages, but the country also contained a large number of ethnic groups which history had often turned into enemies. Although Croats, Slovenes, Serbs, Macedonians and Montenegrins constituted the country's major ethnic groups, important German, Hungarian, Bulgarian, Albanian and Turkish minorities added to Yugoslavia's socio-cultural diversity. This cultural heterogeneity prevented the development of common political and economic views. Prewar Yugoslavs were more motivated by ethnic antagonism than by national awareness. As one writer put it, "the cement that held the Yugoslav system together was comprised of the army, the police and the bureaucracy."[5]

The vast destruction of human and non-human resources brought about by the war greatly weakened an already poor economy. Yugoslavia ranked second in Europe, after Poland, in the extent of war damages suffered. It has been estimated that the total damage to property caused by the hostilities represented in value the aggregate of fifty years of Yugoslav prewar national income.[6] The number of Yugoslav lives lost directly because of the war amounted to 1.7 million or 10.8% of the total population. The loss included almost one-third of all the industrial workers in the country. Communications and transportation systems were seriously damaged. The number of locomotives in operation in 1945 was 24% of that of 1939; the number of railroad cars had been reduced by 84% and that of river-going ships by 88%. 63% of all first-class roads had been destroyed or seriously damaged. Only two ports could be used. The extent of war damage to industrial capacity is best shown by industrial output indices in 1945. Taking 1939 as the base year, the 1945 index for coal output was 46; for crude iron, the index was 20; it was 29 for crude steel, 20 for cement and 15 for electric power.[7] 20.5% of total prewar housing lay in ruin and 289,000 farms had been destroyed.

The First Revolutionary Reforms

Industrial production in 1945 represented on the average only 25% of that of 1939. The Tito govermnemt, in order to avoid any internal strife and unrest which could retard the process of economic reconstruction, generally followed policies of tolerance and moderation. In this, the Communist Party of Yugoslavia, the C.P.Y., followed the example of the various Communist Parties in Eastern Europe during the period 1945 to 1948.[8] Moderation in the pace of reforms was, however, not as necessary for the C.P.Y. as it was for other Communist Parties and Communist-dominated governments in Eastern Europe. Soviet military might had not imposed the Tito government upon the Yugoslavs. For most Yugoslavs, Tito in 1945 represented the great national hero who valiantly fought for the honor and the liberation of his country. Outnumbered by the enemy, and with little help from the Allied Powers, Tito and his *partizani* succeeded in driving the German invaders out of the country. The *partizani* represented all of the various ethnic groups in the country and they did not give preference to any one nationality or religion. The followers of Drazha Mihailovich were mostly Serbs; the Fascist *Ustashis* of Ante Pavelich were Croats; the *partizani* were Yugoslavs. As liberators of their country they enjoyed immense prestige throughout the nation and it is only natural that the government Tito eventually formed had the enthusiastic support of the great majority of Yugoslavs. Opposition to the early reform measures of this government was therefore practically non-existent. Since the resistance movement had cut across ethnic lines, common memories of past privations and suffering weakened old ethnic and relogous prejudices. The vision of a better social and economic Marxist future tended to unify Croats, Serbs and other groups and strengthened nationalistic feelings.

At the end of the war, the major goals of the C.P.Y. were to unify the country and to create a Soviet-type economy. Non-Communist, anti-Fascist parties were allowed to join in a "People's Front," a new political organization soon dominated by the C.P.Y. The Soviet industrial economic system was to be duplicated in order to allow the Yugoslavs to enter the Marxist industrial "paradise." In conformity with Soviet economic policies, industrialization had to be pushed as rapidly as possible, regardless of cost and hardship. Communist leaders, university students and intellectuals felt that only industrialization could bring about the desired transformation and the necessary modernization of the economy. In their view, only a total change in the structure of production would raise the productivity of the country's labor force, particularly the productivity of rural labor. Industrialization would allow a mass exodus of labor from the agricultural sector and would move workers to new sectors where their productivity would be higher. New industries were to provide agriculture with better tools and materials and would also widen the internal market for agricultural products.

The potential of industrialization seemed particularly promising given the country's wealth in minerals and the abundance of sources of hydroelectric power. Yugoslavia, when compared to other countries in the Soviet Bloc, also enjoyed certain politico-economic advantages which facilitated its early postwar industrialization efforts. Unlike Russia's former enemies in eastern Europe, Yugoslavia did not have to pay war indemnities to the U.S.S.R. and its economy remained free of Soviet confiscations of capital equipment and of current output. Unlike Poland, Yugoslavia did not have to bear the cost of Soviety military occupation. Unlike Eastern Germany, Yugoslavia did not receive, and therefore did not have to support, large numbers of expatriates and refugees. On the contrary, the German minority which had lived in the country before the war either fled or was expelled. Finally, whereas Lenin had to start his economic reform program in the face of civil strife and economic blockade, Tito was able to initiate the economic transformation of Yugoslavia with the help of U.N.R.R.A. aid. Postwar U.N.R.R.A. aid to Yugoslavia exceeded by 40% per capita that received by Poland or Czechoslovakia.[9] These factors, combined with the genuine popularity of the Communist leadership, allowed the Tito government to initiate socialist planning without recourse to terrorist coercion.

In 1944, before the war had ended, a Law on the Confiscation of Property Belonging to the Enemy and their Collaborators was enacted by the Tito government. Under this law, the government in 1945 took over industries confiscated a few years earlier by the German authorities. Since most of these concerns were foreign-owned before the war, and since once the Germans had left the country no one claimed ownership or volunteered to operate these enterprises, their nationalization did not raise any opposition in the country. The expropriation of collaborators and other "enemies of the people" met with general approval. State ownership was further expanded by the Law on Nationalization of December 1946. This law nationalized all the large industrial and commercial establishments in the country as well as the entire transportation system and all the banks.[10] A second Law on Nationalization of 1948 nationalized all small industrial and commercial establishments not nationalized before. The speed of nationalization in Yugoslavia at that time was much greater than in any other Eastern European country.

Like the laws on nationalization, the Basic Law on Agrarian Reform and Colonization of August 1945 failed to bring about a marked change in the existing economic system. The law attempted to create a land pool out of which collective and state farms could be created. The difficulty was that Yugoslavia lacked large landed estates which could be expropriated. Expropriations primarily involved lands abandoned by the fleeing German minority. The law provided that in the case of cultivators, private property in land could not exceed from 25 to 35 hectares of arable land, the exact maximum size varying with regions in the country, or could not exeeed 45 hectares of both arable and non-arable land. Members of the clergy were not allowed to own more than 10 hectares of land and non-cultivators were limited to between 3 and 5 hectares.[11] Although peasants were put under pressure to join collective farms, 93.8% of all arable land in the country was still in private hands by the end of 1948. State farms held only 3.6% of the arable area and collective farms only 2.6%. Following governmental efforts to speed up the socialization of agriculture in the summer of 1948, the latter percentage figures at the end of 1951 increased respectively to 6% and 20%.[12] The government's moderation in its drive to collectivize agriculture constituted a major departure from the Soviet model and perhaps reflected the government's fear that more coercive measures could lead to a drastic reduction of agricultural output as had happened in the U.S.S.R. in the 1930s.

To complete the set of reform legislation, a Five-Year Plan was adopted in 1947. Yugoslavia, following the Soviet example, decided to adopt central and total economic planning and rejected policies of partial or short-term planning. The policy of centralized planning was sanctioned by the Constitution of 1946, whose Article 15, Chapter IV, provided that:

> "With the aim of protecting the vital interests of the people, promoting national welfare and the correct exploitation of all economic potentials

and forces, the state guides economic activity and development through the general economic plan."

The First Five-Year Plan, 1947-1951

The main objective of the plan was to industrialize the country. Industrialization had not only economic goals, but also social and cultural objectives. It was hoped that the program of industrialization would do away with regional inequalities in economic development and thereby reduce ancient ethnic prejudices due to regional economic differences. Industrialization was to reduce agricultural overpopulation and give employment to at least one million rural workers in the expanded secondary and tertiary sectors. It was meant to facilitate cultural progress and to push up the standard of living of the masses. Briefly, industrialization was to modernize the entire economy.

The planners proposed to triple national income within a period of five years. Gross industrial output was to increase fivefold. The output of certain products was to increase by more than ten times; among these products were crude oil, gasoline, machine-tools, locomotives, railroad cars, cranes, trucks, tractors and bicycles. To achieve this increase in industrial production, the planners determined that investment should represent about 30% of national income. Following the Stalinist model, the Yugoslav Planning Commission decided that most of this investment would go into the expansion of producer-goods industries; the growth of consumer-goods industries and of construc on would be sacrificed for the sake of rapid industrialization. The Plan provided for an increase in industrial output of 494% but personal consumption was to rise by only 53%.[13]

Output targets for agriculture were not as ambitious as those set for industry. Agricultural output was "to reach, and, in the basic branches exceed by an average of 20%, the pre-war agricultural output."[14] Wheat output was to rise by 15% and corn by 20%. Given the abundance of rural workers in the economy and allowing for some improvement in their technical knowledge and in their equipment, these goals did not seem to be unreachable. What the planners failed to realize was that these goals could only be attained if the farmers could be induced to produce more. The government did not succeed in encouraging peasants to expand their output by keeping agricultural prices very low and by withholding from the farmers the raw materials and tools they needed. Investment in agriculture remained inadequate because of the over-emphasis given to industrial development. The figures in Table 6.1 clearly show the weak position of agriculture.

TABLE 6.1

DISTRIBUTION OF TOTAL PLANNED INVESTMENT

1947-1951

Percentages

Electric Power	11
Mining and Metallurgy	11
Other Manufacturing	20
Transport and Communications	26
Agriculture	7
Other	25
	100

Source: United Nations, Economic Commission for Europe, *Economic Survey of Europe in 1953,* Geneva, 1954, p. 110.

The Yugoslav planning system followed in detail the planning techniques of the Soviet Union. The Central Planning Commmission, a federal agency, acquired extensive management powers over the entire economy. Every economic activity was subjected to detailed directives given by the Commission and its subordinated Ministries. These directives were to be faithfully followed by republic and local governmental organizations as well as by the individual enterprises. The Plan was not based on a rational theory of investment but aimed to provide a full utilization of all productive factors in order to achieve, regardless of cost criteria, the determined industrialization objectives. Rigid controls regulated prices, wages, labor and materials allocations and the quantum and type of allowed investments. Workers, although they theoretically owned the factories they worked in, had no voice in the way they were operated. The Ministry-appointed plant director was not allowed any initiative of his own; his task was to comply faithfully with all production and distribution directives coming to him from his superiors.[15]

The Yugoslav Five-Year Plan of 1947 was much more ambitious than the corresponding plans of other countries in the Soviet Bloc. The Yugoslav plan aimed at a yearly rate of growth of gross industrial output of 38%. The corresponding planned rate of growth was 14% in East Germany, 18% in Bulgaria, 13% in Hungary, 17% in Poland, 20%

in Rumania and 9% in Czechoslovakia. Given the relatively backward state of the Yugoslav economy, the extent of war damage it had experienced and the existing shortage of technicians, Yugoslav planners seem to have been unrealistically ambitious.

There were, however, strong reasons justifying the pursuit of high rates of industrial growth. In order to obtain badly needed credits from the Soviet Bloc countries, Yugoslavia had to rapidly expand its exports; this necessitated a rapid increase in productive capacity which could only be provided by a high rate of economic growth. The Yugoslav planners also perceived the potential of greater utilization of sources of hydro-electric power in the country. To justify the large investments needed for the building of new hydro-electric power plants, the industrial sector had to be expanded so that it would be able to efficiently employ the increased output of electric power.[16] Other considerations also dictated the rapid development of the industrial sector. A high birth rate was raising the already high pressure of population on rural resources and it was imperative that industry absorb the excess agricultural population. It was also felt that the rapid industrialization of the economically backward regions was necessary to reduce lingering ethnic antagonisms due in part to economic inequalities. Thus, demographic, political, social and economic reasons induced Yugoslav leaders to give priority to the rapid development of the industrial sector. The error of the planners was not in aiming high; their mistake was to aim excessively high and to assume that sufficient foreign credits would be given to Yugoslavia to allow it to fulfill the targets of the Five-Year Plan.

Although industrial output increased rapidly during the period 1947 to 1951, the targets of the Five-Year Plan were not attained. With 1939 = 100, the indices in Table 6.2 show that although the production of capital goods more than doubled during the time period of the plan, industrial output failed to increase as projected.

Some inherent weaknesses made the implementation of the plan impossible. If industrial output increased by 53% in 1947 and by 24% in 1948, it was largely because of the initial existence of excess industrial capacity. From the moment this surplus capacity disappeared, the rate of growth of industrial output was bound to slow down. Agricultural output, produced mostly by small family farms, increased in a very limited way.

TABLE 6.2

OUTPUT INDICES, 1947-1951
1939 = 100

	1947	1951
Net Industrial Production	121	166
Capital Goods	241	534
Consumer Goods	130	162
Coefficient of Investment in GNP	28	21

Source: U.N., Economic and Social Council, *Planning for Balanced Social and Economic Development in Yugoslavia, op. cit.,* p. 16.

A major reason why the plan's targets could not be attained in 1951 was the expulsion of Yugoslavia from the *Cominform* in 1948. This expulsion led to an economic blockade of Yugoslavia by the Soviet Bloc and to a sudden stoppage of credits and of deliveries of raw materials and equipment to Yugoslavia.

The *Cominform*, the Communist Information Bureau, was established in 1947 by the Communist parties of nine countires, i.e., the Soviet Union, Yugoslavia, Poland, Hungary, Rumania, Bulgaria, Czechoslovakia, Italy and France. The official task of this organization was to facilitate the exchange of information between the various Communist parties. Its true function was quite different in nature. By 1947, Soviet leaders apprehended the possible consequences of the relatively independent and moderate policies followed by the several Communist parties in the Soviet Union's European sphere of influence. Though Moscow had apparently consented to their freedom of action in the early postwar period, the Communist Party of the Soviet Union now feared that this tolerance had weakened the parties' subservience to Russian dictate. It was probably the Soviet desire to control more effectively any nascent nationalist tendencies in the Soviet Bloc that brought about the establishment of *Cominform* in September 1947. The new organization was created to increase uniformity in the policies and aims of the various Communist parties.

It appears strange indeed that the C.P.Y., a party which had tried so hard to transform Yugoslavia into a model satellite country of the U.S.S.R., which was considered as late as 1947 to be one of the top Communist parties in the Soviet Bloc, whose leader was still hailed throughout the Communist world as a great Communist hero and a faithful ally of the Soviet Union, should be expelled from the

Cominform in 1948. The announcement of Yugoslavia's expulsion from the organization appeared on June 28, 1948. The official reasons given for this action were that Yugoslavia had pursued unfriendly policies toward the U.S.S.R., that the C.P.Y. was dominated by the Yugoslav "People's Front" and that Yugoslavia had failed to collectivize agriculture.[17] Tito was suddenly assailed as having been both a secret agent of the Nazi Gestapo and an agent of British and American intelligence during the war.[18]

The conflict between the U.S.S.R. and Yugoslavia was the outcome of some events which had caused disagreement between the governments of these countries before the war had ended. During the years of war, the U.S.S.R., probably to gain the sympathy of its capitalist allies, had tended to support the cause of the Yugoslav royalists and had urged Tito to give emphasis to the nationalist rather than the Communist aspect of his movement. When Tito refused this, the Soviet leadership felt that Tito was sabotaging good relationships between the Soviet Union and the West.[19] It is natural that once the war ended, the U.S.S.R. wanted the Tito government replaced by a Yugoslav Communist leadership more attentive to Moscow's wishes. There may have been some Soviet jealousy of the prestige enjoyed by the independent Yugoslav Communists. Yugoslavs have contended that the expulsion was mostly due to Russia's opposition to Tito's plan of forming a Balkan Federation under Yugoslav leadership, a Federation that would have united Bulgaria and Yugoslavia, and possibly also Albania. The Yugoslav leaders also felt that the Soviet Union had tried to subvert the Yugoslav armed forces and that it opposed the industrialization of Yugoslavia.[20]

The rupture with the *Cominform* had serious economic consequences for Yugoslavia. Its economy was subjected to an economic blockade imposed by the countries of the Soviet Bloc. In 1947, this Bloc had provided, according to *Borba*, 51.8% of Yugoslavia's imports and had received 49.1% of the country's exports. In 1949, these figures were reported to have dropped respectively to 3.2% and 7.7%.[21] The country had to rapidly reorient half of its foreign trade. It had to find new sources of supply for 50% of its imports and new markets for about the same proportion of its exports. All this was to be accomplished without the help of foreign aid and with an economy weakened by the drastic fall of essential imports. For particular commodities, the adjustment was even larger. Almost all the coke and hard coal Yugoslavia imported in 1948 had come from the Soviet Bloc. Eastern Europe in 1948 had been the source of 80% of Yugoslav imports of fertilizers, 85% of pig-iron imports, 60% of imports of petroleum products and almost the entirety of imports of locomotives and railroad cars.[22]

TABLE 6.3

YUGOSLAV FOREIGN TRADE

Percentages of Total

	Imports				Exports			
	1947	1948	1949	1952	1947	1948	1949	1952
U.S.S.R.	22.2	10.8	1.3	—	16.8	15.0	4.6	—
Czechoslovakia	17.6	17.1	6.3	—	18.8	15.9	4.3	—
Hungary	5.0	4.4	3.0	—	8.3	9.0	2.5	—
Poland	3.2	7.4	2.2	—	3.4	7.8	1.8	—
Bulgaria	3.2	1.7	—	—	1.8	1.0	0.1	—
Rumania	0.6	1.7	—	—	0.9	0.6	—	—
Albania	0.2	—	—	—	—	—	—	—
Eastern Germany	4.1	2.6	1.3	—	2.7	1.4	0.3	—
Total Eastern Europe	56.1	45.7	14.0	—	52.7	50.7	13.6	—
United States	4.0	3.4	10.3	19.3	0.1	2.6	8.4	14.7
United Kingdom	5.4	4.6	10.3	6.8	2.7	6.2	21.7	14.1
Western Germany	—	1.6	7.2	20.3	—	0.3	5.5	23.7
Other	34.5	44.7	58.2	53.6	44.5	40.2	50.8	47.5
Total World	100	100	100	100	100	100	100	100

Source: United Nations, E.C.E., *Economic Survey of Europe in 1953, op. cit.*, Part III, Ch. 8, p. 112.

Following Yugoslavia's expulsion from *Cominform*, Eastern European countries stopped honoring scheduled deliveries to Yugoslavia of raw materials and equipment. Industrial projects in Yugoslavia had to be either abandoned or postponed and this caused difficult bottleneck problems to arise in the Yugoslav economy. Yugoslav planners had assumed that the Five-Year Plan would be implemented on the basis of credits extended by Yugoslavia's Communist partners. There had been plans for the U.S.S.R. to build smelting works in Bosnia, for Hungary to erect an aluminum plant in Slovenia and for Czechoslovakia to set up agricultural machinery and tractor factories in the country. All of these plans vanished after the events of 1948. The effects of the economic blockade were worsened by severe droughts in 1950 and 1952. As a result of these difficulties, stagnation plagued the economy from 1950 until 1953. Economic stagnation in this period was further worsened by the changed political situation. As a member of *Cominform,* Yugoslavia had been relatively safe from military attack by either the West or the East. The rupture meant economic and military isolation and Yugoslavia could now fear military attacks by either the West or the East. Military expenditures had to be increased from 1949 on. Defense expenditures represented only between 7% and 8% of national income in 1947 and 1948. In 1951, they had climbed to 20% of national income. Larger military expenditures forced a curtailment of economic investment and a slow-down in the rate of economic growth. After 1950, the targets of the Five-Year Plan had to be revised and lowered.

The Beginning of Institutional Change: 1950-1952

The Soviet-Yugoslav split induced Yugoslav Communists to start questioning the validity and the usefulness of Soviet politico-economic institutions. They now felt free to interpret Marxist ideology independently of Russian views. With the expulsion of Yugoslavia from the *Cominform,* "the era of unquestioned, inflexible application of Soviet dogma came to an end with a vigorous attempt at social experimentation."[23] Yugoslav leaders contended at the time that the Soviet system had degenerated into "bureaucratic state capitalism" and warned all Communists that the powerful bureaucracy of the U.S.S.R. was not only willing to exploit Russian workers by retaining the surplus value of their production, in the very same way it was done in capitalist countries, but that it also engaged in the exploitation of satellite countries for the unjust appropriation of their raw materials. They pointed out that in the Soviet Union the State was not "withering away" as required in a Socialist society, but that on the contrary, it had become larger and more powerful over time.[24]

Although the Five-Year Plan was formally extended until 1952, the Yugoslav government initiated its decentralizing reforms as early as 1950. Centralized, long-term planning was quietly abandoned; instead, the government concentrated on the completion of key industrial projects without setting definite dates for their realization. The guiding purpose of the reform program was the introduction into the country of a new, truly Yugoslav socialist system which would not be based on centralized planning or on State ownership of the means of production. A major cornerstone of the reform program was the establishment of "workers' management councils" in the socialized sector of the economy as well as in the administrative agencies. The first law establishing worker-management in the country was enacted on July 2, 1950.[2] It was followed by a gradual decentralization of public administration; administrative power was transferred to local government organizations. During the following year, there was first a reduction in the burden of the compulsory deliveries of agricultural products and, after a good harvest in that year, the compulsory delivery program was entirely abandoned. Consumer rationing was ended in 1951. The *dinar* was devalued to one-sixth of its earlier official value and the State gave up its foreign trade monopoly.

Gradually, the economy ceased to be a faithful copy of the Soviet model and the new reforms built the foundations of the present Yugoslav system. This system was no longer controlled by a master economic plan regulating in detail every facet of production, distribution and consumption. The market and competition between enterprises were now given a role in the determination of what and how much should be produced.

The new system was inaugurated with the gradual transfer of control over enterprises from the Federal and Republic governments to the newly created workers' councils. The law of 1950 in effect vested the management of enterprises in the socialized sector in the workers and the latter were to operate their enterprises as trustees for society. Society, rather than the State, was the formal owner of all means of production. At first, the functions of the workers' councils were quite limited; workers were given a voice in the management of production operations, but it was only in 1957 that they acquired the right to pass decisions on the distribution of the net income of their enterprises. Until 1953, the director of the enterprise continued to be appointed by a government agency and workers had no say in his selection.

The organization of workers' managerial bodies as provided by the law of 1950 is well described by Professor B. Ward as follows:

> Briefly, the 1950 law provided for two new bodies within the firm in addition to the director: a worker's council (*radnicki savet*) and a management board (*upravni odbor*). The former was to be elected by the entire staff of the firm and was given such rights and duties as the following: approving the basic plan and the annual report (*zavrsri racun*), issuing resolutions about management of the firm and the execution of the plan, selecting and removing members of the management board,

generally supervising the work of the management board . . . . The management board was to be chosen by the workers' council from among its members and was to perform such tasks as making up the basic plan, issuing monthly operating plans, making final decisions on appointments to senior positions within the firm, and deciding questions of labor norms. In general, the board was responsible for carrying out the plan and for the "correct" operation of the firm . . . . The director was appointed by the competent ministry until 1953, when the local people's committee *(narodni odbor,* the local territorial government), in consultation with the workers' council, made the appointment. In general, the director was responsible for the day-to-day operational control of the firm's activities.[26]

Although E. Kardelj described the workers' councils as "the instrument for the withering away of the state and the achievement of communism," the workers' freedom in the management of their enterprises remained quite limited for a number of years.[27] Economic enterprises and the economy as a whole continued to be subjected to the control and guidance of the federal government which retained extensive powers in the areas of price control, finance, income distribution and foreign trade. Within individual enterprises, the continuation of the central plan and the superior technical knowledge of the director and of his staff made real control by the workers over the operation of the enterprise quite rare.[28]

During the late 1940s, the Yugoslav government's agricultural policy did not differ very much from the corresponding policies pursued by other governments in Eastern Europe. The system of compulsory deliveries at low prices was typical of that of other Communist countries; the system was a means to assure food deliveries to the towns, to tax peasants and to discourage the continuation of private land ownership. The Five-Year Plan of 1947 extended little help to agriculture and the government's policy was that the latter should develop on the basis of its own means.

The agricultural sector was largely constituted by smallholdings of less than 5 hectares and these small farms usually had no marketable surplus to sell. The agrarian reform of 1945 had brought about the establishment of 1,000 collective farms, each counting on the average about 50 families. Although these collective farms possessed some of the best arable land in the country, the area of land cultivated by these collectives remained a very small fraction of the total cultivated area in the nation.[29]

In order to disprove the *Cominform* charges, the Yugoslav government decided in 1949 to start a massive collectivization drive in the
agrarian sector. During that year, the number of collective farms expanded by six times.[30] An increase in the speed of collectivization was
also probably pushed in 1949 because of the desire of the government
to control more efficiently the inflation of "free agricultural prices."
The cost index of foodstuffs, had risen from 463 in 1947 to 714 in 1948.
This inflation of foodstuff prices was diminishing the purchasing
power of wage and salary earners at the very same time when the
political difficulties with the Soviet Bloc threatened to bring about
political factionalism in the country.

Though productivity in the socialized agricultural sector was generally higher than in the private one and although collective farms
received preferential tax treatment, Yugoslav peasants showed on the
whole great reluctance to abandon their small, privately held farms.
The coercive collectivization measures of 1949 induced them to oppose
collectivization by reducing output; this trend is shown in Table 6.4.
After 1949, the expansion of agricultural output was handicapped by
the severe droughts of 1950 and 1952 as well as by the shortage of
synthetic fertilizers, largely due to the East European economic blockade. The utilization of fertilizers in 1951 was only one-fifth of that
provided by the Plan of 1947.

TABLE 6.4

PRODUCTIVITY IN AGRICULTURE

Crop	Year	Yield per Hectare		
		State Farm	Collective	Private
Wheat	1949	15.8	14.5	14.0
	1950	14.0	10.6	10.0
	1951	16.3	13.5	12.6
	1952	10.2	8.5	9.3
Corn	1949	19.8	18.6	16.3
	1950	13.7	10.4	9.0
	1951	20.7	18.4	16.6
	1952	9.9	7.4	6.1
Potatoes	1949	88.3	94.3	88.0
	1950	41.3	35.9	44.5
	1951	82.7	71.5	71.8
	1952	54.7	42.0	48.1

Source: Ekonomski Institut, F.N.R.J., *Privreda F.N.R.J. u 1952 godini*, Table 94.

Although UNRRA aid ended in 1947 and although after 1948 Yugoslavia was in great need of expanding exports of agricultural commodities, Table 6.5 shows that it was not until 1957 that the rural sector reached a period of sustained increase in output.

The failure of the 1949 collectivization drive to bring about a rapid expansion in agricultural production and the fear of the consequences of strong peasant opposition to the program induced the government to pass new legislation in March 1953 which allowed individual members of collective farms to leave them, taking with them the land they had contributed to the collective. Peasants responded immediately by leaving the collectives in large numbers. In May 1953, a new agrarian reform program limited private holdings in land to 10 hectares. Land appropriated by the government under the new law was exclusively reserved for transfer to collective and state farms. This law did not see the disappearance of the production inefficiencies due to excessive land fragmentation and did not solve the problem of shortages of raw materials and equipment.

TABLE 6.5

AGRICULTURAL PRODUCTION INDICES
1939 = 100

Year	Index	Year	Index
1947	89	1955	116
1948	103	1956	97
1949	103	1957	140
1950	75	1958	124
1951	106	1959	163
1952	75	1960	146
1953	106	1961	141
1954	94	1962	142

Source: *Statistički Godišnjak F.N.R.J.*, 1962, p. 107.

The Transition Period of 1953 to 1957

1953 not only brought important modifications of the political system of the country, but it also marked the beginning of a new economic system. This system completely abandoned the Soviet planning model. The government's position was that although a highly centralized planning system had been necessary in earlier years to allow the mobilization of sufficient investment for the rapid reconstruction and industrialization of an agrarian economy, the foundations of a new industrial sector had now been erected, and rigid, centralized, compulsory planning had to give way to a new system of "socialist self-government." There were no long-term plans of development during the years 1953 to 1956. Instead, the economy developed under the guidance of annual, indicative plans.

The government's policy was to formulate short-term plans which simply described the general lines of desired investment policy and which contained production, consumption, productivity and employment forecasts. The new Federal Planning Institute, which replaced the old Central Planning Commission, worked out a set of production goals for key industries in the country. These goals were determined with the assistance of planning officials of the Republics and with that of representatives of people's committees and of workers' councils. These production goals were not mandatory and were not legally binding on enterprises. The latter were relatively free to determine their own input and output mix and to formulate their own yearly production plans. The plans of the enterprises were to be drawn with proper consideration being given to market forces. The government's objective was to obtain an interplay between the social ownership of the means of production and free market forces to obtain an efficient allocation of resources at the micro level. The combination of markets and governmental control was to guide the economy toward desired national objectives.

The management board of the enterprise was given great discretion in the formulation of the annual plan for the enterprise. If, however, the enterprise should fail to achieve the goals stipulated by its own plan, then, the pertinent people's committee could take action to assure the efficient operation of the concern. The committee had the power to determine the types and quantities of products the enterprise would have to produce, to fix prices for these products and to appoint a temporary manager for enterprise. The committee could even liquidate the enterprise if the latter continued to operate in an unsatisfactory way.

In order to guide the economy along desired lines, the government retained a number of controls which included direct investment by the federal government in new industry, taxation, foreign trade regulation, the power to impose ceiling prices in monopoly industries and, perhaps most important of all, the control of interest reates which enterprises now had to pay for borrowing capital.

The new economic system that came into being in 1953 changed the way in which investment was financed. Before 1953, investments were simply government grants or budgetary allocations not subject to repayment. From 1953 on, investible funds could only be obtained from the government in the form of loans which had to be repaid and which commanded an interest charge. These loans were provided by "general investment funds" established at the federal, republic and local government levels. Loans were granted on a competitive and selective basis. Individual enterprises had to bid for these funds and the rate of interest was determined by demand and supply. Terms of repayment varied among industries and depended on the relative economic importance attached to them by the government.[31]

Although industry and mining continued to claim the lion's share of total investment during the 1950s, investment in these sectors peaked in 1952, and declined thereafter, both in absolute terms and as a percentage of total gross investment. After 1952, there were noticeable investment increases in agriculture and transport, as shown in Table 6.6.

TABLE 6.6

GROSS INVESTMENT PER ECONOMIC SECTOR
In billions of 1956 Dinars and percentages of gross investment

	1947-1949 Amt.	%	1950-1952 Amt.	%	1953-1956 Amt.	%	1957-1958 Amt.	%
Industry	134.2	51.5	193.5	67.8	192.1	61.9	162.0	43.8
Agriculture	22.8	8.8	17.4	6.1	23.6	7.6	58.7	15.9
Forestry	8.8	3.4	3.3	1.2	5.7	1.8	6.6	1.8
Building	9.9	3.8	10.4	3.6	9.3	3.0	13.7	3.7
Transport	70.1	26.9	52.6	18.4	61.0	19.7	100.4	27.2
Commerce	13.4	5.1	7.1	2.5	15.7	5.1	23.2	6.3
Crafts	1.4	0.5	1.2	0.4	2.9	0.9	5.0	1.3
Total	260.6	100	285.5	100	310.3	100	369.6	100

Source: Investments in the Post-War Economic Development, *Yugoslav Survey*, Vol. 1, No. 1, April 1960, p. 37.

The performance of the economy started improving after 1953, in spite of the continued economic blockade by the Soviet Bloc and in spite of the adverse effects of severe droughts in 1952 and 1954. While national income increased on the average by 1.9% per year during the period 1948-1952, its rate of yearly growth attained 8.4% during the next three years and climbed to 13% in the period 1957-1960.[32] Aggregate investment, as a percentage of national income, continued to be high. The investment rate, which averaged 26.3% per year in the period 1947-1952, averaged 21.6% during 1953-1956 and 20.4% during 1956-1958.

Table 6.7 illustrates the fact that the share of aggregate industrial investment going to basic industries increased until 1952, but declined after that year to the benefit of the hydro-electric power and light industries.

TABLE 6.7

INDUSTRIAL INVESTMENT
Average Yearly Shares in %

	1947-1949	1950-1952	1953-1956	1957-1958
Power	28.2	30.2	34.0	36.6
Basic Industry	47.0	53.4	47.1	31.4
Processing, Light Industries	24.2	16.4	18.9	30.3
Other	0.6	—	—	1.7
Total	100	100	100	100

Source: Investments in the Post-War Economic Development, *Yugoslav Survey, op. cit.* p. 41.

The priority attached to the growth of basic industries during the period of the First Five-Year Plan allowed the economy to operate after 1953 on the basis of a much larger productive capacity than that which existed before the war. Industrial production was also stimulated by more rational and efficient managerial techniques.

TABLE 6.8

PRODUCTION INDICES
1939 = 100

	1950	1951	1952	1953	1954	1955
Total Industrial Output	172	166	164	183	208	242
Production Equipment	510	534	582	757	785	917
Raw Materials	160	153	156	169	193	228
Consumer Goods	165	162	142	160	184	207

Source: *Yugoslav Facts & Views*, No. 28, July 1957, p. 15.

By 1955, Yugoslavia could boast of having built a modern industrial complex within a single decade. New iron and steel works were built between 1948 and 1955. Among the new additions to the industrial sector were the *Ivo Lola Ribar* machine tool factories at Zeleznik, heavy machinery works at Listostroj near Ljubljana, the automobile plant at Maribor, new electrical equipment works in Zagreb and the *Jugovinil* plastics plant in Split. Three-quarters of the industrial capacity was represented by new or rebuilt factories. The entirety of the engineering and electrical equipment industries was new. Yugoslav industrial achievements during the difficult years 1948 to 1955 were indeed impressive. The prewar exportation of non-processed mineral ores had come to an end. The country no longer exported unfinished timber products as it used to do in the 1930s; plywood and furniture factories added to the value of wood products exports. In 1955, the country was able to produce about 75% of its machinery and electrical equipment needs.

And yet, industrial growth during the first half of the 1950s was restrained by a number of severe difficulties. The droughts of 1950, 1952 and 1954 and the continuation of the Soviet Bloc blockade were in themselves great handicaps to economic growth. Inflationary trends after 1950 added further constraints to the speed of economic expansion. A number of factors contributed to inflation. Lack of foreign exchange and high tariffs kept cheaper foreign commodities out of the country while the stepped-up defense program increased the scarcity and the price of a number of products. The absence of effective competition in certain sectors allowed some producers to set near-monopoly prices and people's committees tended to favor the rapid growth of enterprise profits in order to assure to themselves larger tax revenues.[33] Even though new price controls were introduced in the spring of 1955, prices rose on the average by 5.7% per year during the rest of the decade. The price inflation hindered the growth of exports and imposed additional strains on a balance of payments which was unable to avoid the continuation of deficits in spite of the Western aid Yugoslavia started receiving after 1949.[34]

In spite of these difficulties, Yugoslavia achieved in the period 1953 to 1960 one of the highest rates of growth of national income and of industrial production in Europe; see Table 6.9.

The rapid growth of Yugoslav industrial production after 1953 was mostly due to the increase in productive capacity achieved in earlier years. This increase was obtained by sacrificing consumption, housing and agriculture.

During the period 1947 to 1952, total personal consumption declined by 7.8%, while per capita consumption fell by 12%. Although total consumption started rising at an annual rate of 5.5% in the period 1953 to 1956, the rate of growth of aggregate consumption still lagged behind the rate of increase of national income in that period.[35]

TABLE 6.9

AVERAGE ANNUAL RATE OF GROWTH BY
INDIVIDUAL SECTORS IN THE ECONOMY
%

	1948-52	1953-56	1957-60	1948-60
National Income	1.9	8.4	13.0	7.2
Industrial Production	6.4	12.8	14.2	10.7
Agricultural Prod.	−1.5	4.1	10.5	4.9
Building & Construction	−0.9	−2.0	16.2	3.8
Transport	7.9	9.5	13.3	9.6

Source: Federal Executive Council, *Plan of Economic Development of Yugoslavia, 1961-65*, Belgrade, 1961, p. 42.

Investment in housing followed a similar trend. In spite of great housing needs, caused both by wartime destruction and by the migration of people from rural areas to the cities, the priority attached to the industrialization program kept investment in housing quite insignificant until 1960. Though gross national product doubled in the period 1952 to 1960, investment in housing rose during these years from 2.2% to 5.6% of gross national product. In 1960, the value of housing construction still represented only 30.4% of the total value of construction work done in that year.

Agriculture, unlike industry, remained a laggard sector for ten years after the end of the war. Until 1955, agricultural production was practically at a standstill. The area of cultivated land in 1951 was 11% smaller than it had been in 1939. Agricultural stagnation was in part due to peasant opposition to the forced collectivization of 1949, in part, to other causes such as insufficient investment in agriculture, excessive land fragmentation, a climate where the risk of drought is high and, until 1953, exceedingly low prices of agricultural products.

TABLE 6.10

AGRICULTURAL PRODUCTION INDICES
1939 = 100

Year	1947	1948	1949	1950	1951	1952	1953	1954	1955	1956	1957
	93	107	107	78	110	78	110	97	120	100	145

Conclusion

The Yugoslav government, once the war ended, undertook to re-construct and transform the country's economy in the Soviet image. The Five-Year Plan of 1947 gave the State unlimited power in the direction and implementation of economic development. Yugoslavia was to copy faithfully the economic system of the Soviet Union.

Yugoslavia's expulsion from the *Cominform* brought a drastic change in the country's political and economic orientation. The same Yugoslav government now rejected any form of state centralization and embraced a new political philosophy, that of "participatory Socialism." Participatory Socialism meant social, rather than sate ownership of productive property; it meant a substantial control by workers over their activities and the fruit of these activities, as well as a similar control by citizens in general over social life; it connoted a rapid decentralization of political and economic authority. In particular, it implied the abandonment of centralized economic planning and the adoption of the market mechanism for the allocation of resources. Since both Marx and Engels failed to describe the features of the future socialist order and were rather vague about the extent of workers' participation and control in the post-capitalist society, the Tito government could justly claim that its reform program of the early 1950s would have met with the approval of both Marx and Engels. As Marx had written, "What is to be avoided above all is the re-establishing of 'Society' as an abstraction vis-à-vis the individual. The individual *is the social being.*" [36]

If we do not pay much attention to political labels, it appears that the Yugoslav indicative plans of the mid-1950s very closely followed the methods of the French planning system. In 1955, the Yugoslav economic system on the whole bore a greater resemblance to the West German "social market economy" than to the economic systems of

Eastern Europe. Yugoslavia, just like most "neo-capitalist" countries of Western Europe, had embraced a mixed economy in which both public and private initiative played important roles in the process of economic growth.

NOTES

1. Industry in 1939 contributed only 26% of the national income. The small part of industrial production in overall output made capital formation difficult and resulted in low rates of economic growth. Between 1923 and 1939, national income increased on the average by 2.4% a year, while industrial production rose at an average yearly rate of 3.8%. "Investments in the Post-War Economic Development," *Yugoslav Survey*, vol. 1, (April 1960), p. 35.

2. United Nations, Economic Commission for Europe, *Economic Survey of Europe in 1953, Part III (Geneva, 1954), pp. 106-119.*

3. *In 1939*, 44.6% of the population was illiterate and only 50.1% of all children of school age attended school. B. Horvat, "Yugoslav Economic Policy in the Post-War Period: Problems, Ideas, Institutional Developments," *The American Economic Review*, Supplement, (June 1971), p. 71.

4. United Nations, Economic and Social Council, Report on the World Social Situation, *Planning for Balanced Social and Economic Development in Yugoslavia* (New York, April 1962), p. 8.

5. M.G. Zaninovich, *The Development of Socialist Yugoslavia* (Baltimore: The Johns Hopkins Press, 1968), p. 23.

6. C. Bobrowski, *La Yougoslavie Socialiste* (Paris, A. Colin, 1956), p. 67.

7. *Ibid.,*

8. A. B. Ulam, *Titoism and the Cominform* (Cambridge: Harvard University Press, 1952), p. 45. The author notices that during this period the Communist policy of political toleration went so far that in Poland, members of prewar Fascist organizations were allowed to publish newspapers and to engage in various forms of political activity, while as late as February 1948, Clement Gottwald assured Czech peasants and small businessmen that the process of socialization would be gradual and limited.

9. Bobrowski, *La Yougoslavie Socialiste*, p. 69.

10. Zakon o nacionaliji privatnih privrednih preduzeća od 5 Decembra 1946 — Law on Nationalization of Private Economic Enterprises of 5 December 1946 — Law No. 677, *Službeni list F.N.R.J.* — Official Gazette F.P.R.Y. (Dec. 5, 1946), pp. 1245-47.

11. Zakon o agrarnoj reformi i kolonizaciji od 23 Augusta 1945 — Law No. 605, *Službeni list SFJ* (August 28, 1945), pp. 621-24.

12. United Nations, Economic Commission for Europe, *Economic Survey of Europe in 1953* (Geneva, 1954), pp. 106-22.

13. United Nations, Economic and Social Council, *Planning for Social and Economic development in Yugoslavia*, supra, p. 15.

14. Law on the Five-Year Plan, Belgrade, 1947, Article 12.

15. B. Kidric, *Borba* (August 26, 1951), p. 3.

16. The total gross power potential in the country was estimated to be 108 billion kwh of which only 0.9% was available in 1939. United Nations Economic and Social Council, *Planning for Balanced Social and Economic Development in Yugoslavia, p. 10.*

17. *The Cominform communiqué* of June 28, 1948 stated that in Yugoslavia, "where

individual peasant farming predominates, where there is private property in land and where land can be bought and sold, where much of the land is concentrated in the hands of the kulaks . . . there could be no question of correct Marxist policies being applied." A. B. Ulam, *Titoism and the Cominform* (Cambridge: Harvard University Press, 1952), p. 119.

18. *Ibid.*, p. 78.

19. *Ibid.*, p. 76.

20. The Royal Institute of International Affairs, *The Soviet-Yugoslav Dispute* (London and New York: Oxford University Press, 1948).

21. *Borba*, April 28, 1950. The U. N., Economic Commission for Europe, estimates these figures as 56.1% and 52.7% in 1947 and as 14% and 13.6% in 1949.

22. United Nations, Economic Commission for Europe, *Economic Survey of Europe in 1953*, Part III, Ch. 8, p. 111.

23. Zaninovich, *Development of Socialist Yugoslavia*, supra, p. 73.

24. E. Kardelj, "The Meaning and Importance of the Changes in Organization of Economy and Self-Government in Yugoslavia," *The Yugoslav Law* (October — December 1951), p. 37.

25. Osnovini zakon o upravljanju drzavnim privrednim preduzecima i visim prevrednim udruzenjima od stane radnih kolektiva od 2 Jula 1950 — Basic Law on the Administration of State Economic Enterprises and Higher Economic Associations from the Standpoint of Workers Collectives of 2 July 1950 — Law No. 391, *Sluzbeni list FNRJ, VI, 43* (July 5, 1950), pp. 789-93.

26. B. Ward, "Workers' Management in Yugoslavia," *The Journal of Political Economy*, vol. LXV (October 1957), pp. 374-75.

27. E. Kardelj, *Borba* (April 2, 1952), p. 1.

28. Ward, "Workers' Management in Yugoslavia," p. 384.

29. At the end of 1948, the private agricultural sector still represented 93.8% of all arable land. Zaninovich, *Development of Socialist Yugoslavia*, p. 55.

30. The areas of arable land acquired by collective farms were as follows: 1946, 121.5 million hectares; 1948, 324.0 million hectares; 1949, 1,839.9 million hectares. U.N., Economic and Social Council, *Planning for Balanced Social and Economic Development in Yugoslavia*, p. 17.

31. F. W. Neal, *Titoism in Action* (Berkeley: University of California Press, 1952), pp. 127-32.

32. Federal Executive Council, *Plan of Economic Development of Yugoslavia, 1961-1965* (Belgrade, 1961), p. 42.

33. *Borba* (October 30, 1954), p. 1.

34. *Borba* (December 28, 1954), p. 1.

35. Indeed, the share of total consumption in national income fell from 39.1% in 1953 to 35.2% in 1956. It was only after 1957 that the rate of growth of total consumption approximated the rate of growth of national income. United Nations, Economic and Social Council, *Planning for Balanced Social and Economic Development in Yugoslavia*, supra, p. 46.

36. K. Marx, *Economic and Philosophical Manuscripts of 1844* (Moscow: Progress Publishers, 1959), p. 98.

PART II

SINCE 1955

CHAPTER 7

FRANCE UNDER DE GAULLE AND POMPIDOU

General de Gaulle started his seven-year presidency on January 8, 1959. He chose as his Prime Minister his loyal friend Michel Debré, a man dedicated to the preservation of the planning system in France. If de Gaulle's victory at the polls in November, 1958, brought to France a new Republic, planning in the country retained the essence of the procedures developed by Jean Monnet. Although the goals of the national plans changed over time, the calculations and decisions of government planners continued to be reviewed and modified in the days of the Fifth Republic by numerous modernization committees made up by thousands of industrialists, trade union officials, farmers' representatives and independent experts. The concurrence or divergence in the views of both official planners and committee advisors moulded the details of the final draft of plans, a draft which was further scrutinized by government agencies representing various interest groups in the country. Such an agency was the *Conseil Supérieur du Plan* which was charged with the tasks of supervising the execution of the plan and of recommending changes or revisions if it appeared that the plan could not be carried out with success in the prescribed time period. The *Conseil Economique et Social* which had to recommend to the Planning Commission at the start of the planning process a ranking of economic and social investment priorities as well as a desirable global rate of growth, also broadly represented the various economic groups in French society. The continued success of French planning was mainly due to the fact that both businessmen and trade union officials participated in the formulation of the plans, these plans gaining thereby the support of both management and labor.

The first two plans focused on the achievement of economic reconstruction and development. The targets of the First Plan, covering the years 1946 to 1952, were on the whole met in 1952-1953. France returned to the 1929 standard of living by 1950-1951. The Monnet Plan had stressed the development of basic industries. Unlike this plan, the Second Plan attempted to increase productive capacity throughout the entire economy. This plan's duration was four years, 1954 to 1957, and it proposed to raise gross domestic product by 25%. This target was exceeded, gross domestic product increasing by 30% in spite of serious manpower shortages and inflation.[1] It is interesting to notice that during these years the government continued to follow a policy which gave more importance to output growth than to the control of inflation. The authorities felt that businessmen had to be induced to expand production without fear of possible governmental deflationary policies. Balance of payments difficulties were to be solved, at least in part, not by restricting home demand, but through import controls and devaluation.

The Third Plan, covering the years 1958 to 1961, was started under adverse conditions. Inflation and increasing balance of payments difficulties brought the financial crisis of 1958. The plan contemplated an increase in gross domestic product of 27% above the 1956 level; this target was downgraded to 23% in the revised "Interim Plan" for 1960 and 1961, a two-year plan which tried to compensate for the economic slowdown in 1958 and 1959. The revised global rate of growth was achieved in 1961, and aggregate investments did not fall short of the initial targets.[2]

The Third Plan's production and investment objectives were calculated with the help of improved statistical techniques, and an input-output matrix based on the year 1954 was used for the first time by French planners. A great deal of attention was given to the development of a pattern of growth which would favor both internal and external equilibrium. The Plan was a careful attempt to develop a well-integrated national program whose goals now also included the satisfaction of social needs, such as education, health, housing and urban renewal.

Except for agricultural output, the Third Plan's output goals were fulfilled. By 1961, 316,000 housing units had been built instead of the planned 300,000. The overall output of "non-basic" industries fell below the goal set by the Interim Plan but the growth experienced by these industries still indicated that the Third Plan had been carried out with some success.

The Fourth Plan, 1962 to 1965, was the product of a high degree of sophistication applied in the calculations of the statisticians and econometricians of the *Commissariat du Plan* and the *Services des Etudes Economiques et Financières*. Regional planning was carefully integrated into the global plan and cultural and urban investments received top priorities. Social goals commanded as much weight as economic goals and the plan stressed the desirability of a rapid expansion of community services. Projections and achievements of the Fourth Plan are shown in Table 7.1.

TABLE 7.1

THE FOURTH PLAN: PROJECTIONS FOR 1965
AND ACHIEVEMENT LEVELS

	1965 Index 1961 = 100		Annual Growth Rate %	
	Projected	Achieved	Projected	Achieved
Gross domestic output	124	124.1	5.5	5.5
Consumption	122.5	124.6	5.2	5.7
Gross capital formation	130.0	136.6	6.8	8.1
Productive investment	128.0	125.1	5.4	5.8
Housing	125.4	159.2	5.8	12.4
Government	150.0	151.5	10.7	11.0
Imports	123.0	151.1	5.3	10.9
Exports	120.0	130.3	4.7	6.8

Source: United Nations, Economic and Social Council, *Planning for Balanced Social and Economic Development in France*, New York, 1967, p. 21.

This plan, which was to become a model of indicative planning in Europe, tried to present to each decision-making entity in the economy a detailed survey of the country's economic future which could be helpful in guiding the policies of every decision-making unit in France. The main purposes of the plan were to facilitate the coordination of the activities of the various economic sectors and to help in the achievement of socially desirable long-term goals without any impairment of the existing market mechanism. In the words of Pierre Massé, the General Planning Commissioner, the plan expressed "the search for a middle way between attachment to individual freedom and intitiative, and a common development purpose; its principles are naturally less absolute, its methods less simple than in a true market economy or one with complete central planning."[3]

The plan called for growth rates of 24% for aggregate production, 23% for consumption and 50% for community services. Although the successful execution of the plan seemed to be threatened in 1963 by an insufficient growth of productive investment and by inflation, the targets set by the plan were generally met and a global average yearly rate of growth of 5.5% was achieved.

In its methods and coverage, the Fifth Plan, 1966-1970, was similar to its predecessor. The plan purported to follow a "strategy of balanced expansion" which gave emphasis to both economic and social goals. An additional objective was, however, of equal importance. The plan was to promote the strengthening of the competitive capacity of French industry. As in the Monnet Plan, a great deal of attention was given to the future growth of French industry. In this regard, regional development plans were extended far beyond what they had been in the Fourth Plan. The Fifth Plan also included a non-mandatory prices and incomes policy which was to help in the attainment of the plan's economic and social targets and which allowed the planners to state these targets and their forecasts in terms of real monetary values rather than in terms of unadjusted monetary values or in terms of physical quantities. An early warning system, based on a number of economic indicators, was to inform the planning agency about unpredicted changes in trends so that appropriate measures could be taken and targets could be revised at the proper time.[4]

Planning procedures continued to be based on the democratic system developed by Jean Monnet. Modernization committees remained an important instrument in the preparation of the plan. Committee members continued to discuss, verify and correct the initial forecasts prepared by government planners. Some committees specialized in the study of the development of a given economic sector, e.g., agriculture, engineering, railroad transportation. Others dealt with the development of social activities, e.g., education, urban development, health. So-called "horizontal committees" were responsible for national or multi-sectoral problems such as finance and employment. Counting all the members of the various working groups established for each of these committees, over 5,000 persons participated in the preparation of the Fifth Plan.

The consultation by planners with regional committees established in twenty-one regions of the country was a procedural innovation designed to help in the effectiveness of regional planning. These regional economic development committees, CODER, were made up by local office-holders such as mayors and local officials, and by representatives of professional, trade union and social organizations. Half of the membership of these committees had to be composed of members of union, agricultural, and employers' organizations.

The plan aimed at an annual growth rate of 5% for gross domestic output, of 5.8% for productive gross capital formation, of 8.9% for exports and of 4.5% for household consumption.

In spite of the difficulties brought about by the events of May 1968, the targets of the plan were once again attained.

Obstacles to Effective French Planning
A. Inflation

French economic growth in the 1950s and in the 1960s was above average in Europe. Economic growth in France was, however, accompanied by succeeding waves of inflation. France was not the only European country to experience almost chronic inflation during this period, but French inflation tended to be more severe than inflation in other European countries. Between 1950 and 1966, the price index of the French gross national product increased by 143%. The corresponding figures were 69% for West Germany and 80% for the United Kingdom.[5]

Although "cost-push" factors played an important role in the formation of these inflationary waves, it is equally true that these also fed on the unfettered growth of home demand. The government's deliberate choice not to restrict the growth of this demand in any way strengthened the home demand for imports and tended to weaken the growth of exports. The outcome of this price policy was a series of balance of payments crises in the 1950s.

In the period 1950 to 1970, there were three sub-periods of particularly accelerated inflation. While the interval which separated the first sub-period from the second was characterized by relative price stability, the time interval separating the second from the third sub-period witnessed continuous mild inflation. The first of these sub-periods coincided with the start of the Korean War, and a sharp price increase developed between July 1950 and the end of 1951. During this period, the wholesale price index rose by 46%. This index then remained relatively stable until October 1956 when another wave of inflation developed, lasting until December 1959. Between the end of 1956 and the end of 1959, the wholesale price index rose by 27%. The index continued to rise until the spring of 1966, rising on the average by about 2.3% per year. Inflation weakened between the spring of 1966 and the spring of 1968, but a new outburst of inflation pushed up the wholesale price index by 19% between mid-1968 and the beginning of 1970.[6]

The Korean War inflation was principally a "cost-push" type inflation. Between June 1950 and April 1951, the wholesale price index of imports doubled; it then fell by 28% until December 1951. During the second half of 1951, inflation was largely due to a series of government decisions whose result was a marked increase in production costs. The guaranteed minimum wage, the S.M.I.G., was increased by 11.5% in March 1951, and again by 15% in September of the same year. Coal, electricity and railroad transportation prices were also twice increased during the year, the wholesale price of coal increasing by 45% in 1951, that of electricy by 31%, while railroad freight rates rose by 33%. At the same time, the government followed a policy of "easy money" and bank credit expanded by 40% in 1951.[7]

A rapid increase in productive capacity, a moderate growth of domestic demand, an expansion of the agricultural output in the years 1952 to 1954 and relatively modest wage increases contributed to a period of relative price stability between 1952 and 1955. An export boom and wage increases in 1955 started a strong expansion of domestic demand, a demand which was further strengthened by increases in military expenditures in 1956. At the same time, the mobilization of reservists for military operations in Algeria introduced labor shortages in France. In the fall, the Suez crisis brought a sharp increase in the prices of oil products and the wholesale price index of industrial commodities started rising. During the following three years, repeated increases of the minimum guaranteed wage strengthened inflationary forces in the economy; between July, 1957, and November, 1959, the S.M.I.G. was increased six times.

The years 1960-1967 were characterized by mild but persistent inflation, the rate of price inflation varying between 2.3% and 5% per year. A number of "cost-push" factors explain in part this long period of inflation. The cost of imported raw materials rose during most of these years, the index of wholesale prices of imported raw materials increasing by 12% between 1962 and 1967. Prices of domestic agricultural products rose more rapidly during this period than the general price level and increases in the prices of foodstuffs in turn justified increases in the wage level. Finally, government during these years sharply increased the burden of social security taxes imposed on employers. Concurrently, and until 1963, the easy money policy followed by the government added to the "cost-push" elements of the inflation strong "demand-pull" factors.

A change in government policy came in 1963 under the direction of M. Giscard d'Estaing who had become Finance Minister in 1962, a few months before M. Debré was replaced by M. Pompidou as Prime Minister. D'Estaing was not an enthusiastic supporter of the planning system and his stabilization program of 1963 considerably weakened the significance of planning during the remainder of the 1960s. The program introduced strict price controls; prices were generally fixed at the level existing on August 31, 1962. Wages were frozen and the credit boom was stopped through a number of restrictions which were maintained until mid-1965. While the money supply had increased on the average by 16% per year between 1960 and 1963, this rate of increase declined to 7% for the period 1964 and 1967. In spite of these measures, inflationary pressures in the economy did not disappear and a new outburst of inflation was introduced by the events of 1968.

Inflation not only increases prices, but it also brings about disorganizations in the price structure. Prices of different commodities respond differently to the impact of inflationary pressures. The absence of uniformity in the growth of prices tends to make economic calculations and economic forecasts quite difficult and is thus an impediment in the formulation of contracts and economic plans. More important than these interior effects of inflation is the impact of inflation on the balance of payments.

During the years of the First and Second Plans, the French government attached more importance to rapid economic growth than to price stability. A restriction of home demand as a means to combat inflation and a chronic trade deficit was never advocated, even during the early years of the Fifth Republic. The traditional French policy was to remedy balance of payments difficulties through the imposition of import controls, as was done in 1952 and in 1957, through various types of aid to exporters and through devaluation. The franc was devalued by 17.5% in December 1958, and was again devalued in

August 1969. This policy tended to shield French enterprise against adverse international developments and contributed to the maintenance of French firms' willingness to invest.

The entry of France into the European Economic Community forced French planners to pay more attention to the possible effects of increased international competition. The Third Plan gave great emphasis to the development of import-competing industries. At the same time, the devaluation of 1958 allowed France to stabilize externally by the end of the year. The increased competitiveness given by this devaluation to French exports resulted in the maintenance of external equilibrium during the years 1959-1962.

A decline in German demand for French products started weakening French exports in the fall of 1961; at the same time, the value of French imports went on increasing and the French balance of trade was threatened with a deficit in 1963. The stabilization program of 1963 succeeded in stopping the growth of imports and a balance of trade equilibrium was reached at the start of 1965. Large inflows of long-term foreign investments and the repatriation of French capital resulting from a growth of confidence in the stability of the value of the franc, played a large role in maintaining a balance of payments equilibrium in the years 1963 and 1964.

The renewal of inflation in 1968 and the country's economic *malaise* in that year affected adversely the balance of trade. Following General de Gaulle's defeat in the referendum of April 1969, the government once again decided to stop the deterioration of this balance through a new devaluation of the franc, a devaluation whose effect on French exports was strengthened by the revaluation of the D-Mark which followed soon afterward. The change in the official parities of these two currencies gave French exporters a 20% bonus in the German markets and French exports quickly reacted to the advantages offered by the new exchange rates. By the middle of 1970, equilibrium on current balance of payments account was once again restored.

B. The Insufficiency of Investment

Figure 4 shows that after 1954, total investment taken as a percentage of gross domestic product never declined below 20% and in fact

FIGURE 4

GROWTH OF INVESTMENT AS A PERCENTAGE
OF GROSS DOMESTIC PRODUCT

———————Constant Prices   % Rates   — — — — — —Current Prices

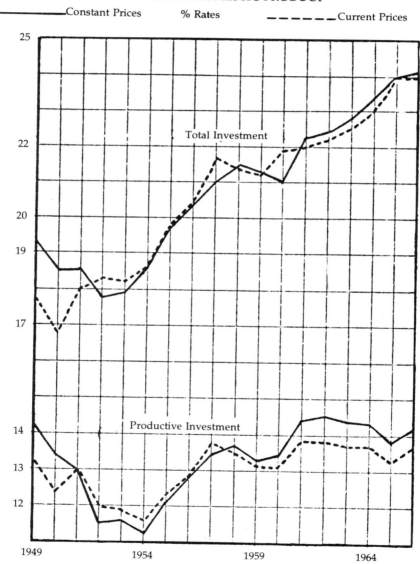

rose gradually to 25% in 1969. Between 1957 and 1960, total domestic investment represented about 21% of the gross domestic product; this ratio increased to 22.7% in 1963, and to 24.1% in 1966. Productive investment tended to follow a parallel trend, although the rate of increase was not as pronounced. Taking productive investment, i.e., investment by producing firms, both public and private, designed to increase their output, to improve their plant and equipment and to raise their productivity, as a percentage of gross domestic product, the ratio was 11.3% in 1954, 14.4% in 1963, and 15% in 1969.

And yet, a major weakness of French private industry throughout the post-war period was its inability to mobilize sufficient capital not only to expand the country's productive capacity, but perhaps more important, to raise French industrial and agricultural productivities. Even though productive investment increased after 1954, the increase was in many instances insufficient to allow the needed gains in productivity required by an economy increasingly subjected to foreign competition. A major modernization of the country's coal and steel industries had been made necessary by France's membership in the European Coal and Steel Community. France, by accepting membership in the European Economic Community, had to agree to a gradual removal of tariff barriers affecting the commerce between itself and the other members of the Common Market, a commerce which was to be totally free of intra-E.E.C. trade restrictions as of 1968. In order to be able to compete with an industrial giant such as the German Federal Republic, French industry, both public and private, needed to expand investment in order to raise French productivity close to the West German level.

In the 1960s, investment in productivity most often meant investment in cybernation. Investment in automation and in computers was expensive and the representative medium-size or small industrial French firm was generally unable to finance the acquisition of this type of equipment. To keep up with technological advances abroad, investment in cybernation had to be supplemented by investment in research. Unlike the case of the United States, the French government played a minor role in financing research and development studies. Only 30% of all research and development investment was financed by the government in France and this public finance tended to support military research projects almost exclusively.[8] In both the 1950s and the 1960s, French private industry faced great difficulties in mobilizing the capital it needed to operate effectively in an environment of ever increasing international competition.

The major sources of private investment are private saving, bank credit, government credit and self-finance. During the post-war years preceding 1954, all of these investment sources were unable to provide the private sector with the funds it needed for expansion and modernization. Inflation discouraged private saving. The mobilization of existing savings by private enterprises was rendered difficult by the fact that until October 1954, new issues of shares of stock and of bonds in excess of 100 million francs by private firms required the permission of the Ministry of Finance. The government, trying to mobilize these savings for imvestment in the public sector, limited the ability of private firms to finance expansion through the sale of stocks and bonds. Bank credit was expensive and small firms were often unable to borrow, banks giving lending preference to large companies. Government lending to the private sector was limited because the authorities chose to direct the bulk of public lending to the nationalized concerns. Finally, the combination of regulated sales prices and rising costs of production resulted in declining profit margins which did not support self-finance for expansion. Self-finance represented only 23% of total investment in the cement industry in 1955, 34% of total investment in the steel industry.

The Pinay deflationary policies of 1952 had initiated a period of relative price stability which was to last until 1956. Price stability brought an expansion of private saving. At the same time, reduced rates of increase in labor, energy and raw materials costs, together with a growing volume of sales made possible by increases in productive capacity, stimulated private investment and allowed firms to raise the share of self-finance in their total investment. A rapid expansion of bank credit after 1955 further boosted investment until 1963.

Between 1963 and 1966, productive investment in the private sector stagnated, a result of the government's stabilization program of 1963. While prices and wages were practically frozen, increasing tax and social security charges made for diminishing profit margins and for a decline in self-finance. During the years 1962 to 1964, self-finance represented 61% of private business investment in France. The corresponding ratio was 68% for Belgium, 80% for the Netherlands and 79% for West Germany.[9]

As productive investment weakened, French firms became more willing to accept the help of foreign çapital and in certain instances, readily sold out managerial control to foreign interests. A notorious example is the take-over by General Electric of *Les Machines Bull* in 1964, a firm that for years had been one of the largest manufacturers of electronic equipment in Europe. From 1959 on, American firms started investing heavily in France, at times setting up their own subsidiaries, at times buying out French firms in spite of governmental opposition. [10]

The insufficiency of French investment in the postwar period is revealed by the relatively small increment in the number of jobs in the economy during the period 1945 to 1965. Three million new jobs were created in France during this period against eleven million in West Germany. Investment deficiencies gave, in turn, cause to rising unemployment, to a diminishing role of French industry within the Common Market and to a slowdown of technological progress. The impact of inadequate investment on technological growth has been described by J. Ardagh as follows:

> One of the most serious results of the shortage of investment has been the lag in scientific research. Although the State spends a fair amount in this field, notably for military purposes, few private firms are conducting nearly enough research to keep them abreast of their world rivals. French opinion has recently woken up to this with a jolt, and the papers have been full of warnings that France spends only 1.5% of her gross national product on research, against 1.8% in Germany, 2.3% in Britain, and well over 3% in both Russia and the U.S.A. The "balance of patents" as it is sometimes called, is severly adverse: that is, France sells only one patent to the U.S. for every five she buys from there; two-thirds of all new patents registered in France are of foreign origin, and France comes only eighth in the world "league table" of originators of patents. [11]

The government's efforts to boost investment after 1965 by increasing public loans had only modest success until 1969. Private firms were unable to obtain all of the finance they desired, largely because over 50% of these loans were extended to nationalized concerns. These private firms strove to finance their modernization, made now imperative by conditions of unrestricted free trade within the area of the E.E.C., by means of bank credit. Bank finance allowed productive investment to rise in 1966. In terms of constant 1963 francs, private productive investment rose from 47 billion francs in 1965 to 52 billion in 1966 and to 60 billion in 1968.[12] This investment expansion was almost entirely based on a increase in the indebtedness of firms. With long-term bank loans commanding an interest rate of over 10%, French production costs were necessarily forced upwards. Compared with the existing situation in rival nations, private investment in France suffered from an excessive recourse to indebtedness and from inadequate self-finance.

C. The Structure of French Industry

French industry is still characterized by an excessive dispersion and by an excessive number of small enterprises trying to survive in the world of the European Common Market by relying on the traditional preferences of the French consumer, by counting on preferential tax treatment and by clinging to an irrational optimism about the economic future. There were 499,000 industrial plants in France in 1963. Average employment per plant was 11 workers, a labor force which was 35% smaller than the corresponding labor force in West Germany. Only 17% of all French industrial establishments employed more than 1,000 workers, as compared with 28% in West Germany and the Netherlands and 25% in Belgium. In 1963, the 50 largest industrial firms in France accounted for only 18% of all industrial sales; in West Germany, the corresponding ratio was 25%.[13]

The 1950s and the 1960s saw a rising trend in the yearly number of mergers and consolidations in France. Although the government encouraged the growth of industrial concentration, this growth was limited by a number of institutional factors. In many industries, particularly in textiles, the prototype firm was a small or medium-size enterprise whose ownership had remained vested during the lives of several generations in one family. For the *patron,* ownership did not only mean direct control and the receipt of dividends, but also represented social standing and prestige in a town or in a region. The firm was the *maison* of the owner and his sons and was to be kept as such for the owner's grandsons. Merger could mean the loss of direct control by the *patron* of a business managed over a long time in the past by men bearing his name. For many French entrepreneurs, the maintenance of traditional ways of doing business appeared to be more important than a higher return on the capital invested in the firm. There was also an apprehension that a merger could lead to the formation of a large concern which could be nationalized some day by the government; this possibility would result in a complete loss of economic and social interests for the present owner-manager. Even the workers opposed mergers. They feared any type of amalgamation which would likely bring about modernization in production techniques, a greater use of labor-saving equipment and a curtailment in the employed labor force.

In France, the survival of small firms was helped by the policies of larger rivals which generally favored the existence of small competitors. In a given industry, prices were set at a level which allowed the small and medium-size firms to survive. The larger firm, operating under conditions of low costs per unit of product, could thereby enjoy substantial profits. The disappearance of small firms would justify a reduction in sales prices which would also diminish the profit margin of the large enterprise.

The government also furthered the maintenance of the traditional industrial structure by giving tax advantages to the small or medium-size firm instead of favoring the large establishment, by granting reimbursements of paid taxes and social security contributions to small exporters and by maintaining tax laws which made the process of merger quite costly.

Compared with the representative size of the industrial firm in other E.E.C. countries, the size of the French firm remained small. The large firm remained the exception in the mechanical industries, in the paper, textile and leather industries, in the sugar refining industry and in many other areas of economic activity. In the textile industry, the average size of the labor force was 91 workers per factory.

Increased international competition in the 1950s forced some sectors of French industry to strive for a higher degree of concentration. The establishment of the European Coal and Steel Community brought an initial step in the direction of merger and large size. A few years later, France's entry into the E.E.C. and the gradual lowering of tariff barriers between the Common Market nations acted as further inducements to merge and consolidate in order to take advantage of large scale economies. In the mid-1960s, the need to produce on a large, internationally competitive scale became more evident when it became clear that conditions of free trade and free competition would apply within the totality of the E.E.C. area as of July 1, 1968. Whereas

modernization and merger still appeared to many French entrepreneurs to amount only to elective luxuries before 1958, industrial
concentration and the adoption of more efficient ways of production
became the *sine qua non* of economic survival after that year.

An initial wave of mergers developed in the early 1950s, a wave
largely limited to the steel industry. A new steel conglomerate, *Sidelor,*
was formed in December 1950 through the merger of the *Aciéries de
Rombas, Forges et Aciéries de la Marine, Aciéries de Saint-Etienne, Aciéries de
Micheville* and the *Aciéries de Pont-à-Mousson.* In October 1953, a new
steel complex resulted from the merger of the steel works of *Longwy,
Senelle-Maubeuge* and *Escaut et Meuse,* the new company taking the
name of *Lorraine-Escaut.* In 1964, the *De Wendel* steel works and *Sidelor*
established a common subsidiary, *Société des Aciéries de Lorraine* or
Sacilor. In 1968, *De Wendel* and *Sidelor* merged.

Merger and amalgamation also developed in other industries in the
1950s. In 1955, the automobile firm *Citroën* acquired 25% of the shares
of its rival, *Pahnard,* and completely took over this firm ten years later.
The airplane manufacturers *Sud-Est* and *Sud-Ouest* merged to form a
new company, *Sud-Aviation.* The government actively encouraged
amalgamation in the shipbuilding industry. The growth of industrial
concentration in the period 1954 to 1962 is shown by the fact that the
number of industrial firms employing more than 200 workers increased by 12% while the number of firms employing less than 50
workers diminished by 18%.

If, on the one hand, modernization and concentration were typical
of the steel, automobile, oil-refining and shipbuilding industries in the
1950s and in the 1960s, many other industries continued to operate on
the basis of thousands of small, uneconomic firms. The survival of the
small family firm had maintained in a large number of industrial
sectors, "the kind of structural defect that holds up economic progress,
and yet its reform requires a more ruthless attack on vested interests
than the Government has yet dared apply."[14]

The Growth of Domestic Output

France reached the levels of production it had attained in 1929 in the
years 1950, 1951. From 1951 on, and until the end of the 1960s, gross
domestic output continued to expand at the average yearly rate of 5%.
Although economic growth in France failed to equal the West German

economic performance, France in the 1950s and in the 1960s was able to maintain a rate of overall economic growth markedly superior to that of the United Kingdom. What makes the postwar French production record particularly interesting is that the yearly growth rate maintained since the end of World War II had never been achieved before 1945. During the entire period 1896 to 1929, French gross domestic output had increased at an average yearly rate of 1.7%; this output not only stopped growing in the 1930s, but actually declined during that decade and the following years of war. The aggregate volume of output in 1946 was 20% smaller than it had been in 1929.[15]

For heuristic reasons, the period 1951 to 1969 can be divided into three sub-periods. During 1951 to 1957, gross domestic product, calculated in terms of 1963 market prices, increased at an average yearly rate of 4.4%. The second sub-period, ending with the stabilization program of 1963, had an average yearly growth rate of 5.4%. The last sub-period, 1963 to 1970, had a corresponding growth rate of 5.1%.

The average yearly growth rate of industrial output for the period 1951 to 1969 was almost identical to the yearly growth rate of gross domestic output in this period. Industrial output grew at an average yearly rate of 5.2%. This rate of growth remained quite stable over the three sub-periods; it was 5% for 1951-1957, 5.3% for 1957-1963 and 5.4% for 1963-1969.[16] Table 7.2 shows gross domestic product for the three sub-periods.

TABLE 7.2

GROSS DOMESTIC PRODUCT AT 1963 PRICES

In billions of Francs

1951	230.17	1961	364.67
1952	236.14	1962	389.02
1953	242.14	1963	411.36
1954	254.82	1964	438.45
1955	269.02	1965	458.84
1956	282.32	1966	484.12
1957	299.19	1967	507.05
1958	306.94	1968	528.56
1959	323.30	1969	572-86
1960	346.09	1970	606.87

Sources: For 1951-1968, OECD, *National Accounts of OECD Countries, 1950-1968*, p. 141; for 1969 and 1970, OECD, *Economic Surveys, France*, Paris, 1972, p. 68.

The expansion of gross domestic output and of industrial output in the postwar period must be evaluated in the light of what happened to the country's active population, i.e., the total population of 15 to 64 years of age, throughout this century. Between 1896 and 1962, France's active population increased by only 0.25 million people, an increase which over a period of more than half a century meant a quasi-stagnation of this population.

As the Table 7.3 shows, France offers the remarkable example of a country which in 1962 had an active population which was smaller than that existing in 1926. Further, the ratio of the active population to total population also gradually declined between the beginning of the century and the end of the 1960s.

TABLE 7.3

EVOLUTION OF ACTIVE POPULATION

Year	Active Population (In Millions)	Percentage of Active to Total Population
1901	19.6	51
1926	20.3	50.5
1946	19.4	48.5
1954	19.6	45.5
1962	19.7	42.5
1968	20.6	41

Source: J.J. Carré et al, *La Croissance Française,* supra, p. 77.

Between 1946 and 1962, the active population increased by only 0.1% per year. A marked change took place after 1962, when this growth rate increased to 0.6%. This change was mainly due to the coming of age of the large number of babies born in the late 1940s. Still, in spite of the postwar baby boom, France employed fewer workers in its "productive" sectors in 1969 than it had employed in the same activities in 1929. The data in Table 7.4 show that 18.2 million persons were employed in the "productive" sector in 1929, whereas only 16.7 million were so employed forty years later.

Given an almost stagnating active population, a population which counted only 230,000 more people in 1969 than in 1929, production increases in the postwar period cannot be explained in terms of an expanding labor force. In the case of France, the growth in production has to be explained in terms of sustained increases in labor productivity after 1945, increases made possible by rapid capital accumulation.

TABLE 7.4

EVOLUTION OF VARIOUS GROUPS IN THE ACTIVE POPULATION

(In 1,000)

Year	Total Active Population	Unemployed	Persons in the Armed Forces	Number Employed in Non-Productive Sectors	Number Employed in Productive Sectors
1929	20,540	240		2,100	18,200
1949	19,500	240	210	2,480	16,570
1951	19,560	230	230	2,520	16,580
1954	19,610	310	310	2,640	16,350
1957	19,880	160	610	2,740	16,370
1962	19,750	230	510	2,910	16,100
1969	20,770	360	250	3,410	16,750

Source: Ibid., p. 80

Between 1949 and 1969, labor productivity defined in terms of production per man-hour increased by 5.2% per year for the entire economy, by 5.3% per year for industry alone.[17] These growth rates were much larger than those experienced by the French economy during all periods prior to 1945; not only were these rates higher, but they maintained their levels in the 1950s and in the 1960s. Labor productivity for the entire economy increased by about 6% per year between 1949 and 1951, by 5% between 1951 and 1963. For industry alone, the corresponding rates were 7% and 4.9%. Overall labor productivity, still defined in terms of production per man-hour, increased at an average yearly rate of 4.9% during the years 1951 to 1957 and at a yearly rate of 5.1% during 1957 to 1969. Gains in productivity were thus maintained in the 1950s and in the 1960s.

The postwar increase in labor productivity was made possible by the sustained growth of net capital, and particularly, by the expansion of net "productive" capital, i.e., the totality of new plant, equipment and transportation facilities of producing enterprises. Since "productive" capital represented at least 60% of global capital, its rate of growth was an important determinant of the rate of increase of labor productivity. French economists have estimated that net "productive" capital grew at an average yearly rate of 3.4% between 1949 and 1966. This rate of growth averaged 4.4% in the 1960.s[18]

The growth of capital was in turn made possible by high and rising levels of aggregate investment. Calculated in terms of 1956 prices, total investment in France represented 19.7% of gross domestic product in

1949, 21% in 1957, 24.1% in 1964 and 25% in 1969. The growth of net "productive" investment paralleled the growth of total investment. The maintenance of such high levels of investment allowed the country to expand rapidly the productive capacity of certain key sectors and thus explains output increases in the face of a stagnating labor force. Although the bulk of this investment went to public enterprises and to large private concerns, the growth of this investment still constituted the principal causal factor of France's postwar economic growth.

The Young Farmers' Revolution

In the 1950s, the standard of living of the French peasant tended to deteriorate as prices of fertilizers, of agricultural machinery and of industrial goods in general increased much more rapidly than prices of agricultural commodities. Increases in agricultural productivity were unable to offset the deterioration in the terms of trade of the agricultural sector. Productivity increases were slowed down by the inefficient methods of production carried on four-fifths of the country's farms whose size did not exceed 50 acres and by the strong conservatism of the French *paysan*. Most French farmers were simply not interested in the possibility of producing more efficiently. Throughout the 1950s, peasants opposed the government's policy of *remembrement*, a policy which attempted to induce peasants to voluntarily exchange their scattered plots of land for the purpose of land consolidation. The peasant found it difficult to exchange the *parcelles* he had inherited from countless ancestors, even though the government agreed to pay up to 80% of all the surveying, legal and other costs pertaining to the reorganization of ownership units. Instead of accepting land consolidation and improved methods of production, most peasants chose to continue working in the traditional manner while demanding from government ever higher price support levels for their products. They rallied around conservative right-wing politicians such as Henri Dorgeres and Paul Antier who, instead of being interested in the reorganization and the modernization of French agriculture, felt that their task should be limited to the extraction of desired levels of price support from the governments of the Fourth Republic. When inflation weakened the benefits the peasantry obtained from these supports, farmers turned to political demonstrations usually consisting of road blockages by tractors, the destruction of crops and the spilling of milk.

No one advocated better methods of production and of distribution, least of all the farmers' union, the *Fédération Nationale de Syndicats des Exploitants Agricoles*, the FNSEA.

An organization of young farmers started to press for agricultural reform in the early 1950s. The *Jeunesse Agricole Chrétienne*, the JAC, had been organized by priests in the 1930s to stop the spread of atheism and Marxism in the rural sector. The religious orientation of this organization faded away during the war years when the young JAC leaders started replacing communal Bible readings by studies of modern farming techniques, economics and accounting. In 1957, the leader of the JAC, Michel Debatisse, succeeded in taking over the youth section of the FNSEA and organized it into a militant propaganda organization which urged farmers throughout France to abandon traditional ways of production and to modernize. This *Centre National des Jeunes Agriculteurs*, the CNJA, soon received the support of many technocrats who came to power with de Gaulle in 1958. Debatisse became a member of the government's *Conseil Economique et Social*. Michel Debré was very sympathetic to the ideas of the CNJA.

In August 1961, de Gaulle appointed a new Minister of Agriculture, Edgard Pisani, a man who also supported the CNJA program. During his four years in office, Pisani gave the force of law to reforms long advocated by the CNJA and the JAC. The "Pisani Laws" established an agency for the buying and the redistributing of land, encouraged the formation of farmers' production and distribution cooperatives and set up a new fund to facilitate the retirement of old farmers. A number of regional agencies, the *Sociétés d'Aménagement Foncier et d'Establissement Rural*, SAFERs, were set up to buy land when it was offered for sale. The agency was to make improvement on the land it purchased before it resold it to able farmers. The government also financed the formation of cooperatives, the *Sociétés d'Intérêt Collectif Agricole*, the SICAS.

These initial steps toward agricultural improvement were not taken everywhere in France. Lack of money and bureaucratic delays weakened the effectiveness of these laws where they were applied; in certain areas such as Brittany and parts of the Massif Central, no reformative effort touched agriculture and the farmer went on working on his scattered plots in the same way his father and grandfather had done it for years. In time, however, the extent of the areas of slow technological progress tended to diminish as old farmers retired and less tradition-minded sons took over the paternal farm.

In spite of their limited impact on French agriculture, the Pisani Laws marked the beginning of the triumph of the ideals of France's young farmers and the start of a slow change in the attitudes of the country's peasantry.

Although the postwar growth of agricultural output has not been as spectacular as the growth of industrial production, the average yearly growth rate of agricultural output was 3%, a satisfactory achievement when compared to pre-1945 growth rates which never exceeded 1% per year. The efforts of the JAC and of the CNJA encouraged the development of mechanized production and the more intensive use of fertilizers. France counted 335,000 tractors in 1956; there were 1,050,000 in 1965. The number of harvesters during this period rose from 38,200 to 104,500.[19] Between 1949 and 1963, agricultural productivity, estimated in terms of production per man-hour, increased by an average of 6.4% per year, twice as fast as in pre-1945 years. These gains in productivity were due to a number of reasons. The expansion of the industrial sector gave employment to an increasing number of farmers and thus allowed a reduction in the size of the farm population. This reduction in the number of farmers was further helped by the government's pension plan for retiring old farmers. The number of these pensions increased from 13,298 in 1965 to 107,390 in 1969. The development of mechanized agriculture contributed in turn to migration out of the agricultural sector. The increased use of mechanized processes was facilitated by a slow growth in the size of the representative farm, as shown in Table 7.5.

TABLE 7.5

NUMBER OF FARMS ACCORDING TO SIZE AND PERCENTAGE OF AGRICULTURAL LAND WORKED

Size of Farms in Hectares	Number of Farms (1,000)			% of Agricultural Land		
	1955	1963	1967	1955	1963	1967
1 — 5	649	454	375	5	4	3
5 — 10	477	364	308	11	8	7
10 — 20	536	485	413	23	22	20
20 — 50	377	394	372	38	37	38
50 — 100	75	85	85	16	17	19
100 and over	20	23	24	10	12	13

Source: J. J. Carré et al, *La Croissance Française*, supra, p. 230.

The French Economy After the "Events of 1968"

The student demonstrations and the strikes which brought the historical barricades back to Paris in 1968 not only brought with them the final retirement of General de Gaulle in 1969, but, quite curiously, gave also cause to the beginning of a major investment boom during the second half of 1968.

Unions struck in May 1968 more for political than for economic reasons. Economic growth in the spring of that year was quite satisfactory; gross domestic product was rising at a yearly rate of 6.5%. At the time the strikes started, only 2.6% of the total labor force was unemployed and a reduction in the inflow of foreign workers promised to improve conditions in the labor market.

Strike activity was ended in June by the so-called *Protocole de Grenelle* settlements which awarded non-agricultural workers a money wage increase of 5% as of June 1, and a further increase of 2.5% to 3% as of October 1. The agreements caused the wages of local government employees to rise by 19% betwen January and October 1968; during the same period of time, the wages and salaries of central government employees and those of workers in the gas, electricity, water, petroleum and textile industries rose by 15%; workers in other manufacturing industries obtained money wage increases varying between 11 and 13%. For the first ten months of 1968, the average increase of money wages in the non-agricultural sector amounted to 10.5%. These wage increases were highly inflationary.[20]

Wage and salary increases were accompanied by a sharp rise in prices. The government allowed significant increases in controlled prices and during the second half of 1968, the prices of gasoline, gas, electricity, railroad and air transport fares, telephone rates and hospital charges were allowed to rise. The Grenelle agreements not only increased the purchasing power of non-agricultural workers, but also aligned the minimum legal wage for agricultural workers with that prevailing for other workers, a change which meant a 56% increase in the minimum legal wage for some 0.7 million agricultural workers. The resulting increase in household incomes, probably associated with widespread expectation of continuing inflation, caused a post-strike spending spree which induced industrialists to expand capacity. Price increases, productivity gains, government subsidies and tax relief to enterprises maintained the level of profit margins unchanged in spite of higher labor costs. The investment boom that started in mid-1968 caused industrial output to surpass in December the pre-strikes volume by 8%. This output increase resulted largely from productivity gains. Employment was also rising; in March, 1969, only 1.9% of the labor force was unemployed.

The 1968 growth of domestic output was also accompanied by a post-strike growth of foreign trade. In December 1968, export values exceeded those of December 1967, by 19.5%. Import values were, however, 23.5% higher than they had been in 1967. The current account balance with non-Franc countries deteriorated and showed a deficit of $300 million at the end of 1968. The weeks of strike activity also witnessed large capital outflows and the resulting deficits on capital account brought in turn large losses of gold and of international reserves. Exchange control had to be reintroduced in November. Balance of payments deficits persisted during the first half of 1969.

Demand continued to rise in spite of substantial price and wage increases during the first two quarters of 1969. Supply bottlenecks developed while external deficits rapidly accumulated. The government adopted restrictive demand management measures in November 1968, but these measures were not strong enough to reduce the rate of growth of domestic demand.

In the summer of 1969,the government finally decided to take stronger action in order to eliminate excess demand in 1970 and in order to achieve external equilibrium. The devaluation of the Franc by 11.1% was to restore external equilibrium. Internally, equilibrium was to be achieved by a tightening of consumer credit and by increases in the cost of credit. The government succeeded in slowing down the rate of increase of real demand during the second half of the year. At the same time, a steady expansion of production eased the imbalance between demand and supply by the end of 1969. External deficits started shrinking as exports soared in response to the August devaluation and as the demand for imports declined. The trade balance actually showed a surplus in December. The last two quarters of 1969 also witnessed a net inflow of capital which furter contributed to the restoration of external balance. This net inflow of capital was constituted in part by the repatriation of French capital from abroad, largley due to higher rates of interest in France, and in part by increased borrowing abroad by French firms, following tighter credit restrictions in the country.

Inflation had not disappeared. Prices continued to rise at the rate of

5% per annum during the second half of 1969. Wages rose even faster. Inflation, however, did not affect the continuation of the investment boom. During the last quarter of 1969, industrial output was still expanding at an annual rate of 5 to 6%.[21] The continuing investment boom seemed to support M. Pompidou's forecast that France would double its industrial capacity in the 1970's.

Under the Pompidou administration investment emphasis no longer favored the spending of vast resources for the completion of prestige projects. Both government officials and industrialists seemed to be more aware of the necessity for expansion and modernization of overall industrial activity in order to increase the international competitiveness of French industry in a world in which protective tariff walls were being gradually dismantled. French industrial genius was no longer to be embodied in feats such as the *Concorde* airplane or the Rance tidal dam in Brittany. French industrial achievements were instead revealed by the large exports of the *Renault R-4* automobile which was able to compete successfully with German automobiles in Germany, by the *Moulinex* kitchen appliances which were able to undersell the products of rival foreign firms and the *Poclain* earth-moving equipment which was exported to all of the E.E.C. countries.

Even the trade unions seemed to favor Pompidou's desire to strengthen France's industrial power. There was a *rapprochement* between unions and the conservative *Patronat*. Leaders of the C.G.T. started negotiating with the employers' association and the improved labor-management relations atmosphere brought to the country a post-May 1968 era of labor peace which was vital for the continuation of the investment boom. The possibility of new strike action developing in the country was further reduced by a government innovation in the field of industrial relations. In the public sector, the government entered into contracts with unions, the *contrats de progrès*, which provided that in exchange for guaranteed yearly money wage increases, the unions would not strike during the duration of the contract. These contracts were to serve as examples to be followed in the private sector.

Conclusion

France, unlike the United States, did not experience the problems of "stagflation" in the late 1960s. Throughout the decade, its overall output continued to increase at an average annual rate of 5% under conditions of quasi-full employment. In spite of the resource drain caused by the French colonial wars, the country succeeded in modernizing and in expanding a number of key industrial sectors to such an extent that its participation in the European Common Market did not bring the economic catastrophe predicted by the old protectionists. Whereas in 1960 one-third of all French exports were sold in the Franc zone, less than 10% of these exports went to the Franc zone ten years later. French exports were increasingly re-oriented to the fast growing markets of the E.E.C., while manufactured products assumed a greater importance in French export sales.

Industrially, the country remained weaker than West Germany. With a gross national product only 20% larger than that of France, West Germany in the 1960s exported nearly four times the mechanical and electrical equipment exported by France. While France accounted for 19% of the totality of E.E.C. exports, it provided about 42% of all raw materials exports, but only 17% of all exports of manufactured products.

In spite of Pompidou's efforts to expand French industry, France in 1970 was still a country characterized by a large degree of economic dualism. Two economic worlds co-existed in the France of M. Pompidou. There was the world of the industrial, progress-minded technocrats, the world of the graduates of the *Ecole Polytechnique,* one of whom is M. Giscard d'Estaing. There was also a separate world made up by large numbers of tradition-loving and protection- urging small farmers, small businessmen, the thousands who had supported Pierre Poujade in the 1950s. This dualism has been described by The Economist as follows:

> France is a country of great inequalities. There is a huge distance between the highest and the lowest, between rich and poor, between the sophisticated technology which has produced Mirage fighters, Concorde planes and colour television, and life in the bidonvilles of Paris or in the mountain farms. The Pompidou policy of accelerated industrial advance, if unchecked, could easily exacerbate these inequalities. Any rational policy, even on the poltical right, must include an attempt to improve the social cohesion of what has always been a rigidly hierarchic, centralized and sectionalist society.[22]

NOTES

1. United Nations, Economic and Social Council, *Planning for Balanced Social and Economic Development in France* (New York, 1967), p. 20.

2. Initial output targets for chemicals and aluminum were surpassed; initial targets were also met by the oil and power industries; they were nearly reached for steel and cement. V. Lutz, *French Planning* (Washington: American Enterprise Institute, 1965), pp. 70-71.

3. United Nations, Economic and Social Council, *Planning for Balanced Social and Economic Development in France*, p. 22.

4. These indicators were the general level of prices, the balance of trade position, the growth of domestic output, the growth of industrial output, the growth of productive investment and employment.

5. OECD, *National Accounts of OECD Countries, 1950-1968* (Paris, 1969), p. 13.

6. J.J. Carré, et al., *La Croissance Française* (Paris: Editions du Seuil, 1972), Ch. 11.

7. *Ibid.*, pp. 448-449.

8. J. Chardonnet, *L'.Economie Française*, Vol. I, *L'Industrie* (Paris: Dalloz, 1970), p. 131.

9. *Ibid.*, p. 139.

10. While IBM, Caterpillar and United Carbon of the United States established their own branches in France, Chrysler Corporation acquired control over Simca and General Mills took over L'Alsacienne, a large French biscuit manufacturing firm. J. Ardagh, *The New French Revolution* (New York: Harper & Row, 1968), p. 39.

11. Ardagh, *The New French Revolution*, pp. 36-37.

12. Chardonnet, *L'Economie Française*, p. 155.

13. In Paris, nine-tenths of all industrial firms in 1963 employed less than 50 workers, While the average size of the employed labor force in large industrial firms employing over 1,000 workers was 2,311 in France, it was 2,600 in the German Federal Republic. Chardonnet, *L'Economie Française*, p. 350.

14. Ardagh, *The New French Revolution*, p. 29.

15. Carré, et al., *La Croissance Française*, p. 32.

16. Growth rates varied among the various industries. They were largest for the energy industries, with the exception of coal, for the chemical industries and for the non-ferrous metallurgical industries. Between 1949 and 1966, the yearly rate of growth was on the average 10.1% for oil refining, 9.5% for the production of electricity, 8% for the output of the chemical industries, 7.9% for that of the non-ferrous metallurgy, but only 2% for coal output. Carrré, et al., *La Crossiance Française*, pp. 43-45.

17. *Ibid.*, p. 109.

18. *Ibid.*, p. 195.

19. P. Coffey, *The Social Economy of France* (New York: St. Martin's Press, 1973), p. 39.

20. OECD, *Economic Surveys, France, 1969*, pp. 6-34.

21. OECD, *Economic Surveys, France, 1970*.

22. *The Economist* (Dec. 2, 1972), Survey, p. 6.

CHAPTER 8

THE END OF NON-PLANNING
IN THE WEST GERMAN ECONOMY

Professors Eucken, von Hayek and Rüstow were some of the German economists who opposed the Nazi regime and who urged their fellow countrymen to reject any economic system based on extensive government controls. Professor Ludwig Erhard belonged to their school of thought and the principal features of his *Soziale Marktwirtschaft* were very much affected by the views of these neo-liberal German economists. In conformity with the type of economic system supported by his mentors, Erhard introduced in 1948 an economy solidly anchored to the institutions of private property and private control of resources, an economy based on the relatively free operation of competitive markets, an economy characterized by the absence of centralized economic planning and by the generally recognized principle that government control over economic activity should be minimized. These economists believed that a high degree of competition in all markets, accompanied by price stability, would best provide for a smooth functioning of the economy and would minimize the need for government anti-cyclical fiscal measures. Monetary policy, on the other hand, was to achieve the important task of preserving price stability by means of adequate controls over the supply of money, including bank credit. If the market system brought about socially undesirable patterns of income and wealth distribution, then taxation and an adequate social security system could be used to provide the needed corrections. Although the social market economy was not a *laissez-faire* economy, it provided nevertheless an environment in which private enterprise could operate quite freely and in which the pursuit of maximum private profits was supported by the State.

Those who have maintained that the successes of the West German economy during the golden years of the 1950s and early 1960s should be largely attributed to the efficient working of a *laissez-faire* market economy, conveniently overlook the fact that the federal government, during both the Adenauer and Erhard administrations, continued to play a major role in the economic life of the country. State participation in the economy, at the federal, *Land* and local levels, remained extensive because of the important role of government as an investor in a large public sector of the West German economy and because of fiscal and monetary policies pursued by public authorities to further economic growth in conformity with desired objectives.

Public expenditures for the development of the State-owned sector, public loans and direct subsidies extended to private enterprises, and tax incentives designed to encourage certain types of economic activity allowed the federal government to manage effectively the level of aggregate demand and to guide the growth of the economy.[1] The federal government did not hesitate to grant tax exemptions to business and industrial firms, to allow them accelerated depreciation allowances and to help them with low-interest loans whenever this help was thought to further the economic objectives of the Bonn government.

If Adenauer's "economic miracle" is said to have been generated by a neo-capitalist system, facts show that this sytem exhibited many features of "State capitalism." The federal government inherited from the pre-World War II years extensive ownership interests in domestic industry and commerce. Although the German Federal Republic never duplicated the post-1945 nationalizations effectuated in France and in Great Britain, a recent study indicates that in the 1960s, the West German federal government owned 40% of the domestic coal and iron ore mining industries, 62% of the electrical industry, 72% of the aluminum industry and 60% of all credit institutions, excepting the central bank which was totally owned by the federal government.[2] Through participation in a number of holding companies, the federal government was able to own assets and to control significant portions of stock in thousands of enterprises. The entire capital stock of the holding company *Vereinigte Industrienunternehmen, A.G.*, (VIAG), was owned by the federal government. Through a subsidiary, *Vereinigte Alumnium Werke*, VIAG controlled over two-thirds of West Germany's aluminum industry. VIAG also held interests in enterprises producing steel, electrical equipment and chemicals.

The federal government further held a 40% interest in *Vereinigte Elektrizitäts und Bergwerke, A.B.*, (VERBA), a holding company ranking among the ten largest companies in West Germany. Through its subsidiaries, e.g. *Hibernia, Preussische Elektrizität, Hugo Stinnes*, etc., VEBA controlled firms producing coal, chemicals, natural gas, petroleum, fertilizers, glass, as well as firms specializing in distribution and trade. Through *Hibernia*, VEBA controlled over 25% of the capital of *Aral*, a major West German gasoline distributor.[3]

The entire capital of *Salzgitter A.G.* was held by the central government. The principal activities of this company centered on mining and on the production of iron and steel; its subsidiaries also produced natural gas, machinery, rails and equipment for ports. The federal government also owned 16% of *Volkswagenwerk*, the largest industrial enterprise in the Federal Republic.[4]

Given the extensive participation of government in the Adenauer and Erhard economies, one may ask whether these economies followed in a meaningful way the economic system prescribed by the post-war German neo-liberal school. Was the West German economic system, as it developed between 1949 and 1966, a true *Soziale Marktwirtschaft* or was it rather a Keynesian-like *Gesteuerte Marktwirtschaft?*

The two fundamental principles of the German neo-liberal school involved the creation and the maintenance of a market-determined price system based on free and true competition and the achievement and preservation of price and wage stability. Economists in this school urged government to protect competition and to shield the economy from the near-monopoly powers and practices of large industrial and commercial combines. Mere State participation in the economy was not seen as a threat to the market system as long as this participation did not disturb the operation of competitive markets and did not interfere with free, market-determined price and wage formation.

These principles were not violated during the 1950s and during a large part of the 1960s. It was only toward the end of the 1960s, when a high degree of industrial and financial concentration finally succeeded in substituting the price and output dictate of the corporate giant for a price mechanism operated by relatively free market forces, that the West German economy repudiated the teachings of Walter Eucken. At the same time, it would be a gross error to believe that the economic success of the German Federal Republic during the golden 1950s was mostly due to the fact that the West German economic system was largely a duplicate of the capitalist nineteenth-century system of Great Britain.

The theoretical model of Erhard's system was not one of *laissez-faire*. The Freiburg School ideas which moulded the West German economic system never condemned State intervention in the economy as long as it aimed at the preservation or the development of what Walter Eucken and Franz Böhm called the "competitive order." What was important for the neo-liberal economists of the Freiburg School was that State action should support and not weaken their proposed system of complete competition. In the works of Eucken, "more or less State activity — this kind of question misses the point. It is not a quantitative but a qualitative problem. . . . The basic principle does not simply require that certain measures of economic policy should be avoided, e.g. State subsidies, the establishment of State monopolies, the freezing of prices, import restriction, etc. It is also insufficient to forbid cartels. The principle is not primarily negative. Far more essential is a positive policy which aims at bringing the market form of complete competition into being, and which thereby fulfills the basic principle. It is here that the policy of the competitive order differs completely from the policy of *laissez faire* which, according to its own basic principles, did not recognize the need for a positive economic policy." [5]

Eucken's concept of "complete competition" differs from the idea of "perfect" or "pure" competition as understood by British economists such as J. Robinson and E. H. Chamberlin. Eucken's "complete competition" does not presuppose the existence of atomistic markets in which numerous producers of similar economic strength, offering identical products at identical prices, sell to numerous buyers. In a more pragmatic way, Eucken simply advocated the economy's return to a competitive operating system. As Böhm put it, "What matters is not the degree to which the conditions of perfect competition are fulfilled, but the opportunity for the free and untrammelled exercise of all competitive energies which, in fact, exist. Every addition to competition is a gain, every diminution a loss. . . . " [6] The goal of these writers was therefore not to attain a state of "perfect competition," but to strive for a more competitive market economy. Any trend toward monopolistic practices should, in their view, be stopped by strong, corrective State action. State intervention was deemed necessary both to maintain and to strengthen the competitive order so that this order could best serve the needs of society. Public intervention for the preservation of price stability was of crucial importance. Governmental social action could be warranted if it did not impair market mechanisms. Eucken, perhaps erroneously, believed that his "competitive order" system would establish in his country the most efficient and the most humane of all workable economic systems.

The Implementation of Eucken's Competitive Order

The Adenauer government seemed to be seriously committed to follow the Freiburg School's recommendation that government should oppose the rise of large, monopolistic combines. Although the government was willing to support Eucken's system, industry and business were not. Eucken had urged the government to protect competition by enacting strong anti-trust laws. The draft of an anti-trust law was introduced as early as 1952, but strong opposition by industry delayed the enactment of final anti-trust legislation until 1957. The 1957 Law against Restraints of Competition was a compromise reached after long years of disagreement by proponents and opponents of Eucken's views. Although the law prohibited in principle agreements in restraint of trade and competition, the statute recognized so many exception cases that it could hardly be used as an effective means to stop the continuing trend toward widening oligopolistic and quasi-monopolistic structures.

The movement toward higher industrial concentration was accelerated in the mid-1960s when the government's position regarding monopolistic practices started softening. The change in the views of the authorities was largely caused by the impact of stronger world competition on German international competitiveness. Their argument now stressed the idea that government should not impair the competitiveness of German firms operating in the international market, particularly in the market of the E.E.C. They pointed out that large size, though it was accompanied by monopoly power at home, was necessary to allow domestic firms to take advantage of economies of scale and to strengthen their ability to compete successfully with large foreign combines.

Growing tolerance on the part of the authorities for industrial mergers and consolidations quickened the pace of industrial concentration in the country. The growth of oligopolistic power was readily observable during the second half of the 1960's. In 1952, the four largest West German chemical firms controlled about 40% of the national market;

twenty years later, the *Hoechst, Bayer, BASF,* and *Henkel* enterprises shared 70% of this market. In the steel industry, the growth of control grew even faster. In 1962, the steel producers *Thyssen, Hoesch A.G., Krupp* and *Salzgitter* provided 58% of the industry's sales; ten years later, these four firms supplied 90% of these sales. During the late 1960s, about 15 retail establishments succeeded in appropriating one-third of the entire national retail trade. Industrial and financial concentration had reached such a level by 1970 that German economists indicated that the entire economy depended on the dictate of about 600 corporate officials who represented the top management of about 130 large industrial, banking, insurance and trading firms in the country.[7] When these large firms started playing the American Big Business "monopoly game," i.e., restricting output and raising prices, even during periods of declining demand, Eucken's "competitive order" ceased to exist in West Germany.

The government's attempts to protect competition in spite of expanding market domination by large corporations are also found in its *Mittelstandpolitik,* its "third estate policy." This policy, inaugurated in 1957, aimed to protect not only the economic position of the middle-class, but also tried to assure the survival of the small and medium-size firms in the economy. The government earmarked millions of marks to achieve this purpose. Federal grants were awarded to finance research and development studies for the benefit of small and medium-size enterprises. Cheap public credits were extended to finance the establishment of new firms of these types. Whenever possible, government contracts were given to these firms. Government further subsidized the costs of vocational training in order to assist the crafts. The *Mittelstandoplitik* tried to strengthen the voice of small shareholders in large corporations. The corporate practice of allocating large parts of profits to secret reserve funds whose existence was only known by insiders was prohibited by the Company Law of 1965. This law also placed limitations on the amount of reserves a corporation could keep. Small shareholders received favorable treatment in the denationalization share sales that followed the divestment of public ownership of certain large enterprises. Low-income buyers were allowed to buy a limited number of shares of these firms at a "social discount." *Volkswagenwerk* was denationalized in 1961 and 1.5 million persons were able to acquire 60% of the share capital of the enterprise. Buyers whose yearly income was lower than 16,000 DM were able to buy *Volkswagenwerk* shares at lower than normal prices. The larger holding company VEBA followed the same fate in 1965 and 2.2 million new shareholders bought 3.7 million VEBA shares; persons earning less than 14,000 DM a year were allowed to buy a maximum of 5 shares per buyer at a substantial discount.[8]

All these measures were unable to stem the growing flow of mergers and amalgamations. In 1969, the Cartel Office in Berlin, a government agency responsible for the registering of all mergers involving firms employing together at least 10,000 workers or having gross sales of at least DM 500 million or controlling 20% or more of the national market, reported that the number of mergers in that year was three times as large as it had been in 1967 and 1968. Large enterprises continued to buy out or force out of the market small and medium-size rivals. In the 1960s, the corporate giant *AEG-Telefunken* absorbed 23 smaller competitors. The construction firm *Deutsche Babcock* acquired control over one-third of the national market by fusing with five rival firms. In the period 1950 to 1970, 130,000 wholesale and retail businessmen and 146 established private bankers lost their independence and became employees of large combines.[9]

The Adenauer Era

The Adenauer government was more successful in the economic than in the political field. The unchanging foreign policy of *Der Alte*, a policy which continuously stressed the idea that only Western military strength would command the respect of a monolithic Communist world and which demanded the non-recognition of the East German government by every country desiring to maintain diplomatic relations with the German Federal Republic, started losing support outside of West Germany in the early 1950s. This policy suffered a major defeat in August 1954 when the French National Assembly voted against the establishment of a European Defense Community, a project that Adenauer had strongly supported. It experienced a further setback in August 1961 when the East Germans proceeded to build the Berlin Wall without any military reaction on the part of the United States. The weakness of Adenauer's policy toward East Germany was revealed in 1963 when the Moscow Test Ban Treaty was signed by a representative of the government of the German Democratic Republic. As a writer put it, Adenauer "did not and could not see that he had become an anachronism in a rapidly changing world, an anachronism who appeared increasingly ludicrous as the last and most rigid 'Cold Warrior' in a world where the Cold War, through by no means ended, was taking on new forms unsuspected in the early 1950s. . ."[10]

It was in the economic field that the Bonn government recorded most successess, successes attributable only in part to the Adenauer-Erhard policies. As was mentioned earlier, American aid, West Germany's rapid integration into the Western bloc following the beginning of the Cold War, a continuous inflow of refugees willing to work 60 or even 70 hours per week and the fact that for many years the country did not have to use resources for military purposes were strong exogenous stimulants of economic growth. From 1951 on, exports were to become the country's principal growth agents.

The following data gives a meaningful sketch of West Germany's rapid economic expansion in the period 1950 to 1963. The West German index of net industrial production rose from 100 in 1950 to 283 in 1963. At the time of Adenauer's resignation from office, the German Federal Republic had become the third largest world producer of iron and steel.[11] It was second only to the United States as a producer of automobiles and ranked third in the world as a shipbuilding nation.[12] Industrial output per man-hour doubled within this period while the cost of living remained relatively stable. West Germany achieved during these years a degree of relative price stability which was not duplicated elsewhere in Europe. Taking 1958 as the base year, the West German cost of living index rose from 85 in 1950 to 112 in 1963, while the same index during the same period increased from 64 to 126 in France, from 68 to 112 in the United Kingdom and from 72 to 117 in Italy.[13] Rapid productivity advances and domestic price stability explain the growing competitiveness of German exports in world markets. Starting in 1951, the West German export curve showed an uninterrupted rise which placed the German Federal Republic in 1960 second to the United States as the leading world exporter. This country, containing only 53% of the area of the German Reich of 1939 and about 75% of its population, accounted in 1960 for one-tenth of the world's exports.

West German economic growth in the 1950s was quite impressive as shown in Table 8.1. Total real gross national product doubled during this decade. Expressed in constant 1954 prices, the gross national product in 1950 was evaluated at DM 113.1 billion; in terms of the same prices, the gross national product rose to DM 233.8 billion in 1960.[14] Real per capita gross national product increased, again in terms of constant 1954 prices, from DM 2,361 in 1950 to DM 4,378 in 1960. The Federal Republic was the most rapidly growing country in Western Europe. Total gross national product increased at the average yearly rate of 7.5%; per capita real product grew at about 6.5% per year. The average gross weekly earnings of industrial workers increased from DM 58.21 in 1950 to DM 149.74 in 1962. This increase in earnings allowed in turn an increase in both private consumption and private saving. Private per capita real consumption increased by about 6.6% per year during the decade.[15]

Between 1950 and 1963, the year of Adenauer's resignation from his position as Chancellor, the number of employed persons in the country rose from 13.8 million to 22 million, while the number of unemployed declined from 1.5 million to 104,500. In 1955 the country reached full employment and full employment was maintained until the recession of 1966.

TABLE 8.1

GROWTH OF WEST GERMAN NATIONAL PRODUCT
In terms of 1954 prices

Year	G.N.P. In billions DM	G.N.P. Index 1950 = 100	Growth Rate of Per Capita G.N.P.
1950	113.1	100.0	27.1
1951	125.0	110.5	9.4
1952	135.4	119.7	7.6
1953	145.6	128.7	6.7
1954	156.4	138.3	6.1
1955	174.4	154.2	10.4
1956	186.4	164.8	5.6
1957	196.5	173.7	4.0
1958	202.9	179.4	2.1
1959	216.5	191.4	5.3
1960	233.8	206.7	6.8

Sources: *Statistisches Jahrbuch 1953*, p. 544; *Ibid 1961*, p. 544.

What made the rapid expansion of the economy possible? West Germany's economic growth in the 1950s was due to two main reasons. The first was a continuously expanding supply of labor. The second was the maintenance of a high gross investment to gross national product ratio. Over the years, the ratio averaged 22%, the actual ratio attaining 26.5% in 1960. Export surpluses permitted additional saving and investment. In the 1950s, these surpluses represented between 2.5% and 4% of gross national product and thus allowed the country to invest as much as between 24% and 29% of aggregate national product.

The high ratio of gross investment to gross national product was made possible by a number of factors. Compared to conditions in other Western European countries, the West German economy in the 1950s was characterized by a relatively low wage share in national income, low ratios of personal consumption to national income and low defense expenditures. Personal consumption, as a percentage of gross national product, declined from 65.8% in 1949 to 57.3% in 1960. The absence of a large military establishment allowed West Germany to devote practically all of its resources to economic growth and modernization. While in the mid-1950s France and the United Kingdom had to allocate over 8% of their gross national product for military purposes, West German defense expenditures in 1956 represented only 2.8% of the gross national product of the country.

The high ratio of investment to national income allowed West Germany to use over 22% each year of its gross national product for gross domestic capital formation. The country's plant and equipment stock was thus allowed to expand rapidly not only in quantitative terms, but also qualitatively. The rapid accumulation of capital not only meant more factories and more machines, but also better factories and better machines. High levels of investment allowed the country to rejuvenate its plant and equipment stock and to generate a rapid growth of labor productivity. 46% of total gross domestic investment was used for the acquisition of new equipment.

West Germany's "golden fifties" must be explained in terms of the conjuncture of a number of factors. A high rate of investment, rapid gains in labor productivity, a low rate of inflation, an expanding labor supply and the ability to produce capital goods in high demand throughout the world combined to produce the prosperous years of the Adenauer administration. The export industries acted as the leading agents of growth. Recurring export booms stimulated investment, created increased employment and boosted profits. They allowed the country to accumulate balance of payments surpluses which contributed to domestic capital formation. Annual export surpluses in the 1950s averaged about $2 billion.

The economy during the period 1951 to 1963 experienced short business cycles of about four or five years' duration. The beginning of the cyclical upswing was initiated by an export boom which was followed by accelerated investment. For a while, wages lagged behind profits, and the reinvestment of profits further boosted investment. As income increases spread over the entire economy, personal consumption expenditures started rising; growing mass consumption brought with it higher prices and rising wages. Monetary policy measures were used by the central bank authorities to tighten credit and stabilize prices. Three cycles of this type can be observed for the years 1951 to 1963, and are shown in Table 8.2

Both traditional and new industries contributed to the West German export boom. Traditional exports such as steel products, chemicals and optical instruments were complemented by new products such as automobiles, electronic equipment and consumer goods.

TABLE 8.2

WEST GERMANY: 1951 — 1963 ECONOMIC TRENDS

Cycle	Annual Rate of Growth of Real G.N.P. %	Annual Rate of Growth of Exports: Constant Prices %	Average Annual Increase in Cost of Living %	Average Annual Rate of Unemployment %
1951-54	8.0	18.5	0.1	5.9
1954-58	7.0	13.4	2.1	3.5
1958-63	5.7	9.2	2.2	1.2

Source: *Statistisches Jahrbuch*, various issues.

The End of a Non-planned Economy

1963 seemed to mark the beginning of a new short cycle. A strengthening of European demand for West German products in that year gave the Federal Republic a trade surplus of $1.2 billion and reduced unemployment to 0.8%. The economic boom, led by exports, continued in 1964 and in 1965. Inflation threatened to get out of hand. Wages were rising faster than the cost of living. Large inflows of foreign capital weakened the effectiveness of monetary policy. To reduce the attractiveness of high West German bond rates to foreign investors, a tax was imposed in 1964 on part of the interest yield accruing to foreign holders of German securities.

The parliamentary elections of 1965 intensified economic pressures in the economy. Before the election, Christian Democrats in the *Bundestag* voted in favor of a number of economic and social programs which required a substantial increase in public expenditure. To avoid budgetary deficits developing from these expensive political pledges, increases in tax revenue in 1966 and in 1967 were obviously necessary. Political considerations brought instead a reduction in income taxes at the beginning of 1965. Dr. Erhard's advice that public spending should not increase faster than national product seemed to be forgotten or ignored by C.D.U. politicians anxious to retain their parliamentary seats. Federal expenditure started exceeding budgetary stipulations and increased faster than national income. The Chancellor did not take any measures to stop these inflationary developments.

The *Bundesbank*, on the other hand, exercising its constitutional right to preserve the value of the currency, decided to pursue a strongly deflationary policy. Harsh credit restrictions were followed by the refusal to allow the government to borrow the money it needed to finance its 1965 election pledges.

The boom peaked in mid-1966 and a weakening export demand coupled with the "tight money" policy of the *Bundesbank* quickly transformed the boom into a recession. The recession lasted through 1967 and brought to the mind of many Germans the question of whether the days of the *Wirtschaftswunder* were over. The economic downswing made the financing of the federal programs quite difficult. As economic growth weakened, tax revenues declined. An unplanned and illegal federal budget deficit threatened to appear in 1966 and was only avoided through the government's postponing of promised programs.

For the economist, the recession of 1966 and 1967 simply represented a dramatic end of the classic business cycle that had started with the traditional export-led boom in 1964. However, the severity of the recession made the average German wonder about the soundness of Erhard's non-planned economic system. Although many people blamed Herr Blessing of the *Bundesbank* for contributing to the deterioration of the economy, many others felt that poorly planned government expenditure programs were the principal cause of the poor state of the economy. Their belief was that government had pumped too much money into the economy in times when it was not necessary to do so, and that it had started pruning its spending programs as soon as economic decline began. They demanded that government abandon this pro-cyclical type of policy and replace it by a wiser short-term management of the economy and by policies which would assure long-term growth.

Rising prices and wage increases which outstripped productivity gains in 1964 and in 1965 induced the Erhard government to introduce in the following year an Economic Stabilization bill which, although mainly designed to help the government control inflation, announced a departure from the government's traditional policy of relying exclusively on monetary policy as a stabilizing instrument. The bill had not yet been voted on in the *Bundestag* when Kiesinger succeeded Erhard in the Chancellery. Kiesinger's "grand coalition" government, a government now including both Christian and Social Democrats, finally passed in June 1967 a "Law for Promoting Stability and Growth in the Economy."[16]

The new Chancellor was confronted with a rapidly deteriorating economy. Real gross national product during the first half of 1967 was 1.5% smaller that it had been one year earlier. Industrial output had declined to its 1965 level. Unemployment had risen from 140,000 at the start of 1966 to 600,000 in the summer of 1967. Although growing unemployment affected mostly immigrant workers, the poor performance of the economy shocked most Germans. The mood of the people in the early days of 1967 was described by *New Statesman* as follows:

> The crisis may have touched relatively few pockets so far, but the crisis of confidence has gone to most heads. As early as August the boss of Siemens electrical works, Dr. Adolf Lohse, was saying 'it is now no longer foolish to speak of the crisis years of 1929 to 1932.' *Der Spiegel* wrote: 'The fashionable colour for managers this season is black.' People have stopped taking sick-leave lightly. At a small engineering firm in Bochum, 372 employees agreed on a 10 per cent wage-cut. A social Democrat MP claims personal acquaintance with a dozen miners who have taken their families across the Elbe . . .[17]

The Minister of Economic Affairs in the Kiesinger government was Professor Karl Schiller, a Keynesian economist who supported both the continuation of the market economy and a high degree of state intervention in this economy to maintain full employment and to assure both stability and growth. His concept of *globale Steuerung*, i.e., "global state intervention," was revealed in an address given by Professor Schiller in Zurich in February 1967. Schiller stated:

> We all know that there are countries with little growth and just as little stability of the price level, and that on the other hand there are countries which have preserved stability despite fast growth. The simple conceptions of the unequivocal association of moderate growth and high stability have meanwhile been refuted. The relationships between the two objectives are more diverse and more complicated than was generally assumed. And an economic policy that sets out to attain both goals simultaneously must take more differentiated action and often apply its instruments in "changing combinations." The beaten track of stop-and-go policy will no longer lead us to our objective. Economic policy in the second half of the 20th century must always be a policy mix.
>
> Such a policy of changing combinations of instruments is now possible only within a synthesis of global control and market economy. The essential macro-decisions in such a system are made by economic and financial policy, but the micro-decisions are left to the market and microeconomic competition.[18]

Schiller's view of the role of government in economic life was thus quite different from the corresponding views of Eucken and Erhard.

Schiller's interventionism became quickly observable. In April 1967, a "Special Investment Budget" was created by the federal government to allow an increase of DM 2.5 billion in public spending. These additional expenditures were to stimulate both public and private investment and the government counted on a Keynesian multiplier-accelerator effect to raise gross national product by a multiple of the additional public expenditures. Since these expenditures came out of a "Special Budget," the constitutional requirement that the main federal budget be balanced was not offended. This legalistic ruse allowed the federal government to engage in deficit finance to facilitate employment increases in industries that had been particularly hard hit by the recession, e.g. the construction and basic industries.[19] The experiment was repeated in late 1967 and early 1968 when the federal government again pumped over DM 5 billion into the economy. Concurrently, investment taxes were reduced. These reflationary policies proved to be successful. By the end of 1967, economic indicators started turning up and by the middle of 1968 the economy had returned to a growth rate of 5%.

The "Law to Promote Stability and Growth of the Economy" of May 1967 officially announced the demise of the *Soziale Marktwirtschaft*. Medium-term, counter-cyclical planning and the use of Keynesian policy instruments formed the core of Professor Schiller's "New Economics." Price stability was no longer the principal goal of government policy. The 1967 law enshrined the four objectives of price stability, full employment, external balance and economic growth. The law provided the federal government with a variety of fiscal policy instruments but placed upon it the responsibility of using them correctly to smooth out the ups and downs of the business cycle. It allowed the Ministry of Finance to borrow up to DM 5 billion in periods of recession to finance extraordinary public expenditure; it allowed the federal government to suspend or restrict the use of accelerated depreciation in times of boom; the federal government was given authority to increase or decrease personal and corporate income taxes by as much as 10% to offset the impact of cyclical trends; with the approval of the *Bundesrat*, the federal goverment could restrict new borrowing by federal, state and local agencies for periods of up to one year. The 1967 Law required in turn that the federal government engage in medium-term fiscal planning. Federal budgets were to be planned for a five year period and these plans were to be re-examined and rolled forward each year, i.e., the base year would be advanced by twelve months each year. These plans were to establish a projection of future expenditure and revenue in the light of the foreseen development of the economy's resources. State and local governments were also required to prepare long-term budgets. Moreover, the federal government was required to submit each year to both houses of Parliament an economic report indicating its economic goals for the coming year, and every two years, a report giving account of the subsidies and grants it had financed. A Council for Anti-Cyclical Policy was established, made up of representatives of the federal, state and local governments as well as representatives of the *Bundesbank*. This *Konjunkturrat* recommended the establishment of a "counter-cyclical reserve fund" by the federal and state governments. On the basis of this recommendation, the federal government acquired the authority to instruct, with the permission of the *Bundesrat*, both federal and state authorities to place up to 3% of the previous year's tax revenue in this fund. The fund was also to be augmented by increases in tax revenue caused by counter-cyclical increases in income taxes. The fund was to be used to finance counter-cyclical expenditures. These expenditures were to be ordered by the federal government with the approval of the *Bundesrat*.

The 1967-1970 Cycle

Economic activity started recovering during the second half of 1967. Economic policy played a major role in the stimulation of domestic demand. The two special federal investment programs accelerated gross fixed asset formation and provided a more favorable business climate for German entrepreneurs. Three-fifths of the initial expenditure of DM 2.5 billion were translated into actual orders during May and June. Orders issued under the second federal investment program, a program started in the fall, added DM 5.3 billion to public spending and boosted aggregate demand in 1968. The income-stimulating effects of these expenditures were, however, somewhat weakened by a number of measures taken by the government in 1967, such as increases in personal and corporate income tax liability, increased employer and employee social security contributions and public expenditure cuts affecting welfare, defense and subsidies to agriculture.

Aggregate demand started expanding more rapidly during the second half of 1968. A sharp rise in exports announced the beginning of a new boom period. Export growth accelerated because of both a strengthening in world trade and the apprehension of a revaluation of the DM. Moreover, a law imposing a 4% tax on the f.o.b. value of certain exports whose delivery would take place after December 23, 1968, induced German exporters to speed-up their deliveries. The growth of exports stimulated manufacturing; whereas the output of manufacturing industries had fallen by 2.5% in 1967, it increased by 12% in 1968. Capacity utilization in industry rose from 76% in January 1967 to 89% in January 1968.[20]

Following the typical pattern of the short-term cycle, wages in 1968 lagged behing profits. Wages and salaries had remained unchanged in 1967; during 1968, although raised by 6 to 8%, they did not increase labor costs per unit of industrial output, given the rapid advances in productivity. The income share going to profits still grew and this growth in turn strengthened the pace of economic recovery.

In spite of an increasing demand for imports, the rapid advance of exports brought a current account surplus of nearly $3 billion at the end

TABLE 8.3

WEST GERMANY: CHANGES IN PRODUCTION BY SECTOR: 1965-1968
Per Cent Change Over Previous Year

	1965	1966	1967	1968
Agriculture and Forestry	-6.2	-0.3	9.8	3.3
Industry	6.8	2.0	-1.7	9.1
Trade and Communications	6.2	1.7	0.6	5.5
Services	5.3	4.5	3.5	2.5
G.D.P.	5.6	2.2	0.3	6.8

Source: OECD, *Economic Surveys, Germany,* Paris, 1969, p.11.

of 1968. This surplus was, however, almost offset by a long-term capital outflow of $2.5 billion. In 1968, the German Federal Republic ceased being net importer of long-term capital.

Demand pressures continued to rise in 1969 and in that year, capacity utilization in industry reached a record level. A rapid increase in the supply fo foreign labor allowed real gross national product to expand at a rate of 8% per year. By the end of 1969, the number of immigrant workers had increased by about 400,000, the total number of such workers reaching 1.6 million at the end of the year. By the end of 1969, the unemployment rate was down to 0.7% and there were six vacant jobs for every unemployed person.[21]

Wage and price increases remained moderate until mid-1969. During the first half of 1969, wages tended to increase by about 6% per year but labor productivity was growing even faster. Many labor-management contracts had been signed during the initial phase of the boom in 1968 and were still very much affected by the recession experience of 1966-1967. Labor unions in 1968 still accepted relatively small wage increases. The slow rise of wages until the summer of 1969 allowed a sharp rise in profits and in investment which contributed to accelerated economic growth but which also made for a growing imbalance in the shares of income going to labor and to profit earners. Labor rebelled in the fall of 1969, and West German industry experienced for the first time a number of wildcat strikes. Trade union leaders started embracing more aggressive wage policies, and employers, concerned with the possibility of having to endure strikes during a period of rapidly rising demand, agreed to re-negotiate labor contracts and granted substantial wage increases averaging between 10% and 12%.[22]

After mid-1969, prices started rising faster, but the rate of price inflation lagged behind the rate of wage inflation. Toward the end of the year, the cost of living index increased at a rate of 6% per year. Wages not only had caught up with the rise in profits, but during the second half of 1969 even exceeded it.

In spite of these inflationary trends, and in spite of the revaluation of the DM by 9.3% in October, fast export growth continued in 1969. If the current account surplus at the end of the year amounted to only $1.8 billion, it was not because of a deterioration of the visible trade balance, but because of a sharp increase in the net deficit of the invisible balance. Germans increased their payments to foreigners for tourism abroad and for the acquisition of foreign services.

At the same time, West Germany was becoming the biggest exporter of long-term capital, the outflow of long-term capital in 1969 amounting to $5.9 billion.

The boom started losing its momentum in 1970. Restrictive demand management policies were used to stabilize prices. The effects of revaluation began to weaken the pull of foreign demand. Prices and wages continued to increase, responding with a lag to the slowdown in the rate of demand expansion. The economy continued to operate under full employment conditions, capacity utilization in industry averaging 93% and the number of foreign workers increasing to 2 million. But the trade surplus did not show an increase over that of the previous year; while the demand for exports weakened, that for imports continued to be strong; the foreign trade multiplier started having a restrictive effect on the economy.

During the years 1967 to 1970 the federal government started using fiscal policy as an important tool of demand management. The effectiveness of the *Bundesbank's* monetary policy was often limited by the fact that banks and industrial concerns could easily borrow abroad. Fiscal policy played a major role in reviving the economy during the second half of 1967. After the recession had been transformed into a boom, fiscal policy changed direction and restrictive measures started being introduced in March 1969. 1969 expenditure plans of the federal government were reduced by about DM 1.8 billion. With the continuation of the boom and the strengthening of inflationary pressures, a more restrictive fiscal policy was adopted early in 1970. Appropriations for public expenditures were temporarily frozen and in May, DM 2.1

billion of these blocked budgetary appropriations were transformed into budgetary cuts. In July, a 10% repayable surcharge on corporate and personal income taxes was imposed and degressive depreciation allowances on investment goods were temporarily suspended.

The central bank's monetary policy tended to support the aims of fiscal policy. The main goal of the *Bundsbank* in 1969 was the reduction of the liquidity of the commercial banks. Minimum reserve requirements for these banks were raised and a high interest differential with the Euro-Dollar market was maintained in order to encourage a high level of capital exports. In March, the central bank increased its discount rate to a postwar record of 7%. Minimum reserve requirements for commercial banks were repeatedly raised. These measures had some success in exerting a depressing effect on domestic demand. As export demand also weakened, it appeared that 1970 marked the end of another typical short-term cycle.

Agriculture, The Laggard Sector

Although the number of people working on the land dropped from 26% of the total labor force in 1950 to 11% in 1966, agricultural per capita income in many areas of West Germany remained in the late 1960s only half of the urban per capita income. The tourist who has seen the abudance of modern agricultural machinery being used by the West German farmer would naturally wonder about the cause of his modest earnings.

The productivity of the farmer has continued to be adversely affected by the small size of his farm and by the fragmentation of his land holdings. Although the technological skills of the farmers were high, the rational use of expensive modern agricultural machinery was limited by the fact that as late as 1968, 84% of all farms over two hectares in size had less than 20 hectares. These small farms covered 57% of the cultivated area in the country.[23] In 1968, 95% of all farms in Rheinland-Pfalz and Baden-Württemberg had less than 20 hectares of arable land.[24] Productivity on these small farms was further limited by the fragmentation of land holdings, high labor inputs, and the crowding of farm houses and other structures in densely populated villages. Excessive fragmentation of holdings, particularly acute in the southwestern regions of the country, impeded the greater rationalization of methods of production.

After the early 1950s, both the federal and state governments attempted to modernize the outdated agrarian structure through the implementation of policies designed to help the farmer to consolidate his holdings, to reduce the number of farms and increase their size and to relocate farm buildings outside the villages. The legal basis for these measures was the Land Consolidation Act, *Flurbereiningungsgesetz*, of 1953. The public financing of projects undertaken under this law was placed on a permanent basis in 1956 with the introduction of annual "Green Plans." The federal Ministry of Agriculture was required to submit each year to the Parliament a report indicating how the agency proposed to improve agriculture during the coming year and the related financial requirements. It had also to submit each year a "Green Report" which explained existing economic conditions in the agricultural sector. Public aid to agriculture, considering that the latter accounts for less than 4% of the gross national product, was enormous. The federal support of agriculture during the second half of the 1960s exceeded DM 3 billion.[25] This aid supported improvements in agricultural structure and in agricultural marketing; it covered fuel subsidies as well as the financing of measures taken to encourage people to abandon farming.

The 1966-1967 recession produced the birth of medium-term agricultural development programs which brought together the efforts and resources of both federal and state governments. In order to induce some farmers to sell their land, thereby making possible an increase in the size of farms, authorities attempted to attract industry into the large farming areas. The idea was to increase the number of non-agricultural jobs in the rural regions in order to encourage peasants to abandon entirely agricultural activity. These efforts did not lack success. The average farm size increased from 8.1 hectares in 1960 to 9.6 hectares in 1969.[26] Optimal farming conditions had, however, not been achieved. It was estimated in 1968 that 5.9 million hectares of agricultural land should still be consolidated; experts also felt that 2.9 million hectares which had already been consolidated required replanning to facilitate productivity increases.[27]

Increases in land productivity were achieved in the 1960s by maintaining a high labor input and by raising the use of capital factors. This entailed the retention of high labor costs in agricultural production. It was suggested in 1970, that if rural family earnings were to increase to two-thirds of the corresponding earnings in the industrial sector, one million farmers would have to leave agricultural activity during the decade of the 1970s.[28] By 1970, the problem of the wide income gap between town and country had not been solved.

Conclusion

The 1967 decision of the West German government to increase its control over economic activity in order to reach the often conflicting goals of price stability, full employment, growth and external balance and its subsequent efforts to do this through the use of counter-cyclical fiscal policy, clearly revealed that Kiesinger's government definitely abandoned whatever was left of Erhard's social market economy. The key principle of the neo-liberal Freiburg School, i e., the idea that public policy should limit itself to the preservation of price stability and to the maintenance of competition, was definitely abandoned.

The 1967 "Law for Promoting Stability and Growth in the Economy" was not the only bell which announced the demise of Erhard's non-planned economic system: the "Big Business" bell sounded even louder.

A major factor in West Germany's remarkable economic performance in the 1950s and in the early 1960s had been the ability of West German industry to reduce its unit costs in times of sluggish growth and to reduce them even further when the economy strengthened. Continous productivity gains gave German exports a great advantage in world markets, particularly because in many other European countries unit costs tended to rise as demand declined because industries would spread the same costs over fewer units of output.

This situation started changing at the close of the 1960s. As market competition gave way to the collusion of oligopolistic corporate giants, firms no longer attached the same importance to the achievement of productivity gains. Large West German firms like *Siemens, Hoesch* and others started learning the big business game of the large American corporation. They observed, for instance, that although General Motors fired one-eight of its workers in 1970 following a drop in sales of 23%, it nevertheless increased the prices of its automobiles by an average of 6.9% and continued to invest in 1971 as if no drop in sales had occurred in the prior year. The lesson was that nothing should slow down the investment plans of large firms. Regardless of economic conditions, they should go on, increasing their productive capacity and their control over markets. In times of declining demand, profits could be maintained and even raised by reducing both the labor force and output and by raising prices.

Monetary and fiscal policies were unable to stop the administered price inflation of the late 1960s. High interest rates had no effect on the policies of corporate giants which financed 70% of their investments through self-finance and which could easily borrow abroad whatever other funds they needed. From 1968 on, inflation was not as much caused by the expansion of domestic and foreign demand as by the growing profit hunger of the large firms. A small group of corporate managers, rather than government officials, seemed to be firmly installed in the driver's seat of the economy. In the words of Dieter Grosser, an economist at the University of Münster, *"Je grösser die Konzentration wirtschaftlicher Macht in Privathand wird, desto schwieriger dürfte es dem Staat werden, eine auf das Gesamtinteresse zielende Politik zu verfolgen."*[29]

NOTES

1. K. S. Pinson, *Modern Germany* (New York: Macmillan, 1966), p. 583.

2. M. Schnitzer, *East and West Germany: A Comparative Economic Analysis* (New York: Praeger, 1972), p. 38.

3. *Ibid.*, p. 67.

4. *Ibid.*, p. 68

5. W. Eucken, *Grundsätze der Wirtschaftspolitik* (Tübingen, J.C.B. Mohr, 1952), pp. 336 and 254.

6. F. Böhm, in *Monopoly and Competition and their Regulation*, ed., E. H. Chamberlin (New York: Macmillan, 1954), p. 157.

7. *Der Spiegel* (January 31, 1972), p. 38.

8. M MacLennan et al., *Economic Planning and Policies in Britain, France and Germany* (New York: Praeger, 1968), p. 66.

9. *Der Spiegel*, p. 30.

10. Pinson, *Modern Germany*, p. 578.

11. Statistisches Bundesamt, *Statistisches Jahrbuch fuer die Bundesrepublik Deutschland 1964* (Wiesbaden, 1964), p. 58.

12. *Statistisches Jahrbuch 1964*, pp. 61n-62n.

13. *Ibid.*, p. 118*.

14. *Statistisches Jahrbuch 1961*, p. 544.

15. H. H. Gotz, *Weil alle besser leben wollen* (Düsseldorf: Econ-Verlag, 1963),262.

16. Gesetz zur Förderung der Stabilität und des Wachstums der Wirtschaft, 8 June 1967.

17. *New Statesman* (6 January 1967), p. 4.

18. From "Stability and Growth as Objectives of Economic Policy," *The German Economic Review*, vol. 5, No. 3 (1967), pp. 177-188.

19. Schnitzer, *East and West Germany*, pp. 101-106.

20. OECD, *Economics Surveys, Germany* (Paris, 1969), p. 11.

21. OECD, *Economic Surveys, Germany* (Paris, 1970), p. 8.

22. OECD, *Economic Surveys, Germany* (Paris, 1970), p. 16.

23. *Bericht der Bundesregierung über die Lage der Landwirtschaft gemäss para. 4 des Landwirtschaftsgesetzes* (Bonn, 1969), p. 142.

24. *Ibid.*

25. Bundesministerium für Wirtschaft und Finanzen, *Leistung in Zahlen, '70* (Bonn, 1971), p. 82.

26. Statistisches Bundesamt, *Agrarstatistische Arbeitsunterlagen, 1968/1969* (Wiesbaden, 1969), p. 22.

27. Bundesministerium für Ernährung, Landwirtschaft und Forsten, *Die Verbesserung der Agrarstruktur in der Bundesrepublik Deutschland, 1967 – 1968* (Bonn, 1969), p. 36.

28. *The Economist* (January 10, 1970), p. xiv.

29. *Der Spiegel* (31 January 1972), p. 38. "The larger the concentration of economic power in private hands, the more difficult it will be for the state to pursue a policy aiming at the collective interest."

CHAPTER 9

BRITAIN EXPERIMENTS
WITH NATIONAL PLANNING

The British economy stagnated during most of the second half of the 1950s. Compared to the growth of other industrial nations, economic growth in Britain continued to rank very low. Both in terms of production and of foreign trade, Britain steadily lost ground to the more rapidly expanding economies of the Continent.

A number of reasons for the relatively slow growth of the British economy in the 1950s have been advanced by British and non-British economists. One line of explanation has given emphasis to the inadequacy of investment expenditure in Britain.[1] The data for the period 1955 to 1960 show that the fraction of gross national product devoted to capital formation was smaller in Britain than in the six countries of the E.E.C. While Britain used 17% of its gross national product for fixed capital investment in 1960, the corresponding ratio was 24% for West Germany. There is not always a consistent, automatic relationship between the level of investment and the rate of economic growth; in most instances, however, insufficient capital investment is a major cause of slow economic growth. A weak investment rate makes for a relatively slow growth of the capital stock and for a relatively rapid obsolescence of this stock. A slow expansion of the capital stock will generate a rate of increase of physical production which may fall short of the rate of increase of demand for output. Inadequate investment can thus produce inflation. During the 1950s, industrial production in Britain rose indeed less than in most European countries. What is worse, the index of industrial production remained almost unchanged in Britain between 1955 and 1958.

Slow economic growth can also be attributed to a number of other factors. The rate of growth of a particular economy depends on the value and on changes in the value of a matrix of variables such as the rate of growth of the labor force, the rapidity of technological advance, improvements in managerial efficiency and changes in the structure of industry. In the case of an open economy, aggregate economic growth may also heavily depend on the level of foreign demand for the exports of the pertinent economy and on quantitative and qualitative changes in this foreign demand.

It has been pointed out, for instance, that the labor supply in Britain in the 1950s was much more inelastic than in other major industrial nations on the Continent. Although France's labor force remained practically unchanged in numbers during the decade, the country was nevertheless able to transfer one-fourth of its agricultural labor from agriculture to industry, adding over two million workers to its industrial labor force. Such a transfer could not be effectuated in Britain where only a very small fraction of the entire labor force was active in agriculture. Refugees from the East continuously expanded the West German labor supply until the erection of the Berlin Wall in 1961. In Britain, the inflexibility of the labor supply, coupled with poor managerial talent in the field of industrial relations, made for a strike-prone economy in which deficient management-labor relations acted as a serious impediment in the achievement of productivity and production gains.

Some writers have given much weight to the conservativeness, the lack of expertise, and the excessive attachment to social and economic traditions of both business managers and trade union leaders as growth-impeding factors. Neither the British employers' associations, i.e., the *British Employers' Confederation*, the *National Association of British Manufacturers*, the *Federation of British Industries and the National Association of Chambers of Commerce*, nor the unions showed great interest in supporting improvements in industrial relations and technology. New techniques too often meant a bothersome change in customary ways of production for business managers and an ominous possibility of job losses for union leaders. The laying off of workers for whatever reason was opposed both by employers and unions. Regardless of the phase of the business cycle, firms continued hoarding labor, so that increased investment was often accompanied by increased under-employment and diminishing productivity in terms of output per man-hour worked. These attitudes were indeed growth-restricting in nature.

The failure of the British manfacturing sector to release labor contributed to the maintenance of a tight labor market; the resulting labor shortages constituted another impediment to rapid economic expansion.[2]

Other explanations of Britain's poor economic peformance in the 1950s have attached much importance to inflation and to government attempts to stop inflation as causes of slow economic growth. The argument holds that price inflation diminished the competitivenes of British exports, while attempts to stop inflation produced declines in the rate of economic growth. It has been shown, however, that there is no consistent relationship between price inflation and the rate of economic growth.[3] The data show that while price inflation in the 1950s was stronger in France than in Britain, French industrial production rose twice as fast as that of Britain. Austria and Norway showed a similar situation. On the other hand, the Netherlands, with less price inflation than Britain, recorded a much higher increase of industrial output. Industrial production in Italy and West Germany rose much faster than in Britain although price inflation in these two countries was much weaker than in Britain.

As pointed out by T. Wilson, it is questionable whether public measures taken to diminish or halt inflation necessarily reduce the rate of economic growth. The idea is that although these measures may have a direct restrictive impact on public and private output plans, these plans could not have been carried out with success even in the absence of the counter-inflation measures. They would have been frustrated by rising prices and shortages. The haphazard effects of inflation would simply take the role of counter-inflation policy. It is only when this policy is unduly severe or lasts for too long that the rate of economic growth will be impaired.[4]

Instead of limiting themselves to an evaluation of Britain's anti-inflationary policies in the 1950s, most of the critics brought under fire the British anti-cyclical policies of this period, the "stop-go" policies of both Labour and Conservative governments. A major goal of these policies was the restoration of external balance following periods of excess demand which often brought with them a rapid increase in imports and a weakening of exports. The balance of payments problem was "solved" by imposing deflationary measures on the economy which would result in a contraction of the home market; a declining domestic demand was expected to encourage producers to sell abroad and to diminish imports. External equilibrium was thus to be gained at the expense of economic growth and full utilization of domestic resources. Once the immediate balance of payments crisis was over, the authorities allowed the economy to expand until the appearance of excess demand brought back the endemic balance of payments problem. The critics of "stop-go" policies claimed that these had a negative effect on growth, largely through their adverse impact on entrepreneurial expectations and domestic investment.[5] These writers claim that the repeated periods of economic recession in the United Kingdom were brought about, not by the effects of spontaneous economic trends, but by deliberate government action. Too many government-ordered "stops" explain the slow growth of the British economy in the 1950s.

TABLE 9.1

GROWTH RATES: 1950 — 1962
Annual Averages

	G.N.P.	G.N.P. per head of population	G.N.P. per head of employed labor force
United Kingdom	2.6	2.1	2.0
Austria	6.0	5.8	4.9
Belgium	2.8	2.2	2.5
Denmark	3.8	2.9	3.2
France	4.4	3.5	4.2
West Germany	7.2	6.2	5.1
Ireland	1.3	1.7	2.6
Italy	6.3	5.7	4.7
Netherlands	4.9	3.6	3.5
Norway	3.6	2.7	3.4
Sweden	3.7	3.1	3.2

Source: O.E.C.D., *Policies for Economic Growth, General Statistics and Manpower Statistics, 1950-1962,* Paris, 1962.

The relatively slow growth of the British economy is shown by Table 9.1. Not only did the United Kingdom stand next to last among the indicated countries in growth of gross national product and product per capita during the 1950s, but it ranked last in growth of product per person employed.

Finally, some economists have attempted to evaluate quantitatively the role of various determinants of growth in both the British and other European economies in the 1950s. This type of approach was based on the recognition that the process and speed of economic growth cannot be explained in terms of monistic causality. Not only are the determinants of growth numerous, not only are they economic and non-economic in nature, but their relative roles in the growth process vary from economy to economy and vary also within a single economy over time. The idea is briefly that the explanation of different growth rates necessarily involves not only an analysis of different combinations of determinants but also a careful study of the possible different role a given determinant plays in each combination. E. F. Denison, in a study of the growth of nine countries during the period 1950 to 1962, attempted to explain differences in growth experience in terms of differences in the rate of increase of various factors of production, i.e., labor, capital and land, and also in terms of technological changes or what he defined more precisely as "changes in output per unit of input."[6] Since in a given economy and over a particular time period the various factors of production do not increase at the same rate, a scheme must be developed which will assign different weights to the factors so that the measure of aggregate factor growth reflects the varying rate of increase of each productive factor. In the Denison study, the weight given to each factor was determined by the share of national income earned by the pertinent factor. For instance, during the period 1950 to 1962, British labor earned 77.8% of national income. It was thus estimated that during this period, labor represented 77.8% of total British factor input. This meant that a 1% increase in labor alone was deemed to increase total factor input by 0.778%.

Denison's conclusion was that "to a considerable extent, conditions beyond the control of the United Kingdom were responsible for higher growth rates in other countries."[7] He noted, for instance, that among the nine countries under study, Britain ranked fifth in regard to the growth of employment, and that furthermore, with unemployment representing only 1.3% of the labor force in 1950, with a moderate natural increase in the population of working age, and without the help of a large inflow of immigrants such as experienced by West Germany, the British government could do little to increase the rate of growth of employment, a rate which vitally affected the rate of growth of total factor input and hence the rate of growth of aggregate output.

The Conservative Government's "Stop-Go" Policy, 1955-1961

The Conservative Chancellors who preceded Mr. Selwyn Lloyd were on the whole opposed to strong government intervention in the economy. They seemed to want to avoid public measures designed to improve the competitive mechanism of the type used in the German Federal Republic, and were not interested in any type of national economic planning aiming at a stimulation of economic growth. The Conservative governments in the second half of the 1950s appeared to want to pursue the goals of price stability, full employment and external balance within the framework of a quasi-*laissez faire* economy, an economy in which monetary policy and the Keynesian adjustment mechanisms of budgetary surpluses or deficits were to act as the sole regulators of economic development. Public regulation was largely intended to rectify sudden deteriorations in the balance of payments and to control wage and price inflation in order to avoid its adverse effect on external balance. In the absence of a balance of payments crisis, the main goal of public regulation was the maintenance of full employment. The obvious consequence of this type of economic policy was a high degree of economic instability. Recessions were imposed by deliberate government action for the sake of external balance. When no longer required, these "stop" periods were transformed into "go" periods by stimulation of monetary and budgetary policies. As one writer put it, "the development of the British economy between 1950 and 1961 followed a very characteristic zig-zag path unlike anything on the Continent."[8]

The relative slow growth of the British economy during these years, and the instability of this growth, induced many industrialists, scholars and even government officials in the early 1960s to urge the abandonment of "stop-go" and the adoption of national planning in order to improve the performance of the economy. The *Federation of British Industries* published in 1961 a report titled "The Next Five Years" in which it requested the government to set up with the help of industrial management and of trade union leaders a national plan in order to achieve price stability and a higher rate of economic growth. In April of the same year, the *National Institute of Economic and Social Research* conducted a conference which studied French planning methods. Planning at the firm level and even at an inter-firm level had existed in Britain in prior years. What economists, businessmen, and others advocated in 1960 and in 1961 was a national plan which would coordinate and harmonize the various plans developed within both the private and the public sectors.

Balance of payments problems influenced in a major way the economic policies of Mssrs. Butler, Macmillan, Thorneycroft and Heathcoat Amory. As tradition would have it, Mr. Butler relied mostly on monetary policy to convert into a surplus the large balance of payments current account deficit which had been brought about by the 1955 boom. The Bank rate was raised from 3% to 3.5% in January and to 4.5% in February. "Hire-purchase" restrictions were reintroduced. In July, the government called on banks to reduce credit.

These anti-inflationary policies were strengthened by Mr. Macmillan who succeeded Mr. Butler as Chancellor of the Exchequer in December 1955. The restriction of home demand was to continue for two years; it was only after mid-1968 that an expansionary policy was resumed. In February 1956, the Bank rate was raised to 5.5%, installment/purchase restrictions were tightened and public expenditure was cut.

Although the Suez crisis generated a speculative outflow of funds, exports continued to expand throughout 1956 while the British demand for imports grew at a slower pace; the balance of payments returned to a surplus on current account. By the end of the year, official assurances that the $2.80 parity would be retained restored confidence in sterling.

Confidence in sterling was to suffer a new blow in 1957. The formation of a European Economic Community was agreed to by the signatories of the Rome Treaty of March 1957. At the time there was discussion regarding the formation of a Free Trade Area whose membership would be larger than that of the E.E.C. The creation of the E.E.C. and the possible establishment of a larger customs union caused world-wide apprehension of changes in exchange rates. Exchange rate policy was to be discussed at an International Monetary Fund meeting in Washington in September and at an O.E.E.C. meeting in Paris one month later. It was then believed that although the West German Mark was undervalued, West Germany would refuse to officially appreciate the Mark against the U.S. Dollar because the large German trade surplus included a large deficit with the Dollar Area. It was expected that the Germans would insist at the International Monetary Fund meeting that the appreciation of the Mark should be obtained indirectly through a devaluation of the British and French currencies. These expectations caused large transfers of funds from

London to West Germany. The loss of British reserves became alarming. The authorities responded by tightening exchange controls, by freezing public investment and by raising the Bank rate to 7%, the highest level it had attained since 1921. In October, Britain received $250 million under a credit extended by the United States Export-Import Bank in December 1956. The crisis had been caused by expectations of a devaluation of sterling. It developed even though the British balance of payments continued to show a surplus on current account in 1957. It caused a decline in industrial production and an increase in unemployment. High interest rates started attracting foreign capital to Britain during the fall and international reserves began rising toward the end of the year.

TABLE 9.2

BALANCE OF PAYMENTS, UNEMPLOYMENT, PRICES
1955 — 1960

	Current Balance £ million	Net Long-Term Capital Inflow (1) £ million	Unemployment % of Labor Force	Retail Price Index: 1963 = 100
1955	−155	−122	1.2	80
1956	+208	−187	1.3	83.8
1957	+233	−106	1.6	86.9
1958	+344	−196	2.2	89.5
1959	+143	−255	2.3	90.1
1960	−265	−192	1.7	91.0

Source: *The British Economy, Key Statistics 1900-1970*, London, The Times Newspaper, Ltd., 1971, Tables F and N. Note: (1) + means net inflow; — means net outflow.

Mr. Thorneycroft resigned in January 1958 and was replaced by Mr. Heathcoat Amory who remained Chancellor of the Exchequer until July 1960. During 1958, the British current account surplus continued to grow even though exports had weakened since the end of 1957; a fall in world commodity prices improved the British terms of trade in such a way that in 1958 the current account showed the largest surplus since the war. In spite of an economic recession in the United States, international reserves rose by £300 million. Policy makers started being concerned about the rate of unemployment which had climbed to 2.2%. Policy gradually became expansionist. The Bank rate was lowered to 5% in June and to 4% by the end of the year. Installment-purchase restrictions were removed. Banks were free to grant as much credit as they wanted. In December, the government allowed free convertibility of sterling held by non-residents and the exchange rate remained fixed at $2.80 to the pound.

The expansionist measures of 1958 started stimulating home demand toward the end of the year. Demand continued to expand in 1959 and industrial production increased by 10% in that year. However, economic recovery generated a sharp increase in imports, and imports rose relative to exports. The current account surplus diminished by £ 200 million and in the following year, this surplus was transformed into the largest deficit experienced in nine years.

Declining exports, rising government expenditure abroad for foreign aid and defense, the declining competitiveness of British shipping and the growth of visible and "invisible" imports were some of the reasons for the appearance of the large balance of payments deficit in 1960. The government once again took corrective action by relying heavily on monetary policy. The Bank rate was raised to 5% in January and to 6% in June. Banks were required to maintain "special deposits" with the Bank of England in order to reduce their liquidity. Installment-purchases restrictions were reimposed and the profits tax was raised. Once again, the rise in production was stopped in order to correct external imbalance.

The revaluations in March 1961 of the West German Mark and the Dutch Florin caused a loss of confidence in sterling and started an outflow of funds from London. To avoid a massive flight from the Pound, the Bank of England, as well as Continental central banks started acquiring and holding on to sterling. These supporting operations cost Britain nearly one-fourth of its international reserves.

Mr. Selwyn Lloyd, Chancellor of the Exchequer since July 1960, resorted once again to "stop-go" to correct the situation. In July 1961, the government announced a 10% surcharge on customs duties, an increase in excise taxes, an increase in the "special deposit" requirements of commercial banks, a freeze of wages in government and in the nationalized industries, reductions in public expenditure and a Bank rate of 7%. Furthermore, the government invited representatives of employers and trade unions to join it in the formulation of a national medium-term economic plan. It had become apparent that the Conservative government had become disenchanted with the performance of the existing economic system and with "stop-go" policy. This line of policy had obviously failed to achieve price stability, external balance and a rate of economic growth comparable to that prevailing in the E.E.C.

Mr. Selwyn Lloyd and the National Economic Development Council

Mr. Lloyd's advocacy of national indicative planning was a drastic departure from traditional Conservative economic views. Suddenly, "planning was no longer a dirty word, or even a music-hall joke on a par with groundnuts or white fish."[9] During the late 1950s the British had become painfully aware of the poor performance of their economy relative to economic growth on the Continent and although in the early 1950s "the irksome restraints of rationing on consumption and of licenses on production were regarded as one of the intolerable and inevitable costs of Socialist muddle and meddle," national planning was generally considered at the end of the decade to be the unavoidable *sine qua non* of economic improvement.[10]

The establishment in 1962 of the *National Economic Development Council*, the NEDC or "Neddie" as the people liked to call it, was not designed to introduce mandatory planning into the United Kingdom. The agency was simply to centralize the "various processes of consultation and forecasting with a view to better co-ordination of ideas and plans."[11] The NEDC was to have only persuasive power. It could not compel government or firms to act in conformity with the recommendations contained in its national plan. At best, it could hope that because various interest groups participated in the drawing of the plan, the plan thus formulated would receive the support of government, business and the trade unions.

The Council was to be made up by twenty members. These were to include three Ministers, the director of the *National Economic Development Office*, NEDO, six employers' representatives, six trade union representatives, two persons representing the nationalized industries and two independent members.

The Council's task was to provide general guidance in the formulation of a five year plan. The actual preparation of the plan was entrusted to the *National Economic Development Office*. NEDO was subdivided into two divisions; the Economics Division was largely staffed by economists coming from the universities or from private research institutes; the Industrial Division was staffed by scientists and engineers. The entire staff consisted of about forty persons, very few of them being government employees. The very limited government representation in NEDO indicated the concern of its Director General, Sir Robert Shone, to keep NEDO as independent of Whitehall influence as possible.

In December 1963, *Economic Development Committees* were attached to NEDO which were to:

> Examine the economic performance, prospects and plans of the industry and assess from time to time the industry's progress in relation to the national growth objectives, and provide information and forecasts to the council on these matters . . . consider ways of improving the industry's economic performance, competitive power and efficiency . . . [12]

In October 1962, NEDO submitted to the Council the outline of a plan of economic development lasting until 1966. This plan was published in February 1963. [13] The plan's projections were based in part on the results of a NEDO inquiry held in the summer of 1962 which covered seventeen branches of British industry. The firms consulted, representing about 40% of the gross national product and 40% of total employment, indicated that they would be able to expand production at a rate of 4.8% per year up to 1966 and that they would obtain annual productivity per worker increases of 4.1% per year. On the basis of this information, the NEDC's first plan aimed at a yearly rate of overall economic growth of 4%, a rate based on the forecast that labor would increase at the yearly rate of 0.8% and that productivity per worker would rise by 3.2% per year.

The plan called for a target rate of growth of exports of 5.1% per year even though exports in prior years had not shown a growth rate exceeding 3%. Planners counted optimistically on rapid gains in productivity and relative price stability at home to make British exports more competitive in world markets. The plan set an annual rate of growth of imports of 4.7%, a rate which was somewhat larger than the targeted yearly rate of growth of the gross national product. An NEDC report published in April 1963 recognized that the successful realization of the plan depended on a rapid increase in exports. [14]

Expansionary measures were gradually adopted in 1962. In March, the Bank rate was reduced from 6% to 5%; the special deposit requirements for commercial banks rate was lowered to 4% at the end of the year. The April 1963 budget was intended to boost a still sluggish economy onto the planned growth path. Government spending was raised, personal direct and indirect taxes were cut and firms obtained liberalized investment allowances.

Government's expansionism in 1962 and 1963 was strengthened by the fact that the balance of payments on current account registered a substantial surplus. The balance of payments started deteriorating largely because exports weakened at a time when a still booming economy maintained a rapid growth in imports. The terms of trade were also moving adversely while long-term capital exports increased over their 1963 level. The 1964 current account deficit was the largest since 1951.

Planning and the Labour Government

The Labour government came to power in October 1964 with a commitment to maintain full employment. At the same time, it inherited from the preceding government serious balance of payments difficulties. Labour critics pointed out that the new Chancellor of the Exchequer, Mr. Callaghan, was unable to tackle properly the dilemma between full employment and external balance. As Graham put it.

> The simplest view of the Labour Government's policy towards the balance of payments is that they failed to devalue early enough. As a result they abandoned their objectives of full employment and growth, and so failure to deal correctly with the balance of payments led to the failure of their other policies . . . Stabilization policy became destabilizing. Industrial policy became an attempt at a series of hidden subsidies to exports or import replacement. Incomes policy was forced into a legally imposed freeze in the second half of 1966 and in 1968 it was used as an instrument of demand management — thereby almost destroying any hope of a *long-run* incomes policy . . . [15]

The government's immediate response to the problem of a rapidly increasing balance of payments deficit was to impose a Temporary Import Charge of 15% on most imports. Small subsidies for exports were granted and the government sought outside assistance to finance the deficit. The government chose an import duty surcharge in preference to a system of quotas on imports in the hope that the surcharge would both reduce imports and provide governments with revenue.

During November 1964, an apprehension developed that the government would devalue the Pound rather than deflate the economy. The November budget was not significantly deflationary and prices and employment continued to rise; by the end of the year, unemployment was as low as 1.7%. Fears of devaluation brought about large outflows of sterling. In order to restore confidence in the currency, the Bank of England announced on November 25 that it had obtained credits amounting to $3 billion from Canada, the United States, Japan, the Bank for International Settlements and a number of Western European banks. The Bank rate was raised to 7%.

The April 1965 budget had only a mildly deflationary impact on the economy. Prices continued to rise and the labor market remained tight. It became apparent that a balance of payments surplus would be realized at the earliest in 1966. Renewed speculation against the Pound brought a new crisis budget in July which imposed tighter exchange controls, new limitations on installment-purchase credit and deferments of public investment. It appeared that the government was returning to "stop-go" policy.

Labour economists and politicians claimed that the Conservative efforts to place the economy on a path of more rapid growth had only led to severe balance of payments deficits. Given the 1964 and 1965 deficits, government action called for a policy which could obtain a satisfactory combination of an adequate level of employment and external balance. The government decided to abandon the 1961-1966 plan and to follow a different one for the period 1965-1970.

The Labour government established in October 1964 a new Ministry which was to function as the government's principal planning machinery. The new *Department of Economic Affairs* was to be responsible not only for the formulation of a new national economic plan, but also for the development of an incomes and prices policy as well as for regional planning. The head of this new agency was Mr. George Brown, who, as First Secretary of State, took precedence over all other Cabinet members, including the Chancellor of the Exchequer.

The Labour party viewed its *National Plan* as something more than a new attempt at indicative planning. The Plan was set to act as a directive in the public sector; in its Foreword, Mr. Brown stated that "the plan for the first time represents a statement of Government policy and a commitment to action by the Government." Since government decided to implement the plan, it also tried to obtain more control over the planning function; this is the reason why the planning process was removed from the relatively independent NEDC and given to DEA.

The Labour plan was presented to the House of Commons in September 1965. Its main objective was stated as follows:

> The Plan is designed to achieve a 25% increase in national output between 1964 and 1970. This objective has been chosen in the light of past trends in national output and output per head and a realistic view of the scope for improving upon these trends. It involves achieving a 4% annual growth rate of output well before 1970 and an annual average of 3.8% between 1964 and 1970. [16]

The plan, contained in a volume of about five hundred pages, included a detailed feasibility study of this growth target. This study tended to reveal the improbability rather than the feasibility of attaining the desired rate of growth and led the planners to recognize that the 25% growth objective "may seem an ambitious aim at a time when balance of payments considerations limit the short-term possibilities for expansion." [17]

The planner's forecast rested on two basic estimates. The first was that manpower would grow at an annual rate of 0.4% between 1964 and 1970; the second was that productivity per worker would rise by 3.4% per year during the same period. Although the productivity estimate involved a large increase, given appropriate policies, the target would not have been unattainable in the presence of external balance. In spite of the actual past performance of the economy, the plan was not overambitious insofar as it concerned the internal economy. The Achilles' heel of the program was the balance of payments. The objective of an annual rate of growth of exports of 5.2% exceeded the corresponding projection of the Conservative plan and seemed quite unattainable in the light of an actual rate of 3.1% which prevailed during the period 1960 to 1964. The government recognized that inflation was a serious obstacle to the expansion of exports; the establishment of a *Prices and Incomes Board* and the enactment of a statutory incomes policy were meant to do away with this difficulty. The government acted in a number of ways in its attempt to remove obstacles to growth. It increased the funds available to the *National Research Corporation* in order to facilitate the adoption by firms of more efficient methods of production and distribution; it financed the establishment of new business schools in the hope of upgrading the quality of business management. *Industrial Training* boards were to finance the improvement of industrial skills.

In spite of all these measures, the government abandoned its plan in July 1966. In the words of one writer, "the Government preferred to sacrifice faster growth and full employment to the existing exchange rate, and not the other way around." [18] Indeed, in spite of the deflationary measures taken in 1965, consumer demand remained strong during the first half of 1966, as did the pressure on resources. Costs and prices were rising rapidly; the balance of payments ceased improving after the first quarter of the year. Installment-purchase credit was restricted in February and the May budget introduced the "selective employment tax" which was expected to have a deflationary impact on the economy in the fall of 1966. The amount of the tax was initially £ 1.25 per week per male employee, 62.5 pence per female or male child employee and 40 pence per female child employee. The burden of the tax differed, however, among various industries. While the construction, distribution and services industries were burdened with the full amount of the tax, the public sector and the transport industries received a 100% refund on their S.E.T. payments. Manufacturing industries received a refund of about 130% of this tax. In May, a *Voluntary Program* was introduced to restrict the export of capital from the United Kingdom to the developed sterling area countries, i.e., Australia, New Zealand, South Africa and the Irish Republic. British firms intending to invest in those countries were required to obtain prior permission to do so from the Bank of England.

Speculation against sterling reappeard in June and July. The Labour government reacted promptly by introducing on July 20 a package of strong deflationary measures. These included a return to a 7% Bank rate, a 10% increase on purchase tax rates, a one-year surcharge of 10% on surtax liabilities, cuts in public investment programs and a six-months freeze of prices, wages, salaries and other income, to be followed by another six months of "severe restraint."

These measures brought an effective end to the *National Plan* and economic planning in the United Kingdom. They revealed that the Labour government had changed its ranking of priorities and that the goals of rapid economic growth and full employment had been subordinated to that of external balance. The Labour government could no longer claim that it could manage the economy better than could its Conservative predecessors.

The 1967 Devaluation and Post-Devaluation Policies

Labour government economic policies followed three main phases during the 1960s. During the first phase, covering the period October 1964 to July 1966, the government gave top priority to the objective of rapid economic expansion. The overall aim of the Labour policy was to implement the *National Plan*. During the second phase, lasting until November 1967, the government substituted external balance for rapid growth as its principal objective and tried to avoid devaluation by means of deflation. Following devaluation in November 1967, the government embraced policies designed to make devaluation effective.

Direct government intervention and fiscal policy were used at first to reduce the existing gap between actual and planned rates of growth. Among the various types of action taken by the government to modernize the structure of the economy and to increase levels of productivity was the establishment of the *Industrial Reorganization Corporation, I.R.C.*, in January 1966. This new agency was given the power to "(i) promote or assist the reorganization or development of any industry; or (ii) if requested so to do by the Secretary of State, establish or develop, or promote or assist the establishment or development of, any industrial entreprise." With financial resources amounting to £ 150 million, the I.R.C. started encouraging mergers which could reduce duplication in production and which could raise productivity by means of economies of scale. This agency was particularly active in the electrical, electronics, ball-bearing and scientific instruments industries.[19]

The *National Board for Prices and Incomes* also attempted to increase market efficiency through the control of monopoly profits. It was able to order a firm to reduce its prices when it found that the firm's market power was excessive. Public outlays for non-military research and development were increased following the enactment of the *Science and Technology Act* of 1965 and the *Industrial Expansion Act* of 1968. The Labour government established in 1965 a Committee of Inquiry, the Geddes Committee, which was charged with the task of recommending measures for the modernization of the shipbuilding industry. These recommendations were embodied in the *Shipbuilding Industry Act* of 1967 which led to the merger of four shipyards and to attempts to modernize what had become, by international standards, a relatively inefficient industry. Government financial assistance was available to support modernization programs.

Among the most important fiscal measures taken by the government to expand economic activity were the replacement of privileged tax treatment granted to firms for the pruchase of capital assets by direct government cash grants and changes in corporate taxation. Both measures were intended to encourage larger investment by firms. As of April 1966, the corporate profits tax was reduced from 56% to 40%; on the other hand, the receipt of dividends by shareholders, generally tax exempt until then, was now treated as ordinary taxable income earned by the recipient.

The government's expansionist predisposition in 1965 was also expressed in the *Monopolies and Mergers Act* of that year. From a legal standpoint, mergers can be viewed as possible antitrust arrangements, as agreements which may result in restraints of trade and of competition. From an economic point of view, mergers can generate economic benefits, largely by producing greater rationality in plant location and operation; a frequent economic benefit brought about by the formation of a merger is the realization of economies of scale which will lower costs per unit of output.

The *Restrictive Trade Practices Act* of 1956 had established a judicial body, the *Restrictive Practices Court*, which was to hear and adjudicate antitrust cases. In order to win, defendants in these cases had to show that the action or agreement under scrutiny satisfied at least one of the "public interest criteria" stipulated by the Act. Not only did they have to show that their action harmonized with one of the explicitly enumerated "public interest gateways," but they had to convince the court that although their action served in some way the public interest, this benefit was not outweighed by possible detrimental economic and social effects.

The *Monopolies and Mergers Act* of 1965 created a procedure of public intervention in monopolistic practices which was not judicial in character. The approach was purely administrative. In the case of mergers, the Board of Trade was to select cases of proposed or effectuated mergers which were to be referred to and studied by the Monopolies Commission. Following its inquiries, the Commission had to recommend to the Board of Trade within a specified period of time whether or not the proposed merger should be prohibited or whether or not an effectuated merger should be dissolved. The Act of 1965 did not specify any "public interest criteria"; no "public interest gateways" were enumerated. The Monopolies Commission was given wide discretion in the determination of what furthered and what hindered the public interest.

In deciding whether or not a particular merger or monopoly offended the public interest, the Commission was free to weigh against the detriment of market power any economic or social benefits generated by these organizations. In its investigations, the Commission relied mostly on economic criteria and looked at the possible technological, financial, managerial and marketing advantages or disadvantages of the pertinent case under study.[20]

The *Monopolies and Mergers Act* was not used by the government to discourage the formation of mergers. Indeed, the number of industrial mergers was larger in 1966 than it had been in the two prior years and the value of assets transferred in 1966 was considerably higher than in earlier years. Mergers went on increasing in 1967 and in 1968.

The July 1966 deflationary measures were an open recognition by the Labour government that long-term expansionary aims had been sacrificed for the sake of short-term balance of payments considerations. And yet these measures, and particularly the absolute standstill imposed on prices and incomes during the second half of the year, were unable to provide a long-run cure for the country's external difficulties. 1966 registered a small current account surplus of 43 million; however, the current account started deteriorating early in 1967 and the surplus was changed into a small deficit during the first half of that year.

A serious balance of payments crisis developed during the second half of 1967. Exports declined, both in volume and in value. Reasons for this fall were both political and economic; the closure of the Suez canal, the Arab boycott which followed the war in the Middle East, dock strikes in London and in Liverpool and a decline in the growth of world trade were all significant variables which adversely affected British exports. The value of total exports fell from £5,047 million in 1966 to £5,029 million in 1967. At the same time, the value of British imports rose from £5,950 million in 1966 to £6,437 in the following year.[21] The rise in imports was largely due to the abolition of T.I.C. in November 1966 and to an increase in Britain's propensity to import. An increase in the net outflow of long-term capital worsened the deterioration of the balance of payments in 1967.

By the end of 1967 it had become apparent that the deflationary policies of 1966 had failed to produce an external surplus; instead of a sizeable surplus required for the repayment of foreign loans which were to mature in the late 1960s and early 1970s, the current account at the end of 1967 showed a deficit of £312 million. This deficit seemed to convince the government that the maintenance of the existing sterling parity and the use of deflation were unable to generate sustained external equilibrium. This view led the government to devalue the pound on November 18, 1967. The new parity rendered the pound equivalent to U.S. $2.40.

TABLE 9.3

BRITISH FOREIGN TRADE AND THE BALANCE OF PAYMENTS:
1960 — 1970

In million £

	Current Account Balance	Net Long-Term Capital Inflow (1)	Value of U.K. Exports (f.o.b.)	Value of U.K. Imports (c.i.f.)
1960	−265	−192	3,648	4,655
1961	− 4	+ 68	3,796	4,547
1962	+112	− 98	3,905	4,627
1963	+114	−149	4,211	4,984
1964	−395	−354	4,411	5,696
1965	− 77	−197	4,728	5,752
1966	+ 43	−106	5,047	5,950
1967	−312	−139	5,029	6,437
1968	−306	− 81	6,182	7,897
1969	+437	− 9	7,039	8,315
1970	+631	−293	7,741	9,048

Source: *The British Economy, Key Statistics 1900-1970*, supra, Tables K and N.
Note: (1) + means net inflow; − means net outflow.

The devaluation, to be effective, required a major shift of resources from home use to activities capable of improving the balance of payments. It was not the government's plan to obtain this shift by means of drastic measures. Policies of the traditional type were followed in order to achieve three main goals. The first goal involved boosting business investment; the second aim was managing overall demand so that the growth of demand would not exceed the rate of capacity growth, i.e., a rate of about 3% per year; finally, in order to strengthen the competitiveness of exports, government proposed to limit the rise of costs.

Demand restraining measures were taken only gradually and it was probably largely due to the government's cautious "stage approach" that a balance of payments deficit persisted during 1968. At the time of devaluation, the Bank rate was raised from 6.5% to 8%; selective restrictions were placed on bank lending and the installment-purchase of automobiles was made costlier. The government also announced a cut of 400 million in public expenditures planned for 1968-1969 and of 450 million for 1969-1970 were announced.

The March 1968 budget provided for an increase in tax rates estimated to add about £923 million to the 1968 tax revenue. At the same time, the policy of voluntary limitations on price and income increases was extended until December 1969. The government obtained larger powers to maintain price and pay stability. Pay increases were only justified when necessary for the furtherance of the "national interest." This meant that a maximum pay increase of 3.5% per year could be granted in those cases where the pay "was too low to maintain a reasonable standard of living" or was "seriously out of line" with typical renumeration for similar work; the increase was justified when required to obtain a necessary redistribution of manpower. Also, in cases of genuine and sufficient increases in productivity, a pay increase exceeding 3.5% per year could be authorized.

In May, bank lending was restricted; banks were asked to limit their total lending to a maximum of 104% of the November 1967 level. The November measures did not weaken consumers' expenditures. As a matter of fact, a consumption boom developed during the first quarter of 1968, largely caused by expectations of rising prices. Output in this period grew at a rate of 2.7% per year; this rate of growth had averaged 1.9% in 1966 and 1.7% in 1967. The accelerated growth of output was made partly possible by a reduction in stocks, and partly by a rise in imports; during the first quarter of 1968, imports grew at a rate of about 6% per year in volume.[22]

Following the March budget, consumers' expenditure and aggregate demand weakened and the growth of output declined. Because manufacturers attempted to rebuild stocks, imports experienced only a slight decline in growth and their growth again became substantial during the third quarter of 1968. Personal consumption expanded after mid-year and it became quite apparent then that the government's devaluation strategy was not providing the expected results. In

November, the government took new deflationary action. The rates of indirect taxes were raised by 10%; an "import deposit scheme" was forced on importers; it required them to deposit 50% of the value of the goods they imported with Customs for a period of six months. Installment-purchase credit and bank lending were futher restricted. In spite of these measures, the deficit on both current and capital account remained near the 1967 level. It appeared that the government had underestimated the growth of home demand in 1968 and that it had overestimated the switch of resources to the balance of payments that was to occur during the same year.

The 1969 budget brought additional increases in taxation. Public expenditure was again restrained. Fear that devaluation was not being as effective as it had been at first expected induced the government to strive for a current account surplus through a further weakening of home demand.

The balance of payments started improving during the first half of 1969. Exports began to expand rapidly, strengthened by both a strong growth in world trade and by the competitive advantage given them by devaluation. While exports grew rapidly in this period, imports remained practically unchanged. The current account improved so rapidly that it registered a surplus of £160 million by mid-year. The government's goal of achieving a surplus on current and long-term capital account of £300 million by March 1970, was attained at the end of 1969. The improvement in the balance of payments was obtained, however, at the price of a very slow growth of output and with the help of continued restrictions on foreign trade. The import deposit scheme was retained for another year and unemployment was allowed to increase from 2.2% in the second quarter of the year to 2.4% in October.

Although the data for 1968 and 1969 recorded large gains in productivity, these gains were not due to the effect of more efficient methods of production utilized in industry, but were largely the result of a reduction in the number of employed industrial workers following the imposition of the Selective Employment Tax and increased social security contributions in 1966 and in 1967. In spite of these gains the growth of domestic output remained well below the National Plan target and failed even to attain the average modest rate of 3% prevailing in earlier years. Except for the external surplus, 1969 was not a year of great economic victories.

TABLE 9.4

ECONOMIC PERFORMANCE: 1964 — 1970

	Level of Unemployment (1,000)	Rate of Price Inflation (%)	Growth of Output (%)
1964	362	3.0	5.5
1965	308	4.8	2.7
1966	323	4.4	2.1
1967	512	3.1	1.8
1968	541	4.0	3.1
1969	535	5.1	1.7
1970	573	7.3	1.7

Source: *National Income and Expenditure, 1970; Department of Employment Gazette.*

The most noticeable development of 1970 was the acceleration of price and wage inflation. During the first half of the year, average earnings rose at the rate of 13% per year while retail prices increased at the rate of 8%.[23] The initial inflationary impulse was generated by the price increases which followed devaluation and the subsequent tax increases. The trade unions, abandoning their policy of restraint, started asking for compensatory wage increases. During the third quarter of 1969, the government allowed large wage increases in the public sector. The unions, sensing a weakening in the government's prices and income policy, asked and obtained similar and even larger wage increases in the private sector. The approach of general elections in June 1970 predisposed the government to grant wage claims; exporters, still favored by the devaluation of 1967 and by inflation abroad, were not in the mood to strongly resist the demands of the trade unions.

The economy started experiencing the problems of "stagflation." While prices and wages were registering their fastest increase since the early 1950s, unemployment continued to remain high in the construction, mining and shipbuilding industries. Total unemployment was larger in 1970 than it had been one year earlier. At the same time, helped by a sharp growth in world trade, the current account surplus continued to increase.

The April 1970 budget was mildly reflationary. Monetary and fiscal policy restraints were relaxed. The Bank rate was reduced from 7.5% to 7% and restrictions on the supply of credit were eased. Personal allowances against the income tax were increased and the rate of deposits on imports was reduced to 30% in May and to 20% in

September. In October, a cut in the income tax was announced, to be effective in April of the following year; at the same time reductions in public expenditure of £300 million in the period 1971-1972 were to neutralize the effects of the tax cut, while reducing the public sector's claims on resources.

After six years of Labour administration, learned economists in the universities or in the government agencies in London could still ask: "*Quo vadis Britannia?*"

Conclusion

There were no good reasons for Britons to feel optimistic in 1970 about the economic future of their country. Although a balance of payments surplus had been attained in 1969 and in 1970, Britain was losing foreign market shares. Unemployment had worsened, and so had inflation. The production and productivity targets of the *National Plan* had not been achieved and what was worse, "planning was many months dead already, or murdered." [24] Britain in 1970 remained one of the slowest growing countries in Europe.

Environmental, structural and managerial analyses of British growth problems in the 1960s have been depressing rather than encouraging. [25] The general mood of British economists at the close of the decade is probably well expressed by the following words of W. Beckerman:

> The productivity target of the National Plan was nowhere in sight of achievement by 1970. Nor did the Government achieve the shift in the pattern of resources in favor of investment that was one of the key objectives of the Plan. And in the field of short-run demand management, the closing years of the Labour Government saw the economy operating with levels of unemployment that were as high as during the worst years of the Conservative Government. . . . [26]

NOTES

1. D. Williams, "The Anatomy of a Crisis: Investment and Output in Britain, 1958-1962," *Banca Nazionale del Lavoro* (March 1963), pp. 108-120; T. Browaldh, "A Swedish View of Britain's Economy," *Three Banks Review* (June 1963), pp. 3-16.

2. J. and A.M. Hackett, *The British Economy, Problems and Prospects* (London: George Allen & Unwin, Ltd., 1967), pp. 33-39.

3. O. Eckstein, "Inflation, The Wage-Price Spiral and Economic Growth," in *The*

Relationship of Prices to Economic Stability and Growth (Washington: United States Government Printing Office, 1958), p. 361.

4. T. Wilson, "Inflation and Growth," *Three Banks Review*, No. 51 (September 1961), pp. 3-21.

5. S. Wells, *British Export Performance: A Comparative Study* (London: Cambridge University Press, 1963), p. 67.

6. E.F. Denison, *Why Growth Rates Differ: Postwar Experience in Nine Western Countries* (Washington: The Brookings Institution, 1967).

7. E.F. Denison, "Economic Growth," *Britain's Economic Prospects*, ed., R.E. Caves (Washington: The Brookings Institution, 1968), p. 263.

8. Hackett, *The British Economy*, p. 44.

9. R. Opie, "Economic Planning and Growth," *The Labour Government's Economic Record, 1964-1970*, ed., W. Beckerman (London: Duckworth, 1972), p. 157.

10. *Ibid.*

11. House of Commons Debates (July 25, 1961), Col. 220.

12. *Board of Trade Journal* (December 13, 1963).

13. *Growth of the United Kingdom Economy to 1966*, NEDC, HMSO (February 1963).

14. NECD, *Conditions Favorable to Faster Growth*, HMSO (April 1963).

15. A. Graham and W. Beckerman, "Economic performance and the Foreign Balance," *The Labour Government's Economic Record, 1964-1970*, p. 11.

16. *The National Plan*, Cmd. 2764, HMSO (September 1964), par. 6.

17. *Ibid.*, p. iii.

18. Opie, "Economic Planning and Growth," p. 171.

19. A. Graham, "Industrial Policy," *The Labour Government's Economic Record, 1964-1970*, pp. 178-217.

20. C.K. Rowley, "Mergers and Public Policy in Great Britain," *Journal of Law and Economics*, vol. II (April 1968), pp. 75-132.

21. *The British Economy, Key Statistics 1900-1970*, Table K, p. 14.

22. OECD, *Economic Surveys, United Kingdom* (Paris, 1968), p. 9.

23. OECD, *Economic Surveys, United Kingdom* (Paris, 1970), p. 5.

24. Opie, "Economic Planning and Growth," *The Labour Government's Economic Record, 1964-1970*, p. 177.

25. G.A. Phillips and R.T. Maddock, *The Growth of the British Economy, 1918-1968* (London: George Allen & Unwin, Ltd., 1973).

26. W. Beckerman, "Objectives and Performance: an Overall View," *The Labour Government's Economic Record, 1964-1970*, p. 68.

CHAPTER 10

THE ITALIAN MOVEMENTS
TOWARD GLOBAL PLANNING
FIRST, "PIANO"; THEN, "FORTE"

Italian writers, specially those writing for the English-speaking public, have tended to emphasize that the high rate of growth experienced
by their country during the 1950s was not the product of global
economic planning but was largely due to the efforts of *l'iniziativa
privata.*[1] An explanation of the economic boom of the 1950s must
necessarily stress the vital role played in the process of growth by the
managerial talent of *Fiat, Romeo, Lancia, Olivetti* and many other privately owned firms. This does not mean that the Italian economic
miracolo must be viewed as having taken place in a predominantly
laissez-faire, market-oriented economy. Public intervention in the
economy was extensive and was facilitated by the existence of a large
public sector of pre-war origin. Throughout the decade, massive public investment supported the high rate of growth of the Italian
economy. The direction this investment took was in turn determined
by a great deal of *ad hoc,* partial, and often uncoordinated planning
undertaken by government and paragovernment agencies. Although
the central government never formulated and implemented in this
period a national economic plan, IRI, the *Cassa per il Mezzogiorno* and
ENI based their investment decisions on both short-term and long-
term plans.[2]

The absence of a national plan at a time when the Cassa and ENI
were each investing over $1 billion in the economy must be understood
in terms of existing political philosophies. Throughout most of his
political life, De Gasperi had manifested little interest in national
planning.[3] The right-wing faction of the Christian Democratic party
feared that the enactment of a national plan would facilitate a return to
the economic tactics of the Fascist state; they supported at most limited
plans relating to chosen geographical or functional sectors. Communists and Socialists took the position that national planning could

242

not be effective unless the state acquired possession of the means of production. It was largely due to the more moderate position taken by the Socialist leader Pietro Nenni and to the support of national planning given by left-wing Christian Democrats such as Amintore Fanfani and Aldo Moro that a coalition government of Christian Democrats and Socialists succeeded in having Parliament approve a national economic plan in the 1960s.

In the 1950s however, the Vanoni proposal of 1955 remained the closest approximation of global planning in Italy. Ezio Vanoni's "Scheme for the Development of Employment and Income in Italy for the Decade 1955-1964" never became an official party or government act. It was never implemented although it was to serve as a blue-print for future plans. It was soon forgotten during the boom years of the second half of the 1950s, years which strengthened the conservative voice of the Christian Democratic party. The years of the economic *miracolo* brought growth rates which exceeded those hoped for by Vanoni and economic prosperity seemed to support the case of those opposed to global planning.

Vanoni's scheme aimed to reduce poverty and unemployment in the country through the creation of four million new jobs in the course of the decade. The proportion of the labor force engaged in agriculture had to be reduced and this would be achieved through increased investment in all sectors of the economy. The achievement of these goals would necessitate an average annual rate of growth of gross national product of 5%, a rate of growth that was to be made possible by high levels of investment, rapidly rising exports and price stability.[4]

The Christian Democratic opposition to total planning contrasted with the party's support of massive investment financed by public or semi-public agencies. Extensive public investment played a key role in the maintenance of high growth rates in the 1950s and in bringing about the economic *miracolo* of the period 1959-1962. As Professor Hildebrand remarked, public investment during the period 1951 to 1959 gave Italy "one of the highest rates of saving in the world" and facilitated a rapid growth of output by "stimulating formerly stagnant markets, creating numerous external economies favorable to lower private costs, and opening up larger internal uses for domestically produced capital goods."[5] Public investment decisions in the 1950s were, of course, the outcome of planning decisions taken by the land reform agencies, by IRA, by the *Cassa* and by ENI.

Politics and Economic Growth in the 1950s

The Christian Democratic Prime Ministers who succeeded De Gasperi continued to believe in the desirability of an Italian economy based on a market system in which production and growth would mainly be guided by the price mechanism. None of them, however, advocated an essentially *laissez-faire* market economy. Indeed, government intervention in the economy grew in the 1950s. Although the various Christian Democratic governments of this period claimed to uphold private enterprise, free international trade and orthodox monetary policy, and although they refrained from taking serious steps leading to national economic planning, they nevertheless approved direct and strong government intervention to reduce poverty and economic backwardness in the South and created ENI in 1953, a gigantic public holding company; ENI, through other holding agencies such as AGIP, SNAM, ANIC and AGIP Nucleare, controlled the production, refining and sale of petroleum products, the production and distribution of natural gas, the hydrochemical industry and the development of nuclear energy. These governments, as was noted earlier, did not object to partial planning by public agencies and to the use of public funds to modernize the industrial structure and to build a more efficient infrastructure.

It was however only in 1960 that the Christian Democratic party ceased courting right-wing parties and, with subsequent Socialist support, started maneuvering toward a more centrally and more comprehensively managed economy. It was only then that the Christian Democrats appeared to remember the words a Christian Democrat had pronounced in 1949: "It is not necessary, because of some fear of Russian-type planning, to have no plan at all. It is not necessary to continue with disordered economic interventions which are in large measure the legacy of Fascism and war. If the Italian people should be given a program of rigorous economic direction, and at the same time they should see swept away at least a portion of existing parapublic, parasitical and damaging bodies, they would heave a huge sigh of satisfaction."[6]

During the 1950s Italy showed the curious example of growing political factionalism accompanied by sustained economic growth, growth which peaked during the years 1959 to 1962, the years of the so-called Italian "economic miracle." A brief sketch of the political trends in the decade of the 1950s may give a more meaningful context to the explanation of economic events in that period.

Until 1957, Christian Democrats continued to form governments on the basis of the traditional *quadripartito* coalition of Christian Democrats, Social Democrats and Liberals, helped by Republican support. This arrangement allowed the governments of Mario Scelba and Antonio Segni to obtain necessary parliamentary majorities without the support of either the Socialists and Communists or the right-wing Monarchists and neo-Fascists. The *quadripartito* arrangement came to an end with the collapse of the Segni government in May 1957. Segni's successor, the Christian Democrat Adone Zoli, formed a single-party government which had to rely on neo-Fascist support to obtain a parliamentary majority.

Early in 1959, Segni formed again a government and continued Zoli's move to the right; Segni's second government was a single-party arrangement, supported by Liberals, Monarchists and neo-Fascists. Segni's successor, Ferdinando Tembroni, continued to depend on right-wing support.

The anti-Fascist demonstratins which occurred in Genoa in June 1960 caused the Christian Democrats to discard right-wing support and to initiate an "opening to the Left" under the leadership of a new Prime Minister, Amintore Fanfani, and of the party's Secretary, Aldo Moro. This strategy had the support of President Gronchi, a man who favored a strong Christian Democratic administration, supported by the Socialists.

In January 1962, Moro, speaking at a Congress of the Christian Democratic party, invited the Socialists to support the government. In February of the same year, Fanfani, who had been Prime Minister since the summer of 1960, formed a new government of Christian Democrats, Social Democrats and Republicans, a government which received the assurance of support from the Socialist party.

In spite of the frequent changes in government leadership, Italy in the 1950s recorded yearly rates of economic growth that were second only to those experienced by West Germany. The Italian rates of economic growth, both on a total and on a *per capita* basis, were in fact the third highest in the world. Furthermore, the Italian growth rates exhibited a remarkable stability when compared to similar rates in other European Countries.

The growth rate tended to accelerate after the mid-1950s and peaked in 1961.[7] This period of sustained economic growth was accompanied by relative price stability and by a rapid improvement in overall labor productivity.

The Italian economic boom of the 1950s has been described as a case of rapid economic growth without full employment, without central planning and without nationalizations.[8] A number of causes can be identified in the explanation of this growth. Firstly, the Italian economy was characterized by the existence of a large pool of unemployed or underemployed labor, largely agricultural labor, which allowed a continuous transfer of manpower from low-productivity to high-productivity sectors. This transfer facilitated rapid growth in that it brought about higher productivity levels and an expanding input of man-hours. C. Kindleberger has explained the Italian economic experience of the 1950s in terms of the W. Lewis model of economic development.[9] The Lewis model involves a two-sector economy. There is a small capitalist industrial sector which constitutes an "island of development surrounded by a sea of backwardness"; the 'sea' is a large, economically backward subsistence sector containing a perfectly elastic supply of labor, a supply which is available in unlimited quantities to the advanced sector. In the subsistence sector, the marginal product of labor is practically nil and labor can thus be siphoned-off this sector without reducing the aggregate substistence output. By offering a wage rate which is slightly higher than that prevailing in the backward sector, the industrial sector can obtain all the labor it wants from the subsistence sector at an unchanging wage rate.

If in the advanced sector the entrepreneurs reinvest their profits in order to create more capital and are able to hire additional labor at a constant wage rate, productivity in the advanced sector will rise and so will profits. As profits continue to be reinvested and as more labor is hired, productivity in the advanced sector goes on increasing and industrial profits continue to grow. This process can continue as long as the labor supply in the subsistence sector remains perfectly elastic and the wage rate in the advanced sector remains unchanged.

There are two main implications in the Lewis model. First, as capital accumulates in the advanced sector, labor productivity in that sector increases. Second, as surplus labor moves out of the backward sector, marginal productivity in that sector will eventually rise. The movement of manpower from the low-productivity to the high-productivity sector will thus improve overall productivity. Kindleberger believes that the existence of this type of economic dualism in Italy formed the mainspring of the country's economic boom in the 1950s.

Another cause of rapid economic growth was the existence of a large public sector which allowed the government to develop productivity-increasing industrial activities by means of a high level of public investment. The Vanoni study of 1955 had predicted that the investment-GNP ratio would increase from 16% in 1951 to 24% in 1964. The target ratio was attained as early as 1960. This remarkable investment performance was made possible, among other factors, by the economy's relative price and wage stability. With wages rising more slowly than productivity throughout the 1950s, profits could increase and rising profits in turn generated Lewis's process of growth. During the decade, industrial wages rose at an annual average of 4.1% while industrial productivity showed yearly gains of 5%.

The increasing share of gross fixed investment and of exports in the country's aggregate demand in the 1950s were complementary agents of growth. While total consumption expenditure increased at a rate of 4.9% per year in this period, gross fixed investment increased by 9.3% and exports grew at the annual rate of 13.8%.[10] The rapidly expanding investment expenditure boosted aggregate demand and provided for a rapid growth in productive capacity.

The high rate of overall economic growth which characterized the 1950s, and especially the years 1959 to 1962, can thus be viewed as resulting from a Lewis-type conjunction of factors such as an excess supply of labor, price and wage stability, a continuous transfer of labor from low-productivity to higher-productivity sectors and high levels of investment made possible by both high profit levels and massive public investment. Rapidly expanding exports gave further strength to the process of growth.[11]

In the 1950s, only Japan and West Germany surpassed Italy's rate of export growth. The rapidity with which exports expanded during the decade allowed this resource-poor country to pay for the equally rapidly increasing imports of raw materials, food and consumer goods. The gradual change in the composition of the exports was as important as their rate of growth. Manufactured products represented nearly three-fourths of all exports in 1961. Clothing, metallurgical products,

TABLE 10.1

ECONOMIC GROWTH INDICATORS
IN CONSTANT PRICES
(In billion lire)

Year	Wholesale Price Index: 1966=100	GNP	GNP Growth Rate %	Total Investment	Exports
1951	92.9	14,473	——	2,649	1,012
1952	87.8	15,022	3.8	2,685	1,190
1953	87.4	16,073	7.0	3,117	1,385
1954	86.5	16,609	3.3	3,391	1,502
1955	87.4	17,711	6.6	4,038	1,695
1956	88.9	18,479	4.3	4,238	1,982
1957	89.8	19,429	5.1	4,567	2,415
1958	88.2	20,377	4.9	4,703	2,475
1959	85.5	21,729	6.6	5,154	2,749
1960	86.3	23,036	6.0	5,967	3,354
1961	86.5	24,843	7.8	6,739	3,838
1962	89.3	26,316	5.9	7,308	4,308

Sources: Banca d'Italia, *Relazione Annuale;* ISTAT, *Annuario Statistico Italiano,* various issues.

chemicals, machinery and vehicles constituted the bulk of these exports.[12] Unlike the United Kingdom, Italy was able to concentrate export growth on those products for which international demand was rising fastest. Italian export firms also excelled in sales efforts, in the servicing and maintenance of their products after their sale and in credit arrangements. More important, Italy's excellent export performance in this period was mainly due to the fact that the country's products remained highly price-competitive during the entire decade. While the export price index of Italian exports fell by 0.5% per year, export prices of other trading nations, with the exception of Japan and Switzerland, rose by 2% to 4% per year during the period 1950 to 1960.[13]

Although Italy's current account balance showed a surplus in every year between 1957 and 1962, the country retained a yearly deficit in the visible trade balance until 1965. The deficit is easily explained by the fact that throughout the 1950s, and until 1965, the value of visible imports continued to exceed the value of visible exports. The current account surplus of the years 1957 to 1962 originated in the net surplus of the invisible trade and remittances accounts. Tourists' expenditures in Italy, emigrants' remittances and the remittances of Italians working temporarily abroad increased from 141 million dollars in 1950 to 1.1 billion dollars in 1961.

Between 1951 and 1961, a yearly net surplus on capital account allowed the country to record balance of payments surpluses, except for the years 1952, 1953 and 1954. The basic balance surplus increased from 86 million dollars in 1956 to 574 million dollars in 1961.[14] This favorable balance of payments trend allowed the country to expand rapidly its gold and international reserves holdings. These holdings increased from $774 million in 1954 to $3.8 billion ten years later. Ample holdings of international reserves allowed the Italians to avoid the growth-depressing effects of British-like "stop-go" policies.

TABLE 10.2

BALANCE OF PAYMENTS ACCOUNTS
(In million dollars)

	1951	1953	1955	1957	1959	1961
Visible Exports	1,642	1,470	1,775	2,478	2,856	4,101
Visible Imports	1,921	2,217	2,454	3,246	2,994	4,679
Balance of Visible Trade	− 279	− 746	− 678	− 768	− 139	− 573
Total Current Account Balance	+ 55	− 217	− 76	+ 36	+ 759	+ 474
Capital Account Balance	+ 53	+ 123	+ 167	+ 216	+ 199	− 170
Basic Balance	+ 122	− 79	+ 72	+ 206	+ 850	+ 574

Sources: Banca d'Italia, *Relazione Annuale*; Banca d'Italia, *Bilancia dei Pagamenti dell' Italia, 1947-1967*.

Planning Proposals, the Nationalization of Electricity and the End of the "Miracolo"

At a Christian Democratic convention held in San Pellegrino in September 1961, Pasquale Saraceno, a major economic policy adviser in the party, warned that the future development of the country could not be left entirely dependent on the free working of the market mechanism. He urged that a planning system be adopted by the government in order to stop the growing economic dualism within the country, a dualism which made for very different economic and social conditions in the North and in the South, as well as in urban and in rural areas. One month later, the left-wing of the Christian Democratic party expressed at a meeting in Rome their support of national economic planning, of fiscal reforms, and of agricultural modernization and called for the nationalization of the electric-power industry.

The Socialists published in turn in January 1962, an economic paper in which they announced their willingness to cooperate with the government in the improvement of an economy based on a market system provided that the Christian Democrats would accept a number of politico-social reforms. The Socialists enumerated the reforms they desired: these included the establishment of regional governments throughout the country, major changes in the system of education, the modernization of agriculture and the development of depressed areas in the country, the nationalization of the electric power companies, the extension of public ownership over the means of production and global economic planning.

In the course of a Christian Democratic congress which was held in Naples during the same month, Aldo Moro gave support to the Socialist claims. Moro argued that the growing gap in the development of the North and South warranted massive public intervention to unify the country economically and pointed out that some sort of planning was necessary to remedy past shortcomings of the market system. He agreed with the Socialists that educational reform was necessary and that public intervention in the field of energy and power should take place for the sake of economic betterment. He invited the Socialists to support the government, a government which would be willing to follow a policy of *rapprochement* with the PSI.

In March, Amintore Fanfani announced in the Chamber of Deputies that his government would introduce bills for the establishment of regional government, for educational reform and for improved social security measures. The Prime Minister also stated that a program of planning was to be developed and that within three months the government would present a bill for the "rational unification" of the electric power industry. Fanfani's speech announced the beginning of the government's "opening to the Left."

The bill relating to the nationalization of electric power companies was presented to Parliament in June 1962 and became law in November. The Parliament also supported the government's proposals touching school, social security and taxation reforms. Fanfani procrastinated however in the formulation of proposals relating to the establishment of regional governments, probably apprehending that in certain areas of the country these would promptly be dominated by a Socialist-Communist coalition.

The Fanfani policies encountered sharp opposition in the course of 1962. Right-wing Christian Democrats and the right-wing parties claimed that the government had extended too many concessions to the Socialists without obtaining from the latter a firm promise that they would no longer vote with the Communists. The PSI in turn protested that Fanfani had failed to honor all of his commitments. The Socialists particularly resented the failure of the government to introduce bills for the establishment of regional governments.

The general election of April 1963 brought serious vote losses to the Christian Democrats and gave the Communists a gain of over one million votes. Fanfani left the government. Following a short-lived single-party caretaker government under the leadership of Giovanni Leone, Aldo Moro succeeded in forming in November a new government of Christian Democrats, Social Democrats, Republicans and Socialists. For the first time since 1947, Socialist Ministers participated in the Cabinet. The "opening to the Left" policy of Fanfani and Moro had succeeded. It was indeed ironic that this government, dedicated so seriously to economic expansion, was suddenly faced by economic problems which had not appeared during many years in the past: inflation and a balance payments crisis.

In the early 1960s, rising trade union aggressiveness and a tighter industrial labor market led finally to sharp industrial wage increases in 1962 and 1963. Although the wage explosion was largely limited to the industrial sector, wage increases also spread to some lower-productivity sectors such as construction and services. Large unemployment and underemployment persisted however in the primary sector. Wage increases started outstripping productivity gains in 1962 and even more so in 1963. The rate of increase of per unit labor cost expanded from 1.2% in 1961 to 5.3% in 1962 and to 15% in 1963. At the same time, aggregate wages and salaries increased by 38% in 1962 and 1963.

Rising labor costs caused a general decline in the profitability of many industries and tended to discourage productive investment. They reduced the competitiveness of Italian exports while inflation induced Italian producers to sell more at home and less abroad.

Wage inflation also brought balance of payments difficulties. After eight years of external surpluses, Italy registered in 1963 a basic balance deficit of $1.2 billion. The rapid increases in wages and salaries boosted consumer expenditure in 1963 and the rapidly advancing consumers' demand had a direct impact on imports. Imports advanced rapidly in 1963 while exports weakened. The resulting deficit on current account was accompanied by a jump in net capital outflow. This outflow reflected both political and economic developments of that time. Intensified strike activity in the country, the results of the 1963 general election, the nationalization of the electricity industry and the imposition of new taxes on corporate dividends scared off potential investors, both Italian and foreign. Investment in the country was further discouraged by the restrictive monetary measures taken by the government in 1963 to restore balance of payments equilibrium.

It seemed as if Vera Lutz had been correct in explaining the end of a decade of rapid and sustained economic growth in Italy. The industrial cost-push inflation limited the transfer of surplus labor out of the backward sector as employers tried to reduce their labor force by adopting labor-saving techniques of production.[15]

TABLE 10.3

BALANCE OF PAYMENTS: SELECTED YEARS
(In million dollars)

	1963	1965	1967	1969	1970
Visible Exports	4,973	7,104	8,605	11,642	11,642
Visible Imports	6,877	6,458	8,626	11,100	13,498
Balance of Visible Trade	−1,903	+646	−21	+542	−381
Total Current Account Balance	−745	+2,209	+1,599	+2,340	+761
Capital Account Balance	−485	−455	−1,023	−3,624	−237
Basic Balance	−1,252	+1,594	+324	−1,391	+356

Source: Banca d'Italia, *Relazione Annuale* (various issues).

Industrial investment rapidly declined after 1963, and brought two years of major economic setback in 1964 and in 1965. Although the economy recovered in 1966, the 1963 level of investment was surpassed only in 1970. After 1963, the pattern and rate of economic growth remained fundamentally different from what they had been in the 1950s. Whereas the economy had grown at an average annual rate of 5.5% in the decade 1952 to 1962, this rate was only 2.9% in 1964 and 3.5% in 1965. It rose to 5.8% in 1966 and to 6.8% in 1967, but from then on, it steadily declined to 1.6% in 1971. 1963 ended the period of the economic *miracolo*.

Recession and Recovery Under Moro's "Centro-Sinistra" Governments: 1964-1968

In November 1963 the new Moro government took over the administration of an economy which was experiencing both a rapid deterioration in its balance of payments and serious inflation. The traditional expansionary monetary policy the government had followed in prior years had only been abandoned in September.

Belated restrictive monetary and fiscal policies were continued in 1964, a year in which great changes occurred in the economy. The boom of 1963 had been replaced by serious recession. The new "tight money" policy of the government led to "stagflation" which lasted until the end of 1965.

The economy started returning in late 1965 to what appeared to be a "normal" path of development, but the disastrous floods of November 1966 postponed until the following year the attainment of one of the major goals of the Moro coalition. After five years of preparation, the Five-Year Economic Development Plan, covering the years 1966 to 1970, finally became law in 1967.

The general election results of May 1968 brought an end to Moro's administration. Once again, as in 1963, Giovanni Leone formed a temporary *monocolore* government, a government which was replaced at the end of the year by a new center-left government under the leadership of the Christian Democrat Mariano Rumor.

It was the Christian Democrats' misfortune to be unable after 1963 to maintain as buoyant an economy as had existed in the 1950s. Erratic economic growth in the 1960s made it impossible for the government to eradicate economic dualism.

The center-left coalition finally collapsed in 1972. The beginning of the 1960s had been characterized by a prosperous and rapidly growing economy; the end of the decade brought renewed inflation, a declining rate of growth, an outburst of strikes and of violence. The causality of this economic and social malaise runs back to the inflation of 1963 and the recession of 1964-1965. Inflationary pressures persisted after 1963 and economic growth was repeatedly threatened by erratic balance of payments developments.

Regarding the rate of increase of prices and wages, the 1964 economy did not differ very much from that of 1963. The rate of increase of hourly earnings in manufacturing continued to exceed the rate of growth of industrial productivity and rising unit labor costs

continued to have an adverse effect on profitability. What differen-
tiated 1964 from 1963, was the decline of aggregate output, investment
and consumer demand. In response to the deflationary policies taken
by the government to restore external balance, the rate of growth of
GNP fell to 2.9% and industrial production declined sharply. 'Stagflation' replaced the 1963 boom; cost inflation continued in the presence
of declining demand.

TABLE 10.4

ECONOMIC GROWTH INDICATORS
IN CONSTANT PRICES
(In billion lire)

	Wholesale Price Index: 1966 = 100	GNP	GNP Growth Rate: %	Total Investment	Exports
1963	93.8	27,679	5.2	7,778	4,753
1964	96.9	28,482	2.9	7,111	5,486
1965	98.5	29,487	3.5	6,576	6,599
1966	100.0	31,193	5.8	6,852	7,394
1967	99.8	33,324	6.8	7,740	7,965
1968	100.2	35,435	6.3	8,087	9,119
1969	104.1	37,424	5.6	8,987	10,545
1970	111.7	39,309	5.0	9,725	11,790

Sources: Banca d'Italia, *Relazione Annuale;* ISTAT, *Annuario Statistico Italiano,* (various issues).

It is interesting to notice that exports continued to grow in spite of
the fact that increasing wages in 1962 and 1963 taken together had
pushed up the cost of Italian industrial production by over one-third.
During the first seven months of 1964, Italy exported 11.9% more
motor vehicles than in the same period one year earlier. This development must be explained by the fact that Italian export industries
absorbed rising labor costs much better than industries producing for
the domestic market; rapidly rising productivity in the export industries permitted these industries to increase their prices by only 2%
between 1962 and 1964.

The single goal of the restrictive monetary policies initiated in September 1963 was the improvement of the balance of payments. In the
achievement of this goal, almost exclusive reliance was placed on
credit restriction. The impact of these policies on the balance of payments was immediate and dramatic. The trade balance deficit of $1.1

billion was replaced by a surplus of $.3 billion in 1964. The net capital outflow of $156 million of 1963 was changed into a net inflow of $466 million. The overall balance of payments surplus of 1964 was expanded in 1965. The curious policy-mix of allowing wages to increase further while restricting credit, accompanied by a $1 billion loan from the United States and several European central banks, had allowed the government to overcome quickly the balance of payments crisis of 1963.

The policy emphasis on credit restriction had a depressing effect on private investment. Private investment expenditure declined sharply during the first half of 1964 and responded poorly to the easing of credit during the second half of the year and during 1965. Declining profitability in industry made for pessimistic business expectations. The absence of an increase in consumers' expenditure during these two years further contributed to the pessimism of these expectations. The weakness of consumers' demand must be explained by the fact that this demand was not stimulated by either significant tax cuts or by rising earnings. Wages, as a share of gross national product, declined in 1965 and in 1966. Aggregate demand could have been boosted by increases in public consumption expenditure but the government appeared unable to use timely and efficient budgetary instruments to stimulate the economy. It was not until 1966 that the economy returned to the typical pre-1963 rate of growth.[16]

The 1966 Italian rate of growth was one of the highest in Western Europe. This high growth rate occurred in a context of relative price stability and seemed to announce a return to the pre-1963 performance of the economy. In contrast with the situation in 1965, private consumer expenditure, expressed in terms of 1963 prices, rose by 5.7%. Gross investment, which had stagnated one year earlier, registered, also in terms of 1963 prices, a rate of increase of 8% for private investment and 6.1% for public investment. Although most of this investment was concentrated on the build-up of inventories, fixed investment rose in real terms by 3.7%.

The modest figure for fixed investment growth concealed a pronounced expansion in industrial investment during the year. While investment in construction continued to stagnate, investment in transport increased by 5% and productive investment, i.e. investment in machinery and other equipment, rose in real terms by over 11%, in contrast to a decline of productive investment of 19% in 1964 and of 18% in 1965.[17] In spite of the rapid recovery of productive investment, its quantum in 1966 was still 26% below that of 1963.

Equally important, the rate of increase of industrial production in 1966 was 11.2%, a rate which compared very favorably with the 4.9% registered for 1965. The industries experiencing the highest rates of output growth were the motor vehicle, the chemical, the textile, the paper and the oil refining industries.

The economy further benefited from relative price stability which gave Italian exports a marked advantage in the world market, especially at a time when competing industrial nations were experiencing strong price and wage pressures. Wholesale prices in Italy remained practically unchanged during the year, while consumer prices rose by only 2.3%, their smallest annual increase since 1960.

The rising internal demand caused imports to expand rapidly. The rate of increase of imports exceeded that of exports; exports in 1966 rose by 11.6%, a rate of growth well below the average annual rate of export growth of 13.8% which had prevailed in the period 1950 to 1963. The relatively modest export growth was largely due to the concurrent strengthening of the domestic market and to the weakening of the West German economy after mid-1966.[18]

The 1966 balance of payments continued to show a current account surplus, a surplus almost identical to that of 1965. A large net capital outflow reduced however the basic balance surplus to $696 million. A number of reasons explain this outflow: Italian repayments of foreign loans, a tightening of monetary conditions abroad, a decline in foreign investment in the country and increases in net private investment abroad made for a capital account deficit of $1.2 billion.

What is remarkable about the growth pattern in 1966 is that, unlike the situation in prior years, economic growth was not led by exports, but was generated by rising domestic demand. Economic recovery in late 1965 had been largely caused by a strong export pull, a pull brought about by the conjunction of a weak domestic demand and a rapidly expanding demand in Italy's foreign markets. The situation changed in 1966. The growth of output was mostly induced by increases in internal real demand.

In spite of the rise of output, employment declined by 1.6% in 1966. This decline was both due to stagnation in non-farm employment and to a continued decrease in agricultural employment. The net outflow of manpower from Italy rose from 282,000 in 1965 to 292,000 in 1966. And yet, in the same year, hours worked in industry increased by about 3% over their 1965 level. The increase in hours worked in industry, accompanied by a lack of growth of the industrial labor force and by a level of industrial investment which was still far below that attained in 1963, led some economists to believe that the growth of output in Italy in 1966 and in subsequent years was not based on investment and productivity increases, but was largely due to an increase in hours worked, to a more intensive use of existing capacity and to deteriorating working conditions.[19]

1967 showed even more clearly than 1966 that exports no longer played the growth-propulsive role they had played in the pre-recession economy. The export rate of growth declined to 7.7%.

Consumption expenditure had about the same impact on the economy it had shown one year earlier. The increase in aggregate demand was largely due to the expansion of gross investment which continued to grow at an increased pace. In absolute terms, gross investment in 1967 reached the level it had attained in 1963, although as a ratio of GNP it fell short of the 24.5% reached in that year. Still, in real terms, gross investment expanded by 11.2% in 1967 and industrial investment grew by 14.8% in value and by 12.4% in volume over what it had been in 1966.[20]

For the first time in many years, the Italian labor force increased in numbers and employment registered a gain of 1.2%. Unemployment declined by 10.4%, compared with an increase of nearly 7% the year before; this is shown in Table 10.5

These favorable developments in the labor market were accompanied by the continuation of relative wage and price stability. Wage increases were contained by the stability of prices and by the fact that many trade union contracts did not expire until the end of the year or until 1968. At the same time, in spite of the expansion of domestic demand, prices remained practically stable, partly because of rapidly increasing imports and partly because of higher levels of domestic production. The wholesale price index registered a slight decline of 0.2% from its 1966 level; although consumer prices advanced by 3.7%, this rate of increase was modest when compared to corresponding rates of 4.6% for 1965, 5.9% for 1964 and 7.5% for 1963.[21]

TABLE 10.5

LABOR FORCE, EMPLOYMENT, UNEMPLOYMENT: 1965-1967

	Thousands			Change 1966 to 1967	
	1965	1966	1967	Thousands	%
Labor Force	19,920	19,653	19,796	+143	+0.7
Employed	19,199	18,884	19,107	+223	+1.2
Agriculture	4,956	4,660	4,556	−104	−2.2
Industry	7,728	7,621	7,782	+161	+2.1
Other	6,515	6,603	6,769	+166	+2.5
Unemployed	721	769	689	−80	−10.4
Unemployment Rate	3.6	3.9	3.5		

Source: Commercial Office of the Italian Embassy, *Italy, An Economic Profile, 1967*, Washington, 1968, p. 41.

Price and wage stability continued in 1968. The easy monetary conditions prevailing in 1967 were on the whole maintained. The overall growth rate declined however, even though it remained well above the growth rate target of 5% established by the Five-Year Economic Development Plan which had been approved finally by parliament in 1967. The economy slowed down during the first half of 1968 because of a decline in private consumption and a stagnating trend in private investment.

During the fall, the government took a number of reflationary measures to stimulate the economy; the authorities decided to expand public investment and to stimulate private investment through fiscal policy. Reviewing the performance of the economy in terms of the Plan's targets, the authorities noted that while productivity had increased faster than expected, fixed investment had risen over the three years 1966 to 1968 by an average yearly rate of only 7.4%, a rate well below the target rate of 10%. And although output had risen at above-target rates, employment had not. In order to boost private productive investment, the government extended special tax allowances to firms and undertook to finance part of the social security contributions of industrial and other enterprises in the South.

Domestic demand started gaining momentum during the second half of the year. The acceleration in the growth of demand was not however generated by private consumption or private investment; the boost in demand was largely created by increases in public investment and by rapidly expanding exports.

For 1968 as a whole, growth was not as spectacular as it had been in 1967. Although gross investment increased by 7.4% in volume, three-quarters of this investment were due to construction. Investment in machinery showed no increase. While public investment rose substantially, private investment remained practically stagnant. Industrial production did not rise as rapidly as in 1967 and although industrial productivity increased by 6%, increases in output per man-hour were mostly due to the employers' efforts to speed up the pace of work in the factory even though production techniques remained unchanged. [22]

Boosted by favorable world trade conditions, exports rose rapidly, their rate of growth attaining 14.5%. With imports rising by only 4.3%, the current account surplus climbed to $2.6 billion. In spite of an all-time high net capital outflow of $1.7 billion, the basic balance recorded a surplus of $627 million.

The favorable trend in foreign trade was offset by a deterioration of the labor market. After improving slightly in 1967, employment fell in 1968, largely because of a more rapid decline in agricultural employment than in 1967. The decline in employment took mostly place in the South and sharpened the economic contrasts between the North and the *Mezzogiorno*. Equally important was the growing discontent of workers in the secondary and tertiary sectors of the economy. A faster tempo of work inside the factory, resulting in a larger number of industrial accidents and often leading to a deterioration of physical and mental health, the lack of adequate housing in overcrowded industrial cities, the worsening of social services, specially in those urban centers which were end-points of southern emigration, and growing differences in the standard of living of the poor and the wealthy filled the

workers with feelings of frustration, feelings which explain the intensification of strike activity in 1969.

Productivity Increases and State Intervention

In both agriculture and industry, the government played an active
role in the improvement of productivity; the modernization of the
economy in the 1950s and in the 1960s was largely due to large-scale
public support.

It has been estimated that the rate of growth of agricultural labor
productivity in the period 1959 to 1966 averaged 7.8% per annum.[23]
This was a high rate of growth by international standards, a rate whose
determinants were increases in capital per worker and improved agricultural methods of production as well as a steady decline in rural
underemployment and rural unemployment. Table 10.6 well sum-
marizes the plural action taken by the land reform agencies to raise
skills and productivity on the new family farms, the *poderi*, they established on expropriated land.

TABLE 10.6

YIELDS OF SELECTED CROPS

	Percent Average Annual Yield	
	1949-1951	1963-1966
Wheat	15.40	20.30
Grapes	3.90	5.60
Corn	18.30	34.10
Oats	10.60	13.40
Sugar Beet	27.40	34.40
Barley	10.50	13.90
Rye	12.90	17.10

Note: Wheat, Barley, Oats, Corn and Rye are expressed in terms of 100 kilograms per hectare. Other
    crops are shown in terms of metric tons per hectare.
Source: United Nations, FAO, *Production Yearbook 1953 and 1966*, Rome.

By 1961, the various land reform *enti* had redistributed 630,000
hectares of land to over 110,000 families. These agencies continued to
invest heavily in agricultural development projects before delivery of
land to farmers took place. As of December 1961, these agencies had
financed the afforestation of 100,000 hectares, had cleared and

ploughed over 500,000 hectares and had completed irrigation projects in the areas representing 37,000 hectares. During 1961 these agencies delivered 71,345 heads of cattle, 29,242 goats and 11,708 pigs to the owners of the newly established farms. These farmers received in addition tools and seeds from the *enti* and could obtain from them thirty-year loans carrying interest of only 3%. They further benefited from the advice they received from the *enti* technicians.[24]

Another major reason for the gains in productivity in the agricultural sector was the continuous decline in the number of unemployed and underemployed in that sector. The elimination of underemployment may have accounted for nearly half of the increase in agricultural labor productivity. The gradual decline of rural surplus labor, combined with steady increases in capital per agricultural worker and the adoption of more efficient methods of production allowed crop yields to rise rapidly in the postwar period.

The transfer of labor from the rural to the other sectors of the economy was facilitated by the rapid growth of the secondary sector. The government played a key role in the expansion of this sector through its investment programs in public corporations or state-holding companies. Nationalized and state-holding industries were a powerful instrument with which the government could engage in economic management and could attempt to achieve the targets set forth by the plan.

The state-holding sector of the economy grew rapidly in the 1960s. The following data reveal the rising importance of public corporations in the economy. Taking 1955 as the base year, the investment index in this sector grew to 218 in 1960 and to 994 in 1971. The share of all public enterprises in total industrial investment advanced from 19% in 1961 to 49% ten years later. These included, in addition to public holding companies such as IRI and ENI, the Electricity Agency — ENEL — , the railways, the Post Office and ANAS — road construction. Public corporations played a particularly active role in the industrialization of the South. During the 1960s, the share of public corporations in total investments in the South increased from 15% to 26%; although, given their capital-intensive nature, the impact of these corporations on employment in the South was quite moderate, they nevertheless played a major part in raising productivity, industrial production and incomes in the *Mezzogiorno*.

Public corporations, although competing in certain instances with private firms, were not established to weaken the market mechanism. Indeed, they were used to increase competition in oligopolistic markets and to induce large private firms to operate more efficiently. They were the agencies through which the government could carry out development programs and solve long-term structural problems in the economy; they were the means by which the government could regulate the flow and the pattern of investment.

It is not easy to compare the performance of the public enterprises with that of private firms. The major objective of the public concerns was not profit maximization. Their role was to maximize long-run social benefits by investing in areas or activities in which private enterprise was unwilling or unable to invest, by testing new production techniques and setting the example in the field of industrial relations, by strengthening competition in certain sectors of the economy and by creating new jobs or maintaining employment.

The state-holding sector at the end of the 1960s was quite large, both in terms of employment and in terms of the number of enterprises in this sector. There were about 350 state-holding enterprises employing about 510,000 workers in Italy and 22,000 workers abroad. The sector included, besides key industries such as steel, chemicals, heavy engineering, shipbuilding and petroleum refining, industries producing electronic equipment, automobiles, films and also banks. The sector operated the *Autostrada del Sole*, tourist spas, *Alitalia*, and the RAI television and radio stations.

THE STRUCTURE OF IRI

Banks and Credit Institutions

Banca Commerciale Italiana
Credito Italiano
Banco di Roma
Banco di Santo Spirito
Credito fondiario sardo
Istituto per lo Sviluppo delle Attività produttive

Specialized Financial Institutions and Subsidiaries

S.T.E.T. (Financial institute for telephone service)
S.T.I.P.E.L. (International Telephone Company for Piedmont and Lombardy)

TEL.VE (Venezia Telephone Corporation)
TI.MO (Eastern Italy Telephone Corporation)
TE.TI (Tyrrhenian Coastal Areas Telephone Company)
S.E.T. (Telephone Management Corporation)

Shipping Companies

Finmare (Maritime Shipping Finance Corporation)
Italia
Lloyd Triestino
Adriatica
Tirrenia

Iron and Steel Enterprises

Finsider (Iron and Steel Finance Corporation)
Italsider
Dalmine
S.I.A.C. (Cornigliano Steel Company)
Terni (Industry and electricity)
Breda-Siderurgica (Iron and steel)
Morteo
Ferromin (Extraction and marketing of iron ore)
Siderurgica Commerciale Italiana (Iron and steel marketing)
Siderexport (Iron and steel export)
Siderurgica Milanese
Sidermar
Cosider (Iron and steel plant installation projects)
Rifornimenti Finsider (Marketing of Finsider products)
Comansider
C.M.F. (Finsider construction subsidiary)
Camentir (Tyrrhenian Cement Corporation)
Cementiere di Livorno (Leghorn Cement Corporation)
ATUB (Brescia Steel and Tube Company)
Montubi (Tube assembly)
Ponteggi Tubolari Dalmine Innocenti (Construction of bridges)

Engineering Industries

Finmeccanica (Engineering Industries Finance Corporation)
Alfa Romeo (Motor vehicles)
S.P.I.C.A.
Ansaldo S. Giorgio (Electrical engineering)
Elettrodomestici S. Giorgio (Electrical household appliances)
Officine elettrodomestiche Triestine

AERFER (Engineering and Aircraft Corporation)
A.V.I.S. (Stabia Engineering and Shipbuilding Company)
Pistoia Engineering and Railway Equipment Company
A.T.E.S. (Electronic Industries of Southern Italy)
Delta
Durkopf Italia
Industrial Machinery Company
Filotecnia Salmoiraghi
Naples Engineering and Foundry Company
S.A.F.O.C. (Gorizia Foundry and Manufacturing Company)
Selenia (Associated Electronic Industries)
Sigme (Italian Missile Manufacturing Company)
Wayne Italia

Electrical Undertakings

Finelettrica (Electricity Industries Finance Corporation)
S.I.P. (Piedmont Financial Institute)
S.M.E. (Financial Institute for Southern Italy)
Terni (Industrial and Electrical Corporation)
S.T.E. (Trentino Electricity Board)
U.N.E.S. (Union of Electricity undertakings)
Vizzola (Lombard Electricity Supply Board)
Puglie Electricity Board
Calabria Electricity Board
Campania Electricity Board
Lucana per Imprese Idroelettriche (Lucca Association of Hydro-electric
     undertakings)
P.C.E. (Piedmont Central Electricity Board)
SENN (National Nuclear Electricity Board)
Agri Hydro-Electricity Board
Germina (National Geological and Mining Institute)

Shipbuilding

Fincantieri (Shipbuilding Industry Finance Corporation)
Ansaldo (Shipbuilding)
Arsenale Triestion (Shipbuilding)
C.N.O.M.V. (Venice shipbuilding and engineering companies)
Cantieri riuniti dell'Adriatico
Esercizio Bacini Napoletani (Shipbuilding company in Naples)
Navalmeccanica (Shipbuilding and engineering company in Naples)
O.A.R.N. (Ship-fitting and ship-repair company)

Miscellaneous

RAI-TV (radio and television)
SIPRA
ERI
FONTI-Cetra (Gramophone records)
Monte Amiata Mineraria (Asbestos)
CELDIT
Montecantini (Chemicals)
SAIVO
Egiziana Fosfati (Egyptian Phosphate Company)
Manifatture Cotoniere Meridionali (Cotton manufacturing in the South)
Il Fabbricone (Woollen Goods)
ALITALIA (Italian National Airlines)
ELIVIE (Italian Helicopter Travel Corporation)
S.A.M. (Mediterranean Airlines
Societa Italiana per il Traforo del Monte Bianco (Mont-Blanc Tunnel Co.)
Italstrade (Highway construction)
Autostrada Firenze-Mare
S.G.A.S. (Operation of hotels in Sicily)
Maccarese
SACAM
SACOS
ILTE
Edindustria Editoriale
IFAP
CAMIN

THE STRUCTURE OF ENI

SNAM (National Oil Pipelines Corporation)
Az. Metanodotti Pandani
Metano Arcore
Metano Borgomanero
Metano Casalpusterlengo
Metano Correggio
Metano S. Angelo Lodigiano
Nuovo Pignone
Agip U.S.A.
Odeodotto del Reno
Oleodotto del Rodano
Südpetrol
Erdöl Raffinerie Jugolstadt

AGIP (Italian Petroleum Corporation)
Idrobitumine Zabban
IROM
Min. Sicilia Orientale
Ravennate Metano
SAMPOC
SAMPOR
SEMI
SERAM
SOIS
SOMICEM
SOMIS
STEI
Vulcano
SOFID
SEGISA
STIEM
Agip A.G. (Sutria)
Agip Argentina
Agip Brazzaville
Agip Cameroun
Agip Casablanca
Agip Dahomey
Agip Djibouti
Agip Ethiopia
Agip A.G. (Germany)
Agip Ghana
Agip Ltd. (Great Britain)
Agip Hellas A.E.
Agip Ivory Coast
Agip Ltd. (Kenya)
Agip Liberia
Agip Madagascar
Agip Mineraria Sudan
Agip Nigeria
Agip Sierra Leone
Agip Somalia
Agip Sudan
Agip S.A. (Switzerland)
Agip Togo
Agip Tunisia
CORI

Gas Orient
IEOC
COPE
Mineraria Somalia
NAOC
Olympiagas
Petrolibia
Asseil
SIRIP
SITEP
SOMIP

ANIS (Chemical Industries)
Anic Gea
Chimica Ravenna
Phillips Carbon Black It.
SALPO
SAPIR
SIPO
STANIC
GHAIP
SAMIR
STIR
Lanerossi
Lebole Euroconf.
Pantalonificio Ital.
Rossifloor
Sapel
Serenella XVII
SMIT
Termotex
Lanerossi Commerciale Europea
Lanerossi G.m.b.h.

AGIP NUCLEARE (Agip Nuclear Industries Corp.)
Sima
Sinterel
Somiren

The organizaton of this sector had a pyramidal structure. At the top, an Interministerial Committee for Economic Planning formulated overall investment programs, programs that were to be implemented by a Ministry of State Participation. This Ministry issued in turn directives to the various *enti* or holding companies in the state-holding sector. The largest *enti* in the system were IRI and ENI, although other holding groups, like EFIM, were also significant.

The *enti* had the task of issuing managerial directives to the enterprises they controlled, although in certain instances, the *enti* operated through subsidiary holding companies. IRI, for instance, acted through specialized holding organizations, the *finanziarias*, such as *Finsider* for iron and steel, *Finmeccanica* for engineering, *Fincantieri* for shipbuilding and *Finmare* for shipping. *Alitalia* and the banks in the IRI group were directly supervised by IRI.

There is no unanimous view in the literature about the quality of the performance of the public corporations. Undoubtedly, they contributed significantly to the modernization of the Italian industrial sector; these enterprises were highly capital-intensive in nature and at the end of the 1960s, the capital per worker employed in public industries was over five times larger than for industry as a whole.[25] How successful public concerns were when compared to similar private enterprises is not easily ascertainable because public and private firms pursued different goals.

The law required public firms to operate with *economicità*. What the term exactly implies is not clear. Some Italian writers have argued that the term does not connote the maximization of profits or profitability. One view is that the term refers only to the requirement that the firm obtain an adequate return on capital invested without need to maximize profits.[26] Another view holds that, at least for public holding companies, the term *economicità* refers only to the company's ability to cover costs from revenues earned and does not imply profitability.[27] A further position is that the term simply refers to the public firm's main goal to serve both the public and the private sectors in the economy by contributing to the solution of short and long-term economic problems.[28] It appears that although the managerial striving for profits in the public concern may not be incompatible with achievement of social goals, the primary objective of the public firm is not the short-run maximization of profits. Furthermore, even though public management may pursue profitability, profits in its firms may be computed in reference to periods exceeding one year or in reference to the aggregate profits of a group of public firms.

What is important is that these firms were an important means by which the government could implement the Five-Year Economic Development Plan and that they introduced industrial activity in areas which did not attract private enterprise. In this regard, they played an important role in the government's efforts to reduce economic dualism in the country.

Renewal of Inflation and Stagnation: 1969 - 1970

The principal objective of the first Five-Year Economic Development Plan was to achieve an annual rate of growth in real terms of 5% under conditions of full employment, price stability and external balance. This objective was attained on the whole during the first three years of the Plan. The economy grew by over 6% per year and prices rose by only 2% or 3%; the economy did not achieve external balance but the large balance of payments surpluses allowed the government to accumulate rapidly foreign reserves.

This situation changed in the summer of 1969. A wave of strikes hit the economy during the second half of the year and caused a loss of 302 million working hours; the economy had never experienced such a yearly loss before. The sudden aggressiveness of the trade unions was not caused by economic developments. The strikes took place even though the rate of unemployment had not risen, even though price increases had been quite moderate and even though no tight labor market existed. The strikes caused sharp rises in prices and wages, a decline in exports and a drop in overall growth to 5%. As in 1963 and in 1964, inflation in 1969 was followed by economic stagnation in 1970.

Responding to the reflationary measures taken by the government in the fall of 1968, economic growth actually accelerated during the first half of 1969. During the second quarter of the year, the rise in real GNP attained a rate of 8%per annum. Both exports and domestic demand strengthened. Economic growth came then to an abrupt stop. During the third quarter, GNP declined in real terms by 0.5% and fell again by 4% in the last quarter. Unfavorable capital movements plunged the balance of payments into a deficit, the first deficit since 1963.

The work stoppages severely affected aggregate investment. While private consumption did not show an appreciable change, total fixed investment declined by 9.8% between the second and the fourth quarters of the year. During the same period, productive investment declined by 12.8%. To this drop in investment was added a fall in the exports of goods and services amounting to 6.1% while imports rose by 6.3%.[29]

The immediate impact of strike activity was on prices and wages. Prices started rising rapidly during the second half of the year, partly because of developing supply bottlenecks and partly because of rising import prices. Prices of iron and steel products increased by as much as 25% and prices of construction materials advanced by nearly 20%. Compared with increases of only 3.5% during the first quarter of the year, wage rates in manufacturing rose by 10% during the last quarter as some wage settlements became effective at that time.

The strikes, the mass demonstrations and the bombings of 1969 puzzled and discouraged domestic and foreign investors and the political center-left coalition. They seemed to announce the beginning of a new period of social and economic difficulties and the end of *Centro-Sinistra* rule.

Conclusion

The principal determinant of Italy's rapid economic growth in the period 1955 to 1962, and again in the years 1966, 1967 and 1968, was wage stability. Wage stability allowed high levels of business profitability and thus stimulated private investment and strengthened the international competitiveness of Italian exports. It encouraged foreigners to invest in the country, contributed to external surpluses, facilitated the growth of output-expanding imports and helped the industrial North to absorb at least part of the large and continuous inflow of workers from the South.

The 1963 inflation brought the collapse of the Italian economic miracle. The post-1965 recovery of the economy was again threatened by inflation in 1969 and in 1970. Inflation in both 1963 and 1969 brought peaks of net capital outflow and had a disastrous effect on the balance of payments. In both years, the wage inflation was not warranted by prevailing economic conditions. The economy was neither characterized by excess demand and rapidly advancing prices, nor by the existence of full employment.

The wage push in both years was the product of trade union aggressiveness and was largely limited to the secondary sector of the economy. Its consequences were well predicted by Vera Lutz. Industrial enterprises turned to more labor-saving methods of production and total employment, including agriculture, declined by 3.8% between 1963 and 1968. This trend made the elimination of southern unemployment and underemployment more difficult and widened the economic gap between North and South. The strikes did not bring the unions closer to their goals of better education, better housing, better health services and better town-planning. Instead, they brought declines in output and exports and a diminished absorption of the southern surplus labor.

If we disregard the years of inflation-caused recession, i.e. 1964, 1965 and 1969, Italian economic performance in the 1950s and in the 1960s remained truly outstanding. Even though planning was made quite difficult by the large southern emigration, and even though most of the *Mezzogiorno* remained an economic desert, Italy continued to record one of the highest growth rates in Western Europe.

The success of Italy's economic performance was due both to the skills of private enterprise in the North and to the willingness of the government to invest heavily in the backward regions of the country. In the 1960s, amalgamation and increased industrial concentration in the North tended to increase and diversify output. The outstanding example was the merger of *Edison,* once a producer of electricity which turned to the production of chemicals after 1962, with the large chemical firm *Montecatini.* The new combine, *Montedison,* became one of the ten largest industrial firms in Europe. Industrial concentration was also favored by the large holding companies, IRI and ENI, and by the nationalized Electricity Agency, ENEL. ENI in 1968 became *Montedison's* controlling shareholder; the large chemical firm was thus able to use ENI's gas and oil resources under favorable conditions. Large size, amalgamation and outstanding managerial talent also permitted northern industry to produce and export automobiles, electric and electronic equipment and other consumer goods which were able to compete with West German and Japanese products. In the very successful automobile industry, *Fiat* was the leader, and it was not long before this firm acquired control over such well-known rivals as *Lancia, Ferrari* and *Maserati.*

Although by 1970 *Fiat* had already invested over 86 billion lire in the establishment of southern plants in Bari, Brindisi and Lecce, northern private industry did not on the whole show great interest in investing in the distant *Mezzogiorno.* The economic development of the South remained largely a matter of public action. Following the example set by De Gasperi, Italian political leaders continued in the attempt to develop the South by means of large public investments. In the 1960s *ENEL* established electricity installations in the South whose cost amounted to 29 billion lire; IRI completed the *Autostrada del Sole,* a highway extending from Milan to Reggio Calabria which was expected to strengthen tourism in the South. Under the Five-Year Plan, investment in southern industry grew at a rate of 18.8%, a rate much higher than the corresponding investment rate in the North.

In spite of these efforts, the government was unable to eradicate the problems of dualism in the economy. Industrial concerns in the South remained "cathedrals in the desert." They were unable to improve employment conditions and the southern wage remained half of the northern one.

Just as his predecessor had understood it twenty years earlier, Emilio Colombo, the man who succeeded Mariano Rumor as Prime Minister in August, 1970, also believed that the poverty of the *Mezzogiorno* was still Italy's main economic problem.

NOTES

1. O. Ornati, "The Italian Economic Miracle and Organized Labor," *Social Research,* vol. 30 (Winter 1963), pp. 519-526.

2. See Chapter 4.

3. De Gasperi apparently became interested in long-range planning shortly before his death and probably encouraged Ezio Vanoni to prepare his ten-year plan. See J. LaPalombara, *Italy, the Politics of Planning* (Syracuse: Syracuse University Press, 1966), p. 59.

4. E. Vanoni, "L'Idea del programma e la sua ispirazione politica," *Discorsi sul programma di sviluppo economico* (Rome: Istituto Poligrafico dello Stato, 1956).

5. G.H. Hildebrand, "Growth and Stability in the Postwar Italian Economy," *The American Economic Review,* vol. LI (May 1961), pp. 390-399, at p. 396.

6. M. Ruini, "Per un efficiente governo democratico in Italia," *Cronache Sociali,* III (February 15, 1949), p. 3.

7. There was a slight decline in the growth rate in 1958.

8. Ornati, "The Italian Economic Miracle and Organized Labor."

9. C. Kindelberger, *Europe's Postwar Growth: The Role of Labour Supply* (Cambridge: Harvard University Press, 1967). See also W. Lewis, "Development with Unlimited Supplies of Labour," *The Manchester School* (May, 1954).

10. ISTA, *Annuario di Contabilità Nazionale 1971* (Rome, 1972).

11. For a study of an export-led theory of Italian growth in the 1950's see R. Stern, *Foreign Trade and Economic Growth in Italy* (New York: Praeger, 1967).

12. In 1961, the dominant exports were non-electric machinery, valued at 300 billion lire, textiles, 276 billion lire, transport equipment, 271 billion lire, chemicals, 164 billion lire, iron and steel, 124 billion lire, and clothing, 101 billion lire. See G.H. Hildebrand, *Growth and Structure in the Economy of Modern Italy* (Cambridge: Harvard University Press, 1965), p. 80.

13. K.J. Allen and A.A. Stevenson, *An Introduction to the Italian Economy*, Glasgow Social and Economic Research Studies, 1 (London, Martin Robertson & Co., Ltd., 1974), pp. 82-83.

14. Banca d'Italia, *Bilancia dei Pagamenti dell 'Italia, 1947-1967* (Rome, 1968).

15. V. Lutz, *Italy, A Study in Economic Development* (London: Oxford University Press, 1962).

16. B. Brovedani, "Italy's Financial Policies in the 'Sixties'," *Banca Nazionale del Lavoro Quarterly Review*, No. 89 (June 1969), pp. 170-189.

17. OECD, *Economic Surveys, Italy* (Paris, 1967), p. 9.

18. 40.6% of Italy's export trade in 1966 was conducted with the EEC, 16.1% with EFTA and 9.3% with the United States. Among the EEC countries, West Germany was Italy's best customer.

19. Allen and Stevenson, *Introduction to the Italian Economy*, p. 65.

20. The ratio of investment in plant and equipment to total fixed investment was 26.5% in 1967, as compared with 25.6% in 1966 and 23.2% in 1965. See Commercial Office of the Italian Embassy, *Italy, an Economic Profile 1967* (Washington, 1968), p. 16.

21. *Ibid.*, p. 44.

22. OECD, *Economic Surveys, Italy* (Paris, 1969).

23. R.M. Lovejoy, "Labor Productivity in Italian Agriculture, 1951-1973," *Industrial and Labor Relations Review*, vol. 21 (July 1968), pp. 570-580.

24. C. Aiello, "The "The Agricultural Sector," *Annals of Public and Co-Operative Economy*, vol. XXXV (1964), pp. 43-56.

25. G. Podbielski, *Italy: Development and Crisis in the Post-War Economy* (Oxford: Clarendon Press, 1974), p. 149.

26. E. Panciera, *Le Macroaziende*, vol. I, *L'Azienda Statale* (Palermo: Abacco, 1957), p. 108.

27. R. Coltelli, "Economicità delle Imprese a Partecipazione Statale," *Rivista Trimestrale di Diritto Publico* (April-June 1961), pp. 433-4.

28. F. Fabbrini, "I Compiti dell' Industria di Stato," *Politica ed Economia* (February 1958), p. 13.

29. OECD, *Economic Surveys, Italy* (Paris, 1970), p. 7.

CHAPTER 11

THE EAST GERMAN ECONOMIC MIRACLE

Throughout the 1950s, East Germany's economic performance continued to be handicapped by adverse demographic trends. An increasingly disadvantageous age structure of the population, illustrated in Table 11.1, meant larger labor shortages, more old age pensioners and a growing participation of women in the labor force. In 1939, out of every one hundred inhabitants in East Germany, 67.5% were of working age, i.e., 15 to 65 years of age. In 1963, this figure was 56.8%. Between 1955 and 1963, East Germany's population declined from 17.8 million to 17.1 million. During this same period, the total number of children under 15 years of age and of pensioners increased from 6.5 million to 7.4 million.[1] Labor shortages were worsened by the continuing emigration out of the country. The number of people leaving the German Democratic Republic tended to vary directly with economic

TABLE 11.1

WORKING AND NONWORKING PERSONS PER 100 INHABITANTS
EAST GERMANY

	% Within Working Age: 15 to 65	Children under 15	Persons over 65	% Under 15 or Over 65
1939	67.5	21.4	11.1	32.5
1946	62.5	24.5	13.0	37.5
1950	63.3	22.9	13.8	36.7
1955	63.2	20.9	15.9	36.8
1956	63.0	20.6	16.4	37.0
1957	62.6	20.6	16.8	37.4
1958	62.3	20.5	17.2	37.7
1959	61.9	20.8	17.3	38.1
1960	61.0	21.4	17.6	39.0
1961	58.5	23.6	17.9	41.5
1962	57.6	24.3	18.1	42.4
1963	56.8	25.0	18.2	43.3

Source: *S.J.D.D.R.*, 1964, Staatsverlag der D.D.R., 1964, Berlin-E, p. 498.

conditions in East Germany. For instance, the exodus reached a peak in 1953, the year of the East Berlin uprising, caused in part by economic factors, but declined by more than one half in 1959, a year of large economic gains in the G.D.R.[2] Emigration statistics are listed in Table 11.2

TABLE 11.2

NUMBER OF EMIGRANTS LEAVING THE G.D.R.
1949-1965

1949	129,245	1957	261,622
1950	197,788	1958	204,092
1951	165,648	1959	143,917
1952	182,393	1960	199,188
1953	331,390	1961	207,026
1954	184,198	1962	21,356
1955	252,870	1963	42,632
1956	279,189	1964	41,876
		1965	29,532

Source: Bundesministerium fuer gesamtdeutsche Fragen, *SBZ von A bis Z*, Bonn, 1966, p. 145.

The rising percentage of women in the active labor force, as shown in Table 11.3, probably explains best why the ratio of births to deaths steadily declined over the years.[3] In 1965, the East German rate of population growth was the second lowest in the world, the lowest being that of Hungary. A curious East German reluctance to import foreign labor until late in the 1960s prevented the elimination of labor shortages. These shortages in turn brought about a larger participation of women in the labor force. A vicious demographic circle ensued, since a rising participation rate of women in the labor force made for a further reduction in fertility rates.

TABLE 11.3

PERCENTAGE OF WOMEN IN EMPLOYED LABOR FORCE

1939	36.7	1962	46.0
1946	44.9	1963	46.0
1948	41.0	1964	46.3
1950	37.0	1965	46.7
1952	42.7	1966	46.9
1955	44.0	1967	47.2
1960	45.0	1968	47.4
1961	45.7	1969	48.0

Source: *S.J.D.D.R., 1967*, p. 65 and *S.J.D.D.R., 1970*, p. 59.

Further economic difficulties were caused by the over-centralized East German planning methods. The duplication of Soviet planning tended to encourage factory managers to fulfill purely quantitative goals through the production of inferior, and very often non-marketable, commodities. The planning system tended to impede experimentation, innovation and technological progress. The result was a deterioration in the East German rate of economic growth in the early 1960s and the adoption in 1963 of some of the ideas prosposed one year earlier in the Soviet Union by Professor E. G. Liberman of the Kharkov Academy of Engineering and Economics.[4]

Major changes in the direction of planning had already occurred in East Germany before 1963. Until the mid-1950s, the planning strategy of the G.D.R. gave development priority to heavy industry in conformity to Stalinist tradition. Large industrial projects were completed such as the new shipyards at Warnemuende, and the special coking facilities at Lauchhammer which were able to transform lignite into metallurgical coke. The first Five-Year Plan aimed almost exclusively to increase the output of steel, heavy machinery, locomotives and ships. A change occurred after 1955. Less importance was given to the further growth of heavy industry. Planning started focusing on the growth of other industries, industries producing light machinery, precision and optical instruments and consumer goods. The policy after 1955 emphasized the need to produce on the basis of comparative advantage and to maximize national income through specialization and international trade.

This change in planning policy was mainly due to the expansion of the activities of the Council for Mutual Economic Assistance, the CMEA, following Stalin's death in 1953. Until 1954, the U.S.S.R. continued to uphold the policy of national autarky and demanded that the other CMEA countries follow the same viewpoint. From 1955 onwards, this policy was modified in the Soviet Union. The autarky principle was no longer to be limited to a single nation, but was to be applied within the Soviet Bloc as a whole. CMEA member countries were now encouraged to specialize and to exchange resources and commodities to further economic efficiency within the entire territory covered by the CMEA. To improve the international socialist division of labor, national economic plans of the various member nations were to be effectively coordinated. The integration and coordination of these national plans had a start in 1956.[5]

East German industrial production also benefited from the end of East German reparation payments to the Soviet Union in 1954. The termination of these payments greatly contributed to a 75% increase in East German industrial output between 1955 and 1963. Industrial output in the G.D.R. doubled between 1950 and 1956. It doubled again during the decade 1956-1966. By 1964, the G.D.R. was producing an industrial output that was larger than that produced by the Third Reich in 1939.

The improved economic performance of the G.D.R. in the 1960s was largely due to the effects of three major politico-economic changes effectuated between 1960 and 1963, changes which were to counteract the decline in economic growth of the early 1960s. The first change affected agriculture. As of 1960, private property in agriculture practically disappeared in the G.D.R. On November 1, 1959, 51% of the cultivable land was still privately owned. One year later, almost 100% of this land was in the possession of LPGs and of state-owned farms. Collectivization of the entirety of the agricultural sector allowed the LPGs to cultivate much larger fields on the basis of modern agricultural methods. The result was a remarkable increase in per-hectare yields after 1962.

The second major change involved the building of the Berlin Wall, ugly and sinister to the western world, but, from the East German point of view, effective in bringing to an end large losses of manpower which for sixteen years had weakened the East German economy.

The last major reform was introduced by Walter Ulbricht in his address to the Sixth Congress of the German Socialist Unity party in January 1963. His proposed reform borrowed heavily from E.G. Liberman's thesis. Ulbricht's economic reform program was adopted in East Germany under the title of "The New Economic System of Planning and Managing the Economy," or, more simply, "The New Economic System."

The New Economic System of 1963

A slow-down of economic growth in the Soviet Union at the start of the 1960s gave rise to extensive debate about needed economic reforms. The various Russian schools of thought at that time admitted that the increased complexity of the economy made the process of decision-making by the top planning hierarchy less efficient. A larger and more sophisticated economy made the task of providing this hierarchy with sufficient and adequately processed information more difficult.

Russian economists differed in their views about the extent and type of necessary economic reform. Members of the Soviet Mathematical Economic Institute and leading Russian mathematicians argued that an extensive use of computers and the development of new programming techniques could increase the efficiency of centralized planning. This group believed that the existing economic system needed no change. All that was needed was to improve the techniques under which economic data were gathered and transferred to the formulators of the central plan.[6] Other economists in the U.S.S.R. felt that their government should abandon over-centralized, mandatory planning and embrace a system of market socialism, following the Yugoslav example.

Khrushchev seemed to support a third school of thought, typified by the ideas of E.G. Liberman. This group proposed to retain centralized planning, but felt that a large number of secondary economic problems could be removed from the consideration of top planners and could be solved by other economic agencies. The top planning hierarchy should be able to concentrate with increased efficiency on the solution of economic problems of major importance. Part of the econommic decision-making process was thus to be delegated to the enterprises. M. Keren describes the Liberman proposals and their adoption in the G.D.R. in the following way:

> The essence of the Liberman proposals has been to give the enterprise freedom of operation, within a centrally determined plan, on whose fulfillment bonus payments will depend. The size of the bonus, on the other hand, is to depend on profitability, i.e., on the proportion of profits to productive assets. The debt of the NES reformers to the Liberman discussion has two facets: the very fact of the Liberman discussion was seen as a green light for reforms in the G.D.R., and many details of the G.D.R. reforms mirrored specific Liberman proposals. However, Liberman's primary interest was micro-economic, in the most restrictive sense of the term. He could allow himself not to be bogged down with problems of the interrelationships between enterprises and the coordination which they entail, and he was not at all concerned with problems of macro-economic balance. The G.D.R. reformers could not disregard these problems and therefore had to go beyond Liberman.[7]

East Germany in 1963 took the lead among the various CMEA countries in the adoption of Liberman-inspired, comprehensive economic reforms. Even though the Liberman ideas had the apparent support of Khrushchev, the East German government was careful to point out that the New Economic System was a logical development of former policies of the Socialist Unity Party and not a break with past policy.[8]

Undoubtedly, Ulbricht's acceptance of economic reforms had political implications. By introducing the New Economic System in 1963, he showed his loyalty to the then existing leader in the Kremlin and his willingness to "destalinize." But there were also important economic reasons for the adoption of NES. The rate of economic growth had started declining during the first years of the 1960s. The inevitable disruptions brought about by the land tenure changes of 1960 and the changes in resource allocations made necessary by the closure of the Berlin border in 1961, caused an unavoidable slow-down. The yearly rate of increase of industrial output fell from a peak of 12% in 1959 to 9% in 1960 and 5.8% in 1961. The decline in the rate of industrial expansion probably best explains why Liberman's ideas were so well received by the East German government.

The NES program of 1963 had little in common with Marxist-Leninist dogma.[9] Following the Liberman scheme, net enterprise profits became the principal indicator of the quality of enterprise management. Although the fulfillment of quantitative targets was retained as a criterion for the award of managerial bonuses, governmental decrees after 1963 assigned greater weight to profitability as an index of good managerial performance.[10] Stalin's faithful allies in East Germany were now prepared to incorporate into their economic system some features of a market economy. Enterprise managers were to make decisions concerning production and sales with greater freedom and their initiative was no longer to be nullified by minute governmental production directives. The soundness of managerial decisions was in turn to be revealed by the quantum of market sales; the efficiency with which managers operated their enterprises was to be shown by profits. Managers were no longer to be subsidized by the State. It appeared that the aim of the reform program was to encourage initiative and experimentation by managers willing to assume new responsibilities and able to produce efficiently under international standards.

Long-range economic plans, *Perspektivplaene*, were to be formulated by the Planning Commission, *Staatliche Plankommission*. These plans were not to give detailed directives, but were simply to indicate general guidelines of economic activity, leaving lower planning agencies, including the individual enterprise, relatively free in the making of production decisions. Eight Ministries responsible to a Council of Ministers and its Presidium, were to undertake more detailed planning on the basis of both the long-term plan and the yearly plans of enterprises. Under these Ministries, eighty associations of socialized concerns, *Vereinigungen Volkseigener Betriebe*, of VVB, were to act as socialist holding companies charged with the supervision of the performance under their control. The VVBs were responsible for the marketing of the products of the enterprises under their control, for market research and advertising, as well as for the quality of the output produced under their supervision. Just as in the case of the individual enterprise, profits constituted the main performance index of the VVB.[11]

The reform program further introduced new comprehensive cost accounting systems and a price reform whose main purpose was to bring prices in the G.D.R. more in line with world prices and with existing relative scarcities. Raw materials prices were raised by an average of 20%. There was also a revaluation of capital equipment and inventories which was completed in 1964.[12] Dynamic pricing was introduced in 1968 in order to relate prices to changing technology and cost conditions.

The data in Table 11.4 show that total industrial output increased by nearly 100% between 1963 and 1970. The New Economic System greatly contributed to the growth of the East German economy in the 1960s, an economy which practically stagnated in the early years of the decade. After 1964, national income started growing at an average rate of 5% per year in spite of a stationary labor force.

The success of the New Economic System, or the Economic System of Socialism, as the reform program was retitled in 1967, cannot be entirely attributed to the larger autonomy enterprises received in 1963. This autonomy was limited in scope and was again restricted in later years when the East German government decided to return gradually to a more centralized planning system. Management's freedom in the investment of after-tax profits in 1963 was still limited by a number of

TABLE 11.4

INDEX OF GROSS INDUSTRIAL OUTPUT

1955 = 100

	1956	1960	1963	1964	1965	1966
Energy and Fuels	108	124	144	153	153	160
Chemical Industry	109	152	188	203	222	241
Metallurgy	109	144	158	169	176	186
Construction Materials	110	174	195	223	241	253
Machinery and Vehicles	110	175	221	237	251	266
Electrical Industry	111	202	260	285	317	351
Light Industry without Textiles	100	146	163	172	179	188
Textile Industry	104	139	147	151	157	166
Total Industry	107	155	183	195	207	220

	1967	1968	1969	1970
Energy and Fuels	167	170	175	181
Chemical Industry	258	280	301	322
Metallurgy	195	207	226	238
Construction Materials	264	280	285	323
Machinery and Vehicles	287	309	332	351
Electrical Industry	378	406	454	501
Light Industry without Textiles	200	211	226	241
Textile Industry	178	180	187	194
Total Industry	235	249	266	282

Source: *S.J.D.D.R., 1972*, p. 114.

directives. Managerial autonomy was further restricted in 1968 when a new type of mandatory planning was introduced. The 1968 program of "planning according to strucutre-determining tasks" gave priority to types of production which would either advance East German technology or which would contribute to the expansion of exports. The new policy marked a return of old economic problems. The development of activities which were not "structure-determining" was neglected. The transport system, commanding low priority, was adversely affected. Shortages in the supply of certain commodities soon developed. Once again, the economy was subject to serious imbalances.[13]

Instead of returning to the 1963 program, party leaders in 1970 decided to solve accumulating economic difficulties by abandoning whatever remained of the New Economic System. A *Resolution on the*

Implementation of the Economic System of Socialism in 1971 recentralized
the allocation system and the entirety of investment planning.

Although during its early years of operation NES helped undoubtedly to boost East German industrial production, industrial growth in
the 1960s was also favored by a greater availablility of industrial raw
materials and by a greater emphasis on those types of industrial production in which East Germany had a comparative advantage within
the CMEA world.

The Role of East German Foreign Trade

Poor in industrial raw materials, the G.D.R. had to depend heavily
on foreign trade in order to be able to import these materials in adequate quantities. To import raw materials on a large scale, the country
had to export on a large scale.

The New Economic System did not abolish the State's control over
international trade. For the East German government, the importance
of foreign trade was not determined alone by the country's demand for
industrial raw materials. It was also hoped that the expansion of
foreign trade would facilitate the attainment of a "technological revolution" in the country. Foreign trade was to be the means by which the
most efficient machinery from the economically advanced countries
could be imported. To facilitate the expansion of the G.D.R.'s foreign
trade, the formulators of NES introduced a number of measures
which, although leaving unaffected the State's monopoly over foreign
trade and foreign exchange transactions, gave greater freedom to
certain enterprises in the earning and disposal of foreign exchange.
These measures principally benefited enterprises producing exporta-
ble commodities. Any enterprise whose exports surpassed the planned volume or value was allowed to retain half of the above-target
foreign exchange it had earned and could utilize this exchange for
commodity imports. Also, any enterprise which through changed
methods of production could reduce its demand for imported raw
materials was to be entitled to retain half of the foreign exchange
thereby saved and could utilize this exchange for the import of improved equipment. Enterprises producing for the export market were
allowed to obtain foreign exchange credits if, through the imports
financed by such credits, they would be able to expand their exports.
The foreign exchange loan was to be repaid through the additional

exchange earned by the enterprise. This policy tended to overlook the fact that in many cases the enterprises in greatest need of foreign exchange to finance the modernization of their plants were enterprises producing solely for the domestic market. The rationale of these measures was to reduce as much as possible the adverse impact of larger imports of machinery on the country's imports of fuels and industrial raw materials.

During the decade 1960-1970, there were only three years during which the G.D.R. recorded an overall negative balance of trade. During this period, the total exports index rose from 100 in 1960 to 188.2 in 1970; the imports index showed a very similar increase by rising from 100 in 1960 to 187.8 in 1970. It is interesting to notice that it was the trade with the western industrial nations which grew fastest between 1960 and 1970. This development reveals the East German eagerness to import from the "capitalist West" the higher technology embodied in western capital goods. Between 1960 and 1970, East German trade with various groups of countries increased as follows: 147.8% with the "industrial capitalist" countries; 113.3% with the CMEA countries; 105.4% with the "socialist countries"; 95.8% with the Soviet Union. [14]

While the share of U.S.S.R. trade in total East German trade declined from 42% in 1960 to 39% in 1970, the share of trade with the industrial capitalist countries increased from 20% to 24%. In 1970, East German trade with the socialist countries represented 71% of the country's total foreign trade and trade with the CMEA countries amounted to 67% of the total trade. East German trade with developing nations represented only about 2.5% of the total East German Trade. [15] In 1970, the Soviet Union was still East Germany's principal trading partner. In 1967, the U.S.S.R. delivered 86% of the East German imports of steel, 82% of the iron ore imports, 88% of the crude oil imports and 90% of the cotton imports. [16] The Soviet Union in turn obtained from East Germany one third of its machinery and equipment imports; the G.D.R. exported to Russia refrigerating equipment, equipment for the construction materials industry, agricultural machinery, photographic equipment, precision instruments and railroad cars. The G.D.R. was also a very important partner for the other CMEA countries; the latter imported from the G.D.R. a large array of industrial products such as motor vehicles, tractors, ships, machinery of various types, electronic equipment, synthetic fertilizers, textiles and consumer durables. In addition, CMEA countries such as Poland, Rumania and Bulgaria benefited from export credits extended by the G.D.R. This trade allowed East Germany to obtain the electric power, the coal, the steel, the bauxite it needed to expand industrial production. Increases in industrial production and exports in turn allowed East Germany's national income to rise. Sales of crude steel, steel bars, machinery, vehicles, musical instruments and precision tools in western markets allowed the G.D.R. to import from the West computers and other industrial machinery that could not be easily acquired within the CMEA market.

TABLE 11.5

EAST GERMAN FOREIGN TRADE
(In million Valuta-Mark)

	Total	With Socialist Countries	With the U.S.S.R.	With Industrial Capitalist Countries	With Developing Countries
1960	18,487.4	13,798.8	7,907.4	3,897.2	791.3
1961	19,034.6	14,279.8	8,326.9	3,842.3	912.6
1962	20,098.5	15,873.0	9,823.5	3,497.2	728.4
1963	21,182.9	16,628.4	10,287.2	3,823.6	730.9
1964	23,373.6	17,853.7	10,897.8	4,628.8	891.1
1965	24,693.2	18,240.8	10,565.7	5,346.2	1,106.1
1966	26,963.8	19,709.1	11,176.0	6,005.5	1,249.1
1967	28,286.1	20,971.9	11,866.8	6,037.5	1,276.6
1968	30,172.6	22,938.6	12,851.6	6,001.4	1,232.6
1969	34,760.8	25,289.0	14,287.7	8,028.9	1,442.7
1970	39,597.4	28,340.1	15,484.5	9,656.0	1,601.4

Source: *S.J.D.D.R., 1972*, pp. 302-303.

Changing terms of trade over the years have not altered markedly the significance of the data in Table 11.5. Although the East German terms of trade with the West have tended to deteriorate slightly, the effects of this trend were more than offset by improving terms of trade with the socialist world. The continuing increase of trade with the West tends to indicate that East German economic policy in the 1960s gave more weight to economic than to political considerations.

Planning and Re-Planning

A second Five-Year Plan, covering the period 1956 to 1960, was abandoned in 1958 and was replaced by a first Seven-Year Plan for the years 1959 to 1965. The main purpose of this change was to better synchronize the planning periods of the various CMEA countries. It became soon apparent that the overambitious goals of this plan could not be attained. The plan attempted to raise both the standard of living and the investment-income ratio, goals which sharply conflicted with each other at a time when many earlier investment projects in the country had not yet been completed and were thus unable to boost national income. Economic difficulties in the years 1960 to 1963 were multiplied by a faulty price policy which kept prices of fuels and industrial raw materials abnormally low and which thus led to a misuse of these scarce factors, and by the economic imbalances which resulted from the emphasis placed on the building of heavy industry. The collectivization of agriculture in 1960 increased emigration out of the G.D.R. and serious labor shortages ensued.

Recognizing that the first Seven-Year Plan was leading to economic disaster, the East German government discarded it in 1962, and in 1963 a new Seven-Year Plan went into effect for the period 1963 to 1970. This new plan was to implement the policies of the New Economic System.

It quickly became apparent that the NES program was beneficial to the economy. A more balanced growth characterized the entire economy from 1964 on. Economic growth during these years was not spectacular, but it was sustained and was not affected by the West German recession of 1966-1967. Economic growth in the G.D.R. was, however, still handicapped by a number of institutional difficulties. The over-regulated East German foreign trade was unable to grow as rapidly as that of the German Federal Republic. A greater concern by the government for an improved standard of living tended to impede an increase in the investment-national income ratio. Insufficient investment in certain sectors of the economy continued to plague it with shortages and low quality products. Although the chemical, electronic, precision instruments and optical goods industries showed high rates of growth after 1964, the construction materials and construction industries, the engineering industries and shipbuilding did not register appreciable growth.

Critics of East German economic policies have pointed out that throughout the 1960s, the G.D.R. was unable to reach the levels of productivity and the living standards of West Germany. Gross domestic product per capita remained about 25% smaller than in the Federal Republic. If told that East German industrial production per capita had doubled since 1939, these critics replied that during the same period of time West German per capita industrial output multiplied by a factor of 2.5. These critics have also argued that the adverse economic effects of the partition of Germany, of Soviet appropriations and of manpower losses should not be taken into account when evaluating the performance of the East German economy during the 1960s. These writers believe that there was no "East German economic miracle" that could be compared to the *Wirtschaftswunder* of the German Federal Republic.

On the other hand, it is a fact that in spite of severe resource scarcities, the East German government succeeded in building an entirely new heavy industry sector within a period of about fifteen years, an accomplishment which not only rendered the East German economy viable, but which also placed this small and once poor economy among the ten largest industrial nations in the world. Entirely new industrial facilities were completed in the 1950s and the 1960s. True, industrial building in West Germany was not slower, but it proceeded in a more favorable economic environment. In spite of shortages in human and non-human capital, the East Germans built the gas and coke works *Schwarze Pumpe* (1959), a new overseas port at Rostock (1960), the cotton spinning mills *Leinefelde* (1963), the synthetic fiber complex *Wilhelm-Pieck-Stadt Guben* (1964) and the automobile plants *Ludwigsfelde* (1965). Although critics have attacked the economic soundness of these projects on the grounds that they were usually built without due regard for construction and operation costs and were in certain instances poorly located, these projects nevertheless permitted East Germany to produce and export along lines of comparative advantages, to rise its capita income and living standards, and to set aside the serious economic handicaps that had weakened it during the first postwar decade.

After the Forced Land Collectivization of 1960

Agriculture remained East Germany's laggard sector in the 1950s. A major cause of the relatively poor performance of this sector was the land reform program of 1945 which resulted in the creation of about 870,000 new small farms of an average size of eighteen acres. On these small units, farmers tried to survive on the basis of a mixed type of production, carried out inefficiently and without the benefit of modern machinery and sufficient fertilizers. Until 1963, the State, in the old

Stalinist fashion, deliberately exploited the agricultural sector to finance the building of new heavy industry. Extremely low prices were paid by the government for the obligatory deliveries of agricultural commodities imposed on farmers. Farm income in East Germany was so low in comparison to income in the other sectors of the economy that poverty induced many skilled East German farmers to flee to the West. Throughout the 1950s, the East German farmer lacked enough mechanized power, tools and fertilizers to allow him to increase yields per hectare; the aggregate utilization of nitrogenous and phosphate-based fertilizers attained their prewar level only in 1957.[17] The end result of such conditions was that food rationing continued in the G.D.R. until May 1958.

Conditions in the agricultural sector rapidly changed after the forced land collectivization of 1960. Total agricultural output in East Germany probably attained the prewar volume only in 1964. After that year, however, and in spite of poor crops in 1966 and 1969, due to adverse weather conditions, agricultural output registered quick and sustained growth during the remainder of the decade. By 1965, East German crop yields were among the highest in Eastern Europe and were comparable to those of the German Federal Republic, France and Italy. Compared to crop yields in these western countries, the G.D.R. in 1965 was leading in pre-hectare yields of wheat, barley and oats. Among Europe's ten leading crop producing nations, East Germany ranked first in per-hectare yields for wheat, barley and oats, second for rye and third for potatoes. Table 11.6 shows the rapid crop yield gains obtained by the G.D.R. in comparison to other countries in Eastern Europe during the period 1966 to 1968.

TABLE 11.6

YIELDS OF BASIC CROPS IN COUNTRIES OF EASTERN EUROPE
(Yields in quintals per hectare)

Country and Crop	1966	1967	1968
Bulgaria			
Wheat	27.9	30.5	24.0
Barley	25.5	25.4	20.0
Maize	38.1	34.3	31.3
Potatoes	113.0	106.0	114.0
Sugar-beet	404.0	342.0	265.0

Czechoslovakia			
Wheat	25.3	27.1	31.6
Rye	20.0	21.6	22.8
Barley	23.4	27.3	29.8
Oats	19.2	22.3	21.4
Maize	32.7	30.3	33.8
Potatoes	134.0	148.0	176.0
Sugar-beet	341.0	376.0	418.0
Eastern Germany			
Cereals	26.1.	31.8	33.4
of which:			
Wheat	31.4	37.8	41.7
Rye	21.3	26.6	26.3
Barley	29.3	34.9	35.6
Potatoes	185.0	205.0	188.0
Sugar-beet	314.0	333.0	344.0
Hungary			
Wheat	21.7	25.9	25.2
Rye	11.0	11.0	12.5
Barley	18.7	20.9	23.4
Maize	31.6	28.5	29.9
Potatoes	122.8	89.4	89.2
Sugar-beet	331.0	324.0	334.0
Poland			
Cereals	18.8	19.4	21.2
of which:			
Wheat	21.5	22.4	24.8
Rye	17.8	17.9	19.8
Barley	20.6	21.6	23.6
Oats	18.8	19.7	20.7
Potatoes	169.0	176.0	185.0
Sugar-beet	313.0	358.0	357.0
Rumania			
Cereals	20.4	20.5	19.2
of which:			
Wheat	16.7	20.0	17.2
Maize	24.4	21.3	21.3
Potatoes	108.0	98.0	116.0
Sugar-beet	225.0	218.0	213.0

Source: U.N. ECE, *Economic Survey of Europe in 1969*, Part II, New York, 1970, p. 32.

The rates of growth of East German livestock and other animal products since 1962 have also been excellent. As shown by the Table 11.7, meat production during these years increased by 41% in the G.D.R. but only by 4% in West Germany.

Meat production had only increased by 2% in the G.D.R. between 1955 and 1962. In 1962, the country produced only 82.4% of its total

TABLE 11.7

MEAT PRODUCTION
(In 1,000 tons)

	1962	1964	1966	Net Change: %
Bulgaria	300	306	387	+29
Czechoslovakia	639	674	680	+6.4
East Germany	854	1,069	1,204	+41
Hungary	571	571	587	+3
Poland	1,818	1,703	1,905	+4.8
Rumania	679	713	715	+5.3
Yugoslavia	622	657	702	+13
USSR	7,780	6,840	8,850	+14
West Germany	2,934	3,012	3,060	+4
Italy	1,260	1,103	1,199	−4.8

Source: USDA, *The Europe and Soviet Agricultural Situation*, Washington, Government Printing Office, 1967, pp. 86, 104.

meat consumption.[18] In 1966, East Germany had become self-sufficient for its meat requirements. Compared with the situation in 1938, the country in 1966 had nearly one-third more cattle, 56% more pigs and the chicken population had almost doubled.[19] Table 11.8 shows that after 1966, the G.D.R. not only continued to increase its meat production, but also maintained a position second only to Poland in the production of milk and eggs.

The record of East German milk production in the 1960s was as good as that of meat output. The events of 1960 and 1961 brought a fall in East Germany's milk production, but from 1964 on, milk output started growing much faster than in the 1950s. Whereas in 1959 the G.D.R. produced 18% more milk than in 1938, by 1966 the production of milk exceeded prewar output by 36%. The quantity of milk per cow per year in 1966 was 21% larger than that in 1938.[20] The difference in the average outputs of milk per cow per year in the two Germanies — 3,088 kilograms in the G.D.R., 3,646 in the G.F.R. — was largely due to the fact that cow fodder in the Federal Republic was richer in protein.

What were the reasons for East Germany's excellent agricultural performance since 1964? First of all, capital investment in agriculture was rapidly expanded in the early 1960s. After fifteen years of severe neglect and exploitation of the agricultural sector, the East German government decided to change its agricultural policy once the entirety of agriculture had been socialized. Capital investment in agriculture

TABLE 11.8

OUTPUT OF LIVESTOCK PRODUCTS, SELECTED COUNTRIES
(Output of meat in 1,000 tons, output of milk in
millions of Litres, output of eggs in millions)

Country & Year	Meat	Milk	Eggs
Bulgaria			
1966	490	1,456	1,490
1967	490	1,562	1,683
1968	534	1,540	1,627
1969	——	1,530	1,530
Czechoslovakia			
1966	1,123	4,404	3,080
1967	1,175	4,205	3,218
1968	1,222	4,417	3,270
1969	——	4,621	3,411
Eastern Germany			
1966	1,660	6,728	3,894
1967	1,731	6,904	3,995
1968	1,798	7,227	4,046
1969	——	——	——
Hungary			
1966	1,220	1,790	2,436
1967	1,211	1,918	2,714
1968	1,351	1,875	2,792
1969	——	1,870	2,600
Poland			
1966	2,625	13,807	6,253
1967	2,130	14,058	6,348
1968	2,160	14,202	6,315
1969	——	14,250	6,400
1970 plan	——	——	——
Rumania			
1966	1,265	3,738	2,814
1967	1,356	4,123	3,011
1968	1,297	3,833	3,113
1969	——	——	——
1970 plan	1,396	4,248	——

Source: U.N., ECE, *Economic Survey of Europe in 1969*, Part II, New York, 1970, p. 34.

increased by about two-thirds between 1960 and 1966.[21] The disappearance of small, inefficient farms and the ability of LPGs to work on
large tracts of land allowed the use of more rational methods of production. From 1965 on, more lime, nitrogen and potash were applied per

hectare of land in the G.D.R. than in West Germany. In 1965, the two countries used the same quantity of phosphate per hectare of culti-vated land.[22] In the G.D.R., total collectivization brought about a rapid development of mechanized agriculture. More machines and more fertilizers in turn generated rising crop yields; this upward trend is shown in Table 11.9.

TABLE 11.9

G.D.R.: CROP YIELDS PER HECTARE
1934/38 - 1970
(In 100 kilograms per hectare)

	Wheat	Rye	Barley	Oats	Sugar Beets	Potatoes
1934/38	24.6	17.1	23.4	21.5	291.0	173.0
1953	27.4	18.7	25.4	24.7	284.0	159.3
1955	30.3	21.8	27.4	25.4	265.9	132.8
1959	31.3	20.7	29.4	23.6	198.9	161.3
1960	34.8	22.5	32.6	28.1	287.6	192.4
1961	27.5	18.2	21.9	24.4	213.8	123.7
1962	31.1	21.3	31.1	28.3	213.8	179.0
1963	30.0	20.4	28.2	25.6	266.0	172.6
1964	31.1	23.0	32.3	26.2	261.3	172.8
1965	36.7	23.2	33.2	29.2	253.1	177.2
1966	31.4	21.3	29.3	26.9	313.5	184.8
1967	37.8	26.6	34.9	31.4	332.6	205.0
1968	41.7	26.3	35.6	33.8	343.8	188.1
1969	35.5	22.4	32.2	30.9	253.2	146.2
1970	35.6	21.8	30.1	26.6	320.1	195.7

Source: *S.J.D.D.R., 1972,* pp. 222, 223.

Another major reason for advances in agricultural productivity was the gradual change in the way the East German farmer viewed the LPG into which he had been forced. Following the transfer of land still in private hands to the LPGs in 1960, the government increased the delivery prices of agricultural products in 1963. The farmer's income rose. By the end of the 1960s he was earning more than many industrial workers. Not only was he pleased by the fact that he had never earned so much money before, but he also appreciated the fact that member-ship in an LPG meant a shorter workday and the possibility of enjoying two or three weeks of vacation per year. A better living standard soon transformed the peasant's opposition to the LPG into an awareness that his economic condition had markedly improved since 1960. The growing willingness of the East German farmer to support the LPG system contributed in a major way to increases in labor productivity. This change in peasants' attitudes is perhaps best revealed by the fact that whereas in 1960 the East German farmer generally preferred to join a cooperative of Type I or Type II so as to retain private ownership over his animals, the trend since then has been to have these cooperatives changed into Type III LPGs, without any compulsion to do so on the part of the government. East Germany's forced collectivization of the entirety of the land succeeded thus in modernizing the agricultural sector and in raising both rural productivity and standards of living.

The Economic Record in the 1960s

Throughout the 1960s, political dogma tended to strengthen the East German government's resolution to increase the share of productivity gains in aggregate output growth by raising economic efficiency in various sectors of the economy. This striving for a "technological revolution" antedated by years the December 1969 resolution of the Central Committee of the Communist Party of the Soviet Union to give more importance to qualitative economic achievements than to the attainment of quantitative economic goals.[23]

The East German effort to achieve more intensive and rational growth in the 1960s is revealed by the trend of its capital-output ratios as shown in Table 11.10. These ratios tended to decline during the decade and indicate therefore that investment allocations were becoming more efficient.

Although in comparison to other economies in the CMEA group, the East German economy in the 1960s did not generate an outstanding rate of growth, increases in labor productivity in the G.D.R. contributed more to growth than in the other six countries. In East Germany, the growth of industrial output appears to have been entirely due to labor productivity increases. Increased labor productivity reflected in turn the improved qualities of the human and non-human capital matrix. Increased productivity was clearly due to policies which channelled investment not only into the accumulation of non-human capital, but which also used investment for the improvement of education and research.

The importance attached by the government to the improvement and wider spread of skills and education is revealed by the following data. Between 1960 and 1970, the number of students graduating from vocational schools increased from 24,544 to 34,778. This represented an increase of 70.57%.[24] The number of students graduating from universities and other institutions of higher learning rose from 15,136 in 1960 to 20,524 in 1970, an increase of 73.75%.[25] In the fields of engineering and architecture, the number of graduates increased from 2,908 to 5,022.

Whether we look at rates of growth of industrial or agricultural outputs, of foreign trade or of labor productivity, it appears that throughout the 1960s, the performance of the East German economy, a

TABLE 11.10

INVESTMENT RATIOS, GROWTH RATES, INCREMENTAL CAPITAL—
OUTPUT RATIOS IN THE CMEA COUNTRIES

	Investment Ratios		Growth Rates		Incremental Capital-Output Ratio	
	1961-1965	1966-1970	1961-1965	1966-1970	1961-1965	1966-1970
Bulgaria	26.7	33.6	6.7	8.6	4.0	3.9
Czechoslovakia	25.4	26.7	1.9	6.9	13.4	3.9
East Germany	20.1	24.1	3.5	5.4	5.7	4.5
Hungary	29.4	32.9	4.5	6.7	6.5	4.9
Poland	23.3	29.4	6.1	6.2	3.8	4.7
Rumania	33.6	36.0	9.0	8.6	3.7	4.2
Soviet Union	23.7	23.8	6.5	7.2	3.6	3.3

Source: U.N., ECE, *Economic Survey of Europe in 1969,* New York, 1970, p. 37.

TABLE 11.11

PERCENTAGE SHARE OF PRODUCTIVITY
GROWTH IN OUTPUT GROWTH

	Industry 1961 - 1965	Industry 1966 - 1970
Bulgaria	63	64
Czechoslovakia	63	84
East Germany	100	89
Hungary	64	57
Poland	61	59
Rumania	55	66
Soviet Union	54	66

Source: U.N., ECE, *Economic Survey of Europe in 1970,* Part II, New York, 1971, p. 71.

small economy quite poor in natural resources and handicapped during many years by adverse politico-economic developments, was in many respects superior to the performances of some of the western economies. The people of the G.D.R. seem to be quite aware of the fact that the improvement in economic conditions they witnessed in the 1960s, the greater availability of education for their children, the frequent conversion by many a peasant of what was once his stable into a garage for his new *Trabant*, were achieved without the help of foreign economic support. Feeling that the West German economic miracle was launched with the help of American dollars, the East German is proud of the fact that economic achievements in his country were entirely due to his efforts, privations and skills. The men and women of the G.D.R. do believe that their government achieved an "economic miracle" in the 1960s, an eastern *Wirtschaftswunder* more remarkable in many ways than that of the German Federal Republic.

NOTES

1. G.D.R., *Statistisches Jahrbuch der Deutschen Demokratischen Republik 1967* (Berlin-E: Staatsverlag der D.D.R., 1967), pp. 498-499. Henceforth denoted as S.J.D.D.R.
2. A. Baring, *Der 17 Juni 1953* (Cologne: Kiepenheuer and Witsch, 1965).
3. G.D.R., *S.J.D.D.R. 1967*, p. 539.
4. For a more detailed study of the Liberman reforms see: E.G. Liberman, *Economic Methods and the Effectiveness of Production* (White Plains: International Arts and Sciences Press, 1972); M. Bornstein, "The Soviet Price Reforms Discussion," *Quarterly Journal of Economics*, vol. 78 (February 1964); A. Zauberman, "Liberman's Rules of the Game for Soviet Industry," *Slavic Review*, vol. 22 (December 1963).
5. A Korbonski, "The Evolution of Comecon," *International Conciliation* (September 1964).
6. E. Neuberger, "Libermanism, Computopia and the Visible Hand: The Question of Informational Efficiency," *The American Economic Review*, vol. LVI (May 1966), pp. 131-44.
7. M. Keren, "The New Economic System in the GDR: An Obituary," *Soviet Studies*, vol. 24, April 1973, pp. 554-587, at p. 556.
8. W. Berger and O. Reinhold, *Zu den wissenschaftlichen Grundlagen des neuen oekonomischen Systems* (Berlin-E: Dietz Verlag, 1966), p. 10.
9. The West German journalist J. Nawrocki reports "dass das Neue Ökonomische System der D.D.R. zunächst überwiegend und in den Grenzen des machtpolitisch Wünschbaren rein pragmatisch begründet worden ist. Die Übereinstimmung mit der kommunistischen Ideologie wurde erst später konstruiert." J. Nawrocki, *Das geplante Wunder* (Hamburg: C. Wegner Verlag, 1967), p. 50.
10. G.D.R., "Verordnung ueber die Bildung und Verwendung des Prämienfonds in den volkseigenen und ihnen gleichgestellten Betrieben und den VVB für das Jahr 1968," *Gesetzblatt der DDR* (1967), Part II, p. 105.
11. G.D.R., *Richtlinie für das Neue Ökonomische System der Planung und Leitung der*

Volkswirtschaft, Beschluss des Präsidiums des Ministerrates der D.D.R. (Berlin-E: Dietz Verlag, 1963), p. 28.

12. H. Bohme, "East German Price Formation under the New Economic System," *Soviet Studies,* (January 1968), pp. 340-358.

13. Professor H. Betz believes that this return to centralized planning was mostly motivated by ideological reasons. According to him, party leaders in the G.D.R. opposed economic decentralization because of political dogmatism. The 1968 events in Czechoslovakia seemed to strengthen the belief of East German leaders that political considerations had to override conflicting economic aims. H. Betz, "East Germany: The Primacy of Dogma over Reform," *Journal of Economic Issues,* vol. VIII, No. 1 (March 1974), pp. 83-96. Professor Keren, on the other hand, believes that the return to centralized planning in the late 1960's was principally motivated by a desire to advance technology and increase the export capacity of the country; if economic growth suffered after 1968, it was not so much because of unwise, dogma-determined policies, but rather because of planning errors and the difficulty of carrying out "taut" plans after that year. M. Keren, "The New Economic System in the G.D.R.: An Obituary," *Soviet Studies.*

14. G.D.R., *S.J.D.D.R.,* 1972, pp. 302-303.

15. *Ibid.,* p. 302.

16. Nawrocki, *Das geplante Wunder,* p. 200.

17. G.D.R., *S.J.D.D.R.,* 1966, p. 281.

18. G.D.R., *S.J.D.D.R.,* 1967, p. 292.

19. *Ibid.,* p. 302.

20. *Ibid.,* pp. 312-313.

21. *Ibid.,* p. 51.

22. *Ibid.,* p. 297 and *Statistiches Jahrbuch fuer die Bundesrepublik Deutschland* 1966), p. 191.

23. The Central Committee of the CPSU stated that "raising the efficiency of production has become a key problem, primarily because there has been a change in the main factors of our economic growth. While previously we were able to develop our economy mainly by using quantitative factors, that is by increasing our manpower numerically and by high rates of growth of capital investments, it is now necessary that above all we rely on qualitative factors of economic growth — the raising of efficiency and the intensity of the national economy." *Pravda* (13 January, 1970).

24. G.D.R., *S.J.D.D.R.,* 1972, p. 388.

25. *Ibid.,* p. 392.

CHAPTER 12

YUGOSLAVIA
TOWARD AN INDUSTRIAL
MIXED ECONOMY

Following the gradual politico-economic changes of the early 1950s, the Yugoslav economy continued to industralize rapidly while adopting more and more the characteristics of a mixed economy. High rates of economic growth were generally recorded in the 1950s and the 1960s. Taking 1952 as the base year, national income in 1968 attained an index figure of 324.[1] Although growth rates varied within sub-periods, national income in the 1950s and 1960s continued to grow faster than in the prewar period.

Yugoslav economic growth was largely the product of rapid industrial expansion. Industrialization was in turn made possible by large investments in fixed assets and by a steady growth of the industrial labor force. During the years 1947 to 1956, industry absorbed over 50% of total gross investment in fixed assets; this proportion declined to 34% between 1957 and 1966, then rose to 36% during the remainder of the 1960s.[2] Between 1952 and 1972, industry more than doubled the number of industrial workers employed. During the first half of this period, increases in industrial output were mostly due to the rapid growth of industrial employment which rose at an average annual rate of 7.5%. During the second half, better industrial facilities and more efficiently organized production and distribution systems allowed a gradual decline in the rate of growth of industrial employment without a slowdown in the expansion rate of industrial output. Between 1962 and 1972, the industrial labor force increased at an average annual rate of 3.4%.[3]

Table 12.1 shows the magnitude of Yugoslavia's industrial growth in the period 1952 to 1972. During these twenty years, the output of the chemical industry increased 32 times; that of the electrical industry, 25 times; that of the petroleum industry, 19 times. Electric power production increased 11 times.

TABLE 12.1

INDUSTRIAL OUTPUT GROWTH BY INDUSTRIES, 1952 - 1972
1952 = 100

Chemicals	3,210
Electrical	2,500
Petroleum	1,890
Pulp and Paper	1,240
Metal-using (Excludes shipbuilding)	1,180
Electricity	1,115
Rubber	1,020
Non-metallic minerals	883
Food	850
Printing	800
Film	758
Ferrous metallurgy	720
Shipbuilding	600
Building materials	600
Textiles	530
Leather and Footwear	506
Non-ferrous metallurgy	457
Wood products	400
Tobacco	236
Coal	225

Source: *Statistički godišnjak Jugoslavije,* 1972, p. 102 and 1971, p. 98.

Within the same period, the country's industrial structure was significantly transformed. In 1952, the textile, leather and footwear, wood, tobacco, food and coal industries provided 49% of the total industrial output; in 1972, these industries contributed only 26% of total industrial production. On the other hand, in 1952 the chemical, electrical, petroleum, pulp and paper, metal-using, electricity and rubber industries produced only 25% of the total industrial output; twenty years later, these industries accounted for almost half the aggregated industrial output.[4]

Even though the rate of growth varied widely among industries as shown in Table 12.1, industrial output as a whole expanded 7.7 times in the period 1952 to 1972. During this time, the industrial labor force increased by 2.8 times, labor productivity rose 2.7 times and capital intensity grew by 2.2 times.

The performance of the agricultural sector was not as spectacular, as shown in Table 12.2. Until 1956, agricultural output did not surpass prewar levels; however, significant gains were recorded from 1957 on when governmental policy toward agriculture changed.

TABLE 12.2

YIELDS OF MAJOR CROPS

Two-year averages in metric quintals/hectare

	1938-1939	1947-1948	1951-1952	1955-1956	1959-1960	1963-1964	1967-1968
Wheat	11.4	11.3	11.0	11.4	18.4	18.5	23.5
Corn	16.4	17.1	11.8	14.4	24.9	25.5	28.1
Sugar Beet	176.0	180.0	139.2	179.3	296.2	297.3	364.1

Source: *Statisticki Godisnjak S.F.R.J.*, 1962, p. 152.

Between 1947 and 1968, national income rose by 3.4 times, i.e., at an average annual rate of 6.03%. During the same period, total population increased by 28%, i.e., at an average annual rate of 1.18%. The total labor force increased by 12%, or by 0.5% per year. Per capita national income grew at an average annual rate of 4.8%.[5]

The increase in aggregate income cannot be explained in terms of a growing labor force alone. True, employment in the socialist sector during the years 1952 to 1968 expanded by 1.4 million; most of this employment increase benefited industry and mining. Yet at the same time, employment in the private sector of the economy declined by about 850,000.[6] Employment expansion could thus not be the key variable explaining income growth. The increase in the national income, as well as in per capita income, in the period 1952 to 1968 must be explained in terms of increased labor productivity.

Industrial Expansion and Labor Productivity

Average labor productivity in the economy as a whole increased in the 1950s and 1960s in response to the continued expansion of the industrial sector which allowed the structure of employment to change in favor of the most productive sectors in the economy, i.e., industry and mining. The new jobs generated by economic growth involved non-agricultural activities and allowed thousands of agrarian workers to switch to a higher productivity occupation. The share of industry and mining in total employment rose from 32.4% in 1952 to 37.7% in 1968.[7] Table 12.3 shows that for the economy as a whole, labor productivity increased by about three times between 1947 and 1968.

The breakdown by sectors indicates that the national income generated by industry rose by almost 5 times between 1952 and 1968. In this period, the industrial labor force expanded by 2.4 times and industrial labor productivity doubled.

TABLE 12.3

GROWTH OF NATIONAL INCOME, EMPLOYMENT AND LABOR
PRODUCTIVITY IN THE YUGOSLAV ECONOMY, 1947 - 1968

	National Income (Million 1966 dinars)	Number of employed and economically active persons (In 1,000)	Labor productivity (National income per employed in dinars)
1947	27,815	6,465	4,300
1948	33,486	6,665	5,020
1949	35,634	6,963	5,120
1950	31,470	6,868	4,580
1951	34,684	6,738	5,150
1952	29,372	6,613	4,440
1953	37,032	6,652	5,570
1954	37,031	6,733	5,500
1955	41,918	6,795	6,170
1956	39,878	6,703	5,950
1957	49,673	6,768	7,340
1958	50,098	6,812	7,350
1959	58,942	6,867	8,580
1960	62,078	6,982	8,890
1961	64,418	7,079	9,100
1962	66,978	7,075	9,470
1963	75,038	7,064	10,620
1964	83,717	7,176	11,670
1965	85,056	7,177	11,850
1966	91,102	7,123	12,790
1967	91,489	7,198	12,760
1968	95,114	7,250	13,119

Source: M. Marković, National Income, Employment and Productivity in the Yugoslav Economy, 1947-1968, *Yugoslav Survey*, May 1970, p. 50.

The continuous growth of the industrial labor force in the 1950s and the steady increase in its productivity were due to the fact that between 1952, when the first Five-Year Plan expired, and 1957, when the second Five-Year Plan was adopted, the investment policy of the government continued to give priority to the completion of key industrial projects. The structure of investment distribution continued to be what it had been in the period of the first Five-Year Plan. As a matter of fact, industry's share in total investment in the period 1952 to 1957 rose from 45.4% to 48.7%. Agriculture's share did not change, but investment in housing, education, health and other social services declined. Higher industrial productivity in this period was obtained at the cost of

TABLE 12.4

GROWTH OF NATIONAL INCOME, EMPLOYMENT AND
PRODUCTIVITY IN YUGOSLAV INDUSTRY, 1952-1968

	Natinal Income (Million 1966 dinars)	Labor Force (In 1,000)	Productivity (National Income per employed in dinars)
1952	6,947	562	12,360
1953	7,616	592	12,860
1954	8,719	671	12,990
1955	9,948	748	13,300
1956	10,895	788	13,830
1957	12,774	856	14,920
1958	14,288	929	15,380
1959	15,965	991	16,110
1960	18,167	1,072	16,950
1961	19,406	1,128	17,200
1962	20,816	1,165	17,870
1963	24,076	1,222	19,700
1964	27,974	1,319	21,210
1965	30,305	1,378	22,010
1966	31,793	1,358	23,410
1967	31,847	1,352	23,550
1968	33,732	1,349	25,005

Source: Same as Table 12.3

a declining standard of living, a greater housing shortage and a deterioration in educational and medical services.

The second Five-Year Plan, covering the period 1957 to 1961, gave priority to new goals emphasizing the improvement of the population's standard of living, increases in agricultural investment, and the development of export and import-substituting industries in order to reduce the balance of payments deficit. The plan did not abandon previous industrialization policies. Table 12.5 shows that investment in fixed assets in industry and mining as a percentage of total gross investment in fixed assets was lower in the period 1957 to 1960 than in the prior period 1947 to 1956. Still, industry and mining continued to claim the largest share of total investment, more than twice the share allocated to the transport and communications sector, and almost twice that of agriculture.

The government felt that the construction of necessary heavy industry had been completed by 1956. Yugoslav planners now had to decide what weights to attach to different goals future industrialization policy

TABLE 12.5

PERCENTAGE COMPOSITION OF GROSS INVESTMENT
IN FIXED ASSETS BY ECONOMIC SECTOR, 1947 - 1965

	1947-1952	1953-1956	1957-1960	1961-1965
Industry & Mining	53.0	58.9	43.1	51.2
Agriculture	17.0	14.2	23.6	17.3
Forestry	2.0	1.9	1.7	1.7
Building	2.7	2.8	3.0	3.1
Transport & Commerce	21.1	15.9	21.3	17.7
Trade & Tourism	3.3	4.9	5.8	7.3
Crafts	0.9	1.4	1.5	1.7

Source: Institute of Investment Economics, *Investicije 1947-1965*, Belgrade, 1967.

could reach. The idea was not to diminish the role of industrilization in the further development of the country; the question was what should be the pattern of future industrialization. Should industrialization policy seek to promote the development of foreign exchange-earning industries, or should it emphasize the growth of import-substituting industries? Should existing enterprises be expanded, or should the government favor the establishment of new enterprises able to produce entirely new products?

Yugoslav leaders agreed on two points. Industrialization should contribute to a high rate of economic growth and it should contribute to the strength of the socialist sector of the economy. The development of light industries, particularly consumer goods industries, provided more growth per dinar invested than the heavy industries. The growth of the consumers' goods output was also deemed necessary for political reasons; the low standard of living could bring about social and political unrest. Economic circumstances also pointed out the desirability of giving priority to the growth of light industries. As Table 12.6 shows, while the capital/output ratio was 2.36 in ferrous metallurgy, it was only 0.65 in the metalworking industry and 0.47 in the textile industry.

The Plan aimed at an increase in industrial output of 68%. While, as already mentioned, the industrial sector as a whole obtained a smaller share of aggregate investment than in earlier years, the proportion of industrial investment going to light industries and the production of electric power increased. Yugoslav planners counted on an increase in the export of finished goods to reduce the balance of payments deficit.

TABLE 12.6

FIXED CAPITAL-OUTPUT RATIOS
1960

Production of electricity	7.04
Coal Production & processing	1.58
Crude oil production & refining	0.82
Ferrous metallurgy	2.36
Nonferrous metallurgy	1.20
Metalworking	0.65
Shipbuilding	1.17
Electrical	0.50
Chemical	1.18
Construction materials	0.94
Timber	0.70
Paper	1.71
Textile	0.47
Leather	0.56
Rubber	0.23
Food	1.28
Tobacco	0.30

Source: *Statistički Godišnjak S.F.R.J.*, 1962, p. 152.

Although this deficit continued to grow, the targets of the Plan were on the whole attained by 1960. Industrial output had grown by 66.4% in only four years. The economy had continued to grow at a rapid pace.

TABLE 12.7

INDICES OF NATIONAL INCOME GROWTH
(In 1960 prices)

	1947-1952	1952-1956	1956-1960	1960-1964	1964-1967
Aggregate growth rate	2.3	7.5	11.8	8.6	4.5
Per capita growth rate	0.9	6.2	10.7	7.4	3.3

Source: Federal Statistical Office, *Jugoslavija 1945-1965*, Belgrade 1965, and *Statistički Godisnjak S.F.R.J.*, 1968 and 1969.

The high rate of growth was due to a number of factors. Not only did the shift in investment priorities to light industries favor industrial growth, but the completion of many factories whose construction had started during or after the period of the first Five-Year Plan allowed a rapid expansion of production after 1956. Industry, from that year on, also started enjoying the benefits of the infrastructure built earlier;

investments in such facilities as power lines and better means of transportation began to yield their fruit. Western foreign aid received in the 1950s, although embarrassing to Yugoslav Communist leaders, allowed the country to import machinery and equipment which could otherwise not have been obtained, given the country's continuous balance of payments deficits.

The second Five-Year Plan was ended in 1960 and a third Five-Year Plan was enacted for the period 1961 to 1965. This plan gave special attention to the further development of sources of energy and to the growth of export and import-replacing industries. Production of electric power, crude oil, copper, aluminum and sugar was to be doubled; that of trucks and tractors was to triple. The plan was abandoned in 1962 in order to reduce imports and to hasten the growth of consumer goods industries. A new Seven-Year Plan was proposed for the period 1964 to 1970, but the government did not approve it. A very flexible Plan was finally adopted for the years 1966 to 1970.

TABLE 12.8

TARGETS OF THE SECOND AND THIRD FIVE-YEAR
PLANS AND ACTUAL ACHIEVEMENTS

Products, Unit		1956 Actual	1961 Planned	1960 Actual	1965 Planned	1964 Actual
Electricity	(1,000 Mwh)	5,047	9,300	8,928	17,500	14,189
Coal	(1,000 tons)	17,101	25,300	22,713	35,000	29,511
Crude Oil	(1,000 tons)	294	850	944	2,200	1,799
Steel	(1,000 tons)	887	1,370	1,442	2,300	1,678
Copper	(1,000 tons)	29.4	40	35.7	77	51.9
Aluminum	(1,000 tons)	14.7	35	25.1	47	34.8
Fertilizers	(1,000 tons)	187	750	418	n.a.	1,581
Cement	(1,000 tons)	1,555	2,400	2,398	4,200	3,039
Trucks	(Items)	2,765	6,000	4,565	13,350	11,443
Tractors	(Items)	2,961	6,450	7,309	20,000	9,423
Cars	(Items)	990	6,000	10,461	30,000	27,845
Sugar	(1,000 tons)	149	331	264	500	330

Sources: *The Five-Year Plan of Economic Development of Yugoslavia, 1957-1961*, p. 155; *The Five-Year Plan of Economic Development of Yugoslavia, 1961-1965*, p. 96, *Statistički Godišnjak, 1966*, pp. 168-174.

Impediments to Faster Economic Growth: Production Inefficiencies, Unemployment and the Balance of Payments

The maintenance of a large ratio of aggregate investment to national income, the receipt of foreign aid from capitalist countries and high tariffs facilitated the expansion of industrial output.[8] Industrial investment, however, was often unwise and led to inefficient production. The federal government, by keeping the prices of energy, raw materials and labor exceedingly low, encouraged republics, communes and enterprises to duplicate economic activities without economic justification and to invest in economically inefficient projects. New factories were often small and poorly equipped. Their high cost methods of production frequently turned out low quality goods which could not compete in foreign markets. For instance, in 1964 two enterprises in Slovenia manufactured 361 automobiles; in the same year three establishments in Serbia produced 388 buses.[9]

In spite of the expansion of industrial activity and the growth of the labor force, unemployment increased in the period 1957 to 1967 and acted as another burden limiting the rate of economic growth. Yugoslav statistics on unemployment cover only those persons seeking jobs who are registered with the state employment agencies. Since many jobless do not register, particularly rural workers, the data tend to underestimate unemployment. Unemployment rates are not given as percentages of the economically active population or as percentages of the labor force, but as percentages of "reported employment." These terms refer to employment in the socialist sector plus private employment reported to the employment agencies; employment data usually exclude employment in private agriculture and in small private enterprises. Table 12.9 shows that except for 1955, 1960 and 1964, unemployment as a percentage of "reported employment" continuously increased.

Unemployment had two main causes. The low priority commanded by agricultural development, rural overpopulation and heavy taxes kept the Yugoslav peasant poor. The young and the ambitious started leaving the villages in large numbers hoping to find a full-time and part-time job in the towns. The largest part of this migration from the villages to the towns was constituted by unskilled workers trying to obtain industrial jobs. Rural male workers, as well as women and youngsters moving from the villages to the cities, tended to represent more than 50% of the urban employed.

The ranks of the unemployed were expanded by the economic reforms of the 1950s and the 1960s. When profit and efficient production methods became the standards of proper managerial performance, a large number of enterprise workers became redundant and

TABLE 12.9

REPORTED EMPLOYMENT AND REGISTERED UNEMPLOYMENT

	Reported Employment (In 1,000)	Annual Rate of Employment Increase	Unemployment (In 1,000)	Unemployment as % of Reported Employment
1952	1,734	—	44.7	2.6
1953	1,836	5.9	81.6	4.4
1954	2,005	9.2	76.2	3.8
1955	2,215	10.5	67.2	3.0
1956	2,212	.0	99.3	4.5
1957	2,392	7.9	115.9	4.8
1958	2,552	6.7	132.0	5.2
1959	2,730	7.0	161.6	5.9
1960	2,970	8.9	159.2	5.4
1961	3,242	9.1	191.3	5.9
1962	3,318	2.3	236.5	7.1
1963	3,390	2.2	230.3	6.8
1964	3,608	6.4	212.5	5.9
1965	3,662	1.5	237.0	6.5
1966	3,582	−2.2	257.6	7.2
1967	3,561	− .6	269.1	7.6

Source: Savenzni Zavod za Statistiku, *Jugoslavija 1945-1964*, and *Statistički Pregled*, Belgrade, 1965, Tables 4-1 and 4-13, and *Statistički Godišnjak, 1968*. Belgrade, 1968, pp. 91, 103.

were dismissed. Whereas the "ton ideology" of the 1940s encouraged enterprises to hire as much labor as possible, technological improvement in the late 1950s and early 1960s tended to reduce the rate of growth of the employed labor force. Long-term unemployment started increasing after 1956. Workers with more than one year of unemployment increased their proportion in total unemployment from 8.1% in 1956 to 20.4% in 1967. In 1956, workers who had been idle for three months or more represented 40% of all jobless; their number increased to 63% of all unemployed in 1967.[10]

During the period of the first Five-Year Plan, balance of payments deficits were mostly due to the import needs of the industrialization program and to the poor performance of the agricultural sector. During the early 1950s, Western aid, to a larger extent than exports, helped the country to import necessary foodstuffs, raw materials and equipment. This aid represented 7.5% of the national income in 1956. The principal aims of the second Five-Year Plan were the lessening of Yugoslavia's dependence on foreign aid and the reduction of the external deficit. Even though the balance of trade in agricultural goods ceased to be negative in 1960 and in spite of the completion of heavy industry projects by 1956, the country's balance of payments deficit continued to grow. This deficit was 73.8% higher in 1960 than in 1956. The emphasis on the production of consumer durable goods after 1961 required even larger imports of machinery, replacement parts and raw materials. Burdened by a system of multiple exchange rates, by low quality production and by a rapidly expanding level of domestic demand, the growth of exports lagged behind that of imports and the balance of payments deficit grew from $212.5 million in 1960 to $434.8 in 1964.

Money, Banking and Prices

During World War II, the occupying powers brought chaos to Yugoslavia's monetary system. Separate central banks were established in Croatia and Serbia. The *dinar* was official currency only in Serbia. Elsewhere, money was constituted by Italian *liras*, by Albanian *francs*, by Bulgarian *levs*, by Croatian *kunas*, by German *marks* and by Hungarian *pengos.*.

The withdrawal of occupation currencies was started before the war had ended. In April 1945, new Yugoslav paper notes, the *novcanice Demokratske Federativne Jugoslavije*, i.e., bank notes of Democratic Federal Yugoslavia, started circulating. Occupation notes had to be exchanged for the new bank notes, commonly known as *DFY dinars*, and later, as "old dinars," between April 20 and July 9, 1945. For purposes of the exchange, the nominal value of occupation notes was discounted by 5% to 70%. Bank deposits were converted into DFY dinars by reducing their nominal amount above 5,000 dinars by 3 to 40%. These operations allowed the government to reduce the aggregate value of notes in circulation; in 1941, this value amounted to 19.5 billion dinars; in 1945, it was 5.8 billion DFY dinars.[11]

In November of 1945, the country adopted a new official name, the Federal People's Republic of Yugoslavia. DFY notes started being withdrawn from circulation in 1947 to be replaced by equivalent notes issued by the National Bank of the Federal People's Republic of Yugoslavia. By 1959, the DFY dinars had disappeared.

Following the Economic reform of 1965, the nominal value of bank notes and coins was reduced by 100%. The 1965 dinar was worth 100 pre-1965 dinars. New dinar bank notes were placed in circulation at the end of 1965 and by the end of 1969, all pre-1965 notes and coins were withdrawn from circulation. Bank deposits and securities were also converted into 1965 dinars as of January 1, 1966.

The exchange rate of the dinar in terms of other currencies also followed a number of changes. In April 1945, the parity of the dinar had been fixed at 17.762 milligrams of gold, the exchange rate in terms of U.S. dollars being 50.6 dinars to the dollar. With the approval of the International Monetary Fund, the parity of the dinar was reduced to 2.9622 milligrams of gold on January 1, 1952. The exchange rate was then fixed at 300 dinars to the dollar. The dinar was again depreciated in January 1961 when the value of the dinar was fixed at 1.1849 milligrams of gold. At the same time, the multiple exchange rates system was abolished and a uniform rate was introduced for all payment transactions with other countries. The rate of exchange became 750 dinars to the dollar. To boost the competitiveness of Yugoslav exports in the international market, the dinar was again devalued in 1965, the value of the dinar becoming 0.7109 milligrams of gold, the resulting rate of exchange being 1,250 dinars to the U.S. dollar. With the adoption of the 1965 dinar, 12.50 1965 dinars exchanged for one U.S. dollar. The dinar was once more devalued in 1971, the rate of exchange being then fixed at 15 dinars to the dollar. The dinar remained an inconvertible currency throughout the entire postwar period.

The banking and credity styem, exclusive functions of the National Bank of Yugoslavia during the period of centralized economic control, were slowly decentralized in the mid-1950s. Up to that time, the National Bank remained the sole financial intermediary in the economy.

Until 1953, the authorities seemed to be little interested in monetary policy; the goal of rapid industrialization commanded much more importance than price-cost stability or balance of payments equilibrium. National Bank officials tried to curb the rate of inflation by issuing detailed microeconomic regulations limiting the liquidity of enterprises and controlling the distribution of their net income. The granting of credit to economic organizations was subject to minute qualitative rules; on the other hand, the National Bank undertook to finance production and trade without quantitative ceilings. If a qualified borrower petitioned for a loan whose purpose was approved by the regulations, the loan would be granted almost automatically.[12]

Following the granting of economic independence to enterprises in the early 1950s, banking and credit policies changed from an emphasis on detailed microeconomic regulations to macroeconomic monetary policy. Indirect monetary controls, such as reserve ratio and discount policies of the central bank, as well as the impact of market forces, were to take the place of centralized management of money and credit. The banking system was to be decentralized, budgetary investment grants were to be abolished and direct credit relationships between the National Bank and economic enterprises were to disappear gradually.

Banking decentralization started in 1955. The National Bank of Yugoslavia continued to implement official monetary and credit policies; it remained the only bank of issue and the bank of the Federal Government. A number of new and specialized banks appeared on the scene, banks which were to take over from the National Bank direct credit relationships with enterprises, socio-political organizations and individuals. Three specialized federal banks were organized. The *Yugoslav Bank for Foreign Trade, Jugobanka*, was established in 1955 to finance the country's foreign trade and export industries. One year later, the *Yugoslav Investment Bank* was founded to handle loans dealing with projects of national interest. The *Yugoslav Agricultural Bank,* established in 1959, was to extend short-term and long-term credits to the agricultural sector. In 1961, six republic banks were set up to finance investment projects in their respective territories. On a more local basis, communal banks could grant both short-term and long-term credit to communal organizations and enterprises.

With the development of this diversified banking system, the practice of "loan auctions" of the early 1950s was soon abandoned. After 1955, the new banks took over the administration of the social investment funds, the federal and republic funds being administered by the Investment and Agricultural Banks, while the funds of districts and communes were handled by the communal banks.

The Economic Reform laws of 1965 reorganized the country's banking system. The new system was constituted by the National Bank and "business banks." By 1966, the banking system in Yugoslavia very much resembled that of England. The National Bank retained most of its earlier functions, except that it could now grant only short-term credit to the new business banks. The actual banking business in the country was to be carried by business banks, classified as investment, commercial and mixed banks. The three federal specialized banks became investment business banks. Communal banks became commercial or mixed banks. Just like business banks in Western Europe, Yugoslavia's banks kept time and sight deposits; commercial banks paid interest on savings accounts. These banks were controlled by the economic and political organizations which had invested in the capital of these banks. Any group of economic and socio-political organizations was allowed to set up a business bank, provided that they endowed it with sufficient initial capital. Subject to regulations, these banks were allowed to sell their own securities, and after 1967, they were also allowed to borrow directly abroad.

Strong governmental controls over the price system were retained in the 1950s and the 1960s. In spite of official claims that the market mechanism was to be given an increasing role in the allocation of resources, direct forms of price control remained in operation until 1970 to assure that economic growth would follow a proper pattern. During the period of centralized government control, measures such as controlled selling prices, fixed margins of profit, and fixed wages and salaries and regulated operational costs were utilized to allocate limited resources in favor of industrial development.

In 1952, with the introduction of the system of self-management, the government declared its willingness to let most prices be determined by supply and demand conditions. The price reform of 1952 allowed many prices to rise, although the prices of industrial raw materials were kept artificially low in order to encourage the development of manufacturing industries. The government did not object to the increase of the prices of foodstuffs and of consumer goods in general since the increases forced a restriction in personal consumption. It was the government's policy to keep the level of consumption low in order to facilitate rapid industrialization. Fiscal policy was also used to achieve this goal. While taxes on consumer goods were high, they were low for raw materials and semi-manufactured goods. This policy had one serious flaw: low raw materials prices increased their scarcity, and scarcity started raising these prices. This inflationary trend was aggravated by the continuing migration of peasants to the towns, because this movement of people boosted the urban demand for agricultural products and resulted in rapidly rising foodstuff prices.

New price controls were introduced as early as 1954. Raw materials, semi-manufactures in short supply and industrial products consumed in large quantities were subject to government-imposed ceiling prices.

Products whose price significantly affected the standard of living or industrial production costs had their prices fixed by government. Profit margins were also regulated. After 1957, the law required enterprises to register any intended price increases with pertinent price control agencies; prices could only be raised if the agency approved the proposed price increases.

Under the Price Control Decree of 1960, communal councils received wide powers to control and regulate prices. These councils were allowed to establish ceiling retail prices, to regulate wholesale prices and to fix allowed profit margins. The Economic Reform of 1965, instead of allowing prices to be determined to a larger extent by market forces, introduced a very comprehensive system of price controls. Both production and trade were covered by this system. The reform placed 80% of all industrial producers' prices under public control; almost all wholesale and retail prices of industrial products, the retail prices of major agricultural products, the prices of health services and rents, as well as transportation and public utilities' rates were regulated by the authorities. Until the end of the decade, direct price control forms continued to be the dominant characteristic of the Yugoslav price system.

Agriculture

From 1957 on, great efforts were made to increase investment in agriculture. As of 1961, agriculture, together with the food and tobacco industries, registered for the first time a positive balance of trade. An expanding agricultural output allowed the value of exports of agricultural products in 1969 to reach $307 million, while the import of these products in the same year amounted to $216 million.

Both total output and crop yields increased rapidly after 1956 in response to increased investment. Although crop yields increased in both the socialized and the private sectors of agriculture, yields were higher in the former because investment and taxation tended to favor socialized agriculture. The law of 1953, which limited to 10 hectares the maximum area of land peasants could privately own, multiplied the number of small, fragmented and inefficient farms in the private sector of agriculture. In most cases, private farms could not provide an adequate standard of living and full employment to the owner and his family. Only 25% of these farms exceeded 5 hectares and 20% of all privately owned farms had only half a hectare of land.[13] The small size and excessive fragmentation of privately held farms forced many peasants to seek off-farm employment in the non-agricultural sectors of the economy. In 1969, 44% of the people earning a living in the private sector of agriculture had part-time jobs outside their farms.[14] Thousands of peasants tried, however, to survive in the villages and a good part of them constituted an underemployed labor force. A United States estimate indicates that in 1965 about one-fourth of Yugoslavia's peasantry was redundant labor and could have been taken off the agricultural sector without loss to agricultural output.[15] Rural overpopulation in the private agricultural sector in turn encouraged the retention of inefficient methods of production and acted as an impediment to increases in labor productivity.

TABLE 12.10

YIELDS AND PRODUCTIVITY BY AGRICULTURAL SECTOR

	Social Holdings			Private Holdings		
	1956-1958	1963-1965	1967-1969	1956-1958	1963-1965	1967-1969
Yields per Hectare Metric quintals:						
Wheat	20.8	29.7	35.8	12.2	18.4	20.1
Corn	34.2	46.2	54.5	16.1	23.0	27.0
Sugar Beet	245.2	357.6	431.6	195.4	243.0	313.0
	1956	1965	1969	1956	1965	1969
Meat Output per Animal (kgs.)						
Per cow	184	270	285	84	150	170
Per sow	553	1,220	1,650	493	639	642
Milk output Per cow (Litres)	1,955	3,018	3,615	1,038	1,050	1,070

Source: *Statistički Godišnjak,* 1970 and earlier issues.

In the socialist sector of agriculture, agricultural organizations of various types were able to cultivate much larger areas of land with more efficient and mechanized techniques than those used by private farmers. In 1967, consumption of commercial fertilizers amounted to 793 kilograms per hectare on socialist holdings, but only to 113 kilograms per hectare on private holdings.[16]

In spite of the growth of agriculture output after 1957, the relative contribution of agriculture to national income continued to decline because of the more rapid increase in industrial output. In terms of 1960 prices, the share of agriculture in national income declined from 31.3% in 1957 to 22.4% in 1962, 20.2% in in 1964 and to 19.2% in 1967. These data show the rapidly increasing importance of Yugoslav industry throughout the 1960s.

The Impact of the 1965 and 1967 Economic Changes

One of the major aims of the Economic Reform of 1965 was to allow the individual enterprise to retain a larger proportion of its income and to permit its managerial board to freely determine how this income should be utilized. In the early 1960s, enterprises retained on the average 46% of the income earned; the remainder was taken by the state in the form of direct and indirect taxes. After 1965, enterprises no longer had to pay direct taxes on income or profits, and they were able to retain for their own use 70% of earned income.[17] Moreover, the 1965 reforms replaced the turnover tax on production by a turnover tax on retail sales. All regulations affecting the distribution of the enterprise's net income were removed. The authorities hoped that the enterprises would utilize their increased after-tax income to invest more heavily in fixed and working capital. This did not happen. Instead, the larger retained incomes were mostly used to increase the personal incomes of employees, specially in those industries where productivity and wages were low.

The reform attempted to encourage self-finance by enterprises and to reduce the dependency of economic organizations on bank credit. Monetary and credit policies were tightened in 1966 and 1967. In 1967, global controls on short-term bank credit replaced the earlier exclusive reliance on selective credit controls. The rediscount facilities of the National Bank were reduced. The total money supply decreased. In the same year, the government decided to liberalize imports, relying on the 1965 devaluation to avoid an import boom.

As industries adapted to the new conditions, the rate of growth of their output first declined, the expansion in industrial output practically stopping in 1967. Import liberalization hurt several low productivity industries, such as the iron and steel and the machine-building industries. Restrictive credit policies forced many enterprises into financial illiquidity. A deteriorating balance of payments further weakened the pace of economic growth. Whereas, in terms of 1966 prices, gross national output had increased at an average annual rate of 7.6% during the years 1959 to 1964, it grew by only 4.5% per year from 1965 to 1969.

FIGURE 5

INDUSTRIAL PRODUCTION
1963 = 100

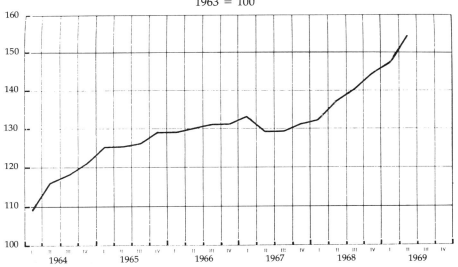

Source: OECD Economic Surveys, *Socialist Federal Republic of Yugoslavia*, Paris, November 1969, p. 17.

A more expansionary monetary policy in 1968 made for a recovery in the rate of growth of industrial output. The ratio of compulsory commercial bank reserves was lowered and the maximum rate of interest charged by these banks was reduced from 10% to 8%; rules restricting consumer credit were relaxed. The money supply increased by 24%. Industrial output responded by rising 11% above the volume attained the previous year. On the other hand, E.E.C. policies made the export of Yugoslav agricultural products more difficult. By raising tariffs on imported agricultural products, the Common Market reduced Yugoslav shipments of beef to Italy. Agricultural output declined by 3.6% in 1968.

Money and credit were again tightened at the end of 1968 to prevent an excessive growth of domestic consumer demand. These "stop-go"

policies were reminiscent of British economic policies during the first
postwar decade. Just like them, they tended to reduce the rate of
investment and to raise the level of unemployment. The result was a
larger flow of emigration which in this period reached the level of
about 70,000 persons per year.

At the same time, a widening trade deficit continued to plague the
balance of payments. While imports were boosted by the liberalization
of 1967, the deterioration of Yugoslavia's export markets made for
export growth lagging behind import growth. The current account
deficit amounted to $41 million in 1966, $82 million in 1967 and $109
million in 1968.

FIGURE 6

FOREIGN TRADE
In million U.S. dollars

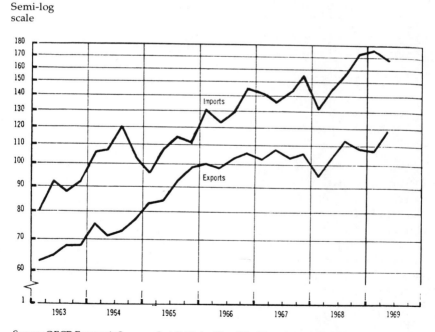

Source: OECD Economic Surveys, *Socialist Federal Republic of Yugoslavia*, Paris, November 1969, p. 24.

The economic slowdown after 1964 induced the Yugoslav government to accept business practices which constituted a serious departure from established Socialist dogma. Before 1967, although enterprises were allowed to found new economic organizations, the parent enterprise could not participate in the management of the new organization it helped to establish, nor could the founding enterprise share in the income of the new concern. Socialist ideology demanded that the enterprise, like the individual, should only earn income from work actually performed by it. An enterprise could not receive part of the income earned by another. This was changed in 1967 when investment income became legal. The founding enterprise could now receive part of the income earned by the organization in which it had invested, provided that this income would be exclusively used for the expansion of the fixed or working capitals of the investing enterprise. A constitutional amendment of 1968 also made it possible for the investing enterprise to participate in the management of the enterprise it had helped to create. There were now two types of enterprises in the country. In the enterprises founded by socio-political organizations, the principle of workers' self-management prevailed; but in enterprises created by other enterprises, management had to be shared with representatives of the founding organizations.[19]

1967 brought another important change in the way new enterprises could be created. After 1967, it became possible for the first time to have a new enterprise partly established on the basis of foreign capital. The principle that Yugoslav workers held socially owned property in trust was conveniently ignored. Private or public foreign "parterns" were allowed to invest in and own up to 49% of the assets of a Yugoslav enterprise. Although foreign investors had to pay a profits tax and had to reinvest in the country a minimum of 20% of their profits, they were allowed, under certain conditions, to repatriate the rest of their profits.

These measures were intended to better technology and to modernize production and sales methods in the country. These measures were only partially successful and economic difficulties did not disappear after their introduction. Inefficient enterprises were not closed down. Inflation was not halted. Skilled workers continued to leave the country.

Economic conditions improved, however, after 1968. Overall industrial production sharply increased during the second half of 1968 and increased again in 1970. Exports rose by 17% in 1969 and by 20% in 1970. This increase in exports was unfortunately more than offset by a rapid rise in the import of basic and semi-finished materials and of consumer goods. The trade deficit increased in 1969 by $660 million. Agricultural output also expanded in 1969, major crops exceeding 1968 production levels by large margins.

The economic expansion which started in mid-1968 did not bring with it significant gains in labor productivity. Output expanded largely on the basis of increased employment. By July 1970, industrial employment was 8.6% higher than it had been two years earlier. At the same time, a strong demand for Yugoslav workers abroad, particularly in Germany, drained surplus labor from the countryside and somewhat alleviated the unemployment problem.

In the socialized sector, personal income per employed was 15% higher in 1969 than a year earlier. Production gains and larger employment, as well as emigrant worker remittances boosted urban incomes; rural incomes were favored by a good harvest in 1969.

Conclusion

The Plan of 1966-1970 was formulated in the light of the Economic Reform of 1965. It was more flexible and indicative than earlier Plans and stressed mostly non-quantifiable objectives, e.g., the freer role of enterprises in regard to production and investment, the more significant role to be played by market forces in production and pricing and the desirability of a more efficient integration of the economy into the international division of labor. Quantitatively, the Plan aimed for a yearly rate of growth of national output of 8%, although a lower rate was expected during the early years of the Plan because of the adjustment difficulties generated by the economic reforms. In fact, the economy grew by about 4.5% per year during the period 1966 to 1968. Economic expansion started, however, to accelerate during the second half of 1968 and economic growth from then on seemed to proceed as predicted by the revised norms of the Plan.

Yugoslavia in the 1960s, just like Great Britain one decade earlier, had to make the difficult choice between, on the one hand, rapid growth, inflation and external disequilibrium, and, on the other, greater price stability, necessary for the expansion of exports, but requiring anti-inflationary monetary and credit policies which acted as a brake on economic growth and adversely affected employment. Restrictive credit policies were largely responsible for the deceleration of the economy between 1966 and 1968.

The reforms of 1965 aimed at the creation of conditions which would facilitate a more efficient allocation of resources, so as to speed up the process of modernization of the Yugoslav economy. It was felt that this goal could be achieved through a further decentralization of the decision-making process and by opening more widely the economy to the effects of market forces. The government relaxed its controls over investment resource allocation, price formation and foreign trade. The reforms, once the period of adjustment was passed, were apparently successful in providing for high rates of growth of output and productivity in an open Socialist economy.

TABLE 12.11

PRODUCTION, EMPLOYMENT AND PRODUCTIVITY

	Structure 1968	Percentage Change from Previous Year			
		1966	1967	1968	1969
National Product	100	6.6	0.9	3.6	9.8
Agriculture	23	16.5	−1.5	−3.4	7.5
Industry	36	3.7	0.1	5.6	11.6
Other	41	3.6	3.2	6.0	9.5
Building	11	4.6	5.8	5.9	10.0
Trade & Tourism	18	4.2	2.1	4.6	9.0
Industrial Employment (million)	1.3	−1.4	−0.4	−0.2	3.6
Industrial Output per Employed		5.2	0.7	6.0	7.1

Source: OECD Economic Surveys, *Yugoslavia*, Paris, November 1970, p. 23.

Compared to the agrarian and backward economy of 1945, the Yugoslav economy had markedly changed by 1970. The industrial sector was now the most important and the most dynamic in the economy, and had achieved one of the highest rates of postwar growth in Europe. As of 1952, this transformation was achieved without the coercive means proper of the Soviet economic system. Mandatory planning was abandoned in Yugoslavia in the 1950s; one decade later, Yugoslavs were free to leave and to re-enter the country.

Rapid industrialization, even under these relatively liberal conditions, had a price. It induced too many peasants to leave the farms for non-agricultural jobs in the towns at a time when the non-agricultural sectors were not yet able to provide everyone with employment. The continuing peasant exodus increased the number of the unemployed while raising the urban demand for foodstuffs. To the problem of rising unemployment was added the problem of inflation. More important, perhaps, in the long-run, is the problem created by the structure of the private agricultural sector. The small, inefficient farms this sector contains have not been able to raise sufficiently agricultural output to curb an inflation based largely on a rising demand for foodstuffs. The rural "minifundia" can only strengthen the growth of redundant agricultural labor. The official policy is to socialize this sector gradually. It is, however, the rapid modernization and rationalization of this sector which will provide the final solution of the country's unemployment and inflation problems. In this regard, the Yugoslav experience resembled the Italian one.

What is typical of the Yugoslav experience is that the Yugoslav economic system, which in 1950 was still almost a duplicate of that of the U.S.S.R., had evolved by mid-1960s into a system which was more similar to that of France than to the economic systems of the Eastern European countries. The indicative Yugoslav and French methods of planning had much in common. So did the pricing policies in both countries. The Yugoslav workers' management system of the 1950s was based on principles analogous to those which underlied the West German *Mitbestimmungsrecht*. In both countries, professional management kept the decision-making prerogative in production and sales. Some argue that Yugoslavia abandoned Socialism in the 1960s. Economic Socialism can be interpreted in many ways. More interesting than the label under which it may be categorized, is the fact that the Yugoslav economy developed into a mixed economy, organized on the basis of both private and public property rights, an economy which resembled in many ways the mixed economies of postwar, "neo-Capitalist" European countries.

NOTES

1. Federal Statistical Office, *Kretanje drustvenog proizvoda i narodnog dohotka Jugoslavije 1952-1958 godine* — Movement of Yugoslavia's Social Product and National Income, 1952-1968 (Belgrade, 1969).

2. Z. Nikolin, "Some Basic Features of Yugoslavia's Industrial Development in 1952-1972," *Yugoslav Survey*, vol. XIV (August 1973), p. 155.

3. *Ibid.*, p. 156.

4. During the period 1952 and 1972, the proportion of total industrial output of the chemical and metal-using industries output rose from 19% in 1952 to 37% in 1972. M. Nikolic, "Changes in the Structure of Industrial Production, 1952-1972," *Yugoslav Survey*, vol. XIV (February 1973), pp. 33-42.

5. B. Marković, "National Income, Employment and Productivity in the Yugoslav Economy, 1947-1968," *Yugoslav Survey*, vol. XI (May 1970), pp. 49-50.

6. *Ibid.*, pp. 50-51.

7. M. Savicević, "Economic Development, 1947-1968," *Yugoslav Survey*, vol. XI (February 1970), pp. 23-42.

8. The proportion of investment in fixed assets to national income was not only kept large, but it was increased until 1965. The ratios, in terms of 1962 prices, averaged 30.6% for the period 1947-1952, 30.8% for 1953-1956, 32.3% for 1957-1960 and 36. 1% for 1961-1965. Institute of Investment Economics, *Investicije 1947-1955* (Belgrade, 1967).

9. Savezni Zavod za Statistiku, *Statistički Bilten-Industrija 1964* (Belgrade, 1965), pp. 28-37.

10. *Statistički Godišnjak S.F.R.J. 1965, Belgrade 1965, p. 115; Ibid., 1968*, Belgrade 1968, p. 307.

11. 'Money in Yugoslavia," *Yugoslav Survey*, vol. XII (November 1971) pp. 43-58.

12. J.J. Hauvonen, "Postwar Developments in Money and Banking in Yugoslavia," *International Monetary Fund Staff Papers*, vol. XVII (November 1970), pp. 13-40.

13. D. Draće, Development of Agriculture, 1945-1970, *Yugoslav Survey*, Vol. XI, November 1970, pp. 13-40.

14. *Ibid.*, pp. 19-21.

15. U.S. Department of Labor, Labor Conditions in Yugoslavia in *Labor Developments Abroad* (Washington, May 1965), p. 5.

16. L. Madžar et al., "Economic Development 1947-1968," *Yugoslav Survey*, vol. XI (February 1970), p. 37.

17. R. Bićanić, *Economic Policy in Socialist Yugoslavia* (New York: Cambridge University Press, 1973), p. 213.

18. Savezni zavod za statistiku, *Samoupravljanje i drustveno-ekonomski razvitak Jugoslavije, 1950-1970* – Self-management and socio-economic development in Yugoslavia, 1950-1970 (Belgrade, 1971), pp. 105-107.

19. Bićanić, *Economic Policy in Socialist Yugoslavia*, pp. 223-224.

BIBLIOGRAPHY

FRANCE

Ardagh, J. *The New French Revolution.* New York: Harper & Row, 1968.

Aron, R. *France, Steadfast and Changing.* Cambridge: Harvard University Press, 1960.

Balassa, B. "Whither French Planning?." *Quarterly Journal of Economics,* Vol. 79, November 1965, pp. 537-54.

Bareau, P. "Economic Miracle in France." *Three Banks Review,* Vol. 49, March 1961, pp. 3-15.

Baum, W.C. *The French Economy and the State.* Princeton: Princeton University Press, 1958.

Carré, J.J. et al. *La Croissance Française.* Paris: Editions du Seuil, 1972.

Chardonnet, J. *L'Economie Française,* Vol. I, *L'Industrie.* Paris: Dalloz, 1970.

De Brulle, D. "Economic Democracy in Nationalized Undertakings in France and Great Britain." *Annals of Public and Cooperative Economics,* Vol. 36, October-December 1965, pp. 461-91.

Eastman, H.C. "The Economic Effects of the French Minimum Wage Law." *American Economic Review,* Vol. 44, June 1954, pp. 369-76.

_____ "The Influence of Government on Labor Relations in France." *Canadian Journal of Economics and Political Science,* Vol. 20, August 1954, pp. 296-307.

Einaudi, M. "Nationalization in France and Italy." *Social Research.* Vol. 15, March 1948, pp. 22-43.

Fournier, H. "The Problem of Controlling Liquidity in France." *Banca Nazionale del Lavoro Quarterly Review,* Vol. 13, December 1960, pp. 317-44.

Franco, G.R. "Some Aspects of Cost-Push Inflation in the French Steel Industry." *American Economist,* Vol. 15, Fall 1971, pp. 4-18.

Gatty, R. "The Consolidation of Farming Lands in France." *Journal of Farm Economics,* Vol. 38, November 1956, pp. 911-22.

Hackett, J. and Hackett, A.M. *Economic Planning in France,* Cambridge: Harvard University Press, 1965.

Hansen, N.M. "French Indicative Planning and the New Industrial State." *Journal of Economic Issues,* December 1969, pp. 79-95.

_____ "Indicative Planning in France: Model for the Future?." *Quarterly Review of Economics and Business,* Vol. 4, 1964, pp. 7-18.

Harlow, J.S. *French Economic Planning: A Challenge to Reason.* Iowa City: University of Iowa Press, 1966.

Kiker, B.F. and Vasconcellos, A.S. "The Performance of the French Economy under Planning, 1949-1964." *Economics of Planning,* Vol. 8, 1968, pp. 157-94.

Kriz, M.A. "Credit Control in France." *American Economic Review*, Vol. 41, March 1951, pp. 85-106.

Landes, D.S. "Observations on France: Economy, Society, and Polity." *World Politics*, Vol. 9, 1957, pp. 329-50.

———— "New Modal Entrepreneurship in France and Problems of Historical Explanation." *Explorations in Entrepreneurial History*, Ser. II, Vol. 1, 1963-64, pp. 56-75.

Lorwin, V.R. "French Trade Unions Since Liberation, 1944-1951." *Industrial and Labor Relations Review*, Vol. 5, July 1952, pp. 524-39.

Lubell, H. "The Role of Investment in Two French Inflations." *Oxford Economic Papers*, N.S., Vol. 7, Feb. 1955, pp. 47-56.

Maclennan, M. et al. *Economic Planning and Policies in Britain, France and Germany*, New York: Praeger, 1968.

Marschak, T. "Capital Budgeting and Pricing in the French Nationalized Industries." *Journal of Business*, Vol. 33, April 1960, pp. 133-56.

Massé, P. "French Methods of Planning." *Journal of Industrial Economics*, Vol. ii, November 1962, pp. 1-17.

———— "The French Plan and Economic Theory." *Econometrica*, Vol. 33, April 1965, pp. 265-76.

McArthur, J.M. and Scott, B.R. *Industrial Planning in France*. Harvard University Graduate School of Business, 1969.

McDonald, J. "National Product and Structural Change in the French Economy," *American Journal of Economics and Sociology*, Vol. 16, 1956-57, pp. 251-80.

Peterson, W.C. "Transfer Expenditures, Taxes and Income Distribution in France." *Quarterly Review of Economics and Business*, No. 3 (1965): 5-21.

Sargent, F.O. "Fragmentation of French Land: Its Nature, Extent and Causes." *Land Economics*, Vol. 28, August 1952, pp. 218-29.

———— "The Persistence of Communal Tenure in French Agriculture." *Agricultural History*, Vol. 32, April 1958, pp. 100-108.

Sheahan, J. *Promotion and Control of Industry in Postwar France*. Cambridge: Harvard University Press, 1963.

Torem, C. and Craig, W.L. "Control of Foreign Investment in France." *Michigan Law Review*, Vol. 66, No. 4, February 1967, p. 670.

Werth, A. *France, 1940-1955*. London: Robert Hale, Ltd., 1956.

Wilson, J.S.G. " Post-War Monetary Policy in France." *Banca Nazionale del Lavoro Quarterly Review*, Vol. 8, March 1955, pp. 16-29.

GERMAN DEMOCRATIC REPUBLIC

Anthon, C.G. "Stalinist Rule in East Germany." *Current History*, May 1963, pp. 265-272.

Apel, H. "East German Miracle?." *Challenge,* Vol. 12, No. 2, November 1963, p. 11.

Betz, H. "East Germany: The Primacy of Dogma over Reform." *Journal of Economic Issues,* Vol. VIII, No. 1, March 1974, pp. 83-96.

Berger, W. and Reinhold, O. *Zu den wissenschaftlichen Grundlagen des Neuen Oekonomischen Systems.* Berlin: Dietz Verlag, 1966.

Bohme, H. "East German Price Formation under the New Economic System." *Soviet Studies,* January 1968, pp. 340-58.

Bottcher, M. "Where Do We Stand with Planning in the New Economic System?." *Eastern European Economics,* Vol. 6, No. 3, (1968): 50-54.

Childs, D. *East Germany.* New York: Praeger, 1969.

Dulles, E.L. *One Germany or Two.* Stanford: Hoover Institution Press, 1970.

German Democratic Republic. Die Landwirtschaft in der DDR. *Heute und Morgen,* Dresden, 1965.

_____ *Zehn Jahre Volkswirtschaft in der Deutschen Demokratischen Republik.* Berlin: Verlag Die Wirtschaft, 1959.

_____ *Zwanzig Jahre ein Freies Land.* Dresden: Voelkersfreundschaft Verlag, 1965.

German Federal Republic. *Sowjetische Bestzungszone von A bis Z.* Bonn: Bundesministerium fuer gesamtdeutsche Fragen, 1966.

Grosser, A. *Germany in Our Time.* New York: Praeger, 1971.

Kohler, H. *Economic Integration in the Soviet Bloc.* New York: Praeger, 1965.

Kolmey, G. "Special Features of the Development of Industry and Foreign Economic Ties of the GDR." *Problems of Economics,* November 1958, pp. 40-45.

Milkulsky, K. "Industrial Management Improvements in the German Democratic Republic." *Problems of Economics,* December 1958, pp. 97-98.

Nawrocki, J. *Das Geplante Wunder.* Hamburg: C. Wegner Verlag, 1967.

Pryor, F.L. "East and West German Governmental Expenditures." *Public Finance,* Vol. 20 (1965): 300-59.

Richert, E. *Das Zweite Deutschland, Ein Staat Der Nicht Sein Darf.* Guetersloh: Sigbert Mohn Verlag, 1964.

Roustang, G. *Développement Economique de l'Allemangne Orientale.* Paris: SEDES, 1963.

Sergeyev, V. "Some Problems of the Development of Domestic Trade in the GDR." *Problems of Economics,* September 1959, pp. 87-90

Smith, J.E. *Germany Beyond the Wall.* Boston: Little, Brown & Co., 1967.

Stolper, W.F. "The "The National Product of East Germany." *Kyklos,* Vol. XII (1959): 131-66.

_____ "The Labor Force and Industrial Development in Soviet Germany," *Quarterly Journal of Economics,* Vol. 71, November 1957, pp. 518-45.

―――― *The Structure of the East German Economy.* Cambridge: Harvard University Press, 1960.

Wunderlich, F. "Agriculture and Farm Labor in the Soviet Zone of Germany." *Social Research,* Vol. 19, June 1952, pp. 198-219.

Zauberman, A. *Industrial Progress in Poland, Czechoslovakia and East Germany, 1937-1962.* London: Oxford University Press, 1964.

GERMAN FEDERAL REPUBLIC

Abs, H.J. "The Structure of the Western German Monetary System." *Economic Journal,* Vol. 60, September 1950, pp. 481-88.

Abosch, H. *The Menace of the Miracle, Germany from Hitler to Adenauer.* New York: Monthly Review Press, 1963.

Adler, H.A. "The Post-War Reorganization of the German Banking System," *Quarterly Journal of Economics,* Vol. 63, August 1949, pp. 322-41.

Albach, H. "New Trends in the Economic Policy of the Federal Republic of Germany," *German Economic Review,* Vol. 7 (1969): 108-28.

Alexander, D.J. "Some Features of West German Policy for Improving the Agricultural Structure." *Journal of Farm Economics,* Vol. 46, November 1964, pp. 791-804.

Alt, P. and Schneider, M. "West Germany's 'Economic Miracle'." *Science and Society,* Vol. XXVI, No. 1 (1962): 46-57.

Balfour, M. *West Germany.* New York: Praeger, 1968.

Bartels, H. "National Product at Constant Prices in the Federal Republic of Germany." *The Review of Income and Wealth,* ser. 14, No. 4, December 1968, pp. 387-402.

Beal, E.F. "Origins of Codetermination." *Industrial and Labor Relations Review,* Vol. 8, July 1955, pp. 483-98.

Brems, H.J. "West German Problems: Price Discipline and Economic Integration." *Quarterly Review of Economics and Business,* Vol. 4 (1964): 51-8.

Bukow, W. "Public Undertakings in the Federal Republic of Germany." *Annals of Public and Cooperative Economy,* Vol. 36, January-March 1965, pp. 7-13.

Dietrich, H.R. *Auf dem Wege zum Neuen Staat.* Stuttgart: Deutsche Verlag Anstalt, 1951.

Emmer, R.E. "West German Monetary Policy, 1948-1951." *Journal of Political Economy,* LXIII, February 1955.

Erhard, L. "Deutsche Wirtschaftspolitik." Dusseldorf: Econ Verlag, 1962.

Fogarty, M.P. "Codetermination and Company Structure in Germany." *British Journal of Industrial Relations,* Vol. 2, March 1964, pp. 79-113.

Grosser, A. *The Colossus Again.* New York: Praeger, 1955.

Gunther, E. "Cartel Policy in Germany." *The German Economic Review,* Vol. II, No. 1 (1964): 16-24.

Hein, J. "Monetary Policy and External Convertibility, The German Experience, 1959-1961." *Economia Internazionale*, Vol. XVII, August 1964, pp. 509-31.

Huddleston, J. "Trade Unions in the German Federal Republic." *The Political Quarterly*, Vol. 38, No. 2, April-June 1967, pp. 165-67.

Kerr, C. "Collective Bargaining in Postwar Germany." *Industrial and Labor Relations Review*, Vol. 5, April 1952, pp. 323-42

Klott, W. "Food and Farming in Germany, Past, Present and Future." *Weltwirtschaftliches Archiv*, Vol. 64 (1950): 111-58.

Krengel, R. "Some Reasons for the Rapid Economic Growth of the German Federal Republic." *Banca Nazionale del Lavoro Quarterly Review*, Vol. 16, March 1963, pp. 121-44.

Kullmer, L. "Problems of the Financial Reform in the Federal Republic of Germany." *German Economic Review* (1969): 53-71.

Lanner, J. "Changes in the Structure of the German Banking System." *Economica*, N.S., Vol. 18, May 1951, pp. 169-83.

Lepinski, F. "The German Trade Union Movement." *International Labor Review*, Vol. LXXIX, No. 1, January 1959, pp. 55-78.

Lutz, F.A. "The German Currency Reform and the Revival of the German Economy." *Economica*, N.S., Vol. 16, May 1949, pp. 122-42.

———— "Germany's Economic Resurgence." *Lloyd's Bank Review*, Vol. 39, January 1956, pp. 12-27.

Maier, K.F. "Has Western Germany a Liberal Market Economy?." *Banca Nazionale del Lavoro Quarterly Review*, Vol. 5, January-March 1952, pp. 37-43.

Marburg, T.F. "Government and Business in Germany, Public Policy Toward Cartels." *Business History Review*, Vol. 38, 1964, pp. 78-101.

Markus, J. "Some Observations on the West German Trade Surplus." *Oxford Economic Papers*, Vol. 17, March 1965, pp. 136-46.

Mayhew, A. "Structural Reform and the Furture of West German Agriculture. "*The Geographical Review*, Vol. LX, No. 1, January 1970, pp. 54-68.

McClellan, G.S. *The Two Germanies.* New York: H.W. Wilson Co., 1959.

McInnis, E. *The Shaping of Postwar Germany.* London: Dent, 1960.

McPherson, W.H. "Codetermination: Germany's Move Toward a New Economy." *Industrial and Labor Relations Review*, Vol. 5, October 1951, pp. 20-32.

Oliver, H.M. "German Neoliberalism." *Quarterly Journal of Economics*, Vol. 74, February 1960, pp. 117-49.

Opie, R.G. "Western Germany's Economic Miracle." *Three Banks Review*, March 1962.

Pounds, N.J.G. *The Economic Pattern of Modern Germany.* New York: Rand McNally & Co., 1963.

Raup, P.M. "The Income Position of West German Agriculture." *Journal of Farm Economics*, Vol. 38, November 1956, pp. 1048-54.

Reichel, H. "Recent Trends in Collective Bargaining in the Federal Republic of Germany." *International Labour Review*, Vol. 104, December 1971, pp. 469-87.

Remlinger, G.V. "Social Change and Social Security in Germany." *Journal of Human Resources*, Vol. 3 (1968): 409-21.

Robertson, W. "The Finance of West Germany's Export Surplus, 1952-58," *Economia Internazionale*, Vol. XIII, August 1960, pp. 529-39.

Roskamp, K.W. *Capital Formation in West Germany*. Detroit: Wayne State University Press, 1965.

Ross, A. "Prosperity and Labor Relations in Europe: The Case of West Germany." *The Quarterly Journal of Economics*, Vol. LXXVI, No. 3, August 1962, pp. 331-59.

Rutz, H. "The Origins of Codetermination." *Industrial and Labor Relations Review*, Vol. 11, July 1958, pp. 615-22.

Schiller, K. "Stability and Growth as Objectives of Economic Policy." *The German Economic Review*, Vol. V, No. 2 (1967): 237-44.

Schiller, O. "Co-operative Promotion of Agricultural Production in the Federal Republic of Germany: A New Approach to Co-operative Farming Methods." *The German Economic Review*, Vol. III, No. 1 (1965): 1-12.

Schmidt, H.G. "Postwar Developments in West German Agriculture, 1945-1953." *Agricultural History*, Vol. 29, October 1955, pp. 147-59.

Schnitzer, M. *East and West Germany: A Comparative Economic Analysis*. New York: Praeger, 1972.

Sherman, H. "The Effect of the Revaluation on Germany's Exports." *Economia Internazionale*, Vol. 17, November 1964, pp. 721-40.

Sohmen, E. "Competition and Growth: The Lesson of West Germany." *American Economic Review*, Vol. XLIX, December 1959, pp. 986-1003.

Wallich, H.C. *Mainsprings of the German Revival*. New Haven: Yale University Press, 1955.

Weber, B. "Post-War Trends in Industrial Output, Employment and Productivity: An International Comparison between Germany and Great Britain." *Scottish Journal of Political Economy*, Vol. 2, June 1955, pp. 166-76.

Weisser, G. "Co-operatives as an Aid to Small Business in Germany," *Law and Contemporary Problems*, Vol. XXIV, No. 1, Winter 1959, pp. 208-21.

Zeitel, G. "Government Loans as an Instrument of Financial Economic Policy." *German Economic Review*, Vol. 6 (1968): 193-216.

Zwing, K. *Soziologie der Gewerkschaftsbewegung*. Jena: Gewerkschafts-Archiv, 1925.

ITALY

Ackley, G. and Spaventa, L. "Emigration and Industrialization in Southern Italy: A Comment." *Banca Nazionale del Lavoro Quarterly Review*, Vol. 15, January 1962, pp. 196-219.

Aiello, C. "The Agricultural Sector." *Annals of Public and Cooperative Economy*, Vol. 35, January-March 1964, pp. 43-56.

Albanese, G. and Onofri, F. "Nuove Strutture Sindicali Nella Programmazione Democratica." *Tempi Moderni*, Vol. V, October-December 1962, pp. 47-57.

Allen, K.J. and Stevenson, A..A. *An Introduction to the Italian Economy*. London: Martin Robertson & Co., 1974.

Apicella, V. "The Development of the Public Sector." *Annals of Public and Cooperative Economy*, Vol. 35, January-March 1964, pp. 5-42.

Baffi, P. *Studi Sulla Moneta*. Milan: Giuffré, 1965.

―――― "Monetary Stability and Economic Development in Italy, 1946-1960," *Banca Nazionale del Lavoro Quarterly Review*, Vol. 14 March 1961, pp. 3-30.

―――― "Monetary Developments in Italy from the War Economy to Limited Convertibility, 1935-1958," *Banca Nazionale del Lavoro Quarterly Review*, Vol. 11, December 1958, pp. 399-483.

Balloni, V., ed. *Lezioni Sulla Politica Economica In Italia*. Milan: Edizioni di Comunità, 1972.

Bandini, M. "Land Reform in Italy." *Banca Nazionale del Lavoro Quarterly Review*, Vol. 5, January-March 1952, pp. 10-27.

―――― "Six Years of Italian Land Reform." *Banca Nazionale del Lavoro Quarterly Review*, Vol. 10, January 1957, pp. 169-213.

Barbero, G. *Riforma Agraria Italiana*. Milan: Feltrinelli, 1960.

Bassevi, G., ed. *La Bilancia Dei Pagamenti*. Bologna: Il Mulino, 1971.

Bresciani-Turroni, C. "Economic Reconstruction in Italy." *Lloyd's Bank Review*, Vol. 7, January 1948, pp. 19-32.

Brovedani, B. "Exchange Rate Structure and Price Levels in Italy, 1947-1948." *Banca Nazionale del Lavoro Quarterly Review*, Vol. 1, July 1948, pp. 369-80.

―――― "Italy's Financial Policies in the Sixties," *Banca Nazionale del Lavoro Quarterly Review*, Vol. 22, June 1969, pp. 170-189.

―――― *Some Observations on Economic Programming in Italy*. *Banca Nazionale del Lavoro Quarterly Review*, Vol. 18, September 1965, pp. 207-234.

Campolongo, A. "Italy's Five-Year Plan Ex-Post." *Banca Nazionale del Lavoro Quarterly Review, Vol. 24, December 1971, pp. 373-81.*

―――― "The Dynamics of Investment in Italy, 1951-1967." *Banca Nazionale del Lavoro Quarterly Review*, Vol. 21, December 1968, pp. 361-96.

Cassese, S. *Partecipazioni Pubbliche Ed Enti Di Gestione*. Milan: Edizioni di Communità, 1962.

Chenery, H.B. "Development Policies for Southern Italy." *Quarterly Journal of Economics,* Vol. 76, November 1962, pp. 515-47.

Clark, M.D. "Governmental Restrictions on Labor Mobility in Italy." *Industrial Labor Relations Review,* Vol. 8, October 1954, pp. 3-18.

———."The Development of the Italian Economy." *Banca Nazionale del Lavoro Quarterly Review,* Vol. 7, September 1954, pp. 125-28.

Clough, S.B. and Saladino, S. *A History of Modern Italy.* New York: Columbia University Press, 1968.

Corazza, G. L. Origini e Strutture Dell' IRI. *Il Mulino,* Vol. VIII, June 1959, pp. 526-77.

Cosmo, G. "State Participation in Business Concerns in Italy." *Banca Nazionale del Lavoro Quarterly Review,* Vol. 4, October-December 1951, pp. 202-12.

D'Aragona, G.G. "A Critical Evaluation of Land Reform in Italy." *Land Economics,* Vol. 30, February 1954, pp. 12-20.

De Rita, G. "La Politica Di Intervento Pubblico." *Il Veltro,* Vol. VI, December 1962, pp. 991-1007.

Fazio, A. "Monetary Base and the Control of Credit in Italy." *Banca Nazionale del Lavoro Quarterly Review,* Vol. 22, June 1969, pp. 146-69.

Ferrari, A. *Perchè Una Politica Di Programmazione?.* Rome: Cinque Lune, 1963.

Foa, B. "The Italian Economy: Growth Factors and Bottlenecks." *Banca Nazionale del Lavoro Quarterly Review,* Vol. 6, October-December 1953, pp. 242-65.

Forte, F. *La Congiuntura In Italia, 1961-1965.* Milan: Etas Kompass, 1966.

Fua, G. *Notes on Italian Economic Growth, 1861-1964.* Milan: Giuffrè, 1966.

———ed., *Lo Sviluppo Economico Italiano.* Milan: F. Angeli, 1969.

Gambino, A. "The Control of Liquidity in Italy." *Banca Nazionale del Lavoro Quarterly Review,* Vol. 13, March 1960, pp. 3-23.

Giugni, G. "Recent Developments in Collective Bargaining in Italy." *International Labor Review,* Vol. 91, No. 4, April 1965, pp. 273-91.

———."Bargaining Units and Labor Organization in Italy." *Industrial and Labor Relations Review,* Vol. 10, No. 3, April 1957, pp. 424-39.

Grindrod, M. *Italy,* New York: Praeger, 1968.

Hildebrand, G. H. *Growth and Structure in the Economy of Modern Italy.* Cambridge: Harvard University Press, 1965.

———."Growth and Stability in the Postwar Italian Economy." *American Economic Review,* Vol. 51, May 1961, pp. 390-99.

Holbik, K. "The Gains and Pains of Economic Integration: The Italian Experience," *Rivista Internazionale di Scienze Economiche e Commerciali,* Vol. 5, April 1958, pp. 326-45.

Jucker, N. *Italy,* London: Thames & Hudson, 1970.

La Malfa, U. *La Politica Economica In Italia, 1946-1962,* Milan: Edizioni di Comunità, 1962.

LaPalombara, J. *Italy, The Politics of Planning.* Syracuse: Syracuse University Press, 1966.

Lutz, V. *Italy, A Study in Economic Development,* London: Oxford University Press, 1962.

―――"The Growth Process in a Dual Economic System," *Banca Nazionale del Lavoro Quarterly Review,* Vol. II, September 1958, pp. 279-324.

―――"Italy as a Study in Development" *Lloyd's Bank Review,* Vol. 58, October 1960, pp. 31-45.

―――"Some Structural Aspects of the Southern Problem: The Complementarity of Emigration and Industrialization." *Banca Nazionale del Lavoro Quarterly Review,* Vol. 14, December 1961, pp. 367-402.

MacDonald, J.S. "Agricultural Organization,and Labor Militancy in Rural Italy, *"Economic History Review,* II, August 1963, p. 75.

Maniatis, G.C. "Evaluation of Operating Efficiency in Italian Public Undertakings," *Economia Internazionale,* Vol. XX, No. 1, February 1967, pp. 111-118.

Menichella, D. "The Contribution of the Banking System to Monetary Equilibrium, and Economic Stability: Italian Experience. *Banca Nazionale del Lavoro Quarterly Review,* Vol. 9, January-June 1956, pp. 5-21.

Mocine, C.R. "Urban Growth and a New Planning Law in Italy." *Land Economics,* Vol. 41, November 1965, pp. 347-53.

Modigliani, F. "Inflation, Balance of Payments Deficit and Their Cure through Monetary Policy: The Italian Example." *Banca Nazionale de Lavoro Quarterly Review,* Vol. 20, March 1967, pp. 3-47.

Nardi, G. "The Policy of Regional Development, A Case Study: Southern Italy," *Banca Nazionale del Lavoro Quarterly Review,* Vol. 13, September 1960, pp. 215-45.

Nobecourt, J. *L'Italie A Vif,* Paris: Editions du Seuil, 1970.

Norman, J. "Politics and Religion in the Italian Labor Movement." *Industrial Labor Relations Review,* Vol. 5, October 1951, pp. 73-91.

Orlando, G. "Agricultural Marketing and the Italian Economy." *The Journal of Marketing,* Vol. XXI, January 1957, pp. 326-29.

Ornati, O. "The Italian Economic Miracle and Organized Labor." *Social Research,* Vol. 30, December 1963, pp. 519-26.

Pennacchietti, A. "Agriculture, Economic Development and the Common Market: Italian Problems." *Banca Nazionale del Lavoro Quarterly Review,* Vol. 12, September 1959, pp. 243-79.

―――"Agriculture in the Italian National Economy." *Banca Nazionale del Lavoro Quarterly Review,* Vol. 18, December 1965, pp. 376-400.

Petrilli, G. "The Institute for Industrial Reconstruction, I.R.I." *Annals of Collective Economy,* Vol. 33, January 1962, pp. 15-19.

Posner, M.V. and Woolf, S.J. *Italian Public Enterprise.* London: Duckworth, 1967.

Raffaele, J. A. "Trade Unionism and Collective Bargaining in Italy." *Social Research*, Vol. 22, Summer 1955, pp. 138-162.

Ruffalo, G. "The Parliamentary Inquiry into Unemployment in Italy." *Banca Nazionale del Lavoro Quarterly Review*, Vol. 6, January-March 1953, pp. 62-73.

Saraceno, P. "I.R.I.: Its Origin and its Position in the Italian Industrial Economy, 1933-1953." *Journal of Industrial Economics*, Vol. III, July 1955, pp. 197-221.

Schachter, G. "Regional Development in the Italian Dual Economy." *Economic Development and Cultural Change*, Vol. 15, July 1967, pp. 398-407.

Spaventa, L. "Effects of Inflation on the Distribution of Income in Italy, 1953-1962." *Banca Nazionale del Lavoro Quarterly Review*, Vol. 16, December 1963, pp. 411-20.

Stern, R. M. "Developments in the Commodity Composition, Market Distribution and Competitiveness of Italy's Foreign Trade, 1955-1963." *Banca Nazionale del Lavoro Quarterly Review*, Vol. 18, March 1965, pp. 58-76.

Sylos-Labini, P. "Prices, Distribution and Investment in Italy, 1951-1966, An Interpretation." *Banca Nazionale del Lavoro Quarterly Review*, Vol. 20, December 1967, pp. 316-75.

Vernucci, A. "The Organization of Exchange Control in Italy." *Banca Nazionale del Lavoro Quarterly Review*, Vol. 7, September 1954, pp. 158-66.

Wheeler, D. L. "Land Reclamation in the Po River Delta in Italy." *Land Economics*, Vol. VLI, November, 1965, pp. 376-82.

UNITED KINGDOM

Aldercroft, D. H. "The Effectiveness of Direct Controls in the British Economy, 1946-1950." *Scottish Journal of Political Economy*, Vcl. 10, June 1963, pp. 226-42.

Balogh, T. "The Problem of the British Balance of Payments." *Oxford Institute of Statistics*, Vol. 19, July 1947, pp. 211-27.

_____ "Britain, O.E.E.C. and th e Restoration of a World Economy." *Oxford Institute of Statistics*, Vol. 11, February-March 1949, pp. 35-52.

Ball, R.J. "Credit Restriction and the Supply of Exports." *Manchester School of Economics and Social Studies*, Vol. 29, May 1961, pp. 161-72.

Ball, R.J. and Drake, P.S. "Export Growth and the Balance of Payments." *Manchester School of Economics and Social Studies*, Vol. 30, May 1962, pp. 105-19.

Barker, T.S. "Devaluation and the Rise in U.K. Prices." *Oxford Institute of*

Economics and Statistics Bulletin, Vol. 30, May 1968, pp. 129-41.

Barker, T.S. and Lecomber, J.R.C. "The Import Content of Final Expenditures for the U.K., 1954-1972." *Oxford Institute of Statistics*, Vol. 32, 1970, pp. 1-18.

Bates, R.W. "Stabilisation Policy and Investment, 1950-1960, With Special Reference to Electricity Supply." *Yorkshire Bulletin of Economic and Social Research*, Vol. 18, May 1966, pp. 3-19.

_____ "Public Investment and Stabilisation." *Scottish Journal of Political Economy*, Vol. 14, June 1967, pp. 138-55.

Beacham, A. "The Restrictive Trade Practices Act, 1956." *Yorkshire Bulletin of Economic and Social Research*, Vol. 11, December 1959, pp. 79-85.

Beckerman, W., ed. *The Labour Government's Economic Record, 1964-1970.* London: Duckworth, 1972.

Bell, G.L. and Berman, L.S. "Changes in the Money Supply in the U.K., 1954 to 1964." *Economica*, Vol. 33, May 1966, pp. 148-65.

Bird, A.R. "The Effect of Agricultural Price Supports on the Balance of Payments in the U.K." *Journal of Farm Economics*, Vol. 39, December 1957, pp. 1714-23.

Blackburn, J.A. "The British Cotton Industry in the Common Market." *Three Banks Review*, Vol. 56, December 1962, pp. 3-22.

Brechling, F. "Trends and Cycles in British Regional Unemployment." *Oxford Economic Papers*, Vol. 73, December 1963, pp. 618-41.

Brittan, S. *Steering the Economy.* Harmondsworth: Penguin, 1964.

Browaldh, T. "A Swedish View of the Britain's Economy." *Three Banks Review*, Vol. 58, June 1963, pp. 3-16.

Brown, A.J. "Culture and British Economic Growth." *British Journal of Sociology*, Vol. 20 (1969): 117-33.

Burrows, P. "Manpower Policy and the Structure of Unemployment in Britain." *Scottish Journal of Political Economy*, Vol. 15, February 1968, pp. 68-83.

Burtle, J.L. and Liepe, W. "Devaluation and the Cost of Living in the United Kingdom." *Review of Economic Studies*, Vol. 17 (1949): 1-28.

Burton, K. "Full Employment, Inflation, and Economic Policy." *Public Finance*, Vol. 12, No. 1 (1957): 67-77.

Cairncross, A.K. "Wage Policy and Inflation." *Scottish Journal of Political Economy*, Vol. 5, June 1958, pp. 145-8.

Campbell, A.D. "Wages and Prices." *Scottish Journal of Political Economy*, Vol. 5, June 1958, pp. 165-7.

Carter, C.F. "The Present Economic Position of Great Britain." *Three Banks Review*, Vol. 44, December 1959, pp. 3-15.

_____ "Problems and Prospects of the Economic Position of Great Britain." *Three Banks Review*, Vol. 45, March 1960, pp. 3-13.

Carter, C.F. and Williams, B.R. "Government Scientific Policy and the Growth of the British Economy." *Manchester School of Economics and Social Studies*, Vol. 32, September 1964, pp. 197-214.

Caves, R.E., ed. *Britain's Economic Prospects*. London: George Allen & Unwin, Ltd., 1968.

Clayton, G. "British Financial Intermediaries in Theory and Practice." *Economic Journal*, Vol. 72, December 1962, pp. 869-86.

Coales, J.F. "Financial Provision for Research and Development in Industry." *Journal of Industrial Economics*, Vol. 5, July 1957, pp. 239-242.

Cole, M. "British Trade Unions and the Labor Government." *Industrial and Labor Relations Review*, Vol. 1, July 1948, pp. 573-78.

Crick, W.F. "Britain's Post-War Economic Policy, 1945-1950." *Canadian Journal of Economics*, Vol. 17, February 1951, pp. 39-49.

Crossley, J.R. "Wage Structure and the Future of Incomes Policy." *Scottish Journal of Political Economy*, Vol. 15, June 1968, pp. 109-28.

Crouch, R.L. "The Inadequacy of the 'New Orthodox' Methods of Monetary Control." *Economic Journal*, Vol. 74, December 1964, pp. 916-34.

————— "Money Supply Theory and the United Kingdom's Monetary Contraction, 1954-56." *Oxford University Institute of Economics and Statistics Bulletin*, Vol. 30, May 1968, pp. 144-52.

Crowling, K. and Metcalf, D. "Labour Transfer from Agriculture: A Regional Analysis." *Manchester School of Economics and Social Studies*, Vol. 36, March 1968, pp. 27-48.

Davis, G. "Regional Unemployment, Labour Availability and Redeployment," *Oxford Economic Papers*, Vol. 19, March 1967, pp. 59-74.

De Brulle, D. "Economic Democracy in Nationalised Undertakings in France and Great Britain." *Annals of Public and Cooperative Economy*, Vol. 36, October-December 1965, pp. 461-91.

Denison, E.F. *Why Growth Rates Differ*. Washington: The Brookings Institution, 1967.

Denman, D.R. "The Paradox of Rural Land Investment in Britain." *Land Economics*, Vol. 32, May 1956, pp. 109-17.

Dennison, S.R. "The Restrictive Trade Practices Court in Action." *Yorkshire Bulletin of Economic and Social Research*, Vol. 11, December 1959, pp. 100-108.

Derrick, P. "Britain's Efforts to Achieve an Effective Incomes Policy." *Annals of Public and Cooperative Economy*, Vol. 39, April-June 1968, pp. 187-94.

Devons, E. "Wage Rate Indexes by Industry, 1948-1965." *Economica*, Vol. 35, November 1968, pp. 392-423.

————— "Economic Planning in War and Peace." *Manchester School of Economics and Social Studies*, Vol. 16, January 1948, pp. 1-28.

Dicks-Mireaux, L.A. "The Interrelationship between Cost and Price Changes,

1946-1959: A Study of Inflation in Postwar Britain." *Oxford Economic Papers*, Vol. 13, October 1961, pp. 267-92.

Dicks-Mireaux, L.A. and Dow, J.C.R. "The Determinants of Wage Inflation: United Kingdom, 1946-1956." *Royal Statistical Society Journal*, Vol. 122, Pt. 2 (1959): 145-84.

Dow, J.C.R. *The Management of the British Economy, 1945-1960.* Cambridge: Cambridge University Press, 1970.

Dow, J.C.R. and Dicks-Mireaux, L.A. "The Excess Demand for Labor: A Study of conditions in Great Britain 1946--56." *Oxford Economic Papers*, Vol. 10, February 1958, pp. 1-33.

Dunning, J.H. and Rowan, D.C. "Interfirm Efficiency Comparisons: U.S. and U.K. Manufacturing Enterprises in Britain." *Banca Nazionale del Lavoro Quarterly Review*, Vol. 21, June 1968, pp. 132-82.

Dunning, J.H. and Thomas, C.J. "Research Development and Trained Manpower in the United Kingdom." *Indian Journal of Economics*, Vol. 38, April 1958, pp. 337-364.

Flanders, M.J. "The Effects of Devaluation on Exports, U.K. 1949-1954." *Oxford Institute of Statistics*, Vol. 25, August 1963, pp. 165-98.

Flanders, A. "Can Britain Have a Wage Policy?." *Scottish Journal of Political Economy*, Vol. 5, June 1958, pp. 115-25.

_____ "Wages Policy and Full Employment in Britain." *Oxford Institute of Statistics*, Vol. 12, July-August 1950, pp. 225-42.

Fisher, D. "The Demand for Money in Britain: Quarterly Results 1951 to 1967." *Manchester School of Economics and Social Studies*, Vol. 22, May 1960, pp. 94-104.

Frankel, M. "Anglo-American Productivity Differences: Their Magnitude and Some Causes." *American Economic Review*, May 1955, pp. 94-112.

_____ "Joint Industrial Planning in Great Britain." *Industrial and Labor Relations Review*, Vol. 11, April 1958, pp. 429-45.

_____ "The Growth of Public Employment in Great Britain." *Economic Development and Cultural Change*, Vol. 5, July 1957, pp. 376-80.

George, K.D. "Changes in British Industrial Concentration, 1951-1958," *Journal of Industrial Relations*, Vol. 15, July 1967, pp. 200-11.

Gurley, J.G. "The Radcliffe Report and Evidence." *American Economic Review*, Vol. 50, September 1960, pp. 672-700.

Hagen, E.E. and White, S.F.T. *Great Britain, Quiet Revolution in Planning.* Syracuse: Syracuse University Press, 1966.

Hall, M. "The New Look in Monopoly Policy." *Oxford University Institute of Statistics Bulletin*, Vol. 18, November 1956, pp. 873-86.

_____ "The U.K. After Devaluation." *American Economic Review*, Vol. 40, December 1950, pp. 864-75.

Hall, Sir R. "Incomes Policy: State of Play." *Three Banks Review*, Vol. 61, March 1964, pp. 13-23.

Hallett, G. "The Economic Position of British Agriculture." *Economic Journal*, Vol. 69, September 1959, pp. 522-42.

Harberger, A.C. "Currency Depreciation, Income, and the Balance of Trade." *Journal of Political Economy*, Vol. 58, February 1950, pp. 47-60.

Harris, S.E. "Devaluation of the Pound Sterling." *Harvard Business Review*, Vol. 27, November 1949, pp. 781-90.

Harrod, R.F. "The British Boom 1954-1955." *Economic Journal*, Vol. 66, March 1956, pp. 1-16.

Harrod, Sir R.F. "Sir Roy Harrod's View of the British Economy: A Note." *Economica*, Vol. 31, November 1964, pp. 423-25.

Hart, P.E. "Business Concentration in the U.K." *Royal Statistical Society Journal*, Vol. 123, No. 1 (1960): 50-58.

Hart, P.E. and Mac Bean, A.I. "Regional Differences in Productivity, Profitability and Growth: A Pilot Study." *Scottish Journal of Political Economy*, Vol. 8, February 1961, pp. 1-11.

Hasson, J.A. "Developments in the British Coal Industry." *Land Economics*, Vol. 38, November 1962, pp. 351-61.

Haver, C.B. "Agricultural Support Measures, Discussion." *Journal of Farm Economics*, Vol. 33, August 1951, pp. 311-19.

Henderson, P.D. "Notes on Public Investment Criteria in the United Kingdom." *Oxford University Institute of Economics and Statistics Bulletin*, Vol. 27, February 1965, pp. 55-89.

Howe, M. "The Iron and Steel Board and Steel Pricing, 1953-1967." *Scottish Journal of Political Economy*, Vol. 15, February 1968, pp. 43-67.

Hughes, J.R.T. "Measuring British Economic Growth." *Journal of Economic History*, Vol. 24, March 1964, pp. 60-82.

Hutton, G. "The U.K. Economy, 1951-1961, Performance and Prospect." *Lloyd's Bank Review*, Vol. 61, July 1961, pp. 1-25.

Jasey, A.E. "The Working of the Radcliffe Monetary System." *Oxford Economic Papers*, Vol. 12, June 1960, pp. 17-80.

Jewkes, J. "The Control of Industrial Monopoly." *Three Banks Review*, Vol. 28, December 1955, pp. 3-20.

————— "British Monopoly Policy, 1944-1956." *Journal of Law and Economics*, Vol. 1, October 1959, pp. 1-19.

Johnson, H.G. "Recent Developments in British Monetary Policy." *American Economic Review*, Suppl., Vol. 43, May 1953, pp. 19-26.

Johnston, J. "An Econometric Model of the U.K." *Review of Economic Studies*, Vol. 29, October 1961, pp. 29-39.

Jones, A. "Prices and Incomes Policy." *Economic Journal*, Vol. 78, December 1968, pp. 799-806.

Kaliski, S.F. "Some Recent Estimates of the Elasticity of Demand for British Exports: An Appraisal and Reconciliation." *Manchester School of Economics and Social Stidies*, Vol. 29, January 1961, pp. 23-42.

Kaldor, N. "The Radcliffe Report," *Review of Economics and Statistics*, Vol. 42, February 1960, pp. 14-19.

Liesner, H.H. "European Common Market and British Industry." *Economic Journal*, Vol. 68, June 1958, pp. 302-16.

Lipton, M. *Assessing Economic Performance*. London: Staples Press, 1968.

Little, I.M.D. "Higgledy-Piggledy Growth." *Oxford University Institute of Economics and Statistics, Bulletin*, Vol. 24, November 1962, pp. 387-412.

Leyshon, A.M. "Import Restrictions in Post-War Britain," *Scottish Journal of Political Economy*, Vol. 4, October 1957, pp. 177-93.

Lydall, H.F. "The Impact of the Credit Squeeze on Small and Medium-Sized Manufacturing Firms." *Economic Journal*, Vol. 67, September 1957, pp. 451-81.

————— "The Growth of Manufacturing Firms." *Oxford University Institute of Statistics Bulletin*, Vol. 21, May 1959, pp. 85-111.

Maddison, A. "How Fast Can Britain Grow?." *Lloyd's Bank Review*, Vol. 79, January 1966, pp. 1-14.

MacDougall, G.D.A. "Inflation in the United Kingdom." *Economic Review*, Vol. 35, December 1959, pp. 371-88.

Mallalieu, W.C. "The Structure of British Private Industry." *Canadian Journal of Economics and Political Science*, Vol. 21, February 1955, pp. 80-87.

Matthews, R.C.O. "Why Has Britain Had Full Employment Since The War?." *Economic Journal*, Vol. 78, September 1968, pp. 555-69.

McKelvey, J.T. "Trade Union Wage Policy in Post-War Britain." *Industrial and Labor Relations Review*, Vol. 6, October 1952, pp. 3-119.

McKersie, R.B. "Incomes Policy in Great Britain." *Industrial Relations Research Association*, Vol. 19, December 1966, pp. 139-48.

Merrett, A.J. and Whittaker, J. "The Profitability of British and American Industry." *Lloyd's Bank Review*, Vol. 83, January 1967, pp. 1-10.

Mitchell, J. "U.K. Balance of Payments, 1946-1955." *Oxford Institute of Statistics*, Vol. 20, February 1958, pp. 29-51.

Mollett, J.A. "Britain's Post-War Agricultural Expansion: Some Economic Problems and Relationships Involved." *Journal of Farm Economics*, Vol. 41, February 1959, pp. 3-15.

Moore, L. "Factors Affecting the Demand for British Exports." *Oxford Institute of Statistics*, Vol. 26, November 1964, pp. 343-59.

Nash, E.F. "The Competitive Position of British Agriculture." *Journal of Agricultural Economics,* Vol. II, No. 3, June 1955.

Needleman, L. "Growth, Investment and Efficiency in Britain: Some Policy Suggestions." *Scottish Journal of Political Economy*, Vol. 9, November

1962, pp. 169-92.

Nevin, E. "The Cost Structure of British Manufacturing, 1948-61." *Economic Journal*, Vol. 73, December 1963, pp. 642-64.

Nicholson, R.J. "Capital Stock, Employment and Output in British Industry, 1948-1964." *Yorkshire Bulletin of Economic and Social Research*, Vol. 18, November 1966, pp. 65-85.

Paish, F.W. "Britain's Economic Problem." *American Economic Review*, Vol. 38, March 1948, pp. 118-21.

_____ "Inflation in the U.K., 1948-1957." *Economic New Series*, Vol. 25, May 1958, pp. 94-105.

_____ "Studies in an Inflationary Economy, The United Kingdom 1948-1961." New York: St. Martin's Press, 1966.

Parker, J.E.S. "Profitability and Growth of British Industrial Firms." *Manchester School of Economics and Social Studies*, Vol. 32, May 1964, pp. 113-29.

Peacock, A.T. and Wiseman, J. "The Past and Future of Public Spending." *Lloyd's Bank Review*, Vol. 60, April 1960, pp. 1-20.

Phillips, G.A. and Maddock, R.T. *The Growth of the British Economy, 1918-1968.* London: George Allen & Unwin, Ltd., 1973.

Please, S. "The Counter-Cyclical Behavior of Public Investment in the U.K. since the War." *Public Finance*, Vol. 14 (1959): 264-80.

Pollard, S. *The Development of the British Economy, 1914-1967.* 2d ed. New York: St. Martin's Press, 1969.

Pratten, C.F. "The Merger Boom in Manufacturing Industry." *Lloyd's Bank Review*, Vol. 90, October 1968, pp. 39-55.

Prest, A.R. "The British Economy, 1945-1960." *Manchester School of Economics and Social Studies*, Vol. 33, May 1965, pp. 141-47.

_____ "Sense and Nonsense in Budgetary Policy." *Economic Journal*, Vol. 78, March 1968, pp. 1-18.

Prest, A.R. and Coppock, D.J. *The U.K. Economy, A Manual of Applied Economics*, 4th ed. London: Weidenfed & Nicolson, 1966.

Reddaway, W.B. "Movements in the Real Product of the U.K., 1946-1949." *Royal Statistical Society Journal*, Vol. 113, Pt. 4 (1950): 435-63.

Robertson, D.J. "Guideposts and Norms: Contrasts in U.S. and U.K. Wage Policy." *Three Banks Review*, Vol. 72, December 1966, pp. 3-29.

Robinson, D. "Implementing an Incomes Policy." *Industrial Review*, Vol. 8, October 1968, pp. 73-90.

_____ "Wage Rates, Wage Income and Wages Policy." *Oxford Institute of Statistics*, Vol. 25, February 1963, pp. 47-76.

Rostas, L. "Changes in the Productivity of British Industry, 1945-1950." *Economic Journal*, Vol. 62, March 1952, pp. 15-24

Rowley, C.K. "Mergers and Public Policy in Great Britain." *Journal of Law and*

Economics, Vol. II, April 1968, pp. 75-132.

Rowley, J.C.R. "Fixed Capital Formation in the British Economy, 1956-1965." *Economic Studies*, Vol. 38, July 1971, pp. 369-76.

Sanders, C.T. "The Development and Problems of Economic Planning in Great Britain." *Weltwirtschaftliches Archiv*, Vol. 92, No. 1 (1964): 57-90.

Sargent, J.R. "Recent Growth Experience in the Economy of the U.K." *Economic Journal*, Vol. 78, March 1968, pp. 19-42.

Sayers, R.S. "Monetary Thought and Monetary Policy in England." *Economic Journal*, Vol. 70, December 1960, pp. 710-24.

Silberston, A. "Hire Purchase Controls and the Demand for Cars." *Economic Journal*, Vol. 73, March 1963, pp. 32-53.

Shepherd, W.G. "British Nationalized Industry: Performance and Policy." *Yale Economic Essays*, Vol. 4 (1964): 183-222.

———— "Changes in British Industrial Concentration, 1951-1958." *Oxford Economic Papers*, Vol. 18, March 1966, pp. 126-32.

Shone, R. "Problems of Planning for Economic Growth in a Mixed Economy." *Economic Journal*, Vol. 75, March 1965, pp. 1-19.

Sultan, P.E. "Full Employment on Trial: A Case Study of British Experience." *Canadian Journal of Economics*, Vol. 19, May 1953, pp. 210-21.

Tanner, J. "British Monetary Policy, 1945-1952." *Weltwirtschaftliches Archiv*, Vol. 71, No. 1 (1953): 90-190.

Taylor, H.C. "Food and Farm Land in Britain." *Land Economics*, Vol. 31, February 1955, pp. 24-34.

Thomas, E. "Recent Changes in British Farm Support Policy." *Journal of Farm Economics*, Vol. 41, December 1959, pp. 1241-49.

Weber, B. "Post-War Trends in Industrial Output, Employment and Productivity, An International Comparison." *Scottish Journal of Political Economy*, Vol. 2, June 1955, pp. 166-76.

Wilson, T. "Science and Industry." *Lloyd's Bank Review*, Vol. 46, October 1957. pp. 34-45.

Williams, D. "Some Aspects of Monetary Policy in England, 1952-58." *Yorkshire Bulletin of Economic and Social Research*, Vol. 12, November 1960, pp. 96-110.

Worswick, G.D.N. and Ady, P.H. *The British Economy, 1945-1950*. London: Oxford University Press, 1952.

———— *The British Economy in the Nineteen-Fifties*. London: Oxford University Press, 1962.

Youngson, A.J. *Britain's Economic Growth, 1920-1966*. 2d ed. London: George Allen & Unwin, Ltd., 1968.

YUGOSLAVIA

Aničić, Z. "Population Changes in Yugoslavia." *Yugoslav Survey*, Vol. 12 (1971): 1-8.

Begtić, M. "Employment, 1952-1966," *Yugoslav Survey*, Vol. 8 (1967): 49-62.

Bićanić, R. "Economic Growth Under Centralized and Decentralized Planning: Yugoslavia, A Case Study." *Economic Development and Cultural Change*, Vol. 6, October 1957, pp. 63-74.

_____ *Economic Policy in Socialist Yugoslavia*. London:Cambridge University Press, 1973.

Bombelles, J.T. *Economic Development of Communist Yugoslavia*. Stanford: Hoover Institution Publications, 1968.

Branković, S. *Impact of Foreign Aid on the Postwar Development of Yugoslavia*, Paris: UNESCO, 1962.

Byrnes, R.F., ed. *Yugoslavia*, New York: Praeger, 1957.

Campbell, J.C. *Tito's Separate Road*. New York: Harper & Row, 1967.

Dedijer, V. *Tito*. New York: Simon and Schuster, 1953.

Dirlam, J.B. and Plummer, J.L. *An Introduction to the Yugoslav Economy*. Columbus: C.E. Merrill Publishing Co., 1973.

Djilas, M. *The New Class*. New York: Praeger, 1957.

Djordevic, J. "A Contribution to the Theory of Social Property." *Socialist Thought in Practice*, No. 24, October-December 1966, pp. 73-100.

Drače, D. "Development of Agriculture, 1945-1970." *Yugoslav Survey*, Vol. 11 (1907): 13-40.

Fisher, J.C. *Yugoslavia-A Multinational State*. San Francisco: Chandler Publishing Co., 1966.

Gorupič, D. "Problems of the System of Financing Investment." *Eastern European Economics*, Vol. 2, No. 3, Spring 1964, pp. 44-59.

Halpern, J. "Peasant Culture and Urbanization in Yugoslavia." *Human Organization*, Vol. 24, Summer 1965.

Hammond, T.T. "Nationalism and National Minorities in Eastern Europe," *Journal of International Affairs*, Vol. XX, No. 1 (1966): 1-13.

Hauvonen, J.J. "Postwar Developments in Money and Banking in Yugoslavia." *International Monetary Fund Staff Papers*, Vol. 17, November 1970, pp. 563-601.

Hoffman, G. W. and Neal, F. W. *Yugoslavia and the New Communism*. New York: The Twentieth Century Fund, 1962.

Horvat, B. *Toward a Theory of the Planned Economy*. Belgrade: Jugoslavenski Institut za Ekonomska Istrazivanja, 1965.

_____ *An Essay on Yugoslav Society*. White Plains: International Arts and Science Press, 1969.

_____ "Yugoslav Economic Policy in the Post-War Period. Problems, Ideas,

Institutional Developments." *American Economic Review,* Vol. 61, June 1971, pp. 69-169.

Horvat, B. and Rascovic, V. "Workers' Management in Yugoslavia: A Comment." *Journal of Political Economy,* Vol. 67, April 1959, pp. 194-98.

Kardelj, E. *Socialism and War.* New York: McGraw-Hill, 1960.

Kerner, R.J., ed., *Yugoslavia.* Berkeley: University of California Press, 1949.

Kolaja, J. *Workers' Councils: The Yugoslav Experience.* New York: Praeger, 1965.

Macesich, G. *Yugoslavia, The Theory and Practice of Development Planning.* University of Virginia Press, 1964.

Madžar, L. "Economic Development, 1947-1968." *Yugoslav Survey,* Vol. 11 (1970): 23-42.

Mandel, E. "Yugoslav Economic Theory." *Monthly Review,* Vol. 11 (1967):40-49.

Marcus, M.R. "Comparative Current Trends in Market Socialism — Czechoslovakia and Yugoslavia." *Marquette Business Review,* Vol. 12, Fall 1968, pp. 121-33.

Markovič, B. "National Income, Employment and Productivity in the Yugoslav Economy, 1947-1968." *Yugoslav Survey,* Vol. 11 (1970): 49-60.

Marsenič, D. "The Price System: Development and Problems." *Yugoslav Survey,* Vol. 14, August 1973, pp. 141-154.

Mesa-Lazo, C. "Unemployment in a Socialist Economy, Yugoslavia." *Industrial Relations,* Vol. 10, February 1971, pp. 49-69.

Mirkovič, M. *Ekonomska Historija Jugoslavije.* Zagreb: Economiski Pregled, 1958.

Mladek, J.V. et al. "The Change in the Yugoslav Economic System." *International Monetary Fund Staff Papers,* Vol. 2, November 1952, pp. 407-38.

Mladenović, M. "Post-War Development in Economically Underdeveloped Republics and Areas." *Yugoslav Survey,* Vol. VI, April-Juen 1965, pp. 2995-3010.

Neal, F.W. *Titoism in Action: The Reforms in Yugoslavia after 1948.* Berkeley: University of California Press, 1958.

Neuberger, E. "Centralization vs. Decentralization: The Case of Yugoslav Banking." *American Slavic and East European Review,* Vol. 18 (1959): 361-73.

Niklic, M. "Changes in the Structure of Industrial Production, 1952-1972." *Yugoslav Survey.* Vol. 14, February 1973, pp. 33-42.

Nikolin, Z. "Some Basic Features of Yugoslavia's Industrial Development, 1952-1972." *Yugoslave Survey,* Vol. 14, August 1973, pp. 155-164.

Pejovich, S. *The Market-Planned Economy of Yugoslavia.* Minneapolis: University of Minnesota Press, 1966.

Sacks, S. "Changes in Industrial Structure in Yugoslavia, 1959-1968," *Journal of*

Political Economy, May-June 1972, pp. 561-74.

Samardzija, M. "The Market and Social Planning in the Yugoslav Economy." *Quarterly Review of Economics and Business,* Vol. 7, Summer 1967, pp. 37-44.

Sichel, W. "The Threat to Market Socialism — The Case of Yugoslavia." *Antitrust Bulletin,* Vol. 16, Summer 1971, pp. 389-414.

Stanovinik, J. "Planning Through the Market." *Foreign Affairs,* Vol. 40, January 1960. pp. 252-63.

Todorovic, S. "Changes in the Structure of Yugoslav Imports, 1965-1972." *Yugoslav Survey,* Vol. 14, February 1973, pp. 79-84.

Tomic, D. "Prices of Agricultural Products." *Yugoslav Survey,* Vol. 14, February 1973, pp. 43-54.

Ulam, A. *Titoism and the Cominform.* Cambridge: Harvard University Press, 1952.

Vanek, J. "Yugoslav Economic Growth and its Conditions." American Economic Review, Vol. LIII, May 1963, pp. 555-61.

Vucinich, W.S., ed. *Contemporary Yugoslavia.* Berkeley: University of California Press, 1969.

Ward, B. "Workers' Management in Yugoslavia." *The Journal of Political Economy,* Vol. 13 (1961): 379-448.

————— "Marxism-Horvatism: A Yugoslav Theory of Socialism." *American Economic Review,* Vol. 57 (1967): 509-23.

Zaninovich, M.G. *The Development of Socialist Yugoslavia.* Baltimore: The Johns Hopkins Press, 1968.

INDEX